# THE TRIBES OF GALWAY
## 1124-1642

Adrian Martyn

by
Adrian Martyn

# CONTENTS

At imdha thra na h-airisi ... Ni cumaing nech a n-innisin do leir acht uate do ilibh dibh ar daigh aesa na n-doene do fhis treotho.

The events indeed are numerous ... No one can relate them all, but a few of the many are given so that the age in which the people lived may be known through them.

Annála Uladh, 1041.

Published by Adrian Martyn. Copyright (C) Adrian Martyn 2016. Maps (C) Adrian Martyn 2016
First published in 2016. Printed by iSupply
No part of this book may be reproduced in any form without the permission of the copyright owner.
ISBN:978-0-9955025-0-5
While every effort has been made to ensure that the details in this book are accurate, the author and printers accept no liability for errors.

# ACKNOWLEDGEMENTS

To those who have long waited for this book, my apologies. I was delayed.

My parents Christy and Noreen (nee McLoughlin) have supported me through a long illness. This book could not have been written without them.

Leonard Doyle, the better half of a great busking duo, for introducing me to the *History of Galway* just before the last bus left for Tirellan, one cold night in February 1996. The late Shevaun Lynam (died 1998), who in June 1996 was the first to tell me my abilities in historical research were a talent, and worth developing. Best. Career. Guidance. Ever.

Jean Kinnane, her brother Jonathan, their father Gerry, and all their family and friends who worked at the late, lamented Net Access Cyber Café (Ireland's first internet café, 1995 to January 2013) at the Olde Malte, off High Street, Galway. Writing this book began there in the summer of 2010. Mary Judy of Dubray's Bookshop, Shop Street, Galway, has been an encourager since 2008, when all seemed impossible.

Very special thanks to Kieran Hoare (Archivist), Margaret Hughes (Senior Library Assistant), Loretta Donohue (Special Collections Librarian), and Aisling Keane (Archivist) of the Special Collections Room, James Hardiman Library, National University of Ireland, Galway. They and the rest of the library staff have been unfailingly helpful in my investigations over the years. The staff of Galway City Library in St. Augustine Street, and Galway Library Headquarters at Island House, Cathedral Square, all aided my investigations which began in their offices in February 1996 when I was twenty-one. Particular thanks are due to Maureen Moran (retired August 2013), Mary Qualter, and Petria Mee in Island House.

The British Library in London for excellent photographic repoductions of the following: "The Circute of the Towne of Gallway" (1589), "St. Augustines Forte neere Galway", (1603?), "A Prospect of Galway" (a and b, 1685), "A Plan of the Town and Fortifications of Galway" (1747).

Professor Nollaig Ó Muraíle eviscerated some major naming errors in Chapter One which is all the better as a result. His work has long been a massive source of inspiration to me. Dr. Freya Verstraten-Veach made many good and useful comments, and was a source of encouragement in dispiriting times. Dr. Joe Mannion clarified obscure points of late sixteenth-century County Galway history. His highly enthused response to the text helped re-light my own, which was then flagging.

Colmán Ó Clabaigh, OFM, stressed that his translation of the *Regestum Monasterii Fratrum Praedicatorum de Athenry* was unfinished, but allowed me to use it anyway. Galway City Heritage Officer Jim Higgins provided photos and drawings of several stone armorials and other monuments he has documented in Galway since the 1970s. I still owe him a pint. Daniel Tietzsch-Tyler for an excellent job on illustrating twelfth-century Gaelic Galway. Marion Coady, who drew the maps that feature here, for grace and professionalism. The first three were based upon Dr. Paul MacCotter's brilliant *Medieval Ireland: Territorial, Political and Economic Divisions* (2008). Paul's kind comments upon viewing the maps were most encouraging. Unintended discrepancies arose as a consequence of finishing the maps in early 2013, and the final text in June 2016. The former contained terms in Modern Gaeilge, the latter in Classical Gaeilge. Attempts to harmonise maps with the text was made, not entirely successfully. Therefore, terms in the text are to be preferred. Breandán Mac Gabhann, Helen Bermingham, Damian Donnellan and the staff of Galway City Museum: Breandán enabled a number of lectures I gave and was a fountain of ideas. Helen located and sourced a number of invaluable images and photos.

The outstanding work of Paul Walsh and Patrick Holland on medieval and early modern Galway saved me years of toil. Paul also sourced a number of useful photographic images. Dr. Diarmuid Ó Rian identified Geoffrey Blake's kinsman as Heinricus/Heinrich/Henry, abbot of Benediktinerabtei unserer Lieben Frau zu den Schotten, Wein (Vienna), from 1393 to 1398. I am especially grateful to Fergus Fahy and Brendan Duffy of NUI Galway for permission to use images from Liber A, aka Galway Corporation book, 1485-1705. Kieran McHugh at ISupply for formatted this book.

I am deeply indebted to Dubhaltach Mac Fhirbhisigh, James Hardiman, Martin Joseph Blake, and Maureen Donovan-O'Sullivan for their unsurpassed works: *Leabhar na nGenealach* (1649-50), *History of Galway* (1820), *Blake Family Records* (1902 and 1905), and *Old Galway* (1942). Hopefully their like will pass this way again. Likewise the many contributors to the *Journal* of the Galway Archaeological and Historical Society. Mile buicious!

The following academics and scholars freely gave their very precious time to critique draft sections of this book according to their disciplines: Professor Nollaig Ó Muraíle (then of National University of Ireland, Galway, now retired), Dr. Freya Verstraten-Veach (University of Hull), Dr. Joseph Mannion (now Board of Directors, Finte na hÉireann/Clans of Ireland), Professor Katharine Simms (Trinity College, Dublin), Dr. Gillian Kenny (TCD), Hanne-Mette Alsos-Raae (NUIG), Dr. Peter Crooks (TCD), Dr. Ian W.S. Campbell, Dr. Eoin Ó Neill (Fluminense Federal University, Niterói), Dr. Matteo Binesco (NUIG), David Etheridge (University of Bristol), Liam Hogan (University of Limerick graduate and Limerick City librarian), Peter Schrijver (University of Utrecht), Richard Warner (retired curator of the Ulster Museum, member of the Royal Irish Academy), Paul Ó Dubtaig (Dublin), and an anonymous reviewer who critiqued the entire text. Their corrections hugely improved this book. Thank you, one and all.

For more informal but still valued reviews, thanks to my cousin Amanda McLoughlin (London), Gerry Hansberry, Dr. Bernard Kelly (University of Edinburgh), Rev. Paddy Towers, Dr. Tyrone Bowes (Irish Origenes.com), George O'Reilly (Dublin, Genealogical Society of Ireland), Councillor Michael Merrigan (Dublin, GSI), Gavin Huban (Mseno, Czech Republic), Ronan Killeen (chairman Athenry Historical Network), Eamon Madden (secretary AHN), Finbarr O'Regan (Athenry), Noel Dilleen (Lisduff), James Martyn Joyce (Ballyloughan), Bernard O'Hara (Galway-Mayo Institute of Technology, retired), and my family.

Thanks also to: Michael Irwin (Thomond Archaeological and Historical Society), Beatrix Faber (Corpus of Electronic Texts), John Joe Conwell (Ireland Reaching Out, and South East Galway Historical and Archaeological Society), Steve Dolan (SEGHAS), Christy Cunniffe (SEGHAS), Professor Michelle Comber (NUIG), Brian Quin (AHN), The Doctor (TARDIS), Professor George Broderick (University of Mannheim), Professor John Collis (University of Aberswyth), Doctor Anne Connon (Ohio Dominican University, USA), Doctor Maurice Gleeson (Family Tree DNA), Professor John Carey, Anna Farmer, Doctor Robyn Mason (RealSim), Anja

Wittnebel and Dragos Barbu (Chat & Net), Pat Mullen (Recess), Maire Mannion (Galway heritage officer), Des, Tom and Tomás Kenny (Kenny's Bookstore, Galway), Professor Colin Veach (University of Hull), Niall O'Brian, Sparky Booker (TCD), Tony 'Sailor' MacDonagh (The Claddagh, valient caretaker of Forthill cemetery), Brian Anton (Boston), Karena Morton (Irish Museum of Country Life), Professor Bárra Ó Donnabháin, Professor Blanca María Prósper (Universidad de Salamanca), Pat McCarthy (The Military History Society of Ireland), Professor Áine Foley (TCD, Freinds of Medieval Dublin), Marion Dowd (Institute of Technology Sligo), Kevin Jordan (Banagher), my grandfather's first cousin Mattie Martyn of Carha, Bullaun (January 1933-April 2013). My apologies if I have forgotten anyone.

Nevertheless, the text is mine and only I am responsible for any errors in it. Every effort has been made to contact the copyright holders of all images displayed in this book. If there are any omissions, please contact me.

I dedicate this book very especially to my niece
Gabrielle Éireann Boeuf
who's comments are still years away!

*The Great East Gate and Clock Tower with SPQR flag, erected 1637-38 by Sir Thomas Blake. Courtesy of NUI, Galway*

# INTRODUCTION – "CONNACHT'S ROME"

When the merchant families of Galway described themselves in a map of the town made about 1664, they drew upon the example of Rome. Its *res publica* motto SPQR is shown on a flag flying from the east gate tower clock, built in 1637-38. Text accompanying the map depicted Galway and its prime families as heirs and equals to the *civitas eterna* (Eternal City):

> *Septem ornant montes Romam, septem ostia Nilum,*
> *tot rutilis stellis splendet in axe Polus.*
> *Galvia, Polo Niloque bis aequas, Roma Conachtae;*
> *Bis septem illustres, has colit illa tribus* [my emphasis].

> *Rome boasts sev'n hills, the Nile its sev'n-fold stream,*
> *around the pole sev'n radiant planets gleam;*
> *Galway, Connacht's Rome, twice equals these;* *
> *she boasts twice sev'n illustrious families* [my emphasis] [1]

Thus, the fourteen families of Athy, Blake, Bodkin, Browne, Darcy, Deane, Font, French, Joyce, Kirwan, Lynch, Martyn, Morris, Skerrett were henceforth tribus Galvia - the Tribes of Galway. The seven *tribus* of Rome were electoral districts containing large groups of unrelated people. The *tribus Galvia* were distinct families of various ethnic and social origins. Both sets of *tribus* were distinguished from other folks by forms of collective citizenship, designated by a community name that set them apart from Others.

The medieval town was home to many families. These fourteen produced Sovereigns and Mayors of Galway, the town's highest rank, marking them further. The popular explanation is that it was a derisive term applied towards the fourteen by English Republicans occupying Galway in the 1650s. Or it might originate in the above Latin verse, the earliest known use of the term. One may have drove the other. Because the term cannot be dated any earlier than this - plus the derogatory, inaccurate use of 'tribal' in Irish contexts - it is used sparingly in this volume.

Galway's reputation was achieved not by wars of conquest but by the hard graft of trade. It was noted as "a town much frequented by foreign businessmen", [2] its merchants described as "shrewd managers of the wealth they have accumulated from trading" [3] "rich, and great adventurers at the sea." [4] Yet with fame came geographic confusion:

> *There is a story that a merchant abroad, who had frequent dealings with the people of this town, once asked an Irishman what part of Galway was Ireland situated.* [5]

The merchants could be allowed leeway for their pride. Over the course of four hundred years, they and their fellow Galwegians survived, and often thrived, against warlords and sieges, recessions and famines, all within a urban outpost at the very edge of western Europe.

This is their story.

* The original translation included the word "Conation" for "Connacht", which I amend above.
1 - Hardiman, 1820, p. 25. 2 - Great Deeds ... , 2014, p. 101. 3 – op. cit., p. 101. 4 - Hardiman, 1820, pp. 21-22. 5 - Great Deeds ... , 2014, p. 103. For the dating of the map, see Fahy, 2013.

*Dun Gaillimhe in the 1100s, as rendered by Daniel Tietzsch-Tyler*

# CHAPTER ONE – STONY RIVER

## *Gaillimh*

Between the *locha* flows the *Gaillimh*.

The river commonly known as late as 1762 as the Gaillimh flows for six kilometres, from *Loch Orbsen* (Lough Corrib) into *Loch Lurgan*, alias *Cuan na Gaillimhe* (Galway Bay). The latter ceased being a freshwater lake after 1700 BC, the process complete by AD 500 at the very latest.

It is tempting to think memory of this process lies behind the term-change from *loch* to *cuan* (a 'bay' and/or a 'harbour'). But *loch* is applied to both inland freshwater and semi-enclosed saltwater lakes in both Ireland and Britain, and Loch Lurgan was the common local name as Gaeilge till at least the 1680s. Probably the term-change only denotes increased maritime activity at a particular space in time, likely due to the town's trading activities. And when Loch Lurgan became Cuan na Gaillimhe/Galway Bay, both past perceptions and 'memory' died. So it goes.

Due west from *Bun Gaillimhe* ('the mouth of the Gaillimh'), Cois Fharraige is an almost straight coastline for upwards of fifty kilometres, breaking up into islands and inlets at Cuan Chasla, facing an *tAigéan Mór* ('the great ocean', the Atlantic). South across the bay is the bare limestone region of *Boireann* ([the] Burren) and the sheer precipices of *Aillte na Mothair* (Cliffs of Moher). The bay's mouth is bounded by an *Oileáin Árann* (the Aran Islands). Storms make howling landfall from thousands of Atlantic leagues, waves smashing into and even over cliffs, reducing Bronze Age hillforts till they crash, lost forever, into the sea.

Gaillimh derives from *Gailleamh* ('stony river'). It refers to the river bed, exposed when the river dried up in 1178, 1190, 1462, 1647, 1683-84. [1] It also pertained to a cataract of rocks through which *bradán* (salmon) leaped. The cataracts were demolished in the 1850s, as was part of the river bed in the 1940s, while salmon, one of the island's earliest inhabitants, now approach extinction. *Gailleamh* remained but the meaning was lost, so a myth was created to explain it:

> the city of Galway took its name from the river, in which was drowned Gaillimh, the daughter of Breasail. [2]

The 'drowning daughter' motif had a wider application. The river marking the east border of what became County Galway was said to previously be called the *Dubhabhainn Bhreá*. It was reputedly renamed *An tSuca* (the Suck) after "Sogca daughter of Cairbre who was drowned in it."

Its true meaning probably derives from the term *suic*, denoting a marsh. [3] This motif may mask a time when the Gaillimh was divine, worshipped as the local Goddess. Rivers such as the Shannon certainly were. The Boyne was personified as *Boand*, wife of *Nuada* and lover of *In Dagda*, two of the island's chief gods. Like Gaillimh and Sogca, she drowned. Who loved Gaillimh is unrecorded.

Loch Orbsen had divine aspects – its namesake, *Orbsen Már*, was an alias for Manannán mac Lír, god-king of the sea. If not purely accidental losses, Bronze and Iron Age swords and items found in the river at *An Daingean* (Dangan, 'the stronghold') could be ritual deposits to a local river deity. [4] But most likely, Gaillimh and the rest were initially names of topographic features. When the original meanings were forgotten, people invented a god or story to explain it. So it goes.

River life included the '*Each Uisge*' ('water horse') alias *dobharchú* (otter [water hound]). [5] The *eascann* (eel), *breac* (trout), and bradán were fished and traded by locals for centuries. The *Cat crainn* (marten), *Easóg* (stoat), and *míol buí* (hare) were all trapped for their fur. Hunting the dobharchú, the *rón* (seal) swam the coast and up its rivers. Tradition among the *Meic Con Ghaola* (Connellys) held that these creatures were their kindred. So strong was this belief that contrary to neighbouring coastal folk, no Mac Con Ghaola would dare kill or eat one. [6]

Larger sea creatures included an *Cráin Dubh* (Killer Whale), an *Liamhán Gréine* (Basking Shark), an *Muc Mhara* (porpoise), an *Deilf* (Dolphin), *míol mór* (whale). They were sometimes hunted by humans, slaughtered if found beached; apparently, Ros a' Mhíl is named from such an incident. At the dawn of the Irish medieval era c. AD 301, the human section of the Irish animal kingdom vied with other dominant species like the *Fia Rua* (red deer, hunted by the Connemara black eagle), *Faolchú* (wolf), *Torc* (boar), and lessers like the *Broc* (badger), *Sionnach* (Fox), *Earc Luachra* (lizard), *Earc Sléibhe* (frog), *Luch Fhéir* (wood mouse) and perhaps *Capaillín Chonamara* (Connamara pony). The turn of the seasons was marked by the arrival of the *Fáinleog* (swallow) in Spring, its Autumn depature coinciding with the arrival of the *Crotach* (curlew).

Nevertheless, merely foraging affected ecosystems. The arrival of the last humans some twelve and a half thousand years ago coincided with the extinctions of the Great Irish deer, hyena, and reindeer - bears survived till about three thousand years ago. From about 4000 BC, agriculturalism gave regions with fertile soil dense if dispersed human populations. *Fásaigh* ('wastelands') might see no humans for decades, and settlements were semi-isolated by rivers, lakes, mountains, bogs, woods.

Yet there was change. Woods became semi-managed, extensive only in localised, agriculturally marginal areas. Bronze Age exploitation three thousand years ago destroyed the forest habitat of Ireland's last bears. Without the cover of pine and hazel trees, rain washed away the soil, creating man-made landscapes such as 'the rocky place' (*Boireann*=the Burren). Yet only in the 1700s did coloniser and colonised alike make deforestation nearly total, creating the unnaturally bare, bleak modern lawnscape. By the early 2000s, intensive agriculture made previously marginal lands viable, if briefly and with much expense.

Drawn-out habitat destruction by the island's apex predator exterminated Irish populations such as *Iolar* (eagle) and *Coileach Fheadha* (Capercaille). Others are severely endangered. Most have been residents for thousands of years, long before the existence of the languages used here to describe them - the island was created some ten thousand years before present. [7] Now ecosystems face collapse and mass Irish extinction slouches closer. So it goes.

The Gaillimh swelled with the waters of Loch Orbsen, *Loch Mesca* (Lough Mask), *Finnloch Cera* (Lough Carra), and their rain-basins. This led to the short Gaillimh river pouring "itself forth ... violently, and with much noise, through a rocky channel" of hard diorite rocks" into the sea." [8]

A kilometre and a half from the sea the Gaillimh ran into a long, high broad ridge, forcing a west-south-west route around it. From there to the sea it fell fully four and more metres. This created exhilaratingly fast currents, ideal for mills but a leap for bradán, making direct sea-to-lake travel impossible for ships, except perhaps via portage (dragging ships along riverbanks). That might explain the presence of vikings on Loch Orbsen in 929 ("The foreigners of *Luimnech* went on Loch Oirbsen, and they plundered the islands of the lake.") [9] and 930 ("The foreigners who were on Loch Oirbsen were slaughtered by the Connachta."). [10]

## (Re)Writing history

The pre-literate, pre-medieval human history of *Éire* (Old Irish *Ériu*, hence 'Ireland') is rendered mythically. *Cnoc Maigh* (Knockmaa, 'hill of the mead'?), [11] near Tuam, was said to contain the tomb of Queen Cessair, legendary leader of Éire's first settlers. Her people were said to be succeeded by Clann Pharthláin, Neimheadh 'sa chlann, and various off-shoots. Yet 'Cessair' and her 'successors' mainly derive from classical sources synthesised during and after the seventh century. It is as if *Lord of the Rings* was believed to depict actual English history. [12]

Likewise, since the 1800s mainstream beliefs about Irish identity assume the Irish are/were 'Celts'. Yet no classical writer ever termed the Irish as *Keltoi* (hence 'Celts').

Far more importantly, neither did the Iron Age, medieval, or early modern Irish.

Literate, highly self-aware, native castes existed in Éire since c. AD 300, fluent in Gaeilge, Latin, Greek, Brythonic and Germanic. Yet in the extensive textual and topographic corpora of Gaelic Éire and Gaelic Britain, neither Greek *Keltoi/Keltai* nor Latin *Celtae* ever appear.

The ethnic Keltoi are almost entirely lost in bad romance. [13] What can be safely said is they existed by c. 500 BC in south-eastern Gaul (now south-eastern France)' the term Keltoi probably originated as a self-descriptive term which the Greeks of Marseilles Hellenised, just as the Romans in Gaul Latinised it. Perhaps the only region where Keltoi had a genuine ethnic application, *Keltike* had urban settlements and economies, literate and sophisticated polities. By the last centuries BC they had expanded culturally and politically into central Gaul, with offshoots in Italia and Hispania. Yet Greeks and Romans used the term imperfectly, akin to 'African', 'European', or 'Asian'. So it was of debatable accuracy even in Gaul, which contained distinct ethnic and linguistic groups such as the Aquitani, Belgae, Ligurians, Germani, who were all Gauls but not Keltoi.

Keltoi and other ethnicities were consumers of La Tène and 'Hallstatt' material cultures; their role in creating them is debatable. No single common culture or people spanned Iron Age Europe. Celtic languages probably originated not in central Europe but along the Gaulish-Italian coast of the Mediterranean [14] (a 'Provençal' or 'Burgundian' Keltike?). The first attested Celtic inscriptions were not by the Keltoi of Gaul, but the Lepontii of Italia. The modern notion that speakers of the Celtic language group are all 'Celts' confuses a group of mutually incomprehensible languages with a single ethnicity, denying the individual identities of Gaeilgeoir, Cymraeg, Brezoneger.

As these terms demonstrate, languages are called after their speakers. Speakers are not called after their languages or language-groups - though English is a Germanic language, English-speakers are not Germans. Neither does speaking English make a person ethnically English, or German. [15]

Greeks and Romans imposed Keltoi/Celtae as a cover-all ethnic stereotype for different peoples and unrelated nations, like the Galatai; the terms were inconsistently applied and had contradictory uses. [16] This mirrored *Indian* in the *West Indies* (the Americas, not west India) and like it, the incomer's terms stuck. Both terms concealed many distinctions of ethnicity and nation - thus inaccurate but convenient, to the incomer - until they were conquered, colonised, *delenda est.*

Their descendants, culturally Roman and Latin-speakers, knew their ancestral identities imperfectly. Their notions of being Keltoi might have being no better than Pocahontas's white, English, Protestant descendants had about being an 'Indian', let alone Powhatan. Even *celtice* vanished sometime after AD 500, during the demise of the (Western) Roman Empire. And so, amid *bagaudae*, Huns, Goths, *foederati*, Burgundians, and Franks, the Keltoi ceased to be, forever.

## Making the Irish 'Celts'

Twelve hundred years later, in the 1700s, the term Celtic was chosen by linguists to describe a group of extant and extinct languages, only correctly classified in the 1860s (perhaps 'Lepontic' would have being a more neutral term). Along with Germanic and Italic, Celtic languages are part of the vast language-group termed Indo-European. This perfectly valid classification and its invaluable discipline, Celtic Studies, has been misunderstood and misapplied ever since.

Up to then, no Irish or British nation claimed any relationship to the extinct Keltoi, nor any common roots for each other - the term for 'foreigner' as Gaeilge is *Gaill* (singular Gall), derived from Irish trade with the Romano-Gauls when they still spoke Celtice. 'Celt(s)' and 'Celtic' do not appear in any Irish or British languages or literatures except as recent Anglo-French imports. Each correctly viewed themselves as distinct living nations, with independent histories, different linguistic and literary traditions, especially extensive for the Gaelic-Irish.

But the European Romantic Movement's ideas about 'Celts' infected developing scholarly paradigms, and was hijacked by politics. In France from 1789, it was used to partition aristocrats ('Franks') from revolutionaries ('Gauls' or 'Celts'). This positive 'racial' construct made *nos ancetres les Gaulois* ('our ancestors the Gauls') the basis of the post-revolutionary French nation-state – ignoring the fact that Keltoi culture and language was long extinct, that the French were not Pagan but Christian, culturally and linguistically Latin with a Germanic ethnym.

This differed from English Celticity, a negative 'racial' construct which derided and homogenised Gaeilgeoiri (Irish, Manx, and Scot) and Cymraeg (Welsh, and Cornish) into 'the Celts'. This was not recognising a common inter-nations identity. None existed. They were lumped together against the dominant ethnicity of the recently created British state (1707), the 'Anglo-Saxons'/Teutons'. Both 'Anglo-Saxon' and 'Celt' borrowed names of historic peoples, but ignored the fact there was little trace of Keltoi in these islands and that the Anglo-Saxons had being conquered and colonised (Europeanised?) by Dane, Norman, and Scot alike.

But history had nothing to do with it. 'Celt vs. Anglo-Saxon' was a heroic political explanation for English imperial dominance in these isles. 'Anglo-Saxons' were superior Protestant white

*Tribes of Galway 1124-1642*

men, predestined masters of a global empire and 'the British Isles' - a term since put to much back-dated and now woefully out-dated use - "'The Isles' became British by monarchical criteria in 1603 and constitutionally in 1801. They ceased to be British in 1949 [1922] ... though few in the British residue have yet cared to notice." [17]

Some of this was aimed at England's old French enemy, homeland of the Keltoi and Celtic languages, but its primary targets were inhabitants of England's 'fringe', Catholics and non-English-speakers. As 'Celts', they were cast as inferior human beings and therefore natural subordinates to a master 'race'. Dominant polities everywhere justify their elite position by demeaning lessers, with "inferiority based on racial [ethnic] classification ... used to justify colonialism." [18] It was a handy way of excusing the brutalities of conquest and colonisation because it was 'inevitable', as the 'Celts' were a 'doomed race'. If like the Romans, the true marker of imperialisation is adopting the conquerors paradigm, then Celticity is a success as descendants of Gaeilgeoiri and Cymraeg proclaim a 'Celtic identity' their ancestors never held.

Understandably, it was positive French Celticity that dazzled Fr. Edward Maginn (1802-49) as a clerical student in France. It was heroically romantic, politically powerful, and from an imperial Catholic state with deep Irish links, so Maginn related Ireland's Gaelic heritage to French Celticity to highlight Ireland's non-Englishness. For the best of motives he nevertheless drew Irish heritage into an stereotype from which it has yet to escape, becoming the first known Irish person to class the Irish as 'Celts'. [19] Evidently, Gaelic culture alone was not enough. A non-English but still imperial Big Brother was needed to make it worthy. In contrast, John O'Donovan (1809-61), a Gaeilgeoir historian whose profound knowledge of Irish heritage was unmatched in his lifetime, does not seem to have used the term at all. Likewise respectful of actual Anglo-Saxon, Brythonic, and Gaelic heritages, philologist J. R.R. Tolkien (1892-1973) forcefully dismissed the 'Celt' and 'Teuton' paradigms as myths, without value. [20]

But scholarship is rarely valued by arts or politics, as both thrive on fiction. For utterly different reasons, Celticity was fashionably *chic* to imperialist and Fenian alike. So within decades, the words 'Irish' and 'Celt' were used by British and Irish, as though they meant the same thing. That it coincided with language shift was not a coincidence. When Gaeilge fell out of majority use in the early-to-mid 1800s, the only popular concepts left were these Anglo-French stereotypes - Celticity is above all Anglocentric. By 1901, the medieval Gaeil were transformed into 'Celts', wearing winged helmets (German) and kilts (British), firmly based on no evidence whatsoever. [21]

The decades either side of 1901 saw the mania of Celticity reach epidemic proportions, with the terms applied to 'race'/'blood', art, magical groups, sports teams, music, even *English*-language literature – in the 1990s it was bafflingly applied to an economy. Celticity has being used for so many things it came to mean whatever people wanted it to mean. And when words can mean any-thing, they become meaning-less. In 1919, partly in response to Celtomania, Irish scholar and nationalist Eoin MacNeill felt obliged to point out that:

> throughout all their early history [histories] and tradition[s] the Irish and Britons
> alike show not the slightest recognition that they were Celtic peoples. We do not

find them acknowledging any kinship with the Gauls, or even with each other ... the term Celtic bears a linguistic and not a racial [ethnic] significance. [22]

Sadly, 'Celt(s)' and Celtic are now so frequently removed from their contexts that they can be binds that tie understanding of Ireland's past. At worst, they are a preposterous fashion and an racial stereotype. As the terms have no historical association with Ireland or the Irish, are loaded with inaccurate connotations, some academics suggest their use in Irish contexts should be abandoned. [23] Few would so far. When used evidentially the terms have excellent applications. Yet there are large gulfs between factual use and mainstream belief, which still infect scholarship - despite claims to the contrary, Bell Beaker culture as a vector for Keltoi and/or Celtic languages in Ireland is "ludicrous", while genetics have found 'Celtic' DNA is not Irish. "The notion of Celtdom has cast a long shadow over meaningful enquiry into the ... Gaelic world." [24]

Summarising the issues, linguist Peter Schrijver writes "Celtic is a well-defined linguistic term, and its application to archaeological cultures and to genes is a metaphor that is bound to cause confusion and misunderstandings." [25] Over several decades, such discrepancies led Irish scholars to query the politicised indoctrination of Celticity into recent Irish identity and heritage. Barry Raftery, [26] John Waddell, [27] Bárra Ó Donnabháin, [28] Jacqueline Cahill-Wilson, [29] and others have all offered useful critiques, the bluntest being that of William O'Brien:

> Are ... the Irish, Celts? The answer is no in terms of our remote origins as we cannot establish any significant racial, ethnic or cultural connection to those Iron Age groups on the Continent called 'Keltoi' by the Classical writers. The Celticity of the Irish lies in later cultural associations connected to the perceived origins of the Irish language and the mythologising of national identity in the modern era. Our direct ancestry lies not in the 'Celtic' Iron Age, but in the history of an indigenous population who origins extended back to the earliest post-Glacial settlement of the island. [30]

## Seanchas nó stair?

Lost in seafóid were the histories and heritages of the Irish, Britons, Angles, Saxons, Franks - most of all the Keltoi, who sadly remain a cliché rather than a people. Old names were sexed up and dumbed down for popular consumption, rarely understood on their own terms. History was understood as a drama, culture was confused with 'blood', ethnicity equated with language.

For example, Gaeilge is considered the 'true' language of the Irish. Yet into the last centuries BC - for over ten thousand years - the Irish were not Gaeilgeoirí. Words such as *Aife*, *Bréifne*, *bradán*, *ciotóg*, *Crufait*, *Grafand*, *faochán*, *gliomach*, *Life*, *partán* - apparently even *Ériu* itself - form part of a curious group of Gaelic lexemes. Curious, because all seemingly derive from a lost language(s) that was not Gaelic, or Celtic, nor even Indo-European. Yet it was an Irish language(s), spoken in Éire until at least AD 500, after which Gaeilge assimilated and overwhelmed it. [31]

Which begs the question; how much of Éire's Gaelic culture is not 'Celtic' but Irish?

Misclassified as 'Celts' for some two hundred years, we have being Irish for over twelve and a

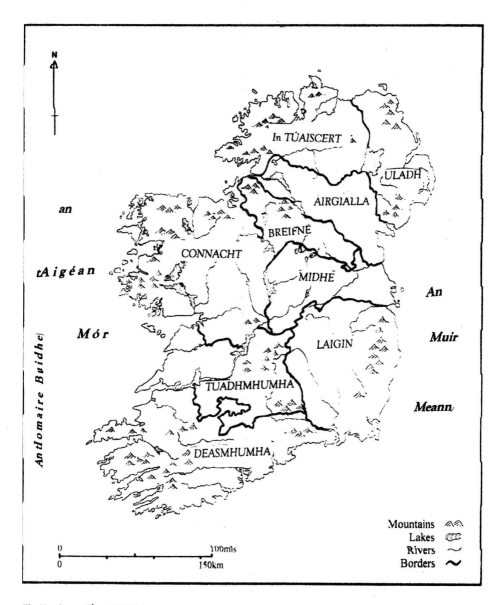

*The Kingdoms of Éire, AD 1166*

half thousand. Being Irish relies upon lives lived on the island, transmitted within and without, no matter what our religions or haplogroups, skin-colours or languages, political affiliations or ethnic backgrounds. The processes that created the Irish, in all our messy complexities, happened in the one and only place the Irish could ever originate - here, on the sea-circled earth of

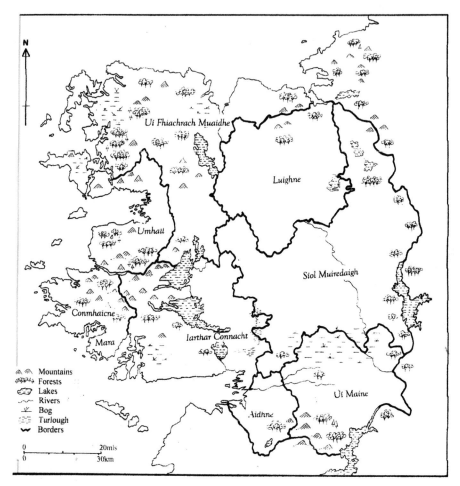

*Connacht and its major Kingdoms and Lordships in the 1100's*

Éire. What makes the Irish is not inherited genetics nor purely culture, but our shared experiences on this island (or perhaps shared *disputed* experiences and *disagreed* remembrances!). They are so powerful that Irish is an identity held by descendants born and raised outside Ireland. On it goes.

Éire's Christian mythologists rewrote the past into a *coimgne* ('harmonization of traditions') that synthesised past events into a 'better' version. [32] No doubt it left out any number of awkward or 'unimportant' bits, as do all national and political myths. The Bible, Greek and Roman epics - themselves deliberate myths - the works of Iberians such as Paulus Orosius (fl. 417) and Isidore of Seville (d. 636) were used as examples and inspiration. They contain vanishingly few references to Éire, but like later notions of Celticity, the literatures dazzled - enough that the mythologists wished to claim kinship with the peoples and cultures that created them. Scythians,

Jews, Egyptians, and Greeks were all tried out as national ancestors. Greek literature was so esteemed in Éire c. AD 800 that scholars attempted to 'prove' Gaeilge derived from Greek!

The prestige of Christian (and therefore Roman) scholarship in Iberia led to a Gaelic, though not Irish, origin legend. A fictional Iberian bearing a suspiciously non-Celtic 'name', míl Espáine, was chosen as the ancestor of the Gaeil - the accidental assonance of Iberia and (H)I(b)ernia must have sealed the deal. It's derivation from the Latin miles Hispaniae ('Spanish soldier') underlines its origin was not Celtic or Iberian but Roman. No profound links were made with Britain or Gaul. [33]

The glamour of this new learning is alluded to in a rémscel ('backstory') of the Táin Bó Cuailnge, where the Cuilmenn - Isidore's derided Etymologiae, published in 640 - is regarded as the 'summit' of all knowledge. [34] Where not suppressed or forgotten, Pagan traditions were rewritten to agree with the Church, its approved books, their political sponsors, and their version of history. [35] The past is endlessly re-spun to justify the ever-changing present, with spin a well-paid profession today.

Bart Jaski observed that "Historical tradition thus provided for what political reality dictated. ... tradition was not sacred to the Irish propagandists ... rather that propaganda was a sacred tradition to them." [36] Orthodoxy survived, dissent died. As always, myth grew bigger than truth. [37]

## The Old Gods and the New

The Fir Bolg were first attested in Irish myth, though apparently based on a genuine Iron Age people. In high medieval times the term was applied to lowly castes who, as 'Fir Bolg', were the most numerous non-Gaeil Irish people. Killimor east of the Sliabh Aughty was then Cill Íomair Bolg ('Iomar's [Fir] Bolg church'). The Bolgthuath Eachtgha, as d'Feraib Bolc, were defined in the 1350s as "lucht freasdail ocus fir duchais"/"serfs and hereditary followers". [38] This denoted

### The creation of Gaelic-Irish surnames
See "A Note on the Emergence of Irish Surnames," F. J. Byrne, 2001, pp. xxxi-xliii.

Form I: ua, Ua/Ó

Colmán [epynom]
|
Aodh mac Colmáin [patronymic]
|
Domnall ua Colmáin [papponymic]
|
Flann Ua Colmáin [surname]

Form II: mac, mac meic, Mac

Áed [epynom]
|
Donnchad mac Áeda [patronymic]
|
Faolán mac meic Áeda/Mac Áeda [papponymic/surname]
|
Lorcan Mac Áeda [surname]

Epynom        = person from whom patronymic, papponymic, and surname, derives.
Patronymic    = term indicating father's name, and thus paternal descent.
Papponymic    = term coined by Francis John Byrne (2001) to indicate grandather's name.
Surname       = term used by someone who is neither son nor grandson of the epynom.

## Clann Fhearghaile and the Uí hAllmhuráin (9th/10th-15th centuries?)

Source: GBIG I, 204.5, pp. 448-449.

Allmhurán [epynom of Ua hAllmhurain, fl. 810?/929-30?]
|
Fear Gallaigh [epynom of Clann Fhearghaile]
|
Cú Ciolle
|
Aodh [first generation surnamed Ua hAllmhurain?]
|
Diarmuid
|
Conchabar *of the battle of Luarach*
|
Domhnall
|
Tadhg *Talchar* [obstinate]
|
Fearghal
|
Aodh
|
Conchabhar
|
Giolla Steafáin *na Fódla* [of Ireland?]
|
Maol Ruanaidh
|
Domhnall
|
Dáibhidh
|
Amhlaoibh
|
Tadhg
|
Giolla Críost
|
Dáibhidh
|
Seónac [post-Norman name]
|
Dabhac

peoples defined by ethnic distinction and caste discrimination. Yet they were still legitimised by being of a fixed community or settled country, hence an *Lucht Túaithe*, 'country folk' - below them were true outsider castes such as an *Lucht Siúl*/'the [walking] travelling folk', and others. By then the 'Fir Bolg' were indistinguishable from Gaeil (singular, Gael) in both language and culture.

In his *Leabhar na nGenealach* and *Cuimre*, scribe and historian Dubhaltach Mac Fhirbhisigh (d. 1671) concluded that the numerous Fir Bolg, *Forshloinnte*, and *Aitheachthuatha*, had been distinct Irish ethnic groups disparaged by their non-Gaeil ancestries. So the Gaeil were the free castes and upper-class nobility, the 'Fir Bolg' derided in terms of 'race' and 'blood'. "Cuma riamh;" observed Mac Fhirbhisigh, "ní fhuil ann acht an teann saorusal 'sa fann daoirísiol, fas seach, are sealaidheacht/It is ever the same; it is only [a matter of] the strong being free and noble and the weak enslaved and lowly, alternately [and] in turn."[39]

An associated group, the mysterious sometimes sinister *Fomoraige* were probably gods, later associated with the sea. Their worshippers must once have been powerful, as their successors demonised them. Philistines, Vandals, and Huns likewise show how an ethnic term can become a slur or baudyman, lasting as a half-forgotten fairy tale, before oblivion.

As an ethnic term, *Fir Bolg* denoted the Dési, Ciarraige, Corcu Loígde, Fortuatha Laigin, and non-Cruthin Ulaid - all classed as Érainn, Óengus Bolg their ancestor deity. [40] No doubt there were originally sharp distinctions between them, but by the high medieval era - when the term as we understand it was seemingly created - they were lumped together, as if a homogeneous group.

In late pre-literate history the term denoted marital frenzy, as *bolg-/*belg-* means '[the] Wrathful', as in 'swollen with wrath/rage'. [41] Possibly it first denoted Óengus, only much later applied to 'his' people. By the 1100s the Érainn had ceased to be while their 'Fir Bolg' descendants held few supreme positions. The language had by then changed so much that only the 'swollen' aspect was understood, so *bolg* came to denote a 'bag', leaving the 'Fir Bolg' to be misremembered as 'men of bags', derided as commoners. Thus it was adapted as a derogatory term for Éire's servile folks. The purpose of the 'Fir Bolg' was to be the 'racial' baudymen that made the Gaeil look good. How this came to be was explained in revisionist, mythic terms, as a religious 'Judgement of the Gods'. The gods concerned, the Tuatha Dé Danann, being those of the Pagan Gaeil.

According to literary legend, the Tuatha Dé Danann - whose arrival in sky ships advertised their divine origins - defeated the all-too human Fir Bolg at the battle of *Maigh Tuired*, near *Cunga* (Cong) on Loch Orbsen's north shore. The Tuatha Dé Danann repartitioned Éire, planting themselves on the best land in the east. The Fir Bolg were expelled to the poorest lands, west beyond the Shannon. Prominent Fir Bolg exiles were the *Tuath mac nÚmóir* ('Úmór's sons' folk'). Some were led to Árann by Aonghus son of Úmór, credited with building an almost Cthulhuic stone fort on what was then the summit of Inis Mór (its actual occupation ended c. 700 BC). Though half has long since collapsed into the Atlantic, it is still *Dún Aonghasa* ('Aonghus's fort'). [42]

That the 'Fir Bolg' may have being native to the areas, not exiles; that an old ethnic nickname was re-applied as a 'racial' caste term; that myth is not history; was irrelevant. The 'manifest destiny' of the Gaeil was to rule. The Fir Bolg were 'fated' to serve. So says myth as written by the victors.

## The nations of Éire

The region west of the Shannon was once [*Cóiced*] *Ól nÉchmacht*, usually understood as '[the province of the] Ol nEchmacht'. Another rendering, 'beyond the marshes/fastness', implies it was originally a geographical term from a midlands view, perhaps only later denoting populations who had no common identity. [43] Equating the 'Fir Ól nÉchmacht' with an western Irish group called the *Nagnatai*, recorded c. AD 130-170 by the geographer Claudius Ptolemaeus, is often cited but not regarded as plausible. Two other western groups were the *Gangani*; and the *Auteni*, inland from the rivers *Ausoba* (the Gaillimh?) and *Senos* (the Shannon?). [44]

These were three of the sixteen ethnic groups Ptolemaeus recorded in second-century Éire;

the possibility exists that there were others unknown to his informants or too 'minor' to record. In the north were the *Erpeditani, Vennicnii, Robogdii, Darini,* and *Voluntii.* In the east were the *Eblani, Cauci, Manapii, Coriondi,* and *Brigantes.* In the south, the *Usdiae, Iverni,* and *Vellabori.* These names are in a language which separated, after the first century AD, into what are now called the Brythonic and Goidelic language groups. [45] Of the kingdoms formed by these Iron Age ethnicities and nations, few overt traces survive. Those that do include partly extant linear earthworks such as the *Cliadh Dubh* in Munster, the *Knockans* in Leinster (almost entirely destroyed in 1997), the *Dorsey* and the *Black Pig's Dyke* in Ulster. These massive works deliberately partitioned landscapes, perhaps acting like the Antonine Wall, Hadrian's Wall, and Offa's Dyke would centuries later in Britain. [46]

By the time native history acquired literacy - and the Tuatha Dé Danann were vanquished by a new Roman god (*'Vae victis!'*) - many Iron Age groups had apparently vanished. Much else had changed. Between the fourth and seventh centuries, what we now call Gaeilge regenerated, drasticly. [47] This is held to be the result of a language shift event - assimilating Éire's native, non-Indo-European language(s), after which the Irish were mostly Gaeilgeoirí. [48] This had huge implications for the transmission of historic knowledge. *History became legend, legend became myth* ... Cataclysmic events were only crudely recalled, in partisan terms. Major and minor details were suppressed, misunderstood, or simply forgotten.

## Luchta Deiscirt Connacht

Seventh-century Éire had ethnic groups called the Cruithin, Dealbhna, Éli, Érainn (*Iverni?*), Laigin, Osraige (*Usdiae?*), Dál Riata, and Ulaid (*Voluntii?*). They in turn had offshoots and subgroups such as the Meadhraighe, Partraighe, and Conmhaicne.

The Conmhaicne ('hound-sons') were scattered all over what would become County Galway – at Dunmore (*Conmhaicne Dúna Móir /Conmhaicne Cenéoil Dubháin*), around Shrule (*in Conmhaicne Cúile Toland*), and near Loughrea at Kilconickny ('the church of the Conmhaicne'). [49] The evangelical bishop, Iarlaithe - better known as Saint Jarlath of Tuam - was of them. [50] One Tribes family, the Kirwans, were descendants of the Conmhaicne.

The most westerly Conmhaicne held the mainland due north of Árainn, the interior marked by mountains called *na Ben Beola*. Known as the *Conmhaicne Mara* ('the Conmhaicne of the sea'), [51] their name now inaccurately applies to all the region west of the Gaillimh, corrupted to Connemara. Their ruling lineage was *Ua Cadhla* (Kealy, Keely). *Muirethaich mac Cadlai, rí Chonmhaicne Mara*, fought for Brian Bóruma at Clontarf in April 1014. He died in 1016, possibly *h-i Purt Chiarain i n-Áraind* ("in Port Ciaráin in Árainn"). [52]

North-east of Conmhaicne Mara were the Partraighe, inhabitants of the lands around Lough Mask and Lough Carra (*Partraighe Cera*), at Cong (*Partraighe in Lacha*), and towards Cruacháin Aigle/Croagh Patrick (*Partrighe in tSléibe*). Almost the only trace of them today is the parish of Partry, and the surname of their kings, *Ua Goirmiallaigh/Goirmghiolla* (Gormally, Gormley). [53] The Darcys, another of Galway's merchant families, traced themselves back to Partrighe.

The Dealbhna apparently took their name from their patron deity, Dealbhaoth of the Tuath

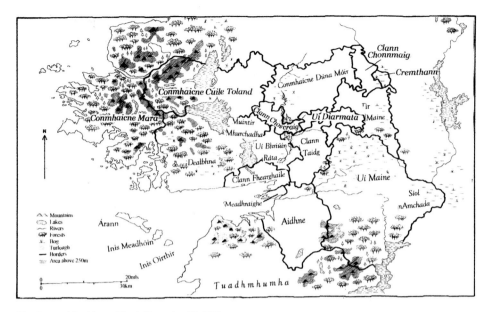

Kingdoms and Lordships of South Connacht, AD 1200

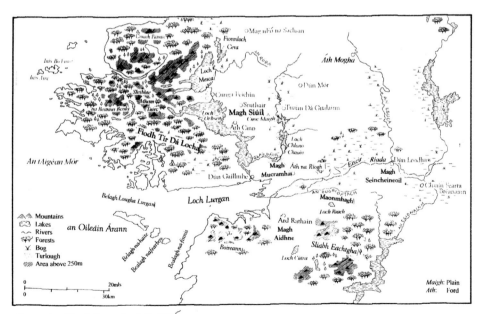

Topography of South Connacht, A.D. 1200

## Muintir Murchadha, 896-1004

Sources: Contemporary annals; the *Banseanchas* (*indicates which individuals); Jaski 2013.
*IC=Iarthar Connacht  UBS=Ui Briuin Seola  T=Thomond  UB=Ui Briuin*
*UBC=Ui Briuin Connacht  C=Connacht  MM=Muintir Murchadha*

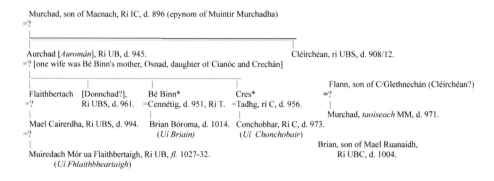

---

## Uí Fhlaithbheartaigh, 1027-1306

Sources: Contemporary annals; the *Banseanchas* (*indicates which individuals); Jaski 2013.
*IC=Iarthar Connacht  UBS=Ui Briuin Seola  UB=Ui Briuin  C=Connacht*

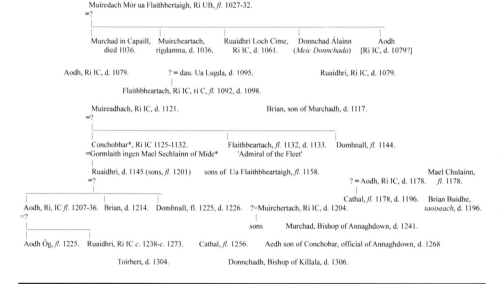

---

Dé, and may once have spanned both banks of the Gaillimh. West of the river was known as *Fiodh Tír Dá Locha* ('the Wasteland [the Wood] of the Land of the Two Lakes', i.e., Loch Orbsen agus Loch Lurgan). [54] It recalls a time when the woods of Dealbhna were dark and deep.

The territory was divided into *Gnó Beag* (parishes of Moycullen, Rahoon, part of Kilannin) and *Gnó Mór* (Kilcummin and most of Kilannin). Gnó Beag's kings bore the surname *Ua* hAdhnaigh (Heeney, Heaney), while those of Gnó Mór - and overkings of all Dealbhna west of the Gaillimh - were surnamed *Mac Con Raoi* (Conroy, 'King' [Con Raoi ='hound of the {battle} plain']). [55]

The history of the Dealbhna east of the Gaillimh is unclear. A late eleventh-century text lists *Ua Faghartaigh* (Faherty) as the surname of the king of "Dealbhna Cúil Fhabhair and Muintir Fhathaigh and Fiodh Luraigh." [56] But these areas were inland and north of the coast. A kindred called the *Clann Fhearghaile* ('Fergal's offspring') are listed in the same text as occupying coastal lands that are now the parishes of St. Nicholas's and Oranmore. Clann Fhearghaile's ruling sept bore the surname *Ua hAllmhuráin* (O'Halloran).

The families of *Ua Con Tuile* (Tully, 'Flood') and *Ua Fearghusa* (Fergus) were apparently junior lineages. [57] Clann Fhearghaile appear to have been firmly suborned by the Uí Bhriúin Eóla, as their ruler is not described as a king in his own right, but as a *taoisich* ('leader', 'lord'). Genetic genealogy in 2013 determined that male Uí hAllmhuráin bore the M222 DNA marker, found from Inis Éoghan to Galway Bay. [58] They were the first certain proprietors of Bun Gaillimhe, but may have ousted the Dealbhna. Who the Dealbhna evicted is utterly unknown.

South of what would become Oranmore were the Meadhraighe, hidden in the placename Maree. The families of *Mág an Ghamhain* (now probably Gannon) and *Mág Catharnaigh* (Carney, Keary) were their rulers. [59] Its not known if they were of the Meadhraighe, were imposed upon them by Clann Fhearghaile, or another group entirely. Rathgurreen in Meadhraighe was the node of a communications network active from at least the fifth to seventh centuries, connecting local land routes with European maritime trade, trading everything from butter to slaves for European goods. An oil lamp, made at Rome in the fourth or fifth century, was excavated there in 1948-49. [60]

North of Clann Fhearghaile was Magh Siúil, the central plain of the Uí Bhriúin Eóla kingdom. Ruled alternately by the rival dynasties of Clann Chosgraigh and Muintir Mhurchadha, its ruler was termed *rí deiscirt Chonnacht* (king of south Connacht). A *crannóg* on Loch Cimbe (Lough Hackett) was a royal residence and perhaps a refuge in stressful times. [61] The chief lineage in each dynasty adopted surnames: *Mac Aodha* (McHugh) for Clann Chosgraigh, and *Ua Flaithbheartaigh* (O'Flaherty) for Muintir Mhurchadha. The Uí Fhlaithbheartaigh were by the 1120s in charge at Bun Gaillimhe and admirals of its fleet, closely attended by their *Mac Donnchadha* (McDonagh) cousins, descendants of Donnchad *Álainn* ('the handsome') Ua Flaithbheartaigh.

South-east of Magh Siúil was Uí Bhriúin Rátha, and the *taoisidheacht* ('lordship') of Clann Taidg, named after its rulers *Ua Thaidg an Teaglaig* (O'Tighe of the household). Their surname suffix denoted they were hereditary marshals to their cousins, the kings of Connacht. Beyond was Uí Diarmata. Its kings were surnamed *Ua Con Cheanainn* (Concannon), overlording the *Mac Scaithghil* (Scahill) of Corca Mogha and other lesser, forgotten folk.

Both Clann Taidg and the Uí Diarmata were septs of the Síol Muiredaigh dynasty, intruding west between the ninth and eleventh centuries, carving their territories from neighbouring kingdoms. Their homeland was Magh nAí in what is now north-central County Roscommon. [62]

East of the river ford called Áth na Ríogh ('Ford of the Kings', now Athenry) to the Shannon spanned Uí Maine. Its kings bore the surnames *Ua Ceallaigh* (O'Kelly) and *Ua Madadháin* (Madden), reigning over a number of unrelated groups such as the Dál Druithe, the Catraighe, and the Soghain. [63] The Soghain were of the Cruithin, found in Connacht, The North, Airgialla, Uladh, and Mide. Soghain families included *Mac an Bhaird* (Ward), *Ua Dubagáin* (Duggan), *Ua Mainnín* (Mannion), all still found in the bounds of their former kingdom. Evidence suggests Cenél nDéigill's Ua Mainnín Kings of Soghain resided in and ruled over the Athenry area till evicted by the Clann Taidg, c. 1135-52. [64]

Between the Sliabh Eachtgha in the east and Loch Lurgan in the west was the kingdom of Aidhne, ruled from the late-sixth century by a branch of the Uí Fhiachrach. The principal families of the dynasty had by the eleventh century adopted the surnames *Ua Cléirigh* (O'Cleary), *Ua hEidhin* (Hynes, Hayes), and *Ua Seachnasaigh* (O'Shaughnessey).

All these families had roles in the story of Galway and its merchants.

## The Irish and the Goídil

The Uí Fhiachrach were a dynasty of one of Éire's notable political confederations, the Connachta. [65] They became so identified with Ól nÉchmacht that it was renamed, being Connacht since at least the 800s. The Uí Fhiachrach were part of a new group termed in Old Irish as the *Goídil* (later Gaeil, singular 'Gael'). They and the older groups all held themselves to be ethnically distinct peoples, identity and politics in Éire remaining deeply localised for centuries yet.

Popular knowledge of these nations is now uncommon, yet their echoes are all around us as all states have ghost populations. The *Laigin* ('the spearmen' [sic]) [66] and the *Ulaid* ('the bearded ones') [67] gave their names to provinces (*Leinster* and *Ulster*). The *Loígis*, a Cruithin folk, were namesakes of County Laois. *Éli* and *Osraighe* ('[kingdom of] the deer people') [68] survived as kingdoms into the sixteenth century, their rulers adopting the surnames *Ua Cearrbaill* (O'Carroll) and *Mac Giolla Pátraic* (FitzPatrick). Osraighe is recalled in the name of a modern diocese, Ossory.

Immigrants from Roman Britannia and 'barbarian' Alba are known to have lived in fifth-century Éire; Pagan and Christian, Latin and Pictish, Saxon and Brythonic-speakers. [69] Irish Pagans worshipped different gods, so sectarian divisions probably existed even between native groups. Each region had its own history and cultural traditions, which with local topography and ecology led to different economic and settlement patterns. Into the 700s, legal practise apparently varied. [70] Some groups were free, others suborned. Each Irish nation had distinct origin legends and do not seem to have recognised any common nationality. [71] And just at the point of Gaelic homogeneity, in the 790s came vikings from Scandinavia and north Britain.

All this reflected the profound political, cultural, ethnic, religious, and linguistic diversity that prevailed in early medieval Ireland. One that was not 'timeless Celticity', but a dynamic melting pot. How real these divisions were as indicators of ethnicity or nationality as we would understand them, is immaterial. They were self-authenticated by communal belief, exactly like today.

### What's in a Name

Between the fourth century BC and the fourth century AD, *Hieriyo, Hibernia, Ierne, Iuverna,* and *Scotia* were terms used by Greek and Roman explorers and writers for Éire. [72] All but *Scotia* were attempts to spell Old Irish *Ériu*, a native geographic term seemingly of non-Indo-European origin to which the Érainn, in a way now unclear, were related. [73] Sub-groups bore prefixes such as *Aes* ('people'), *Fir* ('men'), *Corcu* ('seed'? 'progeny', 'folk'), *Dál* ('posterity'?, 'division'/'portion'[district]), collective suffixes such as *-na*, *-raige* (Dealbhna, Calraige), the gentillics *dercu* or *moccu* ('daughter' or 'son' [of the] -people'). [74] They denoted a ethnic, religious, or political identity, back to a common unifying figure (ancestor, deity) or feature (location, economy, caste, trait). Such terms were mainly used by 'older' folks.

By AD 900, dynasties explicitly dominated. They were denoted by terms such as *Cenél* ('kindred'), *Clann* ('children'/'offspring', 'descendants'), *Muintir* ('family', 'people', 'folk'), *Tellach* ('household'), *Síol* ('seed', 'posterity', anglicised as sept), *Sliocht* ('progeny', 'lineage'), *Uí* ('descendants', 'grandchildren', plural of *ua*). They indicated descent from a collective historic ancestor. [75] Lineage, not 'tribalism', was supreme. But from at least the 940s, even these terms were surpassed, as the Irish introduced an innovation to Europe.

### Europe's first hereditary surnames

Originally, *ua* denoted a grandchild-grandparent relationship. For example, Domnall ua Colmáin indicated that one Domnall was the grandson of a man named Colmán. Domnall's grandson would in turn use the form *ua Domhnaill*, e.g., Aodh ua Domhnaill = Aodh grandson of Domhnall.

The same laws governed the *mac* form. Donnchad mac Áeda denoted a man named Donnchad whose father was named Áed. A son of Donnchad would in turn use the form *mac Donnchada*, e.g., Faolán mac Donnchadha = Faolán son of Donnchad. The suffixes to *ua* and *mac* were in such instances patronymics ('paternal identifiers'), not passed intact to succeeding generations.

Yet by the 940s, men who were *not* sons *or* grandsons of a named man, used *mac* (contracting *mac meic* 'son of the son of') and *ua* forms in hereditary fashion. In written form they were eventually capitalised as Mac and Ua, later Ó. We call them surnames ('sire-names'), indicative of paternal descent. That they were adopted contemporaneously in different parts of the island underlines the astonishing Gaelic cultural homogeneity accomplished by then.

The exact reasons why they were adopted remain debated, but given the classes and power groups among whom they originated, Gaelic-Irish surnames may have been an innovation to restrict ownership of property and privileges to particular lineages. The surnames themselves were titles, and with titles come rights and entitlements, such as kingship (the popular belief, found outside Ireland, that Gaelic surnames were bestowed by Irish kings and lords on their followers is untrue). What can be said is that they arose primarily among Irish ecclesiastical and royal kindreds, and are the oldest hereditary European surnames still in use.

## Kings and High Kings

*Rígdamnai* ('king-material', directly equivalent to Anglo-Saxon *athling*) were men theoretically eligible to become kings, succession depending on their inclusion in the ruling fine ('family', 'kin-

# The Ua Conchobair dynasty, 925-1274

Sources: Contemporary annals; the *Banseanchas*; *Leabhar na nGenealach*; Jaski 2013. Kings of Connacht in **bold**. Purely for clarity, wives and concubines of Tadg (d. 956) and his male descendants are mainly ommited.

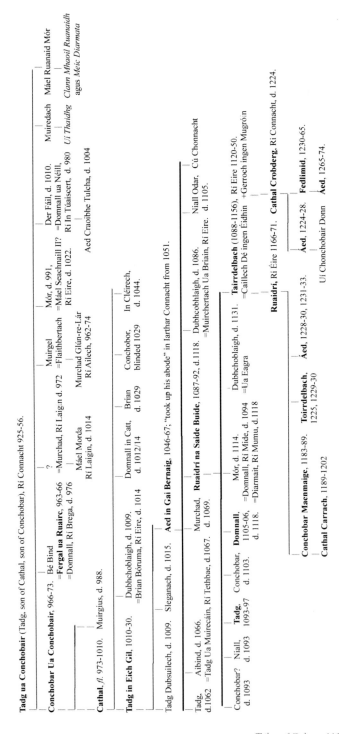

dred'), as was the case in most European societies. Any man descended from a king - up to and including great-grandsons - could become one himself, though mostly sons or brothers of the previous king succeeded. [76] A *rí* ('king') ruled a *túath*, which till replaced by the *tríca cét* in the 11th century was Éire's basic political unit, varying in area. [77] Different types of substantial medieval buildings existed: *ráth/lios, crannóg, cathair,* and *dún*. [78] All have importance in understanding the type and function of Gaelic settlement by the Gaillimhe, the people who lived in them, how, and why.

The *ráth* was the ditch and earth rampart around a site while the *lios* (*les*) was it's yard; both terms came to be used interchangeably. [79] They were domestic settlement enclosures, farmsteads, religious, or industrial so not necessarily associated with kings or even nobles. However, two or more outer ditches and ramparts may have signified a high-status residence of a *rí*. [80]

A *crannóg* was a defensible dwelling built on artificial lake islands, used in Ireland c. 2000 BC – c. AD 1700. They were multi-functional; used as dwellings, to hold hostages or slaves, for fishing or erotic rendezvous. [81] The *cathair* or *cashel* was a ring-shaped stone-walled fortification with at least one internal building consisting of stone, timber, or both. A *dún* ('fort'/'stone fortress') was a garrison used to control the regions in which they were situated. Their ultimate use was to project the prestige and power of their *rí*. [82] And *ríg*, always exclusive to certain lineages, were now further privileged to certain surnames.

## One King To Rule Them All

The lowest type of king was a *rí túaithe* ('local king', 'king of a country'[locality]), subject to a greater ruler termed *rí túath* or *ruiri*. Above them was the highest grade of kingship recognised in Gaelic law, a *rí ruirech* ('regional king') or *rí cóicid* ('provincial king'). [83] The prolific *túatha* were long believed to be the principal kingdoms, yet from as early as the Bronze Age, the island was dominated by indigenous *ruiri* and *rí ruirech*, dynasties and overkingdoms.

Irish society was never static or timeless, anarchic or archaic. Though 'tribal' is often used to describe it, 'dynastic' is more correct. Dynasties are family power groups with lineaged claims on property, titles, lord/kingship. Like elsewhere in Europe, they were the principal social unit and power-brokers, secular and religious, with major dynasts wielding power far beyond their *túatha*. Powerful men want one thing above all - more. And since at least the 600s, some imagined themselves as rulers dominating even regional kings.

From about the mid-seventh century, the kingdoms of In Túaiscert and Mide - located in the north-west and midlands respectively - were ruled by Uí Néill septs who rotated the kingship of Tara between them. The *rí Temair*, 'King of Tara', was recognised as overking of the entire Uí Néill, who were of the Connachta political confederation. Like them, they were a collective of unrelated power groups expressed as a dynasty, and the most powerful of the *Gael*.

The kings of Laigin and Uladh alternated the kingship of Tara prior to the early 500s, but were displaced by the Uí Néill, who all but erased both peoples out of an extensively revised history. [84] Uí Néill rule of Tara was backdated into remote prehistory for historical authenticity, and later invested with an equally fictitious claim to all-Éire rule. This medieval revisionism has been so successful that it is still popularly believed to be true. [85]

These claims were ignored, Cold War-like, by Éire's other superpower, the Eóghanachta, another confederated collective but one for whom the *rí Caisel*, 'King of Cashel', was supreme. The 737 *rígdáil* ('royal conference') at Tir dá Glas between King Cathal of Cashel and King Áed of Tara resulted in a mutual non-agression pact, where each hegemony recognised the other and partitioned Éire into two jurisdictions: *Leth Cuinn* (northern Éire, ruled by Tara) and *Leth Moga* (southern Éire, ruled by Cashel). [86]

The border between the two was marked by the Ice Age natural feature known as the *Escir Riada*, from *Ath Cliath Laigin*, now in Dublin City, to *Áth Cliath Meadhraighe*, now Clarinbridge, County Galway. [87] Though with opposition, until the tenth century the Uí Néill and Eóghanachta remained dominant in their respective jurisdictions. But from the mid-900s, in tandem with upheavals caused by Scandinavian raids, invasions, and settlements, obscure or displaced dynasties such as the Uí Briúin Bréifne and Uí Cheinnselaig successfully gained regional kingships. These conflicts accelerated notions of kingship, so "To keep up with the political developments, the annalists of the tenth century introduce[d] the title of 'high-king' (*ardrí*) as a title of recognition or flattery to denote a powerful king who achieved a remarkable domination over others." [88]

First to make kingship of Éire a mesmerising reality in 854-860, was Máel Seachnaill I of Clann Colmáin. On his death in 862 he became the first man justly described as *rí h-Erenn uile*, 'King of all Ireland' (a comparable *rex totius Britanniae* was not declared until 927). The most infamous was Brian *bóruma* of the Dál gCais (d. 1014). Without any hereditary claim to either Cashel or Tara - Brian was not Gael but an ethnic Déisi - he gained both only to supersede them by proclaiming himself *imperator Scotorum*, 'Emperor of the Irish'. After all, if a King is a Lord of lords, then an Emperor is a King of kings. And *Scotorum* had implications beyond the shores of Éire.

Subsequent Irishmen craved this imperial dream. So much so that in 1125-26 Archbishop Cellach of Ard Macha (Armagh) spent thirteen months all over the island *oc sithughadh fer n-Erenn* ("pacifying the men of Éire") because of *cocaidh mhoir i n-Erinn* ("the great war in Éire").

Conflicts inflict horrors. Escalating horrors devour. Enslavement, displacement, rape, murder were the unprecedented human costs of warfare in Éire during the ninth to twelfth centuries. No wonder that, in describing the island in 1145, a scribe memorably wrote:

> *Coccadh mór isin m-bliadhain-si co m-boí Ere ina fód crithaigh*
> Great war in this year, so that Éire was a trembling sod. [89]

Thus by the 1100s men surnamed Mac Lochlainn, Mac Murchada, Ua Briain, Ua Conchobair, each sought to be the one king to rule them all. Not *ardrí* but *Ri Érenn* - King of Éire.

## Dominions and Partitions

By then, histories were yet again recast. What was previously just *béarla* ('speech', '[the] language') became *Gaeilge* ('language of the Gael'). Like *Gaeilgeoir* ('Gaelic speaker'), it was sub-created from the Middle Irish *Gaeil*. Common practise as languages are generally named after their speakers, not the other way around.

The Gaeil were to Ireland what the English were to Britain. Both were applicable outside each island, have the same 'our island nation'/'united island' dogmas and ignore other ethnicities by privileging one upon whom the 'island nationality' is based: Gaeil=*The* Irish, English=*The* British. Another parallel is the Roman Empire which transformed virtually every conquered nation within and without Italia into Latin-speaking Romans, killing off non-Roman cultures, language groups and identities, forever. Exactly like them, Gaeil was an elite political ethnicity extending downward and outward, consuming all. Such constructions are cold houses for other traditions, because they must. No dogma admits past and present always contain other viable futures - that would undermine the legitimacy of the 'unique tradition'/'the struggle' and its homogenising identity.

The original form of Gaeil, *Goídil*, was adopted during the early-to-mid seventh century. Its Latin equivalent was *Scotti*, while *Hiberionanci/Hibernenses* denoted people in or of Éire. From the 1000s, Gaeil was a generic term increasingly applied by the Irish for themselves. All nationalisms need an Other to look good against, so the Gaeil were contrasted with the *Gaill* (singular *Gall*), a term applied from the 830s to the Scandinavian vikings, and subsequently another Other, the Anglo-Irish. Gaill derived from direct Irish contacts during the fourth to eighth centuries with the Gauls, and denoted a 'foreigner'. [90] Gaeil and Gaill evolved with and because of each Other.

Yet though it came to denote them, *Goídil* was not firstly Irish. It derived from *Gwyddyl*, ('wild men'), [91] a Brythonic term of abuse by the Romano-Britons for the various groups from Éire who raided and invaded Britannia and Alba. It is as if Irish people described the British by the derogative *culchie* (from *coilteach*, 'man of the woods', now meaning 'country fool'), and as if the British adopted it for themselves.

The adoption of Goídil hints it occurred when its original meaning was forgotten or transformed - just as the modern Irish, even Gaeilgeoirí, misunderstand the original meaning of culchie. The unrelated Latin term used by the Romans for the same groups was *Scotti* (hence *Scotia* and 'Scot'). Its original meaning is uncertain, but probably meant something like 'pirate'. It was the Latin term for the Irish, and used by them until about 1200. [92]

As one Irish historian correctly perceived, the adoption of foreign terms indicates "that the Irish had no common [native] word for themselves until they came into contact with foreigners." [93]

So Éire's inhabitants were not one 'race' or a single people, but like the inhabitants of Britain, viewed themselves as distinct nations. These multi-ethnic islanders are best termed *Irish*, just as the Cornish, English, Scots, and Welsh are collectively termed *British* - Manx, Orcadians, and other islanders have their own opinions!

The Greek *ethnos* (plural, *ethnea*) denoted 'a swarm', 'a herd', 'a crowd', 'a rabble', firstly insects or birds, later humans. Ethnicities are group identities, defining 'us - not you', the basis of which varies. 'Civilized' groups are usually termed 'nations', especially if associated with a large territory. 'Primitives' are called 'tribes' if their polity is essentially local. Some or all of the following features are used; a collective name, common laws, a shared history or distinctive culture (language, religion, customs etc.), a specific territory or territories, internal solidarity, a common story or myth of descent, a self-definition again one or more Other(s). [94]

As all are human constructs, all ethnicities can integrate other humans, no matter how 'exclusive' their membership requirements. Like all human constructs, ethnic definitions can be messy, contradictory, and woefully misunderstood outside the ethnos. All are constantly subject to change, indeed to transformation. These last two qualities - not tradition - are the key to their survival. After all, it is tradition that should serve people.

Since the eleventh century, the peoples of Éire were described by a new term - *Iras*, the Old English term which gives us *Irish*, a word directly equivalent to Gaelic *Éireannach*. In time, both Irish and Gaeil were misunderstood to mean the same thing, despite many Gaeil being of Britain.

Yet the Gaeil were not originally a 'race' but a ruling class, the *Féni*. They lived south of the Ulaid and north-west of the Laigin, possibly on "the outskirts of a wooded region on the Meath-Gabrán border." Looking back into late prehistory, an eighth-century text described the prime Irish nations east of the Shannon as *Féni 7 Ulaith 7 Gáilni .i. Laigin* ('Féni, and Ulaid, and Gaileoin or Laigin'). [95]

Interestingly, the Gaelic-Irish law system - misremembered as 'the Brehon laws' - did not have an inclusive term based on a concept of *Éireannach* ('Irish person'). Instead, it was *fénechas* - 'law of the Féni'. This denoted it was law as dictated by a dominant elite. Its lawyers and judges represented not a 'civil service' for a common good, but a 'state service' for a collective few. Féni was almost synonymous with *Goídil* because they defined and denoted an upper-class, warlord-caste. The terms first defined the Connachta, and after they adopted fénechas - perhaps in 737? - the Eóganachta: "the other peoples of Ireland [were] sharply distinguished from them and implicitly relegated to an inferior status." [96]

Thus divisions such as Fir Bolg and Gaeil were not 'race' - though expressed in those terms - but caste, the rulers and the ruled. The Gaeil were the dominant landed aristocracy. The 'Fir Bolg' and others like them were *aithechtuatha* ('commoners'/'vassals'), and *dóertuatha* ('unfree folk') - the labouring peasant population. [97] In a society divided between *nemed* (privileged), *sóer* (free), and *dóer* (unfree), [98] it was a useful technique by the minority to help keep the majority in their place.

There were other reasons for differing terms of identity. Just as the ethnic Gaill were never Gaeil, the Féni were not Érainn, so they had to create a new term for themselves as 'Irish'. Reasons why may have being both ethnic and linguistic - *Bérla Féne* ('language of the Féni', later *Goidelg* hence 'Gaeilge') was originally British. It was contrasted with *iarnbélre* (*Embélre*, 'language of the Érainn', 'the Irish language'), extinct by AD 900 and misremembered as 'the iron [sic] language'. [99] Brythonic Celtic arrived "in Ireland close to or in the first century AD" [100] and termed Gaeilge became the newly-grafted language of all the Irish, as English did from the 17th century. Gaeilge was so named because it was not 'Irish'; it became Irish, as had the Féni. It would do so as long as the Irish wished to be Gaeil. This prestigious common language and culture made the Gaeilgeoirí elite of Éire and Britain see themselves as a nation, even if those in

Britain were *Gall-Goídil* ('foreign Gaeil'). No such fellow-feeling existed with Angelcynn, Brythoniad, or Picti, as they were neither Gaeil or Gaeilgeoiri, nor Irish.

In this way a pre-existing Féni identity was regenerated and renamed, c. AD 650, into a upperclass ethnicity called Goídil, with many more groups than the original Féni. Between 842 and 1286 the meic Alpín dynasty fused Pict, Briton, Gael, Angle, Scandinavian, Norman, into Scot. During the era 878-1065, the House of Wessex fused Saxon, Angle, Frisian, Jute, Briton, and Dane, into English. In Éire from the 600s, the Gaeil attempted to create the dominant, and therefore eventually common, Irish ethnicity. The Gaelic realm was all Éire, the Gaeil were *The Irish* and as the Gaeil were in the British isle then both islands could become *Scottorum*.

Over the centuries, many groups originally unrelated to the dominant polities found it expedient to ally with one or other powerful dynasty. Fabricated pedigrees giving them credible ancestry were supplied to add weight to the political connections. It was a choice between collusive coalition with prospects for further upward mobility, or remaining powerless as the despised unfree.

So just as the gods of the Pagan Gaeil had politically vanquished the 'Fir Bolg', so now did necessity lead to the genealogical assimilation of their descendants.


## Galway's Founder - Toirdhealbhach, Rí Éire

Since the 1700s, Loch Orbsen has being *Lough Corrib*, with the Gaillimh becoming *the Corrib*. A belief now exists that Galway denotes the *Gaill*, who must have built the settlement. Yet Galway was founded not by Gaill but by Gaeil. In 1124, Toirdhealbhach Ua Conchobair built *caistél Gaillme & Caistél Cul Maile & Castél Dúin Leódha* ("the castles of Galway, Collooney, and Ballinasloe"). [101] Whatever may have been previously situated upon the site, Toirdhealbhach created something new and significant. No longer *Bun* Gaillimhe but *Dún* Gaillimhe.

The loanword *caistél* was "undoubtedly used to signify their resemblance to ... the numerous [earth and timber] motte-and-baily castles of England and France that still outnumbered stone keeps in the early twelfth century." [102] The caistél at or within Dún Gaillimhe and those elsewhere in Connacht were sophisticated native innovations, massive stone fortifications, probably decked with timber, "a fusion of the native rath, crannog, and in particular, the cashel traditions." [103]

These were the first buildings in Éire deemed worthy of being called castles, decades before the Norman invasion. And *caistél Gaillme* was perhaps the very first.

Probably born and initially raised at *Tuaim Dá Gualainn* (Tuam), Toirdhealbhach was eighteen when made King of Connacht in 1106 by his uncle, Muirchertach Ua Briain. As the then King of Éire, Muirchertach intended Toirdhealbhach to be his puppet ruler of Connacht, firmly under his control. Instead, Toirdhealbhach spent the next fourteen years accruing the resources necessary to become his uncle's equal, then his successor. By 1120, Toirdhealbhach Ua Conchobair was King of Éire. This was a title he held in actuality (with opposition) till 1150, and one he was diplomatically accorded upon his death in 1156. An 1121 letter of King Henri I of England, concerning the *rex Hiberniae*, almost certainly indicates Toirdhealbhach. [104]

The exact location of the caistél - also called *caislen Duin Gaillme* ('the castle of Fort Galway') [105] - is uncertain. Galway's Norman castle was beside and under what is now Quay Street, so it might have been built upon the site - or was itself the caistél? Indeed the dún may have existed in some form before the caistél was added to it, as was certainly the case at Duín Leódha. The family Toirdhealbhach installed as its constables were among his admirals, so it appears the caistél or dún was one of the kingdom's naval bases. A retrospective annal mentions *loinges Duin Gaillmhe, Chonmaicne Mara/the fleets of Dun Gaillmhe, of Conmhaicne mara* as active on the Atlantic in 1154. [106] Contemporary annals record their earliest deployments under Toirdhealbhach:

> 1124: "A *great fleet* [was brought] *by Tairdelbach to Rinn Luimnigh and he devastated and plundered Desmumu* [south Munster]."

> 1127: "A *great fleet led by the king of Ireland, Toirdhealbhach Ó Conchobhair—190 ships his number—to ravage and lay waste Munster. So he laid waste the plain of Munster as far as Sliabh Cain and Ard Pádraig and Uí Conaill, and he carried off many droves and many people were killed there. A battle of two fleets at sea, to wit, the fleet of Connacht and the fleet of Munster, and the Munstermen were routed and slaughtered.*"

> 1130: "A *thwart-hosting by Toirdhealbhach Ó Conchobhair, king of Ireland, into the south of Ireland and into the north thereof, till they reached Tory Island* [Tory, County Donegal] *and carried off kine and many captives, and then the fleet in the south plundered Dairbri* [Valencia Island, County Kerry] *and Inis Mór and carried off captives.*"

> 1131: "*The fleet of Tairdelbach to Ros Ailithir* [Carberry, Co. Cork] *and devastated Desmumu.*"

> 1132: "A *great fleet led by Toirdhealbhach Ó Conchobhair, king of Ireland, on Lough Derg, to ravage Munster, and it made many preys in Munster and wasted it greatly.*" [107]

Retaliation followed. In 1132, King Cormac Mac Carthaig of Deasmhumha led a combined land-and-sea expedition to Dún Gaillimhe, where his army and fleet

> demolished the castle... plundered and burned the town. The defeat of An Cloidhe on the following day on Iarthar Connacht by the same fleet, and Conchobhar Ua Flaithbheartaigh, king of Iarthar Connacht, was killed, with slaughter of his people. [108]

Ua Flaithbheartaigh was Toirdhealbhach's vassal in Dún Gaillimhe. In 1051, Toirdhealbhach's grandfather ousted and blinded the King of Uí Bhriúin Eóla, Amalgaidh mac Cathal of Clann Chosgraigh. Much of their territory he seized himself, henceforth residing in the area. [109] This forced the Uí Fhlaithbheartaigh into Dealbhna and Conmhaicne Mara, evicting the Meic Chon Raoi, Uí hAdhnaigh, and Uí Cadhla. Muintir Mhurchadha overlordship west of

Loch Orbsen incorporated Deablhna into *Iarthar Connacht* ('the west of Connacht'), later known as Iar Connacht.

Early in Toirdhealbhach's life, the ruler of Iarthar Connacht was Flaithbertach Ua Flaithbeartaigh. Toirdhealbhach's father, Ruaidrí *na Saide Buide* ('of the Yellow Birch') was Ua Flaithbertaigh's foster-father, and godfather to seven of Ua Flaithbeartaigh's children. Ruaidrí was repaid with Flaithbertach blinding him and seizing the kingship of Connacht. [110] Toirdhealbhach ensured no Ua Flaithbeartaigh would ever again rise so high above his station.

## The Lion in the West

Toirdhealbhach Ua Conchobair was fifty years King of Connacht, one of the longest reigns of any European monarch. He dominated Irish politics in the early to mid-1100s, leading armies and navies all over Éire for months on end, dictating treaties, subjugating entire kingdoms. A superb military commander by any standards, his victory at Móin Mór in 1151 was among the most decisive in Irish history, inflicting 7000 enemy casualties. In 1154, a day-long battle off Inis Eoghain saw his Connacht fleet - including units from Dun Gaillimhe and Conmhaicne Mara - engage those of Cenél Eoghain, the Kingdom of the Isles, and possibly Scotland. Connacht was victorious. [111] Four of his seven wives were of Éire's leading dynasties, including two sets of sisters. He sired at least twenty-six children, and didn't think it too many. [112]

Toirdhealbhach created a six-mile long diversion of An tSuca in 1139 around Dún Leodha. [113] He built abbeys, bridges over the Shannon, imposed taxes, made land grants, sponsored the creation of new dioceses, and works of religious art such as the Corpus Missal and the Cross of Cong. [114] An innovative tyrant, his creation of castles was novel in Éire, as was his apparent wish to introduce male primogeniture (the right of the first-born son to inherit all the father's estate). [115] This concept was outrageous to Gaelic laws of succession, but was eventually adopted all over Europe.

Yet kingship requires a peculiar form of ruthlessness. When in 1135 a son, Áed, rebelled, Toirdhealbhach blinded him. [116]

At the height of his power, Toirdhealbhach ruled from the Atlantic to the Irish Sea. Alliances were made by fosterage, marriage, coercion, self-interest. Commercial and political networks connected him with fellow-rulers in Britain, Francia, and Scandinavia. He reorganised lordships and kingdoms as suited him, carving out a well-defended personal domain within Connacht, an imperium that he would have span all Éire. Dún Mór was its *caput*, Tuaim Dá Gualainn the seat of its archbishop, and Dún Gaillimhe its main port - military and merchant.

Quite an achievement for what is perceived as the 'timeless' western 'fringe' of twelfth-century Europe, but was a dynamic society ruled as aggressively as those in 'feudal' Europe.

## Gaelic Galway, Fomorian Éire

The full extent of Dún Gaillimhe's trade, and its classification as a 'town', is uncertain. Much later local tradition described it as "a small community, composed of a few families of fishermen and merchants" [117] but this may be reading history backwards. A very few clues suggest that contacts were broadly similar to later times. Wine was imported into pre-Norman Ireland, with ware of Bristol origin, dating 1175x1250, found in Galway during archaeological excavations. [118] If such trade existed, then later merchants built upon pre-existing networks.

Most intriguing is a speculative grant in 1201 of *Dungalue* by King Johan sanz Terre of England (r. 1199-1216) to a Richard Tirel. [119] This pre-dated de Burgh's settlement by thirty years, but shows that as Lord of Ireland Johan believed it had potential, perhaps already exploited. Areas we now consider remote were connected by sea lanes that by-passed and surpassed land routes. This was the key to Galway's survival in later times.

Maritime legal tracts, *Muirbretha* ('sea judgements') and *Cáin Inbir* ('estuary law'), detailed a king's revenue from trade, shipwrecks, and fishing - including salmon, a lucrative commodity. [120] No doubt Toirdhealbhach exploited such resources as useful funding for his island-wide strategies (nurturing them is another issue). It is difficult seeing so aggressive a king allowing its revenues going solely to his Ui Flaithbeartaigh vassals. Instead his son, King Cathal Crobdearg (r.1189-1224), was described as *flaith Gaillbhe/Galway's prince*. [121] Poetic, yet implying political control.

Archaeologist Eamonn Kelly has argued "coastal areas of Connemara came under Scandinavian control" [122] in the ninth century, citing annalistic references, archaeological finds, and Scandinavian linguistic evidence in placenames from Inishbofin to Ardoileán. A legacy may have being "shipbuilding technology that endured into the high medieval period, in vessels used for trade, piracy and warfare by the O'Malleys ... and O'Flahertys." [123] Be that as it may, Irish merchants had long been trading abroad, particularly with Éire's German neighbours in Britain, and Europe. Éire's coast and islands were centres of extensive maritime networks for millennia. [124] Scandinavian influences, co-opted or suborned, may have only enhanced deeply entrenched traditions. What we can say is that the Irish - and by implication the first Galwegians - were more intrepidly Fomorian than now realised. How else could a African Barbary ape end up in Iron Age Éire? [125] The sea vessel depicted in the first-century AD Broighter hoard depicts an

> ocean-going vessel .. Elaborately equipped with mast and yard-arm ... oars and rowers' benches, steering oar, grappling hook ... Eighteen oarsmen are implied, two more to man the steering oars. There would have been ample room in such a craft for passengers, provisions, and baggage besides. [126]

From the late 200s, Irish groups raided Britannia, turning the *muir meann* ('the middle sea') into 'Mare Hiberniae'/the Irish Sea. They were termed geographically as *Hiberni* in AD 297; by activity? as *Scotti* in 314; as Irish *nationes* of *Attacotti* and *Scotti* in 367. [127] Such interactions gave Irish groups a continuing knowledge of Roman civilization on their own terms (self-Romanisation?). As with vikings centuries later, many were firstly 'smash and grab' raids stealing everything from gold and silver to women and children. Slavery remained a lucrative trade for Irish kings into the 1100s. Enslaving the boy *Patricius* (Saint Patrick) affected the course of Irish and British history. [128]

The Déisi, the Uí Liathain, and the Laigin all invaded what is now Wales and England. This established Irish kingdoms and communities in Éire's 'near abroad', some Irish kings raiding as far as *an Muir Iocht* - the sea of the Isle of Wight, aka the English channel/la Manche. [129] The Ulaid were once overlords of Manainn ('Isle of Man') [130] while the region not then known as Argyll had maritime ties with the Dál Riata enshrined in dynastic legend.

The exact relationship between the Cruithin of Uladh and the Pictish nations of Alba is uncertain, but Cruithin (Old Irish for '[north] Briton') was used in Éire instead of the Latin *Picti*. [131] At any rate it was the *Scotti* Dál Riata of Uladh who made Gaeilge a prestige language of Alba, giving the kingdom its modern name - Scotland (*Scotia*, 'land of the Irish').

Along Britain's west coast stand memorial stones, bearing inscriptions from Primitive Irish (spoken to c. AD 600) in Ogam, a Gaelic alphabet carefully constructed c. AD 300. They are testaments to an Irish presence otherwise almost vanished from British history. [132] While Pagans in Éire existed into the 700s, [133] the Irish were becoming Christian before Bishops Palladius of Gaul (*fl.* 431- *af.* 434) and Patricius of Brittania (dates unknown), intensifying Irish international trade and communications. Adomnán (c. 624-704) noted various types of Irish ships regularly voyaging to Britain and the continent. [134] Frankish sources state Irish ships sailed to Her island on the Loire, [135] merchants purchasing salt from Noirmoutier monastery to sell in Éire.

Dicuil (c. 760-af. 825), an Irish scholar at the court of the Germanic King of Francia, Karl der Grosse ('Charlemagne'), recorded that Irish monks had settled on the Faroes and Iceland. When Scandinavians settled Iceland in the tenth-century, they found traces Irish settlements. [136] Yet the most spectacular voyage - according to legend! - was led by *Brenden moccu Alti* ('Brendan son of the Altraighe'), better known as Brendan the Navigator (c. 484-577). [137]

Like the later merchants of Galway, Brendan travelled all around Éire, Britain, and Gaul. His disciples included Macutus, founder and namesake of St Malo, a Breton town familiar to later Galwegians. In April 567, Brendan and his companions set off from Árann across "isand ocián n-imechtrach" ("the outer ocean", the Atlantic). After many adventures, they successfully made landfall. An account of the voyage, *Navigatio Sancti Brendani Abbatis* ('Voyage of St. Brendan the Abbot'), and romances based upon it, enjoyed a huge European audience during Toirdhealbhach's lifetime, translated into French, German, Dutch, English, Italian, Occitan, Catalan, and Norse. Then and now, readers have been entertained by sixth-century Irish explorers in volcanic Iceland and fog-laden Greenland, surviving icebergs, whales, and reaching North America. Such voyages are plausible. In 1976/77 English sailor Tim Severin and his crew of three created a ship out of materials Brendan would have used and crossed the Atlantic. [138] What if Toirdhealbhach had turned his ambitions outwards, and sent the fleet of Dún Gaillmhe around the Atlantic?

## Uniting Kingdoms

Toirdhealbhach Ua Conchobair died at Dún Mór in the spring of 1156, aged seventy-eight. At *Dyflin* (Dublin) in the spring of 1166, his son Ruaidrí took the kingship of Éire. [139] In two generations, the Uí Chonchobair had risen from among the least of the regional dynasties to surprise winners in an ongoing game of thrones. Gaelic-Irish monarchs were aggressively modern; such aristocrats drove European state-formation. King Ruaidrí had everything at his disposal to create a Gaelgeoir, feudalised, European island kingdom. And from it could arise a new nation.

The church of Éire was fully attuned to western Europe's religious reform movement, driven not by external forces but by the Irish themselves. Far from the 'barbarity' or 'Celticity' depicted in popular medieval and modern accounts, reforming Christianity in eleventh- and twelfth-century Éire was orthodox, progressive, moral, and enlightened. [140]

Titles such as *errí* ('viceroy', '[royal] governor'), *taisech an coblaigh* ('admiral of the fleet'), *cancellarius* ('chancellor'), *rechtaire* ('[royal] steward'), *notarius* ('notary'), demonstrate would-be Irish emperors deployed royal power - governance, military musters, taxation, legislation - as imperially as their insular and continental counterparts. *Catha marcshluaigh* (cavalry battalions), *formna fer* (elite troops), *daingne* (fortifications), professional mercenaries, better armour and improved weaponry gave them the means to implement and consolidate such powers. [141] Lesser rulers and polities were suborned within overkingdoms. Charters demonstrate these overkings were developing that which all states rely - bureaucracy. [142] As in 'England' and 'Scotland', accumulating administrative, military, economic and religious institutions made major Irish kingdoms politically uniform, more territorially defined, and fewer.

Dyflin near *Ath Cliath* was the wealthiest port on the Irish Sea, and the largest Scandinavian settlement in Europe, including Scandinavia. Controlled by Gaelic-Irish kings from 1052, it dominated trade between Éire and Britain, its most lucrative commodities been clothing, horses, cattle, and slaves. Imports would have included salt and wine from Aquitaine's coastal provinces of Poitou and Gascoigne. Dún Gaillmhe was even then a likely destination of such ships and their goods. Dyflin's merchant fleet traded with most west European capitals, as well as more exotic destinations such as Iceland and Greenland, north Africa, Russia, and Constantinople.

Its navy was the single most powerful military machine on the Irish Sea, useful for any Irish *imperator* wishing to gain British subjects. Such a city was well-suited to become the capital of any European kingdom. [143] Coinage had been in circulation for over two hundred years. Diplomatic, political and ecclesiastical contacts existed between Éire and her neighbours in Britain, as well as Francia, Germania, Scandinavia, and Rome. Some *Ríg Érenn* (Kings of Éire) exercised influence and overlordship in Éire's Brythonic and Germanic fringe, thanks to Dyflin's fleet. It could be to the Irish what London was for the English - the economic power-base of an island imperium.

A well-established refuge for displaced nobles from Britain, at least four exiled kings of York reigned in Dyflin. Gryffud ap Cynan (d. 1137), Prince of Gwynedd, was born at Swords during his father's exile. Gofraid Méránach, King of the Isle of Man, and Echmarcach, King of Galloway, had memorable stays. Earlier exiles included Dagobert, later King of the Franks. [144]

English exiles since the 600s found Éire a cordial refuge because before the Normans, Irish and English had few conflicting interests and good relations. The Irish introduced and spread Christian civilization among the Pagan English (Britons and many Picts were already Christian), enlettering them with *Scottice scripti*, 'writing in the Irish style'. The English use both innovations today. [145]

Queen Aedith of England (d. 1075) was a Gaeilgeoir, London's then Irish community large enough to make speaking Gaeilge useful. [146] Her brother, Harold Godwinson (later Earl of Wessex), made Dublin his home-in-exile in 1051 before returning to England, becoming King in 1066. After his death, members of the English royal family were made welcome at Dyflin. In 1069, they led its fleet on an Anglo-Irish invasion to liberate occupied England. [147]

Irish clerics and monks continued to be fluent in Latin, spoken even by peasants into the eighteenth-century. [148] Yet literature was now composed almost exclusively in Gaelige, a self-confident assertion of vernacular identity amid outside influences. One of the dominant languages of the isles, Gaeilge overwhelmed Ernbélre, Latin, Pictish, Brythonic, Norse, French, English. Speaking the language and immersion in its culture created a sense of a society defined by being Gaeil and Gaeilgeoir, as opposed to Brythoniad, Angle cynne ('English-kind'), Frank, or Ostman. That this did not lead to a single polity made it no different from British, German, or Scandinavian examples.

The learned classes had since the seventh century been evolving a politicised genealogical dogma, one which found fullest expression in the eleventh-century *Lebor Gabála Érenn* ('Book of the Takings [invasions] of Ireland'). It made the Gaeilgeoirí of Éire and Britain common descendants of one fictional ancestor, *míl Espáine*, a nod to the *Etymologiae*. Just like today, enchanting myth was treated as history, legitimising the dominance of the political groups for whom it was commissioned. It was designed to transcend ethnic and political boundaries, to cultivate a sense of aristocratic ethnicity, useful for any imperium on the island. Or isles.

*Lebor Gabála Érenn* became *The* canonical account of Irish origins, and therefore 'history'. Written and transmitted with religious certainty, it was not seriously critiqued till the 1900s. [149]

All the Uí Chonchobair had to do was retain the kingship and do what no other dynasty had yet done - rule Éire as a nation-state, as a united kingdom (*'Rioghachta uile Eireann'*).

## Last of the High Kings

In 1166 the 'institution' of Rí Érenn was fragile. Like Britain, there was no all-island kingdom or monarchy, only a kingship violently disputed between the major dynasties. While the Irish had a sense of themselves as a nation, it was as Scotti or Gaeil, not Éireannach. Like today, regional, political, dynastic, ethnic, and above all, kinship loyalties were firmer than national fellowship. Nationalism implies 'the nation' share common goals. History shows this has rarely being the case. Even the supposed 'single cultural province' of Gaeldom spanning Éire, Britain, and Man, was split politically, just like Britain's English-speaking populations.

Éire is an island. Its only unity is geographic. Unlike Britain between 1707 and 1800, it has never been a nation-state. Irish 'nationalism' was cultural, not ethnic or political. Like all others, the Irish were and are a nation of nations. But politics is confused with geography, rendered to exclude or ignore significant portions of the Irish - exactly like British. Similarly, Éire had ethnic groups competing for political dominance via militant dynasties in which brutal necessity overrode sentiment. Common nationalism could only be expressed in geographic and cultural terms because, like today, ethnicity and politics divided the Irish. An *imperium Scottorum* could only be created by force, not consent. And for propagandists and their employers, 'unity' was never 'fellowship' but a euphemism for domination - a *pax Scottorum* enforced by the sharp end of an axe. Little wonder it was resisted.

Even so, failure was not inevitable. Irish overkings had to think in imperial terms, as imperialism has always been a more usual political process than national fellowship, everywhere. Kings, kingships, and kingdoms came first. Nations, nation-states, and empires emerged as a result, all containing ghost populations and extinct polities. Gaeil was a way of realising this, just as religious sectarianism (Catholic and Protestant) and ethnic nationalism (separatist and unionist) would in the future. Dominion over people rather than land was vital, just as in Britain, whose dominant dynasties gradually created regional overkingdoms called Scotland and England, ruled by high-kings. They were not natural national units but bloodily imposed imperiums over diverse peoples (Cornish, *Gall-Ghàidheil*, Jutes, *Anglisc*, *homini Muref*, Saxons, Britons, *Picti*) and independent kingdoms (*Cernow*, Galloway, Kent, Northumbria, Moray, Wessex, *Ail Clut*, Fortriu). All resisted loss of independence, as did those in Éire.

Between 854 and 1171 various Ríg Éire attempted imposing unified rule on an entire island. Only when seen on these terms, as a struggle to resist an Gaelic-Irish imperium, can the 'puzzling' failure to achieve medieval Irish unification be understood. Such island unity was not achieved even in Britain until 1707, yet still failed to erase older identities, only transform them.

Perhaps they were trapped by their propaganda. The unification myth intoxicated, but forced Ríg Éire (and would-be Kings of Britain) into overstretch, constantly defeating practical unity. Smaller, more stable jurisdictions might have eventually consolidated into a greater unit, as happened all over Europe. Eleventh- and twelfth-century Ríg Érenn were like contemporary Kings of France, the German Holy Roman Emperors, and High-Kings of England or Scotland, whose subordinates were all-but independent rulers, only nominally loyal, capable of becoming great kings themselves.

Because it had to be enforced with brutality, Irish political unity was contested. An eleventh-century text lamented: "it is a pity for the Irish" (described not as *Gaeil* but *h-Eireannchaibh*) "that they have the bad habit of fighting among themselves, and that they do not rise all together." [150]

The main regional kingdoms remained; In Tuaisceart, Airgialla, Uladh, Midhe, Laigin, Deasmhumha, Tuadhmhumha, Connacht, Bréifne (the thirty-two counties are English creations). The forces creating a single kingdom and nation out of many was, like Scotland and England, a work-in-progress. Éire's west/east divisions are familiar enough and similar to Britain. Yet as Leth Cuinn and Leth Moga made clear, it's other principal fault-line had similar north/south dimensions.

Few rulers thought 'nationally' as *we* understand it. Only in the very different circumstances of the thirteenth and fourteenth centuries would that begin. Even so, such men have no use for nationalism except in their own image. This is the way the world is run and why some people are run over. Irish kings considered their personal dynastic power foremost, always. And power has no ethics. Consent was not required, only obedience.

Political allegiance remained firmly provisional, local, lineage-based. Loyalty was given to the nearest dynastic lord, each of whom was looking out for himself and his *tighearnais*, 'lordship' (power held by one person and their genealogical or political descendants over other people). Their relationships to their clients and community mattered above all, so each were cajoled or coerced into coalitions supporting national candidates. [151]

And sometimes the price of their allegiance was dear.

Tighernán Ua Ruairc, fearsome King of Bréifne, was a deadly foe of Diarmait Mac Murchada, dread King of Laigin. Vicious rivals since the 1120s, each sought to annex the kingdom of Mide. At Ua Ruairc's insistence, one of Ruaidrí Ua Conchobair's first acts as King of Éire was to exile Mac Murchada (on his death in 1172, Ua Ruairc was King of Bréifne and Mide). [152] This led to Mac Murchada's acquisition of mercenaries to regain Laigin and take for himself the kingship of Éire.

Matters escalated in May 1171 when Mac Murchada died. His heir was his son-in-law, the titular Comte de Pembroke Richard de Clare, alias Strongbow (d. 1176). Like Mac Murchada, his ambitions and those of his followers stretched beyond Laigin into the rest of Éire. Their unforeseen success had unforeseen consequences. England's king, Henri fitz Empress, feared his vassal de Clare might establish a rival kingdom. After all, Henri's great-grandfather duc Guillaume (le Bâtard/le Conquérant) had done exactly while a French vassal.

Irish rulers may have had similar fears. What if King Ruaidrí did as King David I of Scotland (r. 1124-53), King Fergus of Galloway (r. c. 1110-61) - or King Diarmait of Laigin! Namely, make the Normans his vassals to enforce him as king of a kingdom of Éire?

None of the other Irish kings wanted *that* as it would extinguish their kingships. Seeking to escape a King too near, they sought out the son of an Empress generally much further away. So when Henri arrived at Crook near Waterford in October 1171 - escaping the Thomas Beckett affair - he was set to take the pledges of Éire and become *Seigneur d'Irlande* ('Lord of Ireland'). By his departure on 17 April 1172, Henri had, with the blessing of Pope Alexander III, received the willing submission of both the Normans *and* most of Éire's major kings - except King Ruaidrí Ua Conchobair - all of whom paid him "the respect due to an overlord." [153]

In time, descendants of these newcomers came to the Gaillimh and rebuilt the settlement, without an Ua Conchobair, an Ua Flaithbertaigh, or an Ua hAllmhuráin within its walls.

*Galway river traffic at the Wood Quay (by William Joseph Bond, 1870, courtesy of Tom Kenny)*

# CHAPTER TWO – DUNGALUE

## Provosts and Marshals: The Lynchs

A *linch* is Old English for a hillside agricultural terrace, created to control both erosion and the flow of irrigating water. *Lynchet* denotes compressed banks of soil on slopes due to long-term ploughing. *Linchmere, Lydlinch, Redlynch* (in West Sussex, Dorset, Somerset respectively) are place-names recorded in the *Domesday* Book of 1086. [1] One village named *Linch* is in West Sussex. Domesday records that *Wulfric* held it in 1066; twenty years later, held by a *Robert fitz Tetbald*, it was described as follows:

> Then, as now, it was assessed at 5 hides. There is land for 6 ploughs. In demesne is 1 [plough] and
> 7 villains and 5 bordars with 2 ploughs. There is a church, and 2 slaves, and 3 acres of meadow,
> and woodland for 10 pigs. In Chichester, 1 close rendering 10d.

Its 1066 value was £8, afterwards £4 [2] An *Urse de Linches* owned property at Linch in 1194; little else appears to be known of him. Urse derives from the Latin for bear, *ursus*, which is the animal denoted in the Norse name, *Bjorn*. Like many in Norman England, Urse took his surname from his home, de Linces denoting *of Linch*. Burkes and Berminghams do likewise.

The property descended via de Linches's sister to the de Stophams, the widow Isabel de Stopham recorded as holding the manor of Linch in 1291. If de Linches had surviving male-line relatives in the late thirteenth century, they were either elsewhere in the shire, or had perhaps long left England.

By then, Dún Gallimhe was ruled by the de Burgh Earls of Ulster (rendered *de Burgo* in Latin). Guillaume de Burgh of Suffolk arrived in Ireland in 1185. Upon his death in 1206, he held substantial lands in Munster. He is said to have married a daughter of King Domnall Mór Ua Briain of Tuadhmhumha (Thomond); their eldest son was Richard de Burgh. [3]

De Burgh invaded Iarthar Connacht in the 1230s. By his death in 1243, he had pushed his Uí Chonchobair cousins back to Magh nAí and his more distant Uí Flaithbheartaigh kin west of the Gaillimh. Conquests are brutal, involving loss, horror, disorientation, deaths. Locals were suborned, lands stolen and granted to de Burgh's followers as had the Uí Chonchobair before them. So it goes.

The *caistél* was replaced by a Norman one. Dún Gallimhe/*Dungalue* became part of County Connacht, which was all of Connacht save the King's Cantreds (roughly modern County Roscommon), demesne lands of the King of Connacht but held of England's King. Richard Mór de Burgh married Egidia de Lacy. Their eldest surviving son, Walter, became the 1st Earl of Ulster in 1263 "in exchange for the manor of Kilsheelan and other Munster lands". His wife was Aveline, daughter of John fitz Geoffrey, a Chief Governor/Justiciar of Ireland. [4] Earl Walter de Burgh died at Galway castle in 1271. It is from the time of his son, Richard Ruadh de Burgh (*ruadh* = 'red-haired'), that the next surviving references to *Dungalue*/Galway are dated.

Galway town comprised some eleven hectares enclosed by timber and stone walls, one of a

## The de Burgh dynasty, 1160s-1381

Sources: *NHI*, IX, pp. 170-172, 470; *DofB* 3, pp. 3-19; *ODNB* 8, pp. 776-95.

Alice, buried in Walshingham church, Norfolk.
=?[Walter?] de Burgh: held manors of Burgh, Beeston, and Newton in Norfolk; Sotherton in Suffolk.

William de Burgh of Tipperary and Limerick, d. 1206.
=dau.of King Domnaill Mór Ua Briain

Geoffrey, Bishop of Ely, d. 1228.

Thomas, castellan of Norwich, fl. 1215-16.

dau. d. 1243. =de Blunville (issue)

Hubert, Earl of Kent, d. 1243. (issue)

Richard, 1st Lord of Connacht, d. 1243.
=Egidia de Lacy

Hubert, Bishop of Limerick d. 1250.

dau. fl. 1203.

Richard Óge, fl. 1230? (*Burkes of Clanricard*)

Walter, 1st Earl of Ulster, d. 1271.
=Avelina fitz John, d. 1274

cau. =Gerald de Prendergast (issue)

William Óc, d. 1270 =de Exeter
William Liath, d. 1324. =Fionnghuala Ni Briain (*Bourkes of Mayo*)

Aleys =Muirchertach Ó Briain*

Margery =Theobald le Botiller*

dau =Hamon de Vaognes*

Thomas?

Richard, d. 1247
=Alice (of France?) no issue

Egidia/Jill, m. bef. 1296. =James le Steward (*kings of Scotland*)

Theobald, d. 1303.

Richard, 2nd Earl, d. 1326.
=Margaret de Guines, gr-grandau. of Hubert de Burgh

John, d. 1311. =Eliz. de Clare

Matilda =Gilbert de Clare*

Elizabeth =Robert de Bruce*

Eleanor =Thomas de Multon*

Walter d. 1304

Joan, m. 1312, d. 1359. =Thomas fitz John* =Sir John Darcy*

Catherine, m. 1312. =Maurice fitz Thomas*

Thomas d. 1316.

Aveline =John de Bermingham*

Edmund, d. 1338. =Sláine Ní Briain (*Burkes of Limerick*)

William, 3rd Earl, d. 1333.
=Maud of Lancaster

Elizabeth, 4th Countess, 1332-63.
=Prince Lionel, Duke of Clarence, d. 1368.

Phillipa, Duchess of Clarence, Countess of Ulster, Lady of Connacht, 1355-1381.
*married, with issue; titles eventually vested in the Crown.*

*le Stewart: steward of Scotland. *Ó Briain: identity uncertain *le Botiller: arcestor of Earls of Ormond. *de Valognes: grandson? of justicier, 1195-98 *de Clare: 8th Earl Gloucester and 7th Earl Hertford. *de Bruce: Earl of Carrick, King of Scotland. * de Bermingham: 1st Earl of Louth. *de Multon: 1st Baron Moulton of Gillesland. *FitzGerald: 1st Earl of Desmond. FitzGerald: 2nd Earl Kildare. * Darcy: 1st Baron Darcy of Knaith

number of the earl's personal Irish properties. His cousin, Sir William *Liath* ('the grey') de Burgh, deputised in Galway and Connacht while the earl expanded his estates in Ulster or did royal duty abroad. Under Sir William Liath was the Provost, initially a military figure who commanded the defence forces of the settlement. In 1274 the Provost of Galway was *Thomas de Linche*. [5] Later Lynch family tradition recorded the following of the first of their ancestors in Galway:

> William (or according to other accounts, John) de Lynch, was the first settled of the name in Galway, he was married to the daughter and sole heiress of William de Mareschall ... the eldest branch of the family was called Mareschall, until the male line became extinct. [6]

*Walter Marshal* headed a jury held at Athenry in October 1278 (*William de Lenche* is eleventh), while a Justiciary Roll of January 1305 lists *Will. le Marechal of the Galuy.* [7] A 1333 property inquisition mentions a house in the town "which the Earl [of Ulster] bought of William Marescall which renders 11 shillings per annum."[8] *Ballymariscal* ('Marshal's settlement') near Ardrahan, and Marshalspark near Oranmore, may reflect settlement by the family. Familial and professional associations was symbolised by *Nicholas de Linche*. Under his "superintendence" the Great Gate of Galway "and the adjoining works" were erected in 1312. Nicholas's nickname, the *Black Marshall,* [9] was both functional and ancestrally allusive.

Evidently the le Maréchals were a prime family in Galway before the Lynchs. Intermarriage may enabled the latter if - as seems to be the case - the le Maréchals had no male heirs after the 1270s, their property and rights devolving on the female side. Later Lynches similarly prospered with two marriages to the female heirs of the (de) Penrise family, symbolised for centuries after by the Lynch-Penrise arms. So at least at first, marriages and inheritances were more crucial than trade or entrepreneurialism. One enabled the other.

Originally a man charged with the welfare of horses, by 1100 *maréchal* indicated a supervisor of a noble household. The extraordinary Guillaume le Maréchal ('William the Marshal', 1147-1219) elevated the term. An ill-prospected younger son of a second marriage, he went from being a poverty-stricken hearth knight to an undefeated jouster of some five hundred melées, a crusader, and the only man to unhorse King Richard I. Earl of Pembroke by marriage to Isabel, granddaughter of Diarmait Mac Murchada, he ended his career as Regent of England. His rags-to-great riches story was further spread in the *geste* called *l'Historie de Guillaume le Maréchal.* [10] His five sons inherited Isabel's massive Irish estates successively until their extinction, without issue, in 1245. The surname's romance gave renown to unrelated namesakes, no doubt part of the reason why the senior Lynches adopted it. Had this line flourished, Lynch would be as obscure in Galway as Marshal is now. An account of 1815, best described as historical fiction, states:

> The Family of the Galway Lynch's are originally German, from the City of Lintz the Capital of upper Austria from which City probably the Name of Lynch is originally derived.

They claim their Descent from Linceus the Friend of Eneas & who accompanied him when he fled from Troy, & ultimately from Charlemagne who was Emperor of Germany & King of France, by Charlemagne the younger his Son, whose descendants were intermarried with the Dukes of Burgundy, Normandy, France, and with most of the Royal Families of Europe.

Sr. Hugo de Lynch was a General in William the Conqueror's Army and was the first of the Name that came to England with that Monarch in whose Estimation & favour he stood very high and got from him large Estates and possessions in England.

The first of the name of Lynch, who came to Ireland with Henry the Second, or with Strongbow Earl of Pembroke, was a General whose Name was Andrew Lynch, to whom

Lynch Arms, St. Nicholas' Church

Henry gave large Possessions and Estates in Land near Dublin, at a Place called to this day Castleknock, whose youngest Son John Lynch was the first Lynch who came to Connaught in the Viceroyship of John Lackland, the youngest son to Henry the Second and afterwards King of England... and this said John Lynch was the first of that name who settled in the present Town of Galway and from whom all the Galway Lynches are descended. [11]

The le Maréchal connection is reinforced in the same account with the chronologically impossible, socially improbable, factually unencumbered assertion that "This said John Lynch married the Earl of Pembroke's Daughter, which said Earl was Earl Marshall of Ireland." [12] For good measure, a variant associates the family with Lord of Meath Hugues de Lacy (died 1186):

> The family of the Lynches is believed to have descended from the noble race of the Lacys. William de Lacy the 3rd son of Hugh de Lacy (is said) to have given origin to the Lacys in County Limerick, the Lynchs of Knoc, and the Lyches of Galway. Lord ... de Leyns formerly called de Lence the noble proprietor of Knock in Meath is said to have begotten the progenitor of the Galway Lynches who was carried by his nurse into Connacht. He married the sister and heir of Walter Marechall. [13]

These accounts are fabulous and contradictory, demonstrating that when a family is socially elevated, so too are their all-too humble ancestors. Given how few references exist till the 1300s, the family were of little account, contrary to later myths. Yet in the 1500s a Lynch family did re-side at Lynch's Castle, Knock, near Trim in County Meath. [14] Their ancestors were perhaps de Lacy tenants. Some may have sought opportunities elsewhere; *Adam de Lenche* is attested at Limerick in 1257. A namesake and possible descendant is recorded at Athenry in 1341. [15]

A plausible scenario is that about the 1240s/50s, a de Linche - possibly of Meath, perhaps via Limerick - married a Galway woman surnamed le Maréchal, the surname taken from an office held under the de Burghs. He may have been the Thomas de Linche who was mature enough to be Provost by 1274, perhaps only one of a number of occasions he did so. Thomas is said to have held *Buolygarron* (Ballygurran, Athenry?), Ballybane, and *Mote-Lench*, (Moate/Castle Ellen, Athenry?). Much later family tradition called them "Manors" and him a "Lord", though his rank would have being that of a knight and a common one at that.

His presumptive son, William de Linche, is said to have married one of the Uí hAllmhuráin. This may owe more to one Lynch line gaining the Ó hAllmhúráin estates of Barna and *Ohery* in the 1600s, and rewriting it into their 'ancient' family history. [16] Yet the name *Sinolde* (Fionnghuala?) in a Lynch genealogy - if chronologically genuine - hints at some Gaelic background. Men such as le Maréchal and de Linche were probably born and raised in Ireland of Irish mothers, just like de Burgh and many other 'Normans'. Marriage alliances between locals and newcomers made sense on many levels. It helped the former retain some status, and allowed the latter to improve theirs. Power and influence are always worth cultivating, be it by politics, patronage, friendship, or sex.

In 1277, *William de Lenche* was collector of the Galway customs, and member of a jury held at Athenry on Thursday 20 October 1278. [17] *Monsieur Richard de Burg* (2nd Earl of Ulster) granted him in 1273 or 1308 *xxiiii acres de terre en le tenement de Moynedan* in Clann Fhearghaile [18] Perhaps it is no coincidence that it is in the next generation we hear of genuinely impressive family exploits, with Nicholas de Linche supervising the construction of the Great East Gate of Galway in 1312, facing what is now Eyre Square. Achievements may be attributed to one individual but are usually the cumulative effort of generations, as all 'self-made' people have invisible supporters.

The first Lynchs of Galway were men of no great lineage. They did not marry any of the noble brides later attributed to them. Like men without trades the world over before and since, they gained upward mobility though military service, as vassals to a great lord, sergeants, marshals, common knights. Such service led to rewards of property, privileges, and sponsorships, making them men of small-to-middling substance. But they were also like all subsequent founders of Galway's prime families - people from the low-to-middle classes and castes of Irish and British societies, who got a start and made good of it.

## Les Engleis en Yrlande - The English of Ireland

Galway has been described as an English town and while correct, this requires qualification. It was English insofar as its inhabitants were subjects of England's kings and obeyed their laws. Yet from 1066 these kings were not *Angelcynn* ('English-kind') but Normans, people of Scandinavian descent from northern France. With them came natives of Maine and Anjou - kings of England from 1154 were Angevian. While all spoke various forms of langues d'oïl, each saw themselves as ethnically distinct from the each other, and the French, not to mention the English.

Other 'Normans' who came to Britain and Ireland in those years included Bretons from Brittany, who spoke Breton; Flemings from Flanders, who spoke Flemish; Poitivins from Poitou, who spoke lenga d'òc; and Gascons from Gascoigne, some of whom were Basque-speakers. The Norman conquest of l'Angleterre between 1066 and 1217 established four successive French dynasties which firmly imposed their cultures, to the detriment of Old English civilization.

It was facilitated by the greatest land transfer/theft seen in medieval Europe. In 1066 England was held overwhelmingly by Angelcynn and Anglo-Dane. By 1086 it was Norman. Thousands were forcibly dispossessed or exiled, possession enforced with brutality, sometimes harrowing. Its like would not be seen again until seventeenth-century Ireland. English emigration to Éire after 1066, and 1169, was in some respects because of fewer opportunities for property ownership and social mobility in their Norman-dominated homeland (the irony of dispossessed folk enabling themselves by disabling others, often as agents of an imperial power, has too many modern instances alone to cite but it has been a participatory process for generations of Irish people). Additionally, magnates needed them to turn Ireland's mainly pastoral economy into a version of England's more intensively arable one. Those who remained in England became as Frenchified as the Normans themselves.

The Normans so changed English civilization that significant portions of modern English derives from French, as do it's legal terms, government institutions, royal titles, many of its forenames and surnames. [19] For this reason, a common exchange currency in later medieval Ireland and Britain was the French livre (pound), while the Brown Rat was known as the (luach) Francach Donn ('the Brown French (rat)'). Communities in Kilkenny and other Irish areas remained Francophone into the 1320s. Like the Scandinavians and Romans before them, relatively small numbers of Normans had profound effects on the nations of the insularum oceani, 'the islands of the ocean'.

In Éire, they were termed the Gaill. By the 1600s they were also described as Sen Ghall/Old English (first attested c. 1598), English-Irish, Noviores Hiberni/Newer Irish. Their use of French meant that one of the first self-referring literary works concerning them was titled La Geste des Engleis en Yrlande (its modern title is The Deeds of the Normans in Ireland). Further complicating matters, modern historians term them Cambro[Welsh]-Norman, Hiberno-Norman, Anglo-French, Anglo-Norman. In those first generations they recognised they comprised of distinct ethnic groups of Franceis, Flamengs e Normand - "Frenchmen, Flemings and Normans". But predominantly they used the same Frenchified term still used in Britain today - Engles, 'English'.

By the 1340s, those in Ireland called themselves Anglos Hibernos, 'the English of Ireland', also rendered as Anglo-Hiberni,'Anglo-Irish'. [20] Their identity was based on a sense of Englishness centred around ethnicity, language, and loyalty to le Rey Engleterre ('the King of England'), in opposition to being an ethnic Gaeil/Irish. Despite speaking Gaeilge and using fénechas to various degrees, they retained this sense of themselves as a separate middle nation, distinct from both the Iras or Gaeil of Ireland (hence 'Gaelic-Irish'), and the English of Britain. This critical ethnic difference between the two major Irish nations lasted at least into the 1700s. [21] The Gaelic-Irish consistently termed the Angelcynn and later Anglo-French of Britain as Saxain. The latter generally called both Irish nations *(H)Ibernienses or Hibernici*, 'Irish-born', sometimes indiscriminately. [22]

So Galway's 'English' inhabitants were like the Gaelic-Irish themselves, of multiple ancestral strands even if given a single label. England's kings ruled from Berwick on the Scottish border to Bayonne by the Pyrenees, reflected in the surnames of the townsfolk. For example, *Robert Bayon*, collector of Galway's murage from 1278 to 1280, took his name from Bayon-sur-Gironde. [23] *Guillermo de Landes* anglicised his name to *William Longeys* or Long. [24] Both Bayon and de Landes were natives of Gascoigne, possibly Basque.

The le Brit ('the Breton') family were originally of Brittany, perhaps settling in Cornwall after 1066. *William Brit* was killed while Sheriff of Connacht in 1247. They may have renamed the site of the Galway Races - *Ballybrit* ('[le] Brit's settlement'). [25] The surname is now rendered Brett. Other once-Breton families in Ireland may include le *Botiller* (Butler) and le *Poer* (Power). Other Galway bearers of French surnames included Roger Fraunceys [26] (Francis), Alexander Bastard, [27] Geoffrey de la *Va(l)le* (Wall), Walter *Hussee* (Hussey), Walter *Bonaventure*, William *Talun*. [28]

Families originating in Flanders are recalled by surnames like Fleming, Hackett, *de Bronteergast* (de Prendergast). Many took new surnames in Britain and Ireland – de Angle (Nangle, Mac Costello), de Cogan, FitzGerald, de Barri, de la Roche, de Staunton, de Sarsfield, de Weston. *Loinges na fFlémendach* ("the fleet of Flemings") is how one Irish annal chose to describe the invaders of 1169. [29] Despite their significant activities, their ethnicity is hardly recalled.

Old English names should make it easier to trace ethnic English people in Galway, and some exist in surviving records. Thomas *Alwyne*, Seneschal and Receiver of Galway in the mid-1300s, derived his surname from a forename derived from Middle English elements meaning 'noble friend'. [30] Thomas *Dolfin*, collector of the port customs 1303-07, bore a surname of Norse-Northumbrian flavour. [31] Other English surnames included *Lathred, Hereward, Wodelond, Kent,* and *White.* [32]

Yet when coming to Ireland after 1169, French names proliferated. In such a deeply colonised country as England, names like Ealdgyth, Beorhtwulf, Aelfgar, Dedol, Godgifu, and Osmaer were politically and economically disadvantageous, even unfashionable. French surname-forms likewise abounded, utilising *de, fitz,* and *le.* They spoke of geographic origins, paternal forenames, an occupation, appearance, or trait. They are not necessarily helpful in determining ethnicity, or how names and language relied on imitation of the ruling classes (intermarriage with them has always been exceptional). Yet it was mainly these emigrant lower and middle classes peasants, labourers, maids, soldiers, burgesses, common knights, and artisans, that formed the bulk of the 'Normans' in Ireland and made English an Irish language. Its use and accompanying culture, by various ethnic groups in the isles, created a sense of a society defined by being English and speaking English.

For a town that would later pride itself on its Englishness, this ostensible lack of ethnic Angelcynn shows the complex ways peoples and cultures mix, migrate, regenerate (deeply confusing for those who attach ethnic terms to haplogroups). And how entire national cultures change identity from one century to another, yet still be English. Or Irish.

# Yr Brythoniad Ywerddon – The Britons of Ireland

Breythnok ('Briton'), *Cradok, Hostig, Meurig* - these last three were personal names - *le Walyes* ('the Welshman'), *de Kerdyf* ('of Cardiff') and [de?] *Penrise* are found in medieval Irish sources. [33] All allude to *Brythoniad* ('Britons', alias *Cymro* or *Cymrae*), a cover-term for Brythonic-speaking ethnicities in Strathclyde, Cumbria, Wales, and Cornwall, all once Roman Britain. It was an identity rooted in and created by the partial Roman conquest of Britain after AD 43, one which partitioned the island into civilized Brittania and barbarian Alba.

To West Germanic-speakers, Brythoniad were *\*walhaz*, 'foreigner'. It denoted 'Romans' (latin and celtic - speakers), firstly on mainland Europe then the Britons. *Wal*-places from *Walchensee* to *Wales* was where the *wealh* or 'Welsh' lived. The Gaeilge for Brythoniad was *breatnach*. This became a surname itself and an equivalent of the English and Norman terms *Walsh(e)* or *Welsh(e)*.

While other Brythoniad settled in Ywerddon - such as the Cumbrians in Uladh from 1177 - most were natives of places such as Gwyr, Ergyng, Cemais, Brycheiniog, and Morgannwg. All of these were in southern and south-east Wales, where many of the first Normans in Ireland were born and raised, though the purely Brythoniad presence in Ireland much pre-dated 1169.

In Connacht, *Breythnok, Cradok, Hostig, Meurig* and *le Walyes* became Breathnach, Craddock, Hosty, Merrick, and Wallace/Walsh(e)/Welsh(e). Other families of similar ancestry include Barrett, de la Valle/Wall, Griffith, Joyce, Lawless, le Blund, de Lynnot, MacNally, Rice, Sice, and possibly FitzSimmon(d)s. They dimly note emigrant folk with names like Prawst, Hunydd, Anarawd, Esyllt, Idwal, Tegonwy, whose history, culture, and language(s) were neither Irish, English, or Norman, but were subsumed by all, and like the Flemings and Ostmen, forgotten even by their descendants. People in these groups had sexual relations with Irish people, resulting in offspring with multiple ethnic identities. This had enormous, forgotten effects on personal, familial, and political allegiances in medieval Ireland.

# Éireannach na nGallimhe - The Irish of Galway

Nor were the locals necessarily excluded. The sheer preponderance of Gaelic-Irish surnames recorded in medieval Galway town and environs demonstrates a majority of its inhabitants were regional natives. Some families must have been resident before 1124. Descendants are still here. *John Mac Scayn* had a valuable fishery on the Gaillimh c. 1300, kept successively by his son David and grandson Adam as late as 1374. [34] *Thomas son of Walter Kery*, alive in June 1398, may have been a descendent of the Mág Catharnaigh family, proprietors at Maree since before 1100. [35]

The Tierneys (Ui Tighearnaigh) had members become town bailiffs, while a *James Develin* (Ó Doibhilin, or less likely, Ó Docomláin) rose to the summit, serving as town Sovereign. [36] These people must have been granted indentures, letters of denization, or patents enfranchising both themselves and their descendants as full citizens ('freemen'), enabled to own property and trade. Remarkably, they retained their original surnames instead of taking 'English' ones as required. This was not the case for all Gaelic-Irish, many of whom were outside English law or unfree. [37]

Galway's Gaelic families included *Begge* (Small), *Berry* (Ó Béara), *Bollan(d)* (Ó Beolláin), *Branegan* (Ó Branagáin), *Broderick* (Ó Bruadair) *Carr* (gCerr), *Colman* (Ó Colmáin), *Coyne* (Ó Cadhain), Curran (Ó Curráin), Cunningham (Ó or Mac Cuinneagáin), Dermody (Ó Diarmada), Duff (Dubh), Fallon (Ó Fallamhain), Flynn (Ó Floinn), Mc/Glynn (Mág Fhloinn), McFolan (Mac [C]Fuláin), O'Halloran (Ó hAllmhúráin), Hannyn/Hannon (Ó hAinninn), Higgins (Ó hUiginn), Keane (Ó Catháin), Larkin (Ó Lorcáin), Moore (Ó Mordha), Mullen (Ó Maoileáin), Molgan (Ó Mócháin), Nolan (Ó Nualláin), Quinn (Ó Coinne), Quirke (Ó Cuirc). [38]

Notably, they were mainly *aithechtuatha*, from minor, lower-caste families. They could be integrated into the colony because, unlike Gaelic gentry and dynasties, they had no troubling claims to large territorial lordships now held by de Burgh. Some were previously Uí Fhlaithbheartaigh vassals and quite possibly delighted to be rid of them. As was the case with the Angelcynn and Brythoniad, old names faced pressure from ones newly fashionable and politic. So Gerroch, Condmach, Feth fo lige, Goillin, Ulgarc, Echtigern, became rare or unused entirely.

By living among the Gaill, they were not betraying any 'national' allegiance, but seeking to survive and if possible, to thrive. This impulse has driven all families in every space in time.

## High Medieval Galway - multilingual and multinational

French remained a community language among the English of Ireland into the fourteenth century, introducing new terms to Gaeilge such as *gasúr* ('boy', from *garçon*) and *seomra* ('room', from *chambre*). Some Gaelic forenames were originally French. They include Seán (from Jehan/Jean [John]), Eilís (Elise), Nóra (Honora), Sinead (Jeanne), Uilliam [Liam] (Guillaume [William]), Síle (Cecily), Proninsias (François), Róisín (Rohesia), Caitilín (Catelin [C/Kathleen]), Siobhán (Joanne), Eibhlín/Eilín (Aveline [Eileen]), Máire (Marie [Mary]), Séamus (James). The adoption of such names almost always occurred outside the prime Gaelic dynasties, reflecting the contemporary dispositions - and aspirations! - of lower gentry and commons alike. [39]

*Tullaghnafranagh* ('hill of the French') near Ardrahan advertises the presence of medieval French folk. The infamous 1366 Statues of Kilkenny directed the Anglo-Irish (not the Gaeil) to use *la lang Englies et soit nomé par nom Engleys, enterlessant oulterment la manére de nomere usé par Irroies*. Still-current Irish slang terms such as *gurrier* ('brawler') may derive from medieval French, which became the international language of European trade and commerce. As Galwegians traded with French ports, at least basic fluency in French was a necessity. [40]

Brythonic-speakers must have being greatly in evidence, going by the preponderance of surnames such as Breathnach (*Briton*), Wallace (*of Wales*), and Walsh (*Welshman*). The related but distinct dialects and languages of Strathclyde, Cumbria, Wales, Cornwall (*Nichs. the Cornishman* is attested in 1290 [41]) and Brittany, must all have been heard at one time or other. Likewise Middle English dialects, from places as far apart as Kent and Bristol so not always mutually understandable. A hint of an Italian presence is preserved in *Lombard Street*. It recalls a time when money-lenders, some Jewish, were collectively termed 'lombards' after their place of origin - Lombardy, Italy. And Galway had an entire street named after them. [42]

Latin was used at church functions and was an official language used in legal proceedings, rendering de Burgh as *de Burgo*, de Angle as *de Anglo*, usv. A secondary language in Ireland for centuries, Latin had obvious French affinities which may have aided communications between

*Ballydavid Castle, Athenry*

Gaeil and Gaill, as it did with the New English in the 1500s. Multilingualism may not have been exceptional, but in certain settings almost normal. Sailors and merchants speaking Flemish, Occitan, Castillian, Portuguese, Basque, even Iberian Arabic, would have been heard from time to time, as was Gaeilge from other parts of Ireland, as well as na hOiléin, Manainn, and Alba.

Somehow everyone made themselves understood.

All this underlines the multiplicity of Galway's medieval inhabitants, the dynamic way people interacted across cohabiting cultures. Though they defined themselves as English rather than Irish, the latter did live, intermarry, and work alongside the former. The only requirement was that they obeyed the same laws, which is all that any functioning society requires of its peoples.

## Brun, Broun, Browne

The Brownes lived in Athenry's environs for centuries before moving to Galway; bearers of the name are still found there. Rendered variously, the surname mainly indicates an ancestor who had brown hair. In some cases it may be an translation of the Gaelic terms *odhar* or *donn* ('brown-hair'). The placename *Brown* was recorded in Somerset in 1086, alluded to by the surname *de Brown* in medieval Irish exchequer records. [43] According to a family tradition published in 1820, the first Browne to settle in Ireland was

> Phillipus de Browne ... in 1172 appointed Governor of Wexford. In 1178 he went to England, and soon after returned with 60 armed knights, and was a leader at the siege of Limerick. He had three sons, William, who settled in the territory of Clanmorris, in the County of Kerry, and Walter, who settled in the County of Galway, where his posterity still remain; the destination of the third son is not mentioned. [44]

Another tradition stated that

> Sir David Browne, was contemporary with Richard de Burgo [sic], the Red Earl of Ulster, that he died in 1303, and had a son, named Stephen, who settled at Killpatrick, near Dublin, from whence, after a time, a branch of that house settled at Brownstown, near Loughrea, and thence branched forth to Athenry and Galway. [45]

*Phillipus de Browne* is undocumented. *William of Clanmorris* appears to be an attempt to link the family with the Browne Earls of Kenmare (in another source he is given as the ancestor of the Brownes of Clondalkin, Dublin). *Sir David Browne* and *Brownstown* are undocumented. If these accounts are sincere, some of the names and ramifications were distorted by time. Descendants may have given lowly ancestors greater rank and origin than they actually had.

Yet a *Phillip le Brun* is given in some sources as Governor of Wexford town in 1178, and was said to have a brother named William. In the c. 1175 foundation Charter for Dunbrody Abbey *William Brun* was the fourth of eleven witnesses, right after Lady Nesta FitzGerald, wife of Dunbrody's founder (and uncle of Strongbow), Hervé de Monte Morency. Eleventh was *Nicholas son of William Brun*, known from other sources to be alive as late as 1200. [46]

Evidence strongly suggests the Brownes were among the very first Norman settlers of Uí Bairche/Bargy barony under Strongbow and de Monte Morency – a motte at Oldhall may date to the summer of 1169. While not outright lords themselves, they were sheriffs, M.P.'s, and jurors, "providing the military service and generally backboning the continuation of English rule." Brownes were freeholders at Mulrankin from before 1247 to 1654, and were the senior line of the many Browne septs in County Wexford. They were among the last speakers and writers of Yola, an Anglo-Irish language unique to Forth and Bargy that became extinct in the early 1900s. [47]

Phillip and William were said to be two younger sons of *Hugh le Brun*, a supposed native of Poitou who lived in the Welsh marches. Like his fellow marcher, Strongbow, Hugh is said to have backed King Etienne de Blois in The Anarchy (1136-54), earning him no favours under the winner, King Henri II, so they eventually came to Ireland for better prospects. [48] Hugh remains unverified.

The earliest verified Browne in Connacht was *John Brun*, who in 1286 gave a surety that *Matthew le Chepman* [the pedlar] of *Athnery* would hold the peace. [49] John was fined half a mark that year for not attending a legal summons. [50] *Geoffrey Brun, clerk*, sold ten *hogsheads* (barrels) of wine at *le Galuy* [Galway] in 1289, "for supply of the K.[ing]'s castles of Connaught." Geoffrey was paid three hundred pounds to be spent on the maintenance and "the fortifications of the [royal] castles of Roscommon, Randown, and Athlone." [51]

*Walter Brun* held land at *Balyduf* in the manor of Ardrahan in 1289. In 1333, another *Walter Broun* was a free tenant with land at *Ballymcacorthan*, an unidentified location somewhere in Loughrea barony. *Adam Bruen* held land at *Balyduf* in 1289, while *Tancard Brun* is listed as the landholder there in 1321. [52] *Geffrey le Broun* (probably the clerk of 1289) is mentioned in an undated charter of this era concerning *une parcelle de terre en Crosbarry*. [53]

A Gaelic genealogical tract, *Do Bhreathnuibh in Ibh Amhalghaidh mc Fiachrach* ('The Welshmen in Uí Amhalghaidh meic Fiachrach'), states "the Cusacks, Petits, Brownes, and Moores" - along with many other families from Wales - attempted or succeeded in conquering Tirawley in what is now County Mayo. [54] If so, they would have been among the very last conquests before the fourteenth-century colonial decline saw many expelled back to south Connacht. That the author saw no difficulty in listing the Brownes as *Bhreathnuibh* is an interesting if oblique view on how

## Joy of Thomond and south Connacht, 1242-1501

Simon fitz Meredudd, attested Kilfeakle, Co. Tipperary, 1242 [Seóigheach?]

| William Joye, *fl.* 1275/76. | Phillip Joye, *fl.* 1275/76. | Hugh Joye of Seafin, *fl.* 1275/76-1289. | Thomas Joy of Catherskeehaun , *fl.* 1289 |
|---|---|---|---|
| | | | =? (first wife?)      =Juliana (second wife?), *fl.* 1309 |

Gilbert Joye of Limerick, *fl.* 1298     *Symond* (Simon), *fl.* 1301.     Richard, *fl.* 1309. [attested Limerick, 1300?]     Thomas, *fl.* 1321. [ancestor of Clann Seoighe?]

Simon Óg of Craughwell, *fl.* 1321.    Henry (undated) of *Caherhenryhoe*    Robert, victualler at Dublin, *fl.* 1322-33.

Br. Simon Joy of Limerick, *fl.* 1376.    Simon, *amicus fratrum* Athenry, d. 1381.    John Joy, Provost of Athenry, *fl.* 1392.

Thomas Joy, Archdeacon of Tuam, *fl.* 1437-77+ Bermingham of Athenry?

William, Archbishop of Tuam 1485-1501.

the family may, or may not, have viewed themselves in those times.

By then - around 1300 - the Brownes appear to have settled within or around Athenry. The townland of Ballydavid, north of the town, may be the site of an otherwise unknown *David's Castle* [55] - perhaps the person commemorated as *Sir David Browne. John son of Denis*, bailiff of Athenry in 1449, appears to be identical with the *John Brun* who held the same post in 1451. [56] *The Regestum* of Athenry's Dominican Friary records

> The death of the reverend Friar Gilbert Bron, master of the faculty of theology, in the year of the Lord 1451 who ended his life in London ... entered in the convent of Athenry and was professed for that convent and did much good for that convent. [57]

*William Brun* is recorded in a 1523 deed, and is probably the man who was Provost of Athenry in 1527. Though *John Broun* served as one of Galway's customs collectors in 1424, not till 1539-42 did four Brownes of Athenry receive the freedom of Galway, finally settling in the town. [58]

## Joie, Seóighe, Joy(ce)

South of Athenry between Aidhne and Maonmhagh, in Killora and Killogilleen parishes, Joy is first documented in Connacht. Aidhne was granted to Maurice FitzGerald about 1235/36, with settlement commencing about 1240, concentrated in Kinvara, Ardrahan, Killora and Killogilleen. [59] It is within the latter districts that the Joyce properties were situated. Places that can still be identified include Catherskeehaun and Seafin, which in 1289 were held by Thomas Joy and Hugh Joy respectively. [60] In 1309, Thomas's widow, Juliana, sued Thomas's son, Richard, for property at Moycola and Gortnemanagh in Killogilleen. [61] In 1321, a later Thomas Joy was landholder of the property. [62] Richard may have been Thomas's son by his first marriage, while Thomas Joy of 1321 may have being a son of Juliana, or Richard.

# Clann Seóighe

Seóinicín na Gasraighe, son of Seóigheach, son of Sir David, *mac ri Bretain*.

```
  |_____
  |                               |
Dabhac                          Seóinicín
  |                               |
Tomás Ruadh                     Tomás
  |_____         |
  |        |        |            Uilliam
Gearóid  Seaán   Hicinn           |
      (Clann Seoighe)           Seóinicín
                                  |
                                Uilliam
                                  |
                                Tomás Cam
                                  |
                                Tomás Óg
                        (Joyce of Athenry and Galway?)
```

A *Symond Joie* is attested in 1301. [63] Simon Óge Joy of Craughwell, alive in 1321, was proba-bly his son. In 1381 died *Simon Soy*, a benefactor of Athenry's Dominicans, who "gave a parcel of land to them which is called the land Mic gate of Halatun." [64] *John Joy* was Provost of Athenry in 1392. [65] Caherhenryhoe west of Loughrea means '*Henry Joy's residence*'. [66]

All this demonstrates a long-forgotten Joyce presence *east* of the Gaillimh. The folk fame of Duchasa Seóighe/Joyce Country eroded remembrance of other areas of Joyce settlement, and tricked eighteenth-century Tribal Joyces of Galway into thinking their family came from that area.

FitzGerald was a native of Ui Falighe with extensive property in Connacht, including the manor of Lough Mask, within which was Partrighe in tSleibhe and in Laca. The Joys were possi-bly FitzGerald vassals from in south Wales, and were likewise of at least partial Briton origin. [67] According to a genealogy recorded by Mac Fhirbhisigh in the 1660s, they derived from Seóigheach, son of Sir Daibhidh mc rí Bretan/Sir Dáibhidh son of the king of the Britons. [68] At best this indicates descent from a Normanised Welsh lord, or perhaps inflating a family that had no pedigree!

Seóigheach is a nickname, a Gaelic version of the Old French *joie*. This indicates his real name was forgotten by his descendants. He may be *Simon fitz Maurdudd* (correctly Maredudd) at-tested at Kilfeacle, County Tipperary in March 1242. Norman *fitz* - 'fils de'='son of' - instead of the Welsh *ab/ap* -'son of' - indicates a Norman or English father with a Welsh forename, like *Meilyr* de Bermingham of Athenry. Reasons for identifying Simon as the Joy ancestor are as fol-lows.

While a rare Norman name, Simon was used by four Joys in the 1300s. Lacking a surname (*fitz Maurdudd* is a patronymic) may have meant *joie* was applied to him - or *his* ancestor - as a nickname, becoming a surname for his children. Lastly, he is recorded in County Tipperary, where three Joys - Guilliame, Phillipe, Hugues - are documented in 1275-76. Inconclusive, if sug-gestive; he may have being a maternal ancestor, or an esteemed godparent, who's name was passed on.

Seóigheach's only listed son, Seóinicín na Gasraighe, bears an epithet meaning of the *band of youths*, indicating leadership of a military company. [69] This may be why they were planted in the Craughwell area – which straddled the Aidhne-Maonmhagh border - to defend Aidhne's north-east border against the de Burghs, located just a few miles to the east at Loughrea.

The surname Joyce has at least three unrelated origins, and denotes many distinct families. A seventh-century Breton, Judoc - Frenchified as *Josse* - settled in Ponthieu where the settlement of Sainte-Josse-sur-Mer was called after him. The surname Josse (Anglicised as Joyce) can derive both from this and other places called after him, and all the unrelated boys baptised with his name. [70]

In the thirteenth-century a Nottinghamshire family called *de Jorz* are attested, who in the years around 1300 had two Archbishops of Armagh and a Cardinal. De Jorz derives from a place in Brittany. By 1600 it too was Anglicised as Joyce and thus confused with the Irish family. However the derivation of both surnames are distinct, and the families unrelated. [71]

The form *Joy* derives from *joie*, Old French for a cheerful or feckless person. [72] In Gaeilge it is rendered *Seoige*. Like Josse and de Jorz, it was eventually rendered Joyce. This led later Joyces to assume relationships between de Jorz, Joy and Josse that never existed. Likewise, Joyces in Munster are too common and recorded too early to spring from the Clann Seóighe; the latter most probably derive from them, not the other way around.

Two of Seóinicín na Gasraighe's grandchildren were eponymous first cousins, Tomás Ruadh son of Dabhac, and Tomás son of Seóinicín. One of these men must be the *Thomas Joy* of 1289, and identifying one from the other may help distinguish the Tribal Joyces from the Clann Seóighe. In the 1200s the Joys took possession of Partraighe in Lacha and Partrighe in tSleibhe, the central and western districts of Conmhaicne Cúile Toland. Without doubt it included the forceful eviction and/or destruction of the local Partraighe or Conmaicne ruling lineages, if any yet survived. The Joys settlement was probably to prevent the Ui Fhlaithbeartaigh using the Cong isthmus to raid Maigh Eóla and Maigh Eo. Border guards, as apparently they were in the Craughwell district.

So it was that Partrighe in Lacha and Partrighe in tSleibhe lost their original names, as the Joys became Gaelicised as Clann Seoige and the area was henceforth *Duchasa Seóighe* (Joyce County). Memory of its previous population and their heritage was virtually wiped out. Perhaps at least some marriage alliances or vassal relationships resulted. Perhaps not. The area has only so much good land, and to the winner goes the spoils. Losers vanish amid victor's triumphs. To commemorate the family founder in Duchasa Seóighe, each successive chief of Clann Seóighe was know by the title *Mac Tomás*. [73] In some cases this may have resulted in a new surname.

The pedigree of Tomás son of Seóinicín contains only five names after him. In contrast, the lineage of his first cousin, Tomás Ruadh son of Dabhac, proliferates, with all the major septs of Clann Seóighe clearly traced back to him. The lineage of Tomás son of Seóinicín may have been of little importance, or died out. Yet the possibility exists that they are the Joys who stayed in the Craughwell-Athenry area, and never became fully gaelicised. Families outside Gaelic areas were unlikely to patronise *seanchaidh* - professional historians - who would only record lineages that were important, Gaelic, or Gaelicised (despite beliefs to the contrary, genealogy was always a fundamentally literate profession in medieval Ireland).

The reason this line is recorded at all might be because of their ancestral link to Tomás Ruadh Seoige. In 1820 James Hardiman translated and summarised the early portion of an early 1700s Latin history called *Geneologia Domini Gregorii Joyes*, stating that:

> Thomas Joyes, the first of the name that came to Ireland, sailed from Wales in the reign of Edward I and arrived with his fleet at Thomond in Munster, where he married Onoragh O'Brien, daughter of the chief of that district; and from thence, putting to sea, he directed his course to the western parts of Connaught, where he acquired considerable tracts of territory, which his posterity still inhabit. [74]

Thomas is given a son, *Mac [na] Marah* ('son of the sea'), who can be dismissed as fiction because his father is documented as alive in either 1289 or 1321, while Mac Marah's son, William, died as a young man in 1507. This demonstrates that by the early 1700s the Joyce Tribe of Galway had forgotten their actual origins, and naturally enough presumed William came from Duchasa Seoighe. Leaving aside the circumstances of Thomas Joy's/ Tomás Ruadh Seoige's arrival in Ireland, it places his settlement of Partrighe in tSleibhe and Partrighe in Laca in the reign of Édouard I (1272-1307). Joy's lord, FitzGerald, died in 1286, [75] so settlement of the region had probably being secured by then. However, marriage to an Ó Briain and other details are only attested in the *Geneologia*; they may be authentic but should be used with caution. [76]

In 1299, FitzGerald property in Connacht was transferred to de Burgh. [77] This could explain and date Caherhenryhoe, which is not in Aidhne but Maonmhagh, containing de Burgh's personal manor of Loughrea (Caherhenryhoe was beside the Earl's hunting lodge at Tooloobaun).

Tomás may have been following the example of his grandfather, a indentured mercenary who settled and patrolled a new frontier. De Burgh would have found him useful in proximity to uncertain subjects such as the Ui Fhlaithbheartaigh and Ui Mháille. For Tomás, taming a wild frontier may have been more exciting than tending to estates in an area pacified before he was born. Perhaps his actions were a result of being a younger son with few other prospects. He may have been the senior Seóighe, but a junior Joy.

Lastly, there is always the possibility that despite at first bearing the same surname, the families of Joyce and Seoige were as unrelated as most people surnamed Murphy or Smith.

Not until 1507 can any Joyce be located in Galway town. While it's possible that they were a sept of Clann Seóighe, it is probable they were Joys of the Craughwell district, some of whom moved to Athenry, then Galway. In fact it is even more likely as, unlike the Clann Seóighe, they would have been familiar with English language and culture because they never abandoned them. The different cultures their ancestors chose made each view the other as alien.

# Universal Soldiers: The Skerretts

*Robert Huscard* held land in Connacht under de Burgh in 1242, [78] marking him as one of the earliest settlers. A later *Robert Huscard* was Justice of the Common Pleas at Dublin in 1280. [79] Given the surname's scarcity, they must have been relatives of some degree. *Adam Huscard* was in Connacht in 1286 when he was fined half a mark for not attending a summons. [80]

One *Huscarl* of Eastrip in Bruton, Somerset, is attested from 1042 to 1066. His descendant, *Roger Huscarl*, was a Royal Justice in Ireland from 1222 till his return to England in 1227. No doubt junior family members accompanied him, and some seem to have stayed after his departure. [81] These years coincide with de Burgh's initial excursions into Connacht. In 1289 *Eadmundus Huskard* held land at Raruddy near Loughrea (close to Henry Joy), and Duniry near Portumna, while in 1333 *Richard Huskard* held land at Kilcaimin, Ardfry, south of Oranmore. [82]

"*Dominius* Walter Husgard and Lady Joanna his wife" financed the building of the cloister at Athenry Friary, "and they are buried in the next arch beside the altar of Saint Mary." As in the case of Thomas de Linche, *dominius* ('lord') indicates status rather than rank, almost certainly indicating a knight, middling rather than common. [83] *Richard Scared* or *Skeret* was Provost of Athenry in 1378. Thought to be a son of Walter and Joanna, he held the property at Ardfry, as well as land at Maree and Claregalway. Some land in the later area was donated to the friars to build upon. [84]

Skerrett, alias Huskard, derives from *husceorl*, a Danish term denoting a military retainer in Danish-occupied England after 1015. [85] While the term was Danish, English kings and lords had household troops prior to 1015 so it was probably a new term for an old office, not one that necessarily denoted Danish ethnicity. Yet it had some ethnic resonance, as Canute spread his Danish followers all over England from 1015, and they remained after the kingdom reverted to English rule in 1042. *Huscarla* formed the backbone of subsequent English armies; those of King Harold II refused to abandon his body at Hastings, and were killed to the last man.

The first Huskard therefore seems to have taken his surname from an official military position held in a noble household in early eleventh-century England. As Somerset lay well beyond the Danelaw (the main area of Scandinavian settlement in England), the family may have been once Britons of Dumnonia or Saxons of Wessex. Skerretts continued to hold the office of Provost - *Walter Skeret* in 1414 and 1417, *John Skeret* between 1476-1484. [86] Perhaps they were one of the few families from whom officers could be drawn, perhaps they were hereditarily good at the job.

## Caddel, alias le Blake

*Richard Caddel* is first recorded in 1278 as owning a castle and land at *Ballymacroe* (now Frenchfort, Oranmore) ten miles due east of Galway. South of Athenry is *Farranblake* ('Blake's field' [estate?]), the Blakes holding property there, in nearby Mulpit, and within the town. [87] His original surname, *Caddel*, derived from a popular Brythonic forename [88] - the *Fragmentary An-*

*nals of Ireland* record the death of "Cadell son of Rhodri, king of Britain", in 909. [89] Richard's nickname *le blake* – a mixture of French and Old English – means 'the dark', and describes a man of especially black hair or sallow skin. This physical trait became the basis of his new surname.

He is recorded as Provost of Galway in 1290 and 1312, and Sheriff of Connacht 1303-06. Men surnamed *le Blake*, alias Cadel, were found at Blakestown in County Kildare, and Fyrmayl in County Kilkenny. Sir William *Cadel* (fl. 1270s-1290s) held land in Kildare and Carlow, and as Seneschal in both places and Kilkenny, was likewise active in service to greater men. [90]

Richard's immediate descendants by his wife Emeline (her surname is unknown) were second only to the Lynchs in the town's early social order, and remained among the most prominent of Galway's families into the twentieth century. As their history would show, they did so both by been adept at business, and - when occasion demanded - ruthlessness.

One near-unique issue concerning the Blake family is their successful preservation of many of the family's legal and personal records. The earliest, dated 1315, concerns Richard and his wife Emeline. The last, some fourteen generations later, date to the 1700s. Each of the Tribes probably had similar archives, but only those of the Blakes survive, published in two volumes by a descendant in 1902 and 1905 as *Blake Family Records* (sadly never republished). Such documents are nearly non-existent for Connacht, providing glimpses of lives otherwise utterly lost in time. [91]

## Lineage proliferation

Within generations, there were so many Lynchs and Blakes that the suffix *fitz* came into general use. Thus two John Lynch's would be distinguished as John Lynch fitz Stephen, and John Lynch fitz Thomas. Useful, except when each had a similarly-named father *and* grandfather! In doing so, these most Anglo of Galway's families were displaying a trait of the most powerful Gaelic dynasties - lineage proliferation. What enabled this, what rooted these families enough to survive recessions and thrive in booms while others did not, was property ownership. The acreage was small, but lucrative, given their urban location. As historian Kieran Hoare has pointed out:

> there can be little doubt that the rents generated from properties either controlled or owned by merchants in or near port-towns would have been a regular source of income, unlike the risky business of trading. ... control of property and the cash rents from it propelled them into positions of power within their towns. [92]

A similar grasp on *tighearnais*, 'lordship', enabled many Gaelic-Irish dynasties to likewise endure, thus proliferate their lineage and perpetuate their surname. Similar militant origins lay behind these families and dynasties. Both wealth and poverty can be inherited, the latter when the former is inaccessible. And despite their differing cultural applications and outlooks, both major Irish nations shared exactly the same concerns as those of Britain and elsewhere in Europe - transmitting rights agnatically, i.e., via the male line. Like their societies, Irish families were primarily defined by male strength, further so by (male) attachment to and claims on property (lordship is a property). These families and their properties were defined, logo-like, by sire-names.

The Irish are stereotyped as obsessed with property ownership, but there is a cultural reason for it, perhaps of greater time-depth than suspected. Not only deriving from our recent history, but maybe from losses incurred under the vanished imperiums of long-forgotten Irish kings and lords.

## Galway merchandise

Up to about 1270, Galway was mainly a military settlement, used to enforce Earl Walter's rule. The Countess's dower accounts, in the decade after Walter's death, show her income derived from rent obtained via the burgesses, salmon and eel fishing, and revenue from the mill. But a toll or murage levied in 1278 of four pence per *tun* on hides, fish, wine, salt, wool, and cloth, paid for the construction of "Walls towards the sea, and a tower beyond the great gate." [93] Income was sufficient in 1282 to repair Galway castle. [94] This underlined the revenue that trade could generate, and what could be done with it. It may not be coincidence that it is in 1296 St. Francis's Abbey was founded, beyond the town's north wall on a small island cut off from the town by now built-over tributaries of the Gallimh. The text of a second such levy, a grant called a murage charter, indicates the bewildering variety of goods that passed through the town:

> For every crannock of whatsoever kind of corn, malt, meal, and salt, for sale, one penny.
> For every crannock of wayde for sale, two pence.
> For every crannock of corker and symack for sale, one penny.
> For every crannock of bark for sale, one halfpenny.
> For twelve crannocks of every kind of coals for sale, one penny.
> For twelve crannocks of lime for sale, one halfpenny.
> For every horse, mare, hobby, ox or cow for sale, one halfpenny.
> For ten sheep, goats or pigs for sale, one penny.
> For five bacon hogs for sale, one halfpenny.
> For ten woolfells for sale, one halfpenny.
> For every hide of horse or mare, hobby, ox and cow, fresh, salt or tanned for sale, one farthing.
> For every one hundred lamb-skins, goat-skins, hare-skins, wolf-skins, cat-skins, and squirrel-skins for sale, one half-penny. [95]

The text goes on, cataloguing a mind-numbing list of other taxable goods:

Goat-skins ... hare-skins ... wolf-skins ... cat-skins ... squirrel-skins ... hides of stags, hinds, bucks and does ... mill-stones ... wool ... herrings ... large fish ... eels ... salmon ... lamprey ... ashes ... tun of honey cloth ... Irish cloth, sale-wyche and worstede ... canvas ... felt caps ... carpet ... Irish cloak ... large boards ... sandals ... pitch and rosin ... tallow, grease, butter, and cheese ... onions ... garlic ... brush-wood ... timber ...dishes and wooden platters ... ropes for tackling ships ... hinges ... cordewane ... scalpyn and dried fish ... hemp and flax ... lamp oil ... [96]

The English were culturally predisposed to see Gaelic Ireland as underdeveloped 'wilderness'. Yet as the Irish had been agriculturalists and managing the environment for some five thousand years by then, the production of rural goods was obviously down to a fine art. These were then shipped from Galway for sale in places such as Bristol and London, Nantes and San Sebastian, as well as more local centres such as Waterford and Dublin.

*The 'Blue Galway Mantle' -*
*See colour plates*

Irish exports such as salmon and the *broit* or *brát* (aka 'the mantle', possibly a Norse term) were almost always guaranteed sales in any foreign market. [97] An enveloping all-body, weather-proof outer wool cloak, the brát was used in many forms in Ireland since Pagan times, resembling the late-medieval west European gaberdine. Variants included the poncho-like *fallaing* and the leather *cochall*. Regarded as part of the Irish national dress, they continued in use into the early 1700s (since c. 1901 the British tartan kilt is wrongly thought to be Irish).

Fur-lined *mantelles de Hiberniae* were very popular exports to medieval Britain. Waist-length half mantles appear to have been made specifically for Continental export. Their popularity abroad was of long-standing; Irish merchants sold them in Cambridge markets as long ago as the 960s [98] They came in many colours and types (lined, 'blanket', tufted). Some were *blue Galway mantles*, with others described as "russet-brown and purple, with matching or 'prettily variegated' fringes of silk or fine wool ... green, red, yellow and other light colours, with a variety of fringes." [99]

The brát was so practical it was adopted by the *Anglos Hibernos*, so fashionable that bráta were worn in the 1460s by the English royal family, [100] so lucrative that in 1482 the Pope's agent exported them. [101] So inadaquate was English clothing in sixteenth-century Ireland that all the above were worn by English armies, culturally assimilating them and aiding political conquest.

The forces of supply/demand and surplus exchange - capitalism - were well understood in pre-Reformation Europe. Goods were rendered desirable if uncommon, unobtainable, or necessary in areas interested in their purchase. Profit was made by purchase of relatively low-cost goods in one region, and their

*Medieval wine production (Courtesy of Wikipedia Commons)*

sale at higher prices in another - buy low, sell high, cheat or smuggle if necessary.

*Bradán* (salmon) is one of the few words in Gaeilge preserving elements from Ireland's previous language(s) [102] Every year, salmon swam upriver from the saltwater Atlantic, leapt the rocky cataracts spanning the freshwater of the Gaillimh, and into the loch to spawn. Midway between the town and St. Francis's Abbey was *Inchora mor*, otherwise known as "The great cataracts, where salmon are taken up." They were so plentiful that they could be caught by spears thrown from the West Bridge, and were netted between it and Shepisend's mills. [103]

Elsewhere was *Cora na b'mraher*, "the little cataracts [sic]... where Eels are taken." *The fish shambles*, Fisher's Lane, "the market for fresh water fish", show their economic importance locally and abroad. [104] Christian Holy Days imposed dietry restrictions, making fish a necessary foodsource for up to one-third of the year. And Galway had access to a lake, river, and bay full of them. In turn, the Galway merchants sold foreign goods on the Irish market, including wine ... *English or foreign linen cloth ... cloth of silk ... iron ... steel ... nails ... horse-shoes ... clout-nails for carts ... tin, brass and copper ... olive oil for ointment ... coloured glass ... white glass ... averdupois* [miscellaneous merchandise sold by weight]. [105]

## Road and river trade networks

For such a system to function, there had to be fairly sophisticated networks connecting communities. The town's hinterland - west as far as the Rahoon Hills, east as far as Cloonacauneen or Doughiska - could not supply enough exports for even one year. Galway's merchants could

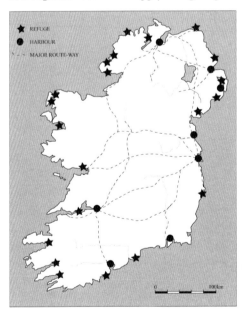 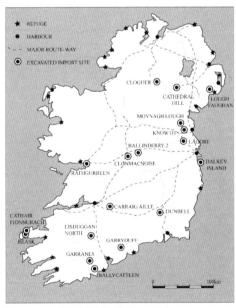

O Lochlainn's routeways, plus natural harbours and refuges as mapped by Warner 1976 (from Comber 2008, 155).

Select excavated Early Medieval sites producing average or extensive evidence of foreign trade, with Warner's 1976 map overlaid (from Comber 2008, 165).

*Tribes of Galway 1124-1642*

only have these amounts if they were able to access deep into Gaelic territories, amid families such as those mentioned in Chapter One. Trade was conducted in 'havens' far beyond the towns, where the 'grey merchants' [106] acted as middlemen between the communities. Relics may have survived in fairs such as Maum Cross and Spancil Hill. Named from road dust on their clothes, 'grey merchants' could be of any nation, perhaps in turn explaining why the Galwegians were of mixed origins.

Both the havens and networks most probably dated back to the numerous trading sites and communication routeways that had evolved in Gaelic Éire. Gravel roads, bridges and causeways, all constructed by Gaelic kings, continued to be used in Norman Ireland.

Gaelic Ireland had five principal major *slighe* ('highways'): an tSlighe Mhór ('the great highway') followed the Escir Riada across Ireland, closest to Galway and Athenry at Kiltullagh and Clarenbridge (with Loch Lurgan being the next stage of any commerical route). A *slige* denoted 'a road cut through a forest', demonstrating it and other types of roads were deliberately created, not a mere *bóthar* ('cow path'). Since the 700s, various types of *leabhar slighedh* ('road [map] book') were used to guide travellers in unfamiliar areas. Thus "the sophistication of the infrastructure ... made the Norman [invasion] of Ireland so rapid." [107] Likewise, post-invasion trade expanded upon this Gaelic-Irish infrastructure; it did not create it.

Archaeologist Michelle Comber has made a very plausible case for early medieval Éire been connected by a national network of routeways and *oénaig* ('fairs'). The latter can be described as communal gatherings or assemblies, "primarily convened for social, administrative and legal reasons, yet often [incorporating] trade as a secondary activity." [108]

*Faiche an Aonaigh* ('the Fairgreen', then north Eyre Square, lastly off Boherbeg) shows an *oénach* just beyond Galway's walls. Likewise Fairhill, now within The Claddagh. Though only documented from the 1700s, both may have medieval ancestry. This is hinted at in another Claddagh placename, Bettystown - 'settlement of the *biatach*."

A regional oénach was the fair of Maonmhagh, which saw a full-scale battle in 1135; faction-fights were a feature of Irish fairs into the 1900s. [109] Fairs at Ballinasloe and Turloughmore, horse-races at Rashane near Craughwell, and Gurrauns near Tuam, may have their roots in such oénaig. [110] Perhaps too the Galway Races, which has seen much political horse-trading.

Such festive occasions were tremendously popular, politically neutral-ish, social events. Thus they were perfect venues for commercial merchants of all backgrounds.

Loch Orbsen was a semi-enclosed freshwater economic unit. Commodities were shipped down the Gaillimh to the wood quay, just beyond the north wall. Goods from Loch Orbsen's hinterland districts - Iar Connacht, Muintir Murchada – had an urban (and by extension, foreign) market increasingly rare in medieval Connacht after the 1340s. Timber, turf, butter, charcoal, fodder, barley, wool, flax, all found a ready market at river's end. [111]

The more sizeable boats carried small animals such as hens, sheep, goats, pigs. Individual horses and cattle were tethered on a rope and made to swim. The sometimes huge Irish *cott* (dugout canoe) survived as "the normal method of transport on Irish inland waters" into the 1680s; "some of those in use on the Shannon could carry sixty or eighty men". [112] Economic migrants in search of work arrived annually, like today attracted by the settlement's labour market. Foreign goods brought into Galway were no doubt transported into the interior by the same means in reverse. River transport was probably a preferred, and now overlooked, form of transportation.

## Maritime highways

But it was Galway's status as a seaport that truly made its prospects. Loch Lurgan was a highway linking it to markets at home and abroad. Into the 1900s "culture, commerce, contagion, and conflict generally moved faster by sea than by land." And on "[an] ocian mór nemforcendach" ("the great endless ocean"), prospects and possibilities were quite literally *nemforcendach* [113]

Just as modern highways are busy with vehicles, Loch Lurgan must have teemed with traffic. Not only was it an economic network itself, as a maritime loch it enabled Galway's ships to venture to Bristol, London, Southampton, (in England), Bruges and Sluys (Flanders), Lubeck (Germany), Calais, Dieppe, and Rouen (Normandy), Morlaix, Nantes, St Malo (Brittany), La Rochelle, Bordeaux (Gascognie), Bilbao, Lisbon, San Sebastian (Iberia). [114]

Seafarers had a broader world view than many medieval people, most of whom lived and died in the same district as their ancestors and descendants - working to live kept them put; maritime work took sailors away. Seafarers were used to the rise and fall of waves shifting their balance. This only occurred to landlubbers after an excess of *usquebagh* (whiskey) at the local *sheebeen* (drinking house). Where a farmer turned left a seafarer turned to *port*, measured in *fathoms* and *leagues*, and looked *fore* and *aft* instead of ahead and behind. Long voyages were *plane sailing* so long as the pilot navigated correctly, avoided *hefty weather* and *grounding* at low tide. If the voyage ended well, a sailor so-minded could get *stowered*, with or without a *mot* (or two).

They could sail greater distances in a single day than most land dwellers travelled in a year, and when the wind was good at speeds that would leave stallions standing. Their lives were full of far-away places, strange nations and incomprehensible languages, exotic, seemingly full of adventure.

On the other hand, few land dwellers faced the daily possibility of death by drowning, murder

or mutilation by pirates. Harsh winds and cold rains famished the blood. If shipwrecked, their vessel became their tomb; even those who could swim might end up dashed to bits against rocks on a strange shore. None but the tides of Manannán would ever know their fate.

Stamina and endurance were prized traits among people regularly pushed to their physical and mental limits. Just offloading/on-loading cargo could be backbreaking or hernia-inducing. Winding sails in or out while on an unsteady sea

*Saint Nicholas's, Galway, about 1664, Courtesy of NUI, Galway*

*Tribes of Galway 1124-1642*

was far from easy, especially if a change in direction was urgent. Hands rapidly callused, and tempers likewise. It was and remains a hard life, but is sometimes exhilarating, especially for the young in fact and heart.

Like any community, Galway's merchants used specialised expressions and terms rarely used or understood outside their context. Words such as *dicker, hides, tun* [115] were verbal shorthand to describe the various commodities they traded every working day. Hides were animal skins, mainly cattle but including anything from a squirrel to a wolf. A *dicker* was ten such hides and a last consisted of twenty dickers, usually those of three-year old cows. [116]

A *tun* was a unit of measurement consisting of two hundred and fifty-two gallons, of anything from wine to honey. But it could also denote a barrel or cask. The *ell*, measuring one and a quarter yards or forty-five inches, was used in relation to types of cloth, usually linen. *Pilchards* were sardines while *sack* was not a bag but a type of wine, usually 'white'. Wine was also useful as a preservative for fish and eels, both of which were valuable exports. Salmon was especially valued both on national and foreign markets, and Galway had a river full of them.

While ship design had improved, basic navigation techniques were unchanged since Brendan the Navigator. *Littus ama; altum alii teneant*/Love the shore; let others go to the deep [117] was advice followed for untold generations. Keep the shore in sight, always, watch for familiar landmarks, strange ships, and changing weather. Purely regional voyages would take them north along the coast to Umall, Tir Amalghaidh, and Tir Conaill, or south to Boireann, Corco Duibne, and beyond. Ports such as Cork, Waterford, Dublin, and Carrickfergus were also destinations for the different classes of ship sailed by medieval Galwegians: barques, carricks, galleys, and cogs. The cog was a sea vessel since the 1150s and widely used on the Atlantic, Irish Sea, and North Sea in the high medieval era. [118] It became the main emblem of the town's coat of arms.

Since at least 1277, Diarmuid Mór Ó Briain of Tromra, ruler of Árann, received

> 12 tuns of wine yearly, as a tribute from the merchants of the town, in consideration of protecting the harbour and trade from all pirates and privateers, by maintaining a suitable maritime force for the purpose. [119]

It was necessary and worthwhile as Diarmuid Mór and his descendants, the Clann Teige Uí Bhriain of Árann, controlled the 'roads' in and out of Loch Lurgan: *Belagh-Lougha Lurgan* (between Conmhaicne Mara and Árann), *Belagh-na-haite* (between Árann and Inismean), Bealagh na-fearboy/fergab (between Inis Mean and "the east island ... Inisoirthir"), and *Bealagh-na-finnis* between Inishoirthir and Thomond, named after a notorious wreck-prone rock. All four converged into one, Bealach na Gaillimhe, the Galway road(s) or The Roads. [120]

This mutually beneficial relationship lasted three hundred years. Loch Lurgan was a vital economic unit that could literally demand its pounds of flesh. When in 1565 Diarmuid Mór's descendant, Mathghamhain Ó Briain, "was treacherously slain in his own town of Aircín, in Aran, by his own associates and relations ... the chief men of Galway ... set out to revenge this misdeed." Driven by them into Thomond, his murderers were captured by Sir Domnaill Ó Briain, who "hanged some of them, and burned others, according as their evil practices deserved." [121]

# The Roads and Saint Nicholas

This maritime tradition is reflected in the name of the town's parish church. St. Nicholas is the patron saint of merchants, sailors, and prostitutes. Today he is best known as Santa Claus. The generally accepted foundation date of c. 1320 is an educated best guess. An unnamed "Galway church" is attested in 1302-06. [122] Prize-winning research by Jim McKeon indicates that like other newly English settlements, a church was built soon after conquest, with "significant patronage" regularly expanding it until "By the fourteenth century, despite [or because of] its frontier location ... it was amongst the largest parish churches in Ireland." [123] So who paid for all this, and how?

Anyone approaching or departing Galway by sea even today can clearly see St. Nicholas's from far out into the bay. It remains the tallest structure in the medieval heart of the town. And given how crucial landmarks were to medieval seamen, this cannot be a coincidence. Both the *caistél* (probably) and the castle (certainly) were situated in an *seanceathrú* ('old quarter'), the Flood Street-Kirwan's Lane area. While defensibly by river and docks, they were much too low to aid navigation.

But St. Nicholas's was carefully placed on what is still recognisably the highest ground within the medieval town. Even today, when seen from the islands of Altanagh just across the river, from the summit of Tonabrocky in the west, it towers above other buildings. Shipmasters would have found it useful for measuring distances and vectors from offshore. As Galway was bringing in good returns by the 1270s, it would have been sensible to invest in a structure that not only spoke to the settlement's spiritual side but played a very useful role in topographical guidance for her sailors. In more ways than one it was the town's compass, and one of the few Irish churches to be adorned with carvings of mermaids. [124] And it wears them well.

Knowledge of sea-depths and tide was essential for shipmasters. Buoys (wooden barrels in medieval times) [125] and posts were guides to the channel, indicating depth, shoals, or sandbanks. Yet sometimes all efforts were shipwrecked, as states the *Annals of Connacht* for 1310: "xx tunda fina do cur for tir i Moig Cetne/Twenty tuns of wine were washed ashore in Mag Cetne" [126] There were surely many Galway voyages that met such Fomorian ends.

# Wine, Fortune, and Fame

All this demonstrates that there was a thirst in Ireland for wine, and one of long standing. *Tairired na Désse*, a late eighth-century origin tale, demonstrates active Irish trade with pre-viking Francia, spun in a way that both indulged and 'solved' alcaholic overindulgence:

> two jars full of wine which had been brought to them from the lands of France, together with the food of France for he who would eat and drink it would be intoxicated and sober at the same time. [127]

Poitiu and Gascoigne in Aquitaine also produced salt, used to preserve one of Galway's main exports, fish. Wine was the intoxication of choice for Galway's high medieval customers. Though many less prestigious commodities were traded in greater proportions or of similar value, wine spread Galway's fortune and fame more than any other over the subsequent three hundred years.

Accounts survive of the Galway customs in the late 1200s. In most years they averaged eighteen to twenty pounds, but in 1296-97, it was sixty-eight pounds, seven shillings and one penny, a record that would not be bettered for nearly a century. [128] All this was welcome income to the *lord of the aforesaid town of Galway and his heirs*. [129] However, the Lordship of Galway was soon a matter of great urgency to the townsfolk, when a single murder would bring about a great reckoning.

*Mermaid, exterior of St Nicholas's church*

*Athenry Coat of Arms (courtesy of Athenry Arts & Heritage Centre)*

# CHAPTER THREE – A GAME OF THRONES

## *Living and Dying in Interesting Times*

It was the policy of le Rey Édouard I d'Angleterre, in his capacity as Seigneur d'Irlande, to use its resources not for Ireland's benefit but for his imperial military campaigns abroad. In his conquest of Wales in 1282, and from 1295 in his campaigns in Scotland and France, Édouard "ignored signs ... that his war policy might produce an adverse effect in Ireland, and ... recklessly exploited the colony, regardless of consequence." [1] A modern biographer glumly but accurately noted that

> Edward was never very much concerned with affairs in Ireland ... [2] [his] main concern with Ireland was probably simply as a source of funds and supplies ... Gascony was always to be much more important to Edward than Ireland. [3]

In 1296, nearly three thousand Irishmen fought in Scotland at a cost of £7,500 to the Irish exchequer. Expeditions of 1301 and 1303 exceeded £6,000 and £8,000 each. Huge quantities of oats and wheat were shipped from Ireland to Gascoigne for Édouard's French wars. [4] These royal commands were a dereliction of duty. For a greater game, Ireland was deprived of men and material better used locally. Commands from absent rulers continued to cause tension between the English of Ireland and England for the rest of the medieval era. Law and order began to break down as criminals acted with impunity in the absence of lawmen abroad on royal duty.

There were other reasons for concern. Bad weather regularly destroyed harvests, causing some half-a-dozen severe and extreme famines in Ireland between 1270 and 1300. [5] In some years

> *it was excessively wet, full of rain and wind so that summer and autumn seemed almost to have become the winter period.* [6]

Disease and heavy snows killed off entire herds of cattle and other stock animals, [7] while violent storms "dispersed haycocks, destroyed houses and caused much damage. [8] ... multitudes of poor people died of cold and hunger and the rich suffered hardship." [9] Subsequent conflicts were not only dynastic or ethnic land wars, but violence over contested resources and sheer physical survival. "Not a thirst for land, but a hunger for food." [10] Irish politics had previously been profoundly influenced by natural forces, and would be again.

All this coincided with the high point of English rule in medieval Ireland. As historian Katharine Simms has remarked:

> just before and after AD 1300 marks the fullest geographical extent of English authority, when Earl Richard de Burgh of Ulster held sway even over remote territories in Donegal and Fermanagh, and English colonists were occupying coastal areas in the modern counties of Clare and Londonderry. In those years there was not a single Irish territory whose

chief was not legally subject either to King Edward I, or to an Anglo-Irish earl or baron. [11]

Qualifying this, Beth Hartland observes:

> Nowhere in the lordship of Ireland were relations between the English or Anglo-Irish and the Irish worked out in precise legal terms. Far from being their feudal lords, the English and Anglo-Irish exercised an undefined overlordship over the Irish. Relations with the Irish, moreover, were a practical, not a theoretical, exercise and the Irish were not always in a subordinate position. [12]

In contrast to the rapid Norman conquest of England, the 'conquest' of Éire was spread over generations, stalled, collapsed, reversed. It had the blow-back effect of strengthening and re-creating Gaeil identity, at least among the upper classes. Conflicts sometimes does. The lesser folk of Éire were all 'Fir Bolg' to the Gaeil. Now they both were all classed as Irish to the English. Distinctions were ignored, lumped together as if all one group. While all Gaelic-Irish had undergone degrees of Anglicisation, and some incorporated into the colony, most remained apart. Regions not settled by the English were home to the most independent Gaelic-Irish. Never fully integrated into the Lordship, they had no stake in its progress. Quite the contrary.

From their refuges dissident septs attacked, competing with each other and the English for territory and resources. Seemingly overnight, lands gained decades before by the Anglos Hibernos were reconquered by the Gaelic-Irish, frequently led by kings and lords utterly hostile to the compromises they imagined their fathers and grandfathers made with the Lordship. [13] Those 'compromises' had been tactical strikes to ensure the survival of personal tighearnais. But the unforeseen result was a massive common strategical error that their descendants understood would end in an island dominated not by the Gaeil of Éire but by the Gaill of Britain. Loss of all significant urban economies was crucial. Rural lordships might survive, but towns enabled the survival of the English and Scottish kingdoms and a serious Irish challenge to both needed lucrative urban bases.

Strife not only between Gaelic dynasties but *within* them meant there could be little realistic joint enterprise. They had rejected unity under various rig Éire for personal domination. Entrenched traditions and dynastic mé féin precluded any long-term unified Gaelic effort.

Even so, the invaders never had it all their own way. Éire was ever seen as *fearond choidhemh* ('sword land') by the Gaeil, to be craved and carved. Finighin Mac Carthaigh had been victorious at the battle of Callan in 1261, briefly re-establishing Deasmuma as an independent kingdom. [14] Likewise, the Wicklow Mountains were home to lineages such as Meic Murchada Caomhánach, the once and future kings of Laigin. [15] The midlands, peripheral Connacht, and much of The North (except Ulster) likewise remained Gaelic enclaves. [16]

From 1258 a new group came from northern Britain, almost in the footsteps of their Cruithin predecessors. Mercenaries for various Gaelic-Irish dynasties of Connacht and Ulster, *gallóclaig(h)* ('foreign youths/warriors'; Anglicised as *Gallowglass*) were Scots-Gàidhlig-speaking descendants of Picts, Britons, Irish, and Scandinavians of Scotland's western isles and highlands. The Meic Domnaill, Meic Suibhne, et al, were further violent factions on an increasingly disturbed island. [17]

An especial disaster for the colonists was the extinction of greater lordships, where massive estates held by a single powerful, resident magnate became extinct in the male line. The properties of dynasties such as Marshal of Leinster, de Clare of Thomond, and de Lacy of Meath, were inherited piecemeal among daughters, grandchildren, and cousins. [18] The inheritors lived mainly in England, and as absentee as the king, were unable or unwilling to move to Ireland and re-establish the productivity of their estates. Often they were then seized by whoever had the strongest sword-arm, Gaelic-Irish, English of Ireland, or something in-between.

Colonial impoverishment was worsened by rising levels of crime, corruption, and emigration, while violent factionalism - a problem since the 1170s - caused internal conflict. [19] 'Degeneracy' [Gaelicisation] among the English of Ireland raised questions of loyalty. Leadership floundered, law and order lapsed. This played into the hands of dissident Gaelic kings and lords, whose competing raids of theft and destruction grew bolder till no revenue could be raised from entire districts. Without it, neither welfare nor security was guaranteed. Its knock-on effect was further emigration and deeper austerity. From 1308 the Irish exchequer experienced a serious decline in revenue. [20]

The result was a series of fractures to English power in Ireland, and Ireland's general prosperity. Any one of these on its own was deeply troubling. Together, they were potentially apocalyptic.

## Ireland's Greatest Knight: Sir John de Athy

Áth Í (hence Athy) in Leinster derives its name from a ford (áth) over an Bhearú (the river Barrow). [21] During the 1200s it became a prosperous market town, perhaps giving a local family the surname de Athy. A possible descent from *Gerald de Athee* of Touraine (fl. 1204-16), a familiar of King Johan, remains intriguing but unproven.

A *William de Athy* was a juror (and by implication a landowner) at Dublin in 1253. From 1270, regular references to men so surnamed are recorded. *John of Athy* was alive in 1270, but dead by Michaelmas 1281. [22] *William fitz John de Athy* was in 1278 described as "sergeant to the K[ing]." and on occasion represented Dunbrody Abbey in legal disputes. [23] In the 1290s, William fitz Thomas de Athy was Seneschal of Kilkenny. [24] *John de Athy* is first recorded in 1310, as sheriff of Limerick. From then to 1312 he was constable of Limerick castle, and had served at least one further term as sheriff by 1315. [25] By 1317 he was knighted. No record of any marriages or children exists, though one William de Athy is described in 1320 as his *valeteus* (personal servant or squire). [26] The confluence of forenames and common royal service suggests a close familial relationship between these men. The lack of references prior to 1270 suggests they were of little consequence beforehand, so either newly risen from the lower classes, recent emigrants, or both.

De Athy's military skills would soon be tested. After his victory over the English at Bannockburn in 1314, King Robert I of Scotland conceived of opening a second front to over-extend the enemy. By exhausting the English of men and resources in both Ireland and Britain, he aimed to force an end to English claims over Scotland, guaranteeing his kingdom's independence. [27] A secondary goal was extending the Scottish imperium. King Robert intended his brother and heir, Edward de Bruce, earl of Carrick, to be made Ireland's king. [28] Ireland and the Irish would bleed for Scotland.

Not for the first or last time in her history, Ireland became the political playground of competing foreign powers. The invasion resurrected the tradition of opposing Irish national groups allying/identifying with different external polities, something which continues today.

## The Scottish invasion of Ireland

In May 1315, Edward de Bruce's fleet invaded Ulster, carrying an army of over six thousand. His Gaelic-Irish supporters were confined to some twelve kings and lords from The North and Ulster such as Ó Neill, Ó Catháin (Keane) and Ó hAnluáin (Hanlon), attracted by the propaganda of a revived Gaelic kingship of Ireland and increased personal power. De Bruce was later joined by disaffected Anglo-Irish families such as de Logan, de Lacy, and de Bisset (now McKeown). [29]

An army marched north and fought against Bruce at *Coinnire* (Connor, Co. Down) in early September. De Bruce won spectacularly. His opponents, Justiciar Edmund le Butler and Earl Richard de Burgh barely escaped. The latter's cousin and deputy in Connacht, Sir William *Liath* ('the grey') de Burgh, captured and brought back to Scotland for ransom on one of "four ships laden with the spoils of Ireland, for the purpose of bringing back more troops." [30] These ships returned with reinforcements to besiege Carrickfergus Castle, where de Athy was apparently constable. [31] Surrounded by thousands of hostile Scots and Irish, the town was burned around the castle. The garrison had no way of retreating except by sea. But the Irish Sea was controlled by the Flemish pirate, Thomas Dun, and his Scottish fleet. [32] No relief came.

Proclaiming himself 'king of Ireland', Edward de Bruce spent the rest of the year destroying Dundalk, Kells, and Trim, defeating every army sent to oppose him, inciting violence wherever he went. Gael and Gall alike were massacred. At Ardee, he burned a church "full of men and women." [33] Even those who submitted to Bruce had their supplies consumed by his forces. This led to desperate conditions in a land already suffering from one of the worst natural disasters of the medieval era, the Great European Famine (1315-18). [34]

And then it got worse.

## The Uí Conchobair Wars

As a result of the invasion, warfare broke out in Connacht between rivals for the kingship, the cousins Fedlimid and Ruaidrí Ó Conchobair. Ruaidrí defeated Fedlimid, and the whole region shook. Almost every significant English settlement west of the Shannon was attacked and destroyed by Ruaidrí, his allies, or opportunists, including the Earl's personal manor of Loughrea. Only Athenry, Clár (Claregalway) and Galway were unscathed, as yet. [35]

> *his Gall friends came to him from every hand, hoping that he would support and succour them, and his Gael friends came into his house likewise, chief among them were Feidlim O Conchobair, king of Connacht, and Muirchertach O Briain, king of Thomond, Maelruanaid Mac Diarmata, king of the Muinter Mailruanaid and Gillibert O Cellaig, king of the Ui Maine, who had all been expelled from the country.* [36]

The Black Marshal of Galway, Nicholas de Linch, numbered among English Connacht's military leadership. So too did former Sheriff, Richard Blake, and his sons Walter, John, Nicholas and Valentine. The Joys and Huskards, both steeped in military traditions, would likewise have armoured up and munstered out. The Brownes may have had the unenviable task of victualling troops in a famine. Gaelic dynasties allied with or subject to the de Burghs - the Uí Mháille, the Uí Fhlaithbheartaigh, the Síol nAmchada and southern Uí Fhiachrach - would have formed part of these units. They spent the autumn and winter fighting a defensive, losing war against Ruaidrí Ó Conchobair. Loughrea barony "was plundered and burned by Tadc O Cellaigh", with the settlement and castle of Aughrim destroyed. [37] Much of the land for miles around Ballinrobe, Claremorris, and Dunmore, was wasted, with the latter town burned. [38]

The *Annals of Connacht* say de Burgh was a wanderer "up and down Ireland all this year, with no power or lordship." [39] His main vassals, Richard de Bermingham, Miles de Cogan, Stephen de Exeter, and deputies such as de Linch and le Blake, led the colonists as best they could. But after defeating Ruaidrí at Templetogher in January 1316, Fedlimid betrayed his English allies and made an all-out attempt to exterminate the colonists and revive the kingdom of Connacht. [40] As a descendant of Toirdhealbhach Ua Conchobair, he received far more support than 'king' Edward de Bruce, and may have intended it as a step to Irish national kingship.

Opposing him were knights such as de Exeter and de Cogan, William de Prendergast, John de Staunton, and other English and Welsh notables such as Robin Lawless, Gerald Gaynard, William Barret and Maurice de Rochefort. But all save Gaynard were killed by Fedlimid near Strade at the annihilation of Ballylahan. [41]

## Gorta Móra/Great Hungers

Back in Carrickfergus, Sir John and the garrison still held out, though supplies were already dangerously low. At terrible risk, they

> *suddenly attacked the Scots by night, and drove them from their camp, and brought away their tents and many other things.* [42]

It was only a brief respite. The Scots returned, the siege continued, the garrison tholed. A summer of almost continuous rain destroyed the harvest; barely a stuicín was saved. The Irish annals provide grim evidence of the combined effects of the war and famine on the population:

*Many afflictions in all parts of Ireland: very many deaths, famine and many strange diseases, murders, and intolerable storms as well. [43]*

Come winter there was "intolerable, destructive bad weather." [44] Because of the summer rains, no more than the odd brishín of turf was dry enough to burn, so there was no heat for comfort, and no fire to bake bread. In any case the destruction of the harvest meant there was no flour. The cold made people sick, lack of food made them starve. Bonds of family, friends, and community were miothered, stretched, and broken. People resorted to horrific means to survive:

*some are said to have taken the bodies of the dead from the graves, to have cooked the bodies in skulls, and to have eaten them; women also devoured their infants. [45]*

By one army or another entire territories were

*beggared and bare from that time on, for therein was no shelter or protection in church sanctuary or lay refuge, but its cattle and corn were snatched from its altars and given to gallóclaigh for the wages due to them. [46]*

At Easter, Sir Thomas de Mandeville set out from Drogheda to relieve Carrickfergus. He successfully battled the Scots and Irish on Maundy Thursday, but an assault on Easter Sunday, 10 April 1316, resulted in his death at the castle gate. [47] De Athy was once more alone in leadership. After some weeks, negotiations with de Bruce began. A contemporary annalist wrote that

*On St. John's Day, [24 June 1316] Bruce came to Carrickfergus, he demands their surrender, as had been agreed upon between them, they asked for life and limb, and that he should send in only thirty, whom they would receive, but when these had entered they put them in chains. [48]*

Yet the Carrickfergus garrison was now so lacking in provisions that when eight of the prisoners died, the garrison are said to have eaten them. [49] On 7 July 1316, salvation seemed at hand with "eight ships laden at Drogheda with necessaries to be sent to those who were besieged in Carrickfergus." [50] Unbelievably, the ships "were stopped by the Earl of Ulster, for the deliverance of William de Burgh, who was a prisoner with the Scots." [51] Matters only worsened for de Athy and his men when later the same month, "Robert Bruce landed in Ireland to aid his brother." [52]

## 'that great rout' - the battle of Athenry

But de Burgh's ransoming of his cousin did have a positive effect. When Sir William Liath was set free, [53] he made straight for Connacht. Given the alarming military situation it is probable he recruited every able man he could find. Thus it is likely that the le Blakes, Brownes, Joys,

*Scale model of Athenry town, AD 1316 (courtesy of Athenry Arts & Heritage Centre)*

de Linches, and Huskards were among the many on the front line of the desperate encounter that followed. King Fedlimid had being busy, the *Annals of Connacht* stating that he had been

> *slaughtering unnumbered people ... [he] plundered the countryside from the castle of Corran [Bally-mote] to the Robe [Ballinrobe], both church and lay property. [54]*

At Meelick "he burned and broke down the castle". Afterwards, he conferred with the two Uí Bhriain contenders for the kingship of Tuadhmhumha, choosing to recognise Donnchad son of Domnaill as king. "He then turned back to Roscommon [castle], intending to raze it." [55] However Fedlimid changed his target upon the return of Sir William Liath de Burgh:

> *On hearing that William Burke had come into Connacht from Scotland [Fedlimid] called upon his subjects to assemble an army to expel him; and the army was assembled from all the regions between Assaroe [Connacht/The North border] and Aughty [Connacht/Munster border]. [56]*

Fedlimid was accompanied by the kings of Uí Maine, Tuadhmhumha, Bréifne, Uí Fhiachrach Muaidhe, Mide, Uí Diarmata, Luigne, Tethba, plus dozens of notable lineages

> *and many more of the king's and lord's sons of Ireland. [They] assembled to him. And they all marched to Athenry. [57]*

*Athenry town seal featuring heads of Fedlimid and Tadhg (courtesy of Athenry Arts & Heritage Centre)*

Lord Athenry, Richard de Bermingham, fought at Templetogher alongside Fedlimid (a Robuc de Bermingham was wounded there). He had in 1312 obtained a murage charter to enclose a greatly expanded Athenry. [58] Now it looked as though it would be strangled at birth. De Bermingham, de Burgh, their mixed Gaill and Gaeil army, faced King Fedlimid's forces who had marched on the tSlighe Mhór "and joined battle with them in front of the town" on Tuesday, 10 August 1316. [59]

In one of the bloodiest battles fought in Ireland since Móin Mór in 1151, the royal army was defeated. The Gaill appear to have suffered light casualties with only one notable, Gerard Gaynard, listed as killed. [60] The Gaeil, on the other hand, suffered a slaughter that the scribe of the *Annals of Connacht* struggled to describe, listing over thirty notable dead and alluding to many more:

> Many of the men of all Ireland about that great field; many a king's son, whom I name not ... was killed in that great rout; my heart rues the fight. [61]

The Annals of Ulster likewise portrayed it as a great feast for crows, maintaining that

> there was not slain in this time in Ireland the amount that was slain there of sons of kings and of chiefs and of many other persons in addition. [62]

The *Regestum* of the Athenry Dominicans recorded "three thousand of the Irish were killed."[63] In Kilkenny, Friar John Clyn stated that "According to a common report a sum total of five ... thousands in all [were killed], the number decapitated was one thousand five hundred." [64] Athenry survived to die another day.

Though various Uí Chonchobair were *Rí Connacht* till 1477, prospective recovery of the overkingdom died with Fedlimid at Athenry. The real beneficiaries were among the ostensible losers; the kings of Tuadhmhumha, Uí Maine, and Uí Fhiachrach Muaidhe. Within decades each were successfully reconstituted as independent kingdoms, existing as such for the next two hundred and fifty years. Descendants of their leading lineages survive as titled aristocracy today.

The heads of King Fedlimid of Connacht and King Tadhg of Uí Maine were mounted over the town's main gate. This image remains the coat of arms of Athenry today.

# Admiral of the Irish Sea

Meanwhile, the soldiers in Carrickfergus Castle were reduced to eating leather. De Athy eventually travelled under safe conduct to Coleraine where he negotiated surrender with Bruce. Around 12 September, after a siege last fourteen months, "Carrickfergus ... surrendered to the Scots, life and limb being granted to those who were in it." [65] The garrison marched south to Dublin, [66] but there was little time for rest. De Athy was appointed *Admiral of the Irish Sea* and sent off to find and fight Thomas Dun and his fleet. An Irish Exchequer payment of early 1317 reads

*Athy arms, courtesy of Jim Higgins*

> *The Keeping Of The Sea In The War Against The Scots: Richard de Celario, king's clerk, appointed to pay necessary expenses for the maintenance of John de Athy, knight, and the men at arms and sailors in his company staying by order of the king for the safer keeping of the Irish Sea, to suppress the malice and rebellion of the Scottish enemies, for these expenses, by writ of privy seal and indenture of receipt: £13 10s.* [67]

Finally, on 2 July 1317, there was a reckoning somewhere on the Irish Sea:

> *Sir John de Athy met at sea Thomas Don, a famous pirate, who he took prisoner; there were slain of those who were with him, about forty, but he brought his head and the heads of the rest to Dublin.* [68]

It was a famous victory, important as Dun had made maritime supply of areas under English control a virtual impossibility. Nevertheless, it was not until Saturday 14 October 1318 that Edward de Bruce's forces were defeated near Faughart in County Louth. The victor, Sir John de Bermingham, was a cousin of Lord Athenry and was created Earl of Louth for ending the war. [69] The Gaelic Annals of Connacht scorned the Scot who would have been Ri Érenn:

> *Edward Bruce ... was the common ruin of the Gaels and Galls of Ireland ... never was a better deed done for the Irish ("d'feraib hErenn") than this since the beginning of the world and the banishing of the Fomorians from Ireland ... For in this Bruce's time, for three years and a half, falsehood and famine and homicide filled the country, and undoubtedly men ate each other in Ireland.* [70]

For King Robert, the invasion was at best a painful expense. While it weakened the English in Ireland and perhaps aided Scotland's independence, it cost of thousands of men including one he could least he could least afford to lose, his only male heir. It likewise failed to create a useful

Scottish imperium even in Ulster. Not for another three hundred years would another king of the *Scottorum nacio* intervene so directly in Ireland.

## In victory, defeat

As is ever the case, the price of victory was high. Many English settlements were ruined and abandoned. Refugees crowded into secure towns such as Athenry and Galway. Others, continuing a trend established for decades, quit Ireland as a place accursed. Emigration continued the rest of the century as the colony contracted. Loss of people and property meant a fall in revenue, enforced austerity leaving the Lordship to fund and defend itself with fewer resources. The *fásaigh* regenerated as land fell out of cultivation around deserted settlements. Many areas saw the English entirely expelled by triumphant Gaeil, who in turn displaced weaker Irish septs.

Among the casualties was Richard de Burgh, whose fortunes never fully recovered. He died in July 1326, aged sixty-seven. His successor as 5th Lord of Connacht and 3rd Earl of Ulster was his under-age grandson, fourteen-year old William *Donn* ('brown-haired') de Burgh. [71]

By then, Sir John de Athy had reached the pinnacle of his career. On 7 March 1325, Sir Robert de Morlee deputed him as his *chere bacheler*, to serve and in his name execute, the duties of the Marshalry of Ireland. [72] Sir John de Athy was officially Ireland's greatest knight.

De Athy remained Constable of Carrickfergus till at least Easter 1326. By August of that year he was Constable of Trim Castle. Paid a wage of one shilling per day, his responsibilities included guarding two hostages of *Meyler McGohegan*, returning to Carrickfergus sometime after September. Payments to him as Constable of Carrickfergus continued till June 1328. [73] After this, he was Keeper or Constable of Roscommon Castle from March 1331 to March 1333, and again to September 1335. [74] This was his first recorded tour of duty beyond the Shannon, perhaps connected to the de Burgh civil war then desolating western Connacht.

In 1334 he was recalled to naval duty as "John de Athy, captain and admiral of the king's fleet of all ships in all ports and other places in Ireland" [75] during King Édouard III's Scottish expedition. It was such a dismal failure that Édouard went off to France to start the (first) Hundred Year's Wars (1337-1453). It too eventually ended in a decisive English defeat, but in making the French their principal Other in that era, the English re-created their own national identity. The basis of it remains current and was reinforced by the (second) Hundred Year's Wars (1688-1815).

Sir John was "for his expenses in connection with the arresting of ships in various ports there in 1334-35" given "as a gift: £2." Sometime after 29 September 1341 he was awarded forty pounds and fourteen shillings "in part payment of fee" [76] while four times constable of Roscommon Castle between 1332 and 1335. Such gifts seem to have been sorely needed by Sir John, whose personal finances resembled that of the colony. In a revealing document, it was stated that in 1339 he was present at the court of the Mayor of London and William de Carleton, clerk. Sir John "acknowledged his debt of £10 to Henry de Birchesle, to be repaid by All Saints then upcoming." [77] However, in 1344, de Carleton noted

*he has not observed these terms. Therefore, they pray that the Chancellor will write to the Sheriff of*

Short of travelling to Ireland, it is unlikely that they received the monies, and in any case, de Athy seems to have been unable to provide even for himself any more. In a list of *The King's Gifts and Grants* given between 29 September 1341 and 5 May 1343, it is recorded that

> *John de Athy, now grown old, deprived of his sight and impoverished, granted to him by the deputy justiciar and council in aid of his maintenance: £5.* [79]

A final reference to him, dated between May 1343 and September 1344, reads "John de Athy, enfeebled by old age, as a gift for his good service: £5." [80] The old Irish knight died somewhere on the frontier between Gaeil and Gaill, as distressed in person as the lordship he served.

In these years the Athys became associated with Athenry and Galway. *Mary Athy* is given in a Lynch genealogy as the wife of Thomas, a son of William de Lenche. *William de Atthy* was a juror (implying local land ownership) at a land inquisition held at *Athneri* on 31 December 1333. He seems identical with the *William son of Richard de Athy* – Sir John's *valetus* of 1320? – described as "of Athenry" in 1342. An Elias de Athy attested in that space and time, their exact relationship unknown. [81] A later William de Athy was Treasurer of Connacht in December 1388, [82] while John Athy is listed in a customs licence dated 13 April 1404. [83] In this John's lifetime, the family would reach its apex, before they were overcome by a feud of Shakespearian intensity.

## A family of blood

Earl William Donn came into possession of his estates in 1328 but almost immediately was disputing with his cousin, Walter de Burgh, son of Sir William Liath. The latter's family deputised for the earl in Connacht for decades, becoming too familiar in their power. Open warfare between the cousins broke out in 1330 and lasted till November of the following year, when Earl William captured Walter and two of his brothers. Imprisoned in Northburgh Castle on Inis Éoghan, Walter was allowed to starve to death. [84]

Finally secure, Earl William further extended his Ulster estates into The North. 6 June 1333 found him and his trusted squires, John de Logan, Robert fitz Richard and Robert fitz Martin de Mandeville, at Woodburn, Carrickfergus. Without warning, they murdered the Earl in a conspiracy organised by Richard de Mandeville's wife, Gyles - sister of the late Walter de Burgh. [85]

The Earl's murder was a catastrophe; within six months all the earldom west of the Bann was lost. His surviving uncle, Sir Edmund de Burgh of Limerick, attempted to hold Connacht but faced stern opposition from Sir William Liath's surviving son, Sir Edmund *Albanach* ('the Scot'). The two Edmunds fought for supremacy in a war that saw "The entire of the West of Connaught ... desolated." [86] It only ended in 1338 through familial treachery:

> *Edmond Burk, i.e. the son of the Earl of Ulster, was taken prisoner by Edmond Burk; and a stone was tied round his neck, and he was afterwards thrown into Loch-Mesca; and the destruction of the*

Earl William Donn's only surviving child was an infant daughter, Elizabeth, who's mother took her to England for safety. In time, King Édouard III married Countess Elizabeth de Burgh to his son, Lionel, duke of Clarence, in the hope that he would someday regain her estates. But Ireland west of the Shannon was lost. For the next two hundred years, Connacht remained outside the direct realm of English governments more preoccupied by dynastic instability and costly European adventures. Colonial demise saw towns such as Roscommon and Rindoon disappear entirely from exchequer records in the 1340s. [88]

County Connacht dissolved into independent lordships, its offices held of the de Burghs but diminished in scope, becoming purely familial fiefs, and eventually redundant. As late as 1347, a John Prout was appointed coroner for Muintir Murchada, [89] demonstrating that the Headford area still adhered to English law. But the terrible Black Death plagues of 1348-50 and 1361-62 killed a third or more of the population. By the later 1300s, English Connacht slowly withered to the immediate areas of Athenry, Ballinrobe, Loughrea, and Galway.

## Eclipsed

Ireland was repartitioned into dozens of territories regularly at war with each other. The Anglo-Irish were on the defensive, with a siege mentality and fewer resources. At exactly the point when a native *Ri Érenn* might have unified them nationally as Bruce had the Scots, the Gaelic-Irish chose individual dynastic independence. Between then and the sixteenth century they consciously transformed from kings to warlords, the title *ri* replaced in importance by their surname. [90] This demonstrates that not only did Ireland not endure *800 years of* [English] *oppression*, neither was there a unified 'national resistance' or heroic 'Gaelic resurgence'. [91] There were only different factions, each taking personal advantage of a decades-long colonial decline, in gang-warfare writ large. There were no heroes in the house.

This too was the view of the English of Ireland during the reign of Édouard III (1327-77); they placed the blame not on the Gaelic-Irish, but on themselves alone. Principal causes they saw undermining the Lordship was acculturation with the Gaelic-Irish, and unregulated legal activity:

> *By granting charters of peace*
> *To false Englishmen without tenure*
> *This land shall be much undone*
> *But god-parenthood and fosterage*
> *And losing of our language*
> *Have greatly helped there too.* [92]

As the Lordship faded, links with England diminished, especially west of the Shannon where English families assimilated in various degrees. De Exeter became *Mac Siúrtáin* (Jordan); de Angle became *Mac Oisdealbhaigh* (Costello); de Staunton became *Mac an Mhílidh* (McEvilly); de

*Athy's Castle, Market Street in the 1660s, courtesy of NUI, Galway*

Bermingham became *Mac Fheorais* (Corish). Gaelicisation resulted in what was termed 'degeneracy' in its original sense of 'no longer its kind'. Many English did so "in contempt and hatred of the English name and nation", so much so, that "these degenerate families [have] became more mortal enemies than the pure Irish." [93] Thus the de Burghs of Connacht became a *Búrc* (Bourke, Burke), splintering into a dozen septs bearing different surnames - *Mac Giobúin* (Gibbons), *Mac Philbín* (Philbin, Phillips), *Mac Sheóinín* (Jennings), *Mac Hugo* (McCooge, Cooke), *Mac Báitéar* (Qualter), to name but a few.

For all outward purposes, the English of Ireland became as Gaelic as the Irish themselves. The process took place over generations rather than years or even decades, with the two cultures and languages coexisting as Gaeilge overlaid English. By the early modern era, English was an endangered Irish language while Gaeilge and its culture predominated among the population till about the 1760s. [94] The council of Ireland, in a letter to Édouard III dated 1351, bleakly stated "the land of Ireland is in continuous war." [95] Galway and its families was on their own.

*James Reagh Dorsey, Mayor of Galway, died 1603, courtesy of Adrian Lead*

# CHAPTER FOUR – COMUNITATIS GALVE

## A Period of Transition

From 1338 until his death in 1375, Sir Edmund Albanach de Burgh was an illegal but very actual lord of Galway. In return for his 'protection', the Galwegians became his clients and gave him his due. Such arrangements have being the basis for entire kingdoms, even empires.

All independence is based on economic wealth. Without it, communities, cities, empires, wither and die. Without opportunity for gaining it, people work hard all their lives and still die in poverty, labouring just to live. Economic set-ups favour the enabled few while disabling the rest, so they must exploit systems fixed in someone else's favour. By the mid-1300s the Galwegians had to maximise their economic potential to become independent of the local warlords and their 'dues'. One way was exploiting tensions between Sir Edmund and Galway's lawful lords, Countess Elizabeth and Duke Lionel. In 1361, their presence in Ireland was used by "the bailiffs and good men of Galway" to obtain a murage charter. [1] In the long view, all sides benefited. The Crown still had a loyal town. Galway was able to repair and raise further stones walls to improve its security and thereby protect its economy. Sir Edmond Albanach received a better due (*chíos*, 'tax'). Government investment in business enterprise is the single greatest alliance in capitalism.

By 1375 Galway had become a staple port, meaning that in return for a levy paid to the Crown, the merchants were allowed to export leather and raw wool to ports in Britain and Europe. But it was short-lived; the crown withdrew staple status in 1377, possibly due to intervention by Sir Edmond's son and successor, Sir Thomas, to stifle Galway's nascent independence. Some merchants found another outlet by opening up trade links with Iberia, particularly Navarre, Castille, and Portugal, perhaps even Islamic Granada. [2] This placed the Galwegians directly in touch with the nascent Portuguese and Spanish global empires which within generations stretched from Africa to Asia, from the Americas back to Europe - *an Spáinneach Geal* ('the white Spaniard', aka the potato) most probably came from Peru to Ireland by the 1580s via Iberia, as its anim Gaeilge implies. Atlantic commerce renamed na Ben Beola in Conmhaicne Mara; "called by marriners the twelve stakes, being the first land they discover as they come from the [Spanish] maine." [3] They have being the Twelve Bens ever since.

From the 1420s Portugal seized tropical Atlantic islands such as the Azores, the Canaries, Cape Verde, Madeira. Their fruit, olive oil, wine, and sugar were traded to Galway. Access to the Mediterranean and its goods possibly preceded Aragon and Castille's 'reconquest' of Granada and subsequent creation of Spain. In the Americas and Asia from the 1490s, united under a single monarchy from 1580 to 1640, Iberia's global empires laid paths the Dutch, English, and French each followed and emulated. Galwegians settling in Portugal, Spain, and their colonies had their surnames recast as *Bodquin, Esqueret, Frens, Quiroban, de la Fuente, Bruno, Lince*. Their stories and those of other Irish await researchers to delve into voluminous archives.

Not all were so productive. Withdrawal of the staple caused huge resentment in Galway, Henry Blake lead a town faction that in 1385 they caused "damages and destructions that were

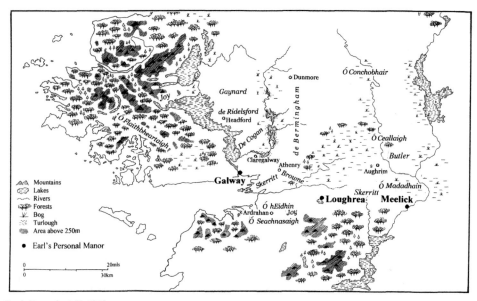

*South Connacht A.D. 1316*

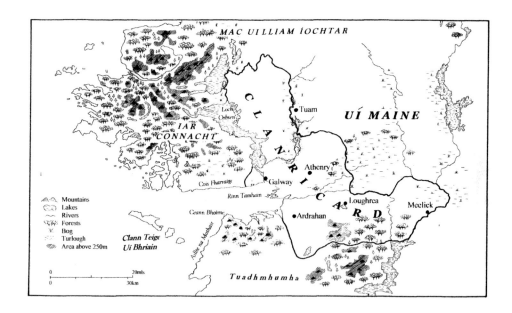

*South Connacht A.D. 1416*

perpetrated in the town of Galway." [4] Blake fought the law and the law lost, pardoned in 1395 for

> *all manner of treasons, felonies, homicides, burnings, receivings, trespasses, contempts, rebellions, conspiracies, champarties, falsities, deceptions, extortions, oppressions, ambidextries, false allegiances and misprisions.* [5]

An oblique view of *realpolitik* can be glimpsed in chancery documents. One, dated January 1387, asked that *William Athy and Stephen Dyvelyne* be pardoned for various "seditions, felonies, extortions, oppressions [etc.], at the request of Thomas s. of Edmund Burgh." [6] Another, dated April 1387, asked that *Geoffrey Blake, Stephen Dyvelyne and William Seman* be appointed as supervisors and receivers of *le coket* customs, while in December 1388, William Athy was appointed Treasurer of Connacht. [7] These posts would have been impossible to hold without the goodwill of Sir Thomas, who no doubt aided Henry Blake's legal rehabilitation.

## 'Comunitatis Galve'

But by the 1390s the de Burghs of Connacht had splintered into two rival septs. Sir William Liath's descendants, based in north Connacht, became known as the *Meic Uilliam Íochtar a Búrca* ('the lower [northern] Bourkes'). Descendants of Richard Óg de Burgh - an illegitimate son of the first William de Burgh - became the *Meic Uilliam Eighter a Búrca* ('the upper [southern] Burkes'). Based in the town of Loughrea, the latter became popularly known as the *Clann Ricard* ('Richard's family'/'offspring'). Their territory and lord were both known as Clanricard. [8]

In 1399 Galway "was taken and plundered by Ulick Burke [of Clanricard] and innumerable were the spoils taken from it, both gold and silver, and all kinds of goods." [9] From this point, successive Clanricards overlorded. Unlike the Galwegians, they had resources enabling them to hire armed forces and professional Scottish mercenaries. If the Galwegians were not to be drawn into a conflict they could not win, accommodations had to be made with each Clanricard, as well as Ó Flaithbheartaigh, Ó Briain, and other lords.

> [So] if the Crown had to reconcile itself to the loss of Connaught, it was all the more anxious to keep the town of Galway, and consequently it now deemed it expedient in the English interest to grant the town fresh liberties. [10]

In 1396 King Richard II granted Galway its first royal charter of incorporation. Recognising it as "the key of those parts of the K[ing].'s land of Ire[land]" situated between "Irish enemies and English rebels" [11] the grant gave Galwegians more independence in their day-to-day affairs with the surrounding lordships, and allowed English rule a foothold in its most lonely outpost. Significantly, the previous de Burgh arms were replaced. Instead, the 1396 Seal of Galway incorporated a version of the Lynch arms. But at some point in the following decades, this was replaced by the cog as the prime symbol of the town and its people, surrounded by the Latin legend DE:COMU-

NITATIS:VILL:DE:GALVE:INCONAICIA - "The Community of the Town of Galway in Con-nacht." (see cover illustration) Thus Galway "became a haven of security for many who, because of the native resurgence, found life in the country districts more than they could bear." [12]

## Chief Millers of Galway - The Martyns

During the decades either side of 1400, the Bodkins and Martyns are recorded in the town. The first Martyn identified as of Galway is recorded in the following document:

> A.D. 1365, June 2. Joan, daughter and heir of William Sepishend, chief miller of the mills of the town of Galway, gave and confirmed to Thomas Martyn, and his heirs, all the profits and emolu-ments arising out of the said mills of Galway, descended to her by hereditary right; to hold as freely and quietly as her said father, John her grandfather and William her great grandfather, held the same of the Lords Walter, Richard and William de Burgh, late Earls of Ulster and Lords of Con-naught. [13]

These mills were located on the site of what is now Blake's Castle and Jury's Hotel, and are re-called in *Martyn's Mill Lane*, which connects Quay Street to Kirwan's Lane. Of *Thomas Martyn's* background nothing is known. The surname derives from a fourth-century bishop of Tours, Mar-tinius of Pannonia (now Hungary). Originally a Roman legionnaire named after Mars, the Roman god of war, Martinius was a militant evangelist among the Gauls. After his death in 397 he became a patron saint of Gaul, Martin becoming a popular baptismal forename. This led in turn to Martin becoming a surname all over western Europe. In high medieval Ireland, the sur-names Mac Giolla Máirtin, Fitz Martyn, Mac/Ó Mael Martáin, de Castlemartin, Ó Martáin, de Saint Martin, Martin(e), Martyn(e), are all attested. It is still a popular Irish forename.

Thomas Martyn appears after decades of civil disturbance and two lethal attacks of the Black Death, all of which may have devastated Joan Sepishend's family. [14] Events may have depleted the town elite enough for 'new blood' to take their place, as happened at the time all over Eu-rope. Yet the change from an established 'auld stock' family like Sepishend to a nouveau like Mar-tyn could not take place without the wishes of the town's elites being taken into account. They had to be assured that something so fundamental to the town's welfare and economy as its mills - where grain became flour and flour became their daily bread - would be in fully capable hands. Ten years later, Martyn is recorded in a property dispute, perhaps concerning the mills:

> 1375, August 16, the Lord Justice of Ireland, being at Limeryk, constituted Clemens Laveragh and John Baudekyn, clerks, to enquire and determine a certain transgression on Nicholas Calf, burgess of Galvy, by Thomas Martyn; and also to take assize of novel desseizen, which said Nicholas ar-raied against said Thomas and Margaret his wife, concerning tenements in Galvy. [15]

Another source states Thomas's wife was *Margaret Balagh Lenche*. Galway's premier family had bound the new chief miller to themselves. Evidently, Martyn would do.

# 'Hospita Fratum' - Margaret Balagh Lenche

Thomas Martyn was dead by 1386 (the plague reoccurred in 1383), and was buried in the Dominican Friary of Athenry. That may hold a clue to his origins; the Uí Mhairtín were a Soghain sept, whose homeland lay north of Athenry. [16] Yet it may only signify his personal devotion, that of his wife, or that Dominicans would not have a base in Galway for another hundred years. He was survived by sons Thomas and William, and his widow Margaret *Balagh*. [17] Her nickname derives from the Gaelic term *ballach* ('spotted', 'speckled'), indicating Margaret may have survived the plague, smallpox, or scabies but was left facially scarred. On the other hand, a John *Ballach* Lenche was Provost of Galway 1357-58, [18] so the nickname might indicate a hereditary physical trait. As an acquaintance of dozens of Margaret's female Martyn descendants, I prefer to believe for them she had a face beguiled by freckles.

Margaret sought and obtained the protection of the lieutenant-Chief Governor of Ireland. An abstract of a document written at Le Naas (Naas, Co. Kildare) on 28 November 1386, states:

> As various damages and injuries have been inflicted on Margaret Balagh Lenche and Thomas Martyne, her son, by their enemies of the parts of Connacht, and many more are to be feared, the marquis has taken them, their men and possessions into his special defence and protection. [19]

Who were their enemies? A document written at Dublin in January 1387 ordered *Richard Burgh* and *Henry Blake* to "interfere no further in the said [salmon] fishery [of the town and river of Galway]." [20] Evidently Galway was internally factioned, but perhaps so were the Martyns, if Margaret's husband had being married to Joan Sepishend and had children by her. Whatever aid the distant lieutenant-Chief Governor provided was temporary. In 1401, "Margaret Ballagh of Galway in Ireland" appealed to King Henry IV, giving further detail on the interferences, and her own life:

> She has been subject to a vow of chastity since her youth, but recently evilly-disposed people motivated by envy have done great damage to her goods and chattels and intend to do more damage both to her person and estate and to her possessions. [21]

In common with a number of wives and widows of Connacht, Margaret supported the Athenry Dominicans. Her relative, Sylina Lynch, donated valuable casks of fish and wine to the friars at the start of Lent and Advent for twenty years. [22] Several other Lynchs – James, Christina, William, Thomas, Dominick, Edmund – were noted benefactors of the Athenry friary. [23] Margaret's hospitality to Dominicans visiting Galway earned her the sobriquet hospita fratum - 'hostess of the friars' - who noted that she made a gift of "a most beautiful chalice", and "she was a great almsgiver to all the friars and not only to all the friars but to all those in manifest necessity."[24] Margaret did not remarry, apparently preferring respectable independence: "she lived in honest widowhood for many years distributing her largesse to the poor for love of God." [25] Thomas's other son, *William Martin* is attested in three deeds dated 1398, 1399 and

1407. [26] In them, members of the White and Lawless families, of Galway and Athenry respectively, mortgaged

> certain lands, tenements and fishing-pools ... within the franchises of Galway and Athenry ... two
> eel-weirs situated in the river of Galway ... a tenement within the walls of Galway ... five acres of
> arable land lying without the walls of Galway ... and of other weirs near the ford called Crossin ...
> to William Martin, son of Thomas Martin, burgess of Galway ... for £20. [27]

The deeds indicate that within two generations, the Martyns rose from 'nowhere' to become substantial property-owners. And for at least a dozen years, that rise was nurtured by a woman.

## Poinards and Silks: The Bodkins

Of the clerks constituted by the Lord Justice at Limerick in 1375, *Clement Laveragh* bears the surname of an Athenry family. [28] The second, *John Baudekyn*, is previously undocumented.

The orthodox origin of the surname is that it derives from an Old English term for 1) a short, pointed dagger 2) a type of arrowhead. The former was effective in close quarters combat, while the latter could on occasion penetrate a knight's armour. [29]

A previously unconsidered explanation lies in the text of the 1361 Murage Charter, which lists the levy tolled on silk: "For every cloth of silk or *baudekin* [my emphasis] for sale, one halfpenny." This surprising etymology is confirmed in the *Century Dictionary* which states that a rich, embroidered silk fabric – originally woven with a wrap of gold thread – was known as a *baudekin*. [30] Indeed an inventory of the Archbishop of Tuam in 1286-88 lists as among his possessions "6 choir copes of *baudekin* [my emphasis] and 3 of silk." [31]

This, then, may be the true origin of the name. They were a family who took their surname from trading, or wearing, large quantities of embroidered silk. All the way from China. However, an 18th-century genealogical account, the Bodkin Progeny, gave a heroic etymological origin:

> the Connaught Bodkins anciently called Baudekins, derived that name (as the tradition of their eld-
> ers says) from the fact that a man was slain with a slender poniard (called by the Irish, Baudikin)
> by their progenitor, who thenceforth was designated "buath Baudekin", "of the victory of the
> Poniard. [32]

Yet this may reflect nothing more than the family forgetting the original meaning of their surname, and the creation of an explanation. The seventeenth-century Leabhar na nGenealach has a Bodkin pedigree hinting at a surname bequeathed by adoption or fosterage, commencing with Archbishop of Tuam 1537-72, Christopher Bodkin:

> Airdeasbog Tuama Críostoir Boidicin mac Seaáin m. Risdird mc Semuis m. Risdird m. Semuis m.
> Baiter mc. Semuis m. Adaimh mc Tomais Bobhdacing, do hoileadh in Ath na Riogh ag Bobdacing;
> ona oileamuin aige raitear Boidicin friu, agus ar sliocht Muiris m. Muiris Móir atá.

The archbishop of Tuam Críostóir Boidicín s. Seaán s. Risteard. s. Séamus s. Risteard s. Séamus s. Báitéar s. Séamus s. Ádhamh s. Tomas Bodhacing, who was reared in Áth na Ríogh by Bodhacing; from his rearing they are called 'Boidicín' and are of the lineage of Muiris mac Gearalt mac Muiris Mor. [33]

Áth na Ríogh (Athenry) is claimed as home of the first of the name, of whom the *Progeny* says:

> Thomas, son of Richard, was progenitor of the Bodkins and their surname before the year 1300 in the reign of Edward the 2nd, King of England. [34]

*Bodkin arms, courtesy of Cooke's Restaurant*

Muiris Mor is identified as Maurice fitz Gerald [35] of Flemish Dyfed, from which Normans, Flemings, Bretons, and English gained vast swathes of Wales from 1108. But in the Great Revolt of 1136-37, the Britons rose up under their princes, and won back much of their lost lands. Maurice fought at Crug Mwar under Robert fitz Martin of Cemais. A defeat for the Normans, they rallied under fitz Martin and held Cardigan Castle. [36] But in the decades after, the colony steadily contracted under pressure from Maurice's cousin, Rhys ap Gruffyd, Prince of Dehurbarth (d. 1197).

Thus in 1166, when the exiled King Diarmait of Laigin invited Maurice and his kindred to help him regain his kingdom, they availed of his offer. They had nothing to lose.

Maurice's extended family - fitz Henrys, de Carews, fitz Stephens, de Barrys - participated in and profited from the invasion, becoming principal proprietors in Leinster, Meath and Munster. From him sprang the Earls of Kildare and Desmond, so many claimed him as an ancestor. *The Progeny* and *Leabhar na nGenealach* disagree about the name of Tomas Bodhacing's grandfather - the latter says Maurice (Maurice fitz Gerald had a son called Maurice of Kiltrany, County Wexford), while the Progeny says Thomas (Maurice fitz Gerald likewise had a son named Thomas of Shanid, County Limerick, ancestor of the Earls of Desmond). The *Bodkin Progeny* gives this account of the progenitor:

> Richard, son of Thomas held dominions in Connaught under Lord Rickard de Burgo [sic], in the year 1242 in the reign of Henry the 3rd in England. [37]
> Thomas, son of Richard, was progenitor of the Bodkins and their surname before the year 1300 in the reign of Edward the 2nd. Henry Bodkin, son of said Thomas, lived in the time of Henry the 6th, King of England. Richard Bodkin, in the time of Henry the 7th, King of England, was a citizen of the town of Galway and of Athenry, and possessed the Castle and lands of Tobberskehine, [Tobbernaskeen, Athenry] etc; he was many time Provost of Athenry and from him descend all the Bodkins still surviving in those parts. [38]

# Bodkin Pedigree in Leabhar na nGenealach

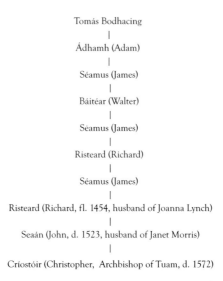

Tomás Bodhacing
|
Ádhamh (Adam)
|
Séamus (James)
|
Báitéar (Walter)
|
Séamus (James)
|
Risteard (Richard)
|
Séamus (James)
|
Risteard (Richard, fl. 1454, husband of Joanna Lynch)
|
Seaán (John, d. 1523, husband of Janet Morris)
|
Críostóir (Christopher, Archbishop of Tuam, d. 1572)

The FitzGerald connection cannot be independently verified. Gaelic genealogies are unreliable for the early generations of Anglo-Irish families, and there are chronological difficulties in reconciling the accounts. Genealogical creativity may be involved! Additionally, that Thomas son of Richard - described as living before 1300 or during the reign of Édouard II (1307-1327) - had a son alive in the reign of Henry VI (1422-71) stretches credulity. However if we interpret *living* to mean born in the era 1300-27, rather than denoting an already *adult* man, then we can allow that Thomas son of Richard is chronologically acceptable. It also links him in time and space to the earliest documented bearer of the surname, *Ysybel Bodykyn*. Her parents are unknown; she may have been a sister or an aunt of Thomas son of Richard. The only secure date that can be associated with her is 1343, the year her husband, *Wyllyn Wallys*, died. Ysybel and Wyllyn are mentioned in the *Regestum* of Athenry's Dominican Friary:

> after the death of her respected husband [she] remained in her old age and widowhood in the infirmary of the said convent and bequeathed the eastern part of the said infirmary. And the said Wyllyn Wallys is buried in the chapel of the Blessed Virgin in his stone tomb with whom is buried his wife and their sons. [39]

*Thomas son of Richard* or *Tomas Bodhacing* did exist. Nicholas Bodkin (fl. 1380x84) is referred to in a contemporary document as *Nicholas son of **Thomas Baudekyn*** [my emphasis]. [40] Other sons may have included *John Baudekyn* the clerk (alive 1375x80), and Henry (alive 1398x1420), named in the *Progeny* as a "son of said Thomas [alive] in the time of Henry the 6th." [41]

*Dominican Friary, Athenry.*

Thus one Thomas, nicknamed *bodkin*, who lived in early-to-mid fourteenth-century Athenry, was claimed by his descendants as a FitzGerald. In 2014, Y-DNA genetic genealogy determined the ancestors of the Bodkins originated in Flanders. [42] Their relationship to the FitzGeralds remains unclear, be they ties of blood, fosterage, or vassal. Yet the Bodkin arms - "Saint Andrew's cross with a leopard's head" [43] - clearly referenced those of FitzGerald. And that is how the family chose to present themselves to the world.

A deed written at Drogheda in September 1421 states that the late "Richard Clerk of Galway" was "also called Richard Bawdekyn". [44] The surname was still in flux, hinting at 'new' origins. Richards son and heir, Walter, gained custody of the islands of *Busheyland and Goteyland* at Galway. Edmond, Robert, and Walter Bodkin were Provosts of Athenry in 1444, 1449 and 1451. [45] They could have been sons of Richard, but the *Bodkin Progeny* states "Richard Bodkin had issue four sons, namely, James, Henry, John and Lawrence, among whom he equally divided his property." [46] Names and precise relationships may have been confused over several generations.

Richard's wife was Joanna Lynch, and their punitive third son was the John Bodkin who served as Mayor of Galway 1518-19. [47] He died in 1523, having married *Janet Mares* (Morris). They had six known children, including Christopher, *Airdeasbog Tuama* 1537-72. [48]

## Roving Merchants

Surviving documents can give us a flavour of the geographical range of these Galwegians. One, dated June 1395 at Westminster, states that Geoffrey Blake of Galway was tried for exporting *hides, wools and wool-fells* to Flanders "contrary to the form of the ordinance of the staple" and not paying customs dues on "eight whole woollen cloths" [49] brought from Bristol to Ireland. Blake's intercessor was his "kinsman", the "abbot of the Irishmen of Vienne in the duchy of

Daustry" (Wein [Vienna], duchy of Austria). The abbot, *Heinrich* (Henry, fl. 1393-98), hoped that "in consideration of the good cheer shown by the said abbot to the king's brother, the earl of Huntingdon, and other lieges of the king when in Daustry", Blake would be pardoned. [50]

A document written at Dublin in July 1415 told the misadventures of "Thomas Lynche, John Athie, William Butler, William Webbe, Edmund Blake of Galway, John Rede, Henry Heryng, and John Omorchowe [Ó Murchadha/Murphy] of Athenry in Connacht, merchants." They loaded a ship of Lübeck at Galway and sailed to Kinsale to pay customs dues on St Laurence's Day, 1413. But:

> *between those towns a great storm arose such that, having been driven onto the high seas, they were unable to approach the town of Kinsale or any other port of Ire[land] to pay their custom, but instead they began their voyage to the port of Sluys in Flanders.* [51]

As a result of this they asked to be pardoned for not paying the customs. A petition to the Chancellor of England of 1465x71 concerns *William Bargayne*, a merchant of Brittany who received some sharp dealing by a Geoffrey Lynch. Bargayne stated he received from

> *Geoffrey Lynche of Ireland, mariner, merchandise valued at £60, which was delivered to the petitioner in Ireland, and for surety of repayment of which he was bound by his bill (written in his own hand) to repay, as soon as he could make his voyage to Portugal and his return to Ireland, which he did therefore and contented the said Geoffrey within a short time after landing back in Ireland. Not being a man predisposed to mistrust, he had no idea of the deceit that might befall him and desired not to have deliverance of the bill, leaving it instead in Geoffrey's custody. Geoffrey began an action of debt upon the bill before the mayor, sheriff and bailiffs of Bristol, intending to recover the £60 anew.* [52]

Bargayne asked for the Chancellor's aid against Lynche. The outcome is unknown.

## The Athy-Blake feud

And other documents raise more questions than can ever be answered. The prime example is the mysterious Athy-Blake feud. James Hardiman related in 1820 that, whatever its exact cause, its end result was the near-annihilation of the Athys by the Blakes. Only one document apparently dealing with it exists so it's worthwhile to quote it in full:

> *Writ of King Henry VI to the Sheriff of Connaught: Whereas divers disputes had previously arisen between John son of Henry Blake, of Galway, and Henry Lynch, William Lynch, William Blake, Walter French, William Dene, Walter Skyret, Nicholas Skyret, Edmund Athy, Thomas Athy, John Laweles, Richard Martyn, Nicholas, Richard and Walter Athy, sons of William Athy, and Walter, son of John Athy; and said John Blake complained that he and his men were in fear both of personal injury and of loss to their goods from the said persons by reason of the said disputes;*

the King, desiring to provide protection to the said John Blake from injury and peril, enjoins the Sheriff to require the said persons to find good sureties under penalty of £100 that no injury or loss shall ensue to the said John Blake from any of them.

If the said persons or any of them refuse to find such surety, then the persons so refusing are to be arrested and imprisoned until they find surety. The Sheriff is directed under penalty of 100 marks to make a return to this writ without delay. Attested by William Welles, Esq., deputy of Leo, Lord Welles, the King's Deputy in Ireland. Dated at Dublin April 13, in the eighteenth year [1440] of the King's reign. [53]

Hardiman dated the event over one hundred years too early, saying "the peace of the town was, about that time, disturbed by some deadly disputes which arose between the rival families of Blake and Athy; and, in the commotions occasioned by them, several of the latter were slain." [54] The full nature of the dispute, with or without star-crossed lovers, is utterly lost to us. Apparently, two families alike in dignity bore grudges that sparked murder, matters perhaps connected to political power - John Athy may have been Sovereign of Galway as many as four times in those decades, and built a castle that if it still stood, would have dwarfed Lynch's Castle.

The King's writ makes plain that John Blake was opposed not just by Athys but by representatives of at least eight other Galway families, including a William Blake. Of the fifteen men named, only six were Athys, yet their family appear to have suffered the most. *Blake and his men dealt with the fear of personal injury and loss to their goods* effectively. The Athys never again rose so high. But John Athy had served as Sovereign at least twice (in September 1428 and July 1444) and memory of this was enough, centuries later, to list them among the Tribes. After all, the *thirteen* Tribes of Galway might be considered unlucky by some.

## Year of the French

The founder of another of Galway family appears in the 1440 document. *Walter French* is said to have been sent to Galway by the king (or at least his Dublin representative) to mediate the feud.

[He] settled near Galway ... where he married the daughter and sole heiress of John Athie, of a worthy family, of great antiquity, and from him are descended the family of the Ffrenches of Connaught. [55]

A date of "about the year 1425" [56] is given for Walter's arrival. He and William Butler of Athenry were appointed at Dublin in July 1420 to be "collectors of the customs of wool, leather, hides, fleeces and lead, and other merchandise liable to custom in Sligo and Galway." [57] The surname derives from the Middle English *frensche*, denoting 1) an ethnic French person, 2) a person whose native language was French, or 3) a nickname for someone who adopted French fashions or culture. The family themselves claimed to originate in "the County of Wexford ... two families of the name settled at different periods in Galway, the first, with Walter French, in the reign of Hen. VI about the year 1425, and the other, with Henry Begg Ffrench, in the reign of Elizabeth." [58]

Frenchs were resident at Ballytory, parish of Tacumshin (in *Fortharta*/Forth barony), County Wexford, since at least 1247. In 1654 Ballytory and Beting townlands were held by their descendants, while the remains of a tower house existed there in 1987. [59] Distant neighbours of the Brownes of Mulrankin, they too would have been Yola speakers. A *John Frenssh* was master of the *Trinite de Drogheda* in 1361, so some of the name were Irish Sea mariners by then. Others were tenant farmers based at Galtrim, County Meath, and Newtown, County Dublin, in the very early 1400s. [60] Mutual relationships remain unknown.

Despite Wexford's distance from Galway, being ports made them inter accessible. Walter may have found his office as Galway's customs collector enough to facilitate property ownership and a good marriage, options perhaps not available in Wexford. Indeed the Frenchs of Wexford never seem to have reached the status as the Brownes of Mulrankin, so perhaps for Walter it was an doubly upward step. It certainly enabled his descendants to flourish in the generations and centuries ahead. Whatever his origins or exact role in the Athy-Blake feud, Walter was esteemed enough to witness deeds between 1440 and 1453, and served as Sovereign of Galway 1445-46. [61]

## Deane, alias Allen

In 1440 *William Dene* is first recorded in Galway. Among the more obscure of the families, they were said to have "came hither from Bristol in the reign of Henry VI" (1421-71). [62] The surname may derive from the clerical office of Dean. It can also denote a *dene*, a Middle English term for a wooded valley (hence the Forest of Dean, near Bristol). [63] This may explain why *William Dene* had two surnames: *Allen* was the original, the epithet *Dene* perhaps meaning 'of Dene' (Old English for 'a clearing' in the woods'?), the area from which they originated. *William Allen*, alias *Den* or *Dene*, died in 1448 while town provost, some months after a new outbreak of the plague. William married Julianne Lynch (daughter of Thomas, who died in 1419); they had at least one son, William Óge Allen/Deane, Sovereign of Galway in 1462 who died in 1478. A deed of April 1451 - where he is called *William Alleyn* – grants him and Edmund Lynch, "merchants of Galway", the lucrative posts of collector of the customs of Galway and Sligo. [64]

It's likely that Edmond Deane (Mayor 1502-04) was a son of William Óge, and was named after a member of his grandmother's family. The prime candidates are Juliane Deane's brother, Edmund (fl. 1451), or her granduncle, Edmond *a Tuane* (fl. 1442-43). He appears to be the "Edmund Aleyne, alias Dene, a Galway merchant", who in 1475 granted two tenements in St Thomas's Street, Bristol, to a fellow Irish merchant in the town. [65]

Edmond's other near relations and in-laws included members of the Penrise, Bodkin, Font, Morris, and Martyn families, indicative of the Deane's early prestige. *Juliana/Ciliana Dene*, a sexual partner of Dominick Dubh Lynch before 1481, was probably Edmond Deane's sister. Dominick Dubh, then Galway's wealthiest merchant, was Edmond's second cousin.

Edmond's terms of office were some of the liveliest for any Mayor of Galway. The town was captured in 1504 by the sixth Clanricard, Uilleag *Fionn* ('fair-haired') a Búrc. He might have held it longer but for abandoning his wife - a daughter of the Earl of Kildare - for the Queen of Uí Maine. Her adulterated husband, Maol Eachlainn Ó Ceallaigh, and the outraged Earl of Kildare, formed a huge military coalition that converged between Athenry and Galway, in the most massive military confrontation seen in Connacht (and possibly Ireland) since the Bruce Wars. It was possibly the largest battle ever fought between Irishmen – at least till the next Turlough Fair.

Uilleag Fionn would have held Galway hostages in his entourage; relatives of Mayor Edmond Deane, bailiffs Conchobair Ó Fallamhain and Uilliam Ó Cíordubháin among the most valuable. Búrc possibly had Galway partisans, perhaps takeing the town with some internal support. Some ten thousand men gathered and fought at Knockdoe (parish of Lackagh) on 19 August 1504. Thousands were killed, Kildare's coalition won, and the following morning the victors made the eight-mile journey to Galway which they seized without a struggle. "They remained for some time together in this town, cheerful and elated after the aforesaid victory." [66] No doubt the thirty *tuns* of fine wine granted by Edmond Deane aided their cheers!

## Font, alias Faunt

*Walter Font*, Provost of Galway 1443-44, was the progenitor of another obscure merchant family. The only background on them is given by Hardiman:

> This family settled in Galway at the beginning of the fifteenth century, they sprung from an ancient English family of Leicestershire. [67]

*Lenfaunt* or *le Enfaunt* suggest an origin with a person who appeared younger than their age, or who was the family 'infant'. The forms *de Fonte* or *de la Faunte* denote an ancestor who lived close to a spring or well. Nominally French, its also of Portuguese, Provençal, and Catalan origin. [68] Bearers of the surname are found in a few references pertaining to the narrow strip of land between the Wicklow mountains and the Irish Sea. Three *de Fonte's* are attested near Wicklow town c. 1227-c.1232. Thomas de Fonte was constable of Castlekevin in 1313-14, while Alexander de Fonte was one of two chief yeomen ('*valletti*') defending Newcastle McKinegan in 1316. [69]

The Fant family (originally *le Enfaunt*) were of Limerick town and county since at least the 1270s, and were recorded there into the 1640s. Like their Galway namesakes, they were predominately merchants. *Walter le Enfaunt* - 'member of the king's household', 'keeper of Kildare castle', 'justice itinerant' - is attested 1275x1308. His son, king's knight Sir *Walter Lenfaunt*, was rewarded with £10 in 1334 "for capturing Simon the White, the king's felon, and delivering him to the king". Both held land in Carlow, Kildare, and Limerick. [70]

Despite this, none of the above can be tied to the Fonts of Galway nor can the purported origin in Leicestershire be verified. A further tantalising link occurs with the prominent Bristol merchant, *William de la Fount* (fl. 1473-95), alive when Galway's trade with Bristol was especially strong. A Gascon, de la Fount settled in Bristol after his family were expelled from English Bordeaux by the French in 1453. He was one of four Bristol merchants who sponsored an expedition in 1481 to find Hy Brasil (they failed). He traded in Ireland, Iceland, Portugal, and Spain in the 1480s-90s, residing in Andalusia in the 1480s where he bought and sold African slaves (Christian Europeans by then traded not in each other but Pagan Africans and Muslim Europeans). He went on pilgrimage to Rome in 1492 and had returned to Bristol by April 1495, dying in May. He was survived by his second wife, two sons and four daughters. [71] The confluence of activities, geography, and surnames are very suggestive but do not prove a link. It is especially tantalising as descendants of the le Enfaunt/Fant family of Limerick are members of a haplogroup which predominates in Sardinia but is also found in Iberia and Gascoigne. [72]

A pedigree of a sept of the Galway Fonts was published by Hardiman, tracing them from Walter to his ninth-generation inclusive descendant, Bridget de Fonte of Boyle, Co. Roscommon (later Mrs. Peter Bath of Knightstown, Co. Meath, died 1778). Hardiman prefaces it with two men – *William de Ffont* (fl. 1409) and his son *Thomas* (fl. 1437) – stating the latter was Walter Font's father. However there seems to be at least one generation missing from the pedigree. Almost none listed can be connected to the handful of Fonts in contemporary sources. And there is nothing to prove William de Ffont or his son were of Galway or any connection to Provost Walter Font.

Walter was Provost of Galway in 1443-44. Interestingly, he married an Evelyn Kirwan, decades *before* the latter family moved to the town, showing that even then the Uí Chíordubháin had a status equal with Galway's main families. Walter and Evelyn had two known children, an unnamed daughter and a son, Thomas. A likely sibling of theirs or perhaps an uncle was *John Font*, portreeve of Galway in 1472. Ms. Font married Geoffrey Lynch and was mother of Anastasia (married Uilliam Ó Cíordubháin), Eveline (married Valentine Blake), Stephen, and James.

Thomas is probably the *Thomas Faute* recorded as one of four Galwegians who received royal Portuguese safe-conducts while visiting Lisbon in 1465. [73] His companions included John and Dominick Lynch; the former was probably his brother-in-law, the latter very likely John's son, Dominick *Dubh* Lynch. By the eighteenth-century, some Fonts had settled in both Lisbon and Cadiz, others as early as the late 1400s. Thomas married Eleanor French and was father of *Martin Faunt* (fl. 1498-1520), the first of three Font Mayors. Adam (fl. 1509-27), the second Font Mayor, was a contemporary of Martin but their exact relationship is unknown. The unusually named *Givane* was Mayor 1569-70. Perhaps they suffered hardships in the turbulent 1500s; a Geoffrey Font was murdered by highwaymen near Galway in 1573. Such long-forgotten losses may be why so little survives on the family.

## Uí Chíordubháin Conmhaicne – the Kirwans

Finnear son of Cumhscraidh was one of six brothers, ancestors to different Conmhaicne lineages. Finnear was ancestor of the Conmhaícne Mag Réin in what are now counties Leitrim and Longford. His great-grandson, Néidhe son of Onchú (ancestor of the Uí Fearghail of Anghaile in what is now Co. Longford) won the battle of Ardrahan in Aidhne, c. AD 800, defeating the Uí Fhiachrach. [74] This suggests a Conmhaicne sept resided in Maonmhagh - around what is now

Loughrea - the kingdom adjacent to Aidhne and its likely principal adversary at Ardrahan.

In southwest Maonmhagh is Kilconickny ('church of the Conmaicne'). They may have settled there as refugees or fighters for Maonmhagh's kings, as in this era the Conmhaicne of Dún Móir and Cúile Toladh were conquered by the Uí Bhriúin after the battle of Shrule in 766. Perhaps it was a way of retaining some independence. Perhaps the hound-sons wanted to go down fighting.

Centuries later, descendants of Néidhe's brother, Luachán, all bore surnames found in south County Galway - Ó Dubhan (Duane), Mac Giolla Shíonaigh (Fox), Ó Maonacháin (Monaghan), Ó Maoil Padraig (FitzPatrick), Meg Muireaghaigh (Murray), Ó Diumsaigh (Dempsey) Ó Finn (Finn), Ó hAininn (Hannon, in Galway in the 1390s), Ó Cíordubháin (Kirwan). [75] These surnames were probably adopted by the 1100s, but have no subsequent pedigrees. By then the Conmhaicne were politically unimportant, recorded by seanchaidh as historical curiosities. Néidhe, Ardrahan, and much about them was forgotten, even by their descendants. Luachán is dimly recalled near Kilconicky at *Túath Lubáin* ('Lubáin's country', now Tooloobaun), probably firstly their sept-name. Yet the *Manuscript History of the Kirwan Family* states they came from Derry in The North (now part of Ulster), being expelled in 1217 by John de Courcy, and fled south:

> ... the family remained at Dunbally from the above period to the year 1488, when William O Kirwan, the owner and proprietor of this castle, was obliged to fly to Galway in consequence of a quarrel that took place between him and Thomas Bermingham, 9th Lord of Athenry.
>
> Tradition states that shortly afterwards he was reinstated in the possession of the castle & lands in consequence of an intermarriage that took place between Thomas Oge Mac Jarvis, his Lordship's fourth son, and Unagh Ní Ciorovane [Úna Ní Cíordubháin], and that the family remained there until 1625, when the lands were seized (that is, were taken possession of legally) by Richard Bermingham, 14th Lord Athenry, and afterwards vested in his son, Moiler Boy Bermingham of Dunmore. The lands of Dunbally were afterwards confiscated after the victory of Cromwell. [76]

The Derry expulsion story is probably not historic, yet their 'Ulster' origin is a dim recall that Conmhaicne were an Ulaid folk. Dunbally is located within what was Conmhaícne Dúna Móir, east of Conmhaícne Cúile Toladh. Both Conmhaicne were conquered by the Uí Bhriúin Eóla by or soon after 800. [77] *Leabhar na nGenealach* records a member of *Clan Fheórais ó Dhun Mór* called *Tomás Óg* (or Dubh) son of *Tomás na Feasóige* ('bearded Thomas'), a great-grandson of the Richard de Bermingham who was victorious at Athenry in 1316. [78]

Dunbally was by then part of the territory of de Bermingham, *alias* Mac Fheórais ('Mac Jarvis'). The patron saint of Tuam, Iarlaithe son of Lugha (fl. 500?), was of the Conmhaícne. His mother, Moingfhinn daughter of Cíordhubhán, belonged to the Ceinéal Cineann/Cíorann, a sept of the Conmhaicne residing in *Cera* (alias Críoch/Ceinéal Meic Earca). According to Leabhar na nGenealach, "From Ciora is Ceinéal Ciroann in the territory of Ceinéal Meic Earca", Ciora being a brother of Finnear mac Cumhscraidh. [79]

The first documented Kirwan, *Dermot O'Kyrvayn*, is listed in the 1420 will of John Óge Blake as owing him "11 marks, 10 shillings and 3 pence." He is the only Ó Cíordubháin to bear a Gaelic forename, hinting at a family already somewhat anglicised. [80] *Walter Kervyk* was one of four King's Justices for Athenry and Galway in 1432. [81] Thomas O'Kyervyke was a burgess of Athenry (eight miles from Túath Lubáin) in 1439, becoming Provost in 1465. [82] By mid-century an Evelyn Kirwan was wife to Provost Walter Font, while a later Eveling Kyruan, wife of Edmund Bodkin, wrote her will in 1500. [83]

All this points to the Uí Chíordubháin already inhabiting the same merchant class as Galway's main families *before* they moved to Galway. Not great lords or landed gentry like the Ui Fhlaithbertaigh or Clanricards, nor the landless peasants and labourers who were the majority population in such lordships, but a small class in the large middle ground between upper and lower.     This class status, transcending ethnic divisions, explains their ability to marry into the town elite and gain its highest offices relatively swiftly. Walter Kervyk's post of King's Justice hints at enfranchisement in Lord Athenry's jurisdiction before 1432.     David and Uilliam Ó Cíordubháin were bailiffs in 1501-2 and 1503-4 respectively, so obviously Galway residents. [84] From Uilliam's marriage to Anastace Lynch was born Tomás *Caoch* Ó Cíordubháin, Mayor in 1534-35 and male progenitor of the senior line. [85] In contrast it took the Uí Dhorchaidhe six generations, probably because they were of a much lower caste even among the Gaelic-Irish.

Most likely, the Ui Chíordhubháin were 'grey merchants' in districts within the territory of Lord Athenry. Familiarity with Anglo-Irish culture no doubt aided their enforced move from Dunbally or Athenry to Galway. Acculturation worked both ways.

## From Crigferter to Galway? Mares/Morris

*John Mares*, town Provost in 1477, [86] was the first recorded of his family. Provosts were somewhat equivalent to nineteenth-century emigrant Irishmen who became policemen on the mean streets of London, or Sheriffs on the American wild west - a Morris descendant, film-maker John Ford, would direct several films set in the latter. Mares's wife was Christina Lynch, indicating an astute alliance with Galway's prime family. Three Morris's were bailiffs between 1486 and 1516. *William Maryse* became Mayor in 1527. Only one other, Andrew in 1587-88, would gain that office.

*Mares* may be the Norman de Mareis (in Latin, *de Marisco*). [87] Derivation from Ó *Muirgheasa* (now Morrissey, found around Athenry) seems unlikely. A family surnamed *O'Morris* are attested north of Athenry since the early 1600s, but their origins are unknown. *MacMuiris*/Morris around Boyle in north County Roscommon were probably Gaelic natives to Maigh Luirg though their origins are also uncertain. In County Mayo, people surnamed Morris are mainly de Prendergast descendants who adopted the surname *Mac Muiris* [88] - rendered Macmorris in Shakespeare's *Henry V*. It is from this family the many Morris's of south Connacht may descend.

The first of the family in Ireland was Sir Maurice de Prendergast (*fl.* 1169-75). His ancestors originated in Flanders, hired by Duc Gilluame of Normandy to aid his conquest of England in 1066. From 1108, these Flemings invaded and settled Dyfed (now Pembrokeshire) in south-west Wales, where Flemish was spoken as late as the 1570s. [89] Sir Maurice derived his surname from

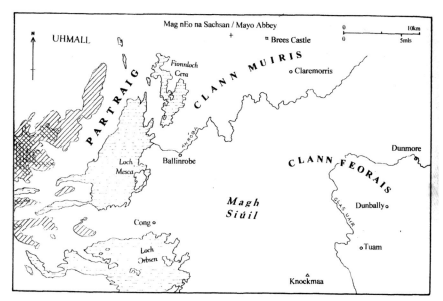

*Partraighe, Clann Muiris and Clann Feorais.*

the village of *Bronteergast* in Flanders. Historian F.X. Martin described him as

> a valiant soldier from Rhos [Haverfordwest area] in South Wales, [he] embarked at Milford with ten men-at-arms and a large body of archers in two ships and landed with the first Anglo-Normans at Bannow Bay on 1st May 1169. [90]

In a famous incident, Sir Maurice was the lone honourable voice against a plan by the Irish and Normans to murder King Domnaill Mac Giolla Patraic of Osraighe, in spite of a safe conduct. Alone, he faced them down in a scene made vivid in *La Geste des Engleis en Yrlande:*

> Morice par sa espé ad juré
> N'i ad vassal si osé
> Que sur le rei a icel jor
> La mein i met ad deshonur,
> Le quel, seit sen u folie,
> Ne seit parmi la teste asuie

> Maurice swore by his sword
> that any vassal who dared
> to lay a hand dishonourably
> on the king that day
> should have his head split open,
> whether it be wisdom or folly to do so. [91]

None of Maurice's companions felt the need to swear otherwise, and all lived to tell the tale. The first of the name in Connacht was Sir Maurice's grandson, Gerald fitz Phillip de Prendergast of Cork and Wexford (dead by 1251). He conquered the trícha cét of *Crích Fer Tíre* (Crigferter), renamed Clanmuiris. This became their core territory, now the parishes of Crossboyne, Kilcolman, Kilvine, [92] as well as land in the parishes of Mayo and Tagheen, all in County Mayo. [93]

Kiltullagh parish (now in County Roscommon) was held from 1268 to at least 1474, [94] while church land in the parish of Balla was incorporated into the lordship sometime prior to 1500. [95] Undoubtedly, many other nearby areas must have attracted their attention in those generations. The manorial headquarters of Crigferter appears to have been located at what is now Castlemacgarrett, and its market town was adjacent, at Burris townland. [96] The family endowed Mayo Abbey, and founded Ballinasmall Abbey near the town of *Clarclanmuiris* (Claremorris). [97]

Gerald married a sister of Walter de Burgh (later 1st Earl of Ulster), but had only female legitimate offspring. He appears to have been "the original lord of Crigferter, who duly placed two of his relatives under him ... sometime in the 1240s, and subsequently surrendered his interest to his overlord," either Richard Mór de Burgh (d. 1243), his eldest son Richard (d. 1248), or Richard's brother Earl Walter (d. 1270). [98] These relatives were Sir David de Prendergast (fl. 1215-60) and William or Gerald, grandfather of a Sir William de Prendergast. Sir David, a younger brother of Gerald, was married to Derbforgaill Ní Carthaigh of Desmond, and died in battle at Coill Berrain in Thomond. Via at least two sons, Sir David's lineage continued in Crigfertir. [99]

William/Gerald represented one of the many obscure junior and/or illigitimate lines of the extended family. His grandson was a Sir William de Prendergast who died early in the 1300s - either *the most famous and illustrious knight in his own time in Erinn* who died in 1306 [100] or the Sir William killed at Ballylahan during the 1315-16 Uí Chonchobair wars. [101] Definite lines of descent are complicated by sure indications that "The Prendergasts clearly ramified early in Crigferter, throwing off many lesser branches" [102] Matters intensified with the withering of Anglo-Irish Connacht in the fourteenth century. The last colonial record occurs in 1347, when

> the three chief men of the Prendergasts submitted to the administration and gave hostages as a pledge of good behaviour (who were then kept in the walled town of Galway and later released). [103] ... the last evidence we have of involvement of the Dublin administration in the affairs of Connacht dates from 1353. After this ... politics descended to the level of clan and lineage power-struggles. [104]

This latter point is emphasised in a notice in the *Regestum* of Athenry Friary. Beside its Great Altar were buried William and Maurice de Prendergast *captains of the nation of Clanmuiris*, [105] Here, 'nation' was understood in its original Latin sense of a *natio* - a family lineage or dynasty. Likewise, the French terms 'captain' and 'chief/chieftain' were applied first to Anglo-Irish lineaes, but eventually erased Gaelic ones even among the Gaelic-Irish themselves.

The first person explicitly recorded bearing the new surname appears to have being *Thomas Mac Maurice* [who] *died in Baile-Locha-Mesca* in 1271, while in 1300 Seonín Óg Mac Muiris "was slain, and many other persons along with him, by Conchobhar, son of Fiachra O'Floinn." [106] The new surname denoted descent from Sir Maurice, a practise reflected by other Anglos Hibernos who adopted surnames commemorating the first of their family in Ireland. [107] It also denoted their Gaelicisation. In 1335 the son of The Mac Muiris was killed during a raid, while in 1341

> *Maidm mor do thabairt do Mac Uilliam Burc ar Clainn Muris, du ar marbad Tomas Mac Muris & Muris mac Seonac Ruaid & secht xx. mar oen riu.*
> A great defeat was inflicted by Mac William Burk on the Clann-Maurice, on which occasion Thomas Mac Maurice, and Maurice, son of Seonac Ruadh, and seven score persons along with them, were slain. [108]

They would have been subject to the Mac Uilliam Íochtar, but resisted him. In 1366 this led to a "Cocad mor etir Gallabib Connacht .i. Mac Uilliam agus Mac Muiris." [109] Clann Muiris allied with Clann Ricard, thus remaining semi-independent from Mac William Íochtar and familiar with Athenry and Galway. Over time, the surname became common in the south Mayo region. [110]

Sometime in the mid-1300s, the original manorial *caput* at Castlemacgarrett and the market town of Burris were abandoned. Henceforth, Mac Muiris resided at Brees Castle in Mayo parish. The castle existed as early as 1367, the title *MacMuiris na mBrigh* designating their lord; an *Uilliam na mBrí* seems to be the Mac Muiris who led the move. [111] Uilliam na mBrí's genealogy reveals *seanchaidh* were unfamiliar with his early ancestors, Clann Muiris incorrectly traced back to the FitzGeralds. Yet it hinted at some vauge understanding that both families were once Flemish.

The Mares family background before 1478 remains obscure and is probably beyond recovery - de Mareis, Ó Muirgheasa, O'Morris, MacMorris, Mac Muiris, or something else? If indeed a Meic Muiris, John Mares evidently had no great prospects in Clanmuiris. Why else move to Galway? Like Shakespeare's Macmorris - the first stage Irishman - he built upon employment beyond his homeland. Via his swear-worthy sword.

## Last of the Fir Bolg: Ó Dorchaidhe/Darcy

Economic motives were the likely reason for the Uí Dhorchaidhe move to Galway town. Natives of Partraighe Cera, [112] tradition in the 1640s stated that Báitéar Riabhach Ó Dorchaidhe was

> *an cedfear d'Ibh Dorchaidhe tainig go Gaillimh, do rer luchta Gaillmhe fén*
> the first man of the Darcys who came to Galway, according to the Galwegians themselves [113]

This migration seems to have occurred sometime in the mid-1400s - The Ó Dorchaidhe was *taoisioch Partraighe* ('leader/lord of Partraighe') as late as 1417. [114] Yet it was not till the 1590s that the Uí Dhorchaidhe/Darcys, joined the town's elite. Why did it take so long?

Historians regard the Partraighe with curiosity. Fr. Paul Walsh held that the name betrayed their "non-Gaelic origin, as no pure Gaelic words commence with P." [115] Francis John Byrne believed them "a remnant of a pre-Celtic [sic] population", "ancestors of the Fir Umaill of Clew Bay" and their kings, the Uí Mháille (O'Malleys), [116] conclusions supported by Mayoman, Nollaig Ó Muraíle. [117] Celticist George Broderick has written that the first element of their name, part-

> has no satisfactory etymology either in Celtic/Indo-European or as a loan-word, and is therefore a borrowing from a non-IE [Indo-European] language. [Furthermore] the loaning language ... must still have been in existence in Ireland at least until c. 500 AD [meaning that] this language would have been spoken alongside [Gaeilge] [into the sixth century] [118]

Another deeply informed Celticist, Peter Schrijver, has remarked of them that

> like some other peoples carrying names in -raige, [they] appear to have been a politically insignificant people inhabiting a prototypical refuge area ... If one were to speculate about who [in Ireland] might be identified as speakers of a disappearing non-Indo-European language around AD 500, it is to such peoples that one would turn. [119]

Distant ancestors of the Partraighe may have created the Neolithic rock art half-hidden by blanket bog on Droim Chagaidh mountion, which sky-scrapes over the Gaelteacht of Tuar mhic Éadaigh. [120] The long-vanished mhic Éadaigh may have been a sept of the Partraighe, but their full identity, like the language of their pre-Gaelic 'Gaelteacht', is lost in time.

The area is dominated by Loughs Mask and Carra, Sliabh Phartraí, strong winds and emigration. Floods on the Corrie river often prevented traffic to and from Castlebar well into the 1900s. Good soil exists around Partry, even up in the derreens and glanna, but large parts are sliabh, caladh, agus móin. Stunning in all weathers, it is popular with anglers, remote and thinly populated. Little wonder some of the last wolves in Connacht found refuge there. [121]

Partraighe Cera was a *túath* within the kingdom of Cera, whose original dynasty had been displaced by a branch of the Uí Fhiachrach Muaidhe in the seventh century. They were replaced by grandsons of Toirdhealbhach Ua Conchobair, ousted themselves during the 1240s by the Lawless and de Staunton families, who were subsequently subject to Mac Uilliam Íochtar. [122] At the bottom of these successive layers of rulers and sub-rulers lay the Uí Dhorchaidhe.

Partraighe Cera was from *Áth na Mallachtain* (Cappaduff East townland, parish of Ballyovey) to *Glaise Ghuirt na Lainne* (Glasfort townland, parish of Ballintober) and from *Caol* (Keel Bridge, parish of Ballyovey) to *Fál* (Killfal, parish of Ballyovey).

*and Ó Goirmiallaigh is their king and Ó Dorchaidhe their chieftain, or the chieftaincy of Ó Dor-*

*chaidhe alone* [123]

This confusion over the rank of the leader of the Uí Dhorchaidhe is reflected in one of the few medieval references to the family while still residing in Partraighe.

*Maith do chosaid fonn na ffear*
*O Dorchaidhe as ard aigneadh*
*críoch Phartraighe na ccal ccuir*
*le crunn altbhuidhe in imoghuin*

*Well did O Dorchaidhe the high-minded*
*defend the land of the men*
*the territory of Partraighe of the smooth hazels*
*with a yellow-socketed spear-shaft in battle* [124]

The Ó Dorchaidhe is tactfully described as a mighty warrior, but given no rank or territory. If even he was without land ownership, what prospects were there for the average Ó Dorchaidhe? Their only remaining local reference is *Knockadorraghy* ('Uí Dhorchaidhe's hill'), north-west of Mayo Abbey. [125] While within the eastern border of Cera, it's a distance away from the known territory of Partraighe. That the only area associated with them was outside their known home area hints at legal subordination, possibly as *manaig* (monastic tenants). Though individual *manach* had some limited legal rights, they were *lucht freasdail* (serfs), unable to be legally independent. All indicative of the Uí Dhorchaidhe been classed as *dóer* (unfree), caste among the 'Fir Bolg'.

Báitéar Riabhach was the first Ó Dorchaidhe to settle in Galway, but did he already have connections within the town? The Uí Thighearnaigh were one of three families who held kingship over Cera, possibly the same as the Galway Tierneys. [126] Likewise, Lawless is attested both in Cera from 1241, and in fifteenth-century Galway. [127] Intriguingly, Knockadorraghy five kilometeres from Brees Castle, the Meic Muiris caput. Is it entirely coincidence that Mares and Ó Dorchaidhe appear in Galway within the same era? Every Provost needs soldiers, even one with nothing more than *le crunn altbhuidhe in imoghuin/a yellow-socketed spear-shaft*. At some point an Ó Dorchaidhe married a Develin (another north Connacht surname), a family who had at least one Sovereign of Galway, James Develin, in 1461-62. [128] The Develins died out in the male line

*and the Darcys of Galway are their generall heirs. The Develin's arms, still extant, [in 1684] carved in stone in James Reagh Darcy's house in Abby-gate street, is the same with the Dillon's arms.* [129]

Gaining property via marriage enabled wealth and social rise, like the Lynchs before them. Furthermore, "the rents generated from properties [were] a regular source of income, unlike the risky business of trading." [130] It was probably the most vital aspect for all the prime families. Access to greater trade offered further prospects unobtainable back in Partraighe. Yet whereas the first Uí Chíordubháin in Galway married into the town's elite and gained Corporation offices within years, it took the Uí Dhorchaidhe six generations. This is likely because the Uí Chíordubháin were already a family of similar class and caste to Galway's main families, whereas the Uí Dhorchaidhe were not. Their rise was even less 'inevitable'. Not till the lifetime of Báitéar Riabhach's great-great-great grandson, James Reagh Dorsey (fl. 1582-1603), did the family move into Galway's upper ranks, enabled by marriages, property acquisition, government sponsorship, and changing from Catholic to Protestant. Change, and not a moment too soon.

## Why some Irish became English

Why did some medieval Irish choose to become English? Their reasons were the same as post-independence and home rule generations who emigrated - and continue to emigrate - to Britain. Their birth society had nothing to offer them.

The "status of the great mass of the population in Gaelic Ireland, the actual cultivators and labourers ... was very low indeed." [131] It was not inflexible but like the system that succeded it, Gaelic Ireland was a heirarchy run by and for its elite. Surface differences aside, it was like other European societies - patriarchal, elitist, sexualized. Its biases were aristocratic, its prejudices towards the commons. Thus vast swathes of Gaeilgeoiri were technically not Gaeil, because it was fundamentally an upper-class caste and this sense of the term existed well into the 1700s.

The lowest castes, of whatever ethnicity, were demeaned as an Other 'race', as 'Fir Bolg' - or worse again as Lucht Siúl, the contrast of *Lucht Túaithe*, 'country folk' [the settled communites]. The situation was similar to that of landlords and tenents in 19th-century Ireland, where surnames like Burke and Daly were borne by titled major landlords and their peasant tenents. All were ethnic Irish, but partitioned by caste and class. If similar tensions existed in medieval times, they were suppressed by methods familiar to Earls Clanricard and Barons Dunsandle.

The Gaelic elite's negative values - violence as politics, the contempt of the enabled for the disabled - were reflected downwards, dressed as 'virtues', and linger in Irish culture. Fixity of rent and tenure did not exist. Physical force and invented tradition legitimised tighearnais. Consent was not required, only obedience. Gaelic Ireland's upper castes kept peasants firmly in their place:

> [Gaelic lordship] was dependent upon a 'strong man' who could impose his will ... through political and military persuasion. ... the levying of various revenues and exactions [were] his only by extortion and intimidation. ... the lords exercised a more or less imperial jurisdiction over all those born within their territories ... the harsh grasping nature of their rule produced a two-tiered society consisting of the more prosperous landowners and privileged professional groups on the one hand, and the great mass of the local inhabitants, 'the depressed classes', on the other ... institutions such as the brehon law and public assemblies, and officials such as the hereditary marshals and rent collectors, existed to give order and structure to local life and enforce the rule of the lord. [132]

The family of historian, Dubhaltach Mac Fhirbhisigh (d. 1671), served Gaelic lords for some five hundred years. On the exercise of power, in a statement now dignified as Mac Fhirbhisigh's Law, he observed that *the great princes, when their families and their kindreds multiply, tend to oppress, wither and despoil their clients and followers.* [133] A similarly unsentimental description of Gaelic lordship describes a system that "[had] no underclass of prosperous tenant farmers ... to demand beneficial leases ... Instead there was a mass peasantry subsisting as tenants-at-will ... With no leases to honour ... where all land was owned by the ruling lineage and its adherents, and farmed on its behalf, there was no concept of tenant's rights; ... all the peasants were serfs." [134]

Not only was there no equality in Gaelic law, there was no notion of it - the popular idea of benificial 'Irish ways and Irish laws' never existed. It was difficult or impossible for Gaelic lower castes to better themselves because of fénechas, which distinguished between *nobiles agus ignobiles*. Indeed the hard agricultural work they did was previously preformed by slaves. People "who had no legal status and little or few material possessions [were] bound to their lord [preforming] hard manual labour." [135] Lacking eduction or access to a skilled profession doomed generations to being unskilled labourers and maid-servants, infantry fodder and prostitutes.

If dóer were wounded or killed, compensation was paid to their lord as they were viewed as his property. The servile and unfree in Gaelic society became so via debt, servitude, or conquest in war, but the condition became hereditary with almost no legal way out. [136] In a system with a built-in generational disablement against lower castes, one option was opting out of the system entirely.

Writing of his male-line ancestors the Meic hArtáin Gion Ais of Uladh, Patrick Guinness, a descendant of Ireland's notable brewing dynasty, bluntly described their choices:

> [While] many preferred to remain in a tight, interrelated community in which they were well-known than to be poor in a place where nobody knew them ... they could never gain much wealth in the long term. The underlying reason for this helotry is clear, yet it is seldom mentioned; it was the cycle of being born into a poor family in a poor place, something that was true all over Europe. Some, however, found ways to break that cycle. [137]

One way out for marginalised Gaelic families was to migrate to *Galltacht* enclaves and towns such as Athenry and Galway. The Gaelicisation deplored by the fourteenth-century English of Ireland could be a two-way street, leading to Anglicisation, and fortune for some:

> For the *Gaedheal*, this society offered opportunities for social mobility that his own did not. Bound by his patrilineal ancestry ... a 'low-born' person in the *Gaedhealtacht* could rarely penetrate the professional orders or the ruling or ecclesiastical clans if he were not born into them. To put it another way, a commoner could rarely aspire to be anything more than a labourer, a tiller of the soil or a tender of cattle. [138]

This was incentive for lower-class Gaelic-Irish, especially so for women. As second-class people even among elite Gaelic society, they may have played a forgotten role in driving such migrations if they believed Anglo-Irish society held better prospects for their children, male and female. [139] Nor was Galway exceptional - exactly the same process occoured in Limerick, Drogheda, Cork, Dublin, Wexford. Among the medieval Irish emigrating to Britain, and elsewhere in Europe.

Life for most people has been one of exhaustive toil, especially in marginal areas best left to wild creatures, till they too were pushed out. They were inhabited when people had nowhere else to go, and abandoned as soon as they did. Life in a thatched mud and wattle *bothán*, amid farm animals, their piss and shit, are abandoned by every people at the earliest opportunity.

The poorest in Gaelic Ireland were badly-dressed, near-naked. [140] Half died before their mid-thirties, at which age women were toothless and physically ravaged from multiple pregnancies - if they survived. [141] Childhood was a brutalised nightmare from which few escaped. Disease, violence, famine, were frequent interludes from regular hardship and everyday squalor, as well as keeping actual wolves and human animals from the door; the romanticised 'Fianna' derive from the dreaded, heathen *díbergaig*, whose main activities were unromantic raids of rape and murder. [142]

Life is harsh and full of effort. Support-systems (families, marriage, religeon, paid employment) are essential for survival in a world that is unfair and cruel. Odds are always stacked in favour of the 'great' and lesser folk know it. They leave little trace in death because they have less in life, are more susceptible to the tragedy of time. Their choices are few, often harsh. While excessive wealth may indeed demean, poverty entirely diminishes.

Not that Anglo Ireland was a worker's paradise! It too was a society acutly aware of status and likewise built on it. Galway's merchant oligarchs zealously defended their rights and privilages. Like people in all times they were a middling mix of good and bad, with secular saints and petty monsters. They had an underclass of tenents and servants, artisans and labourers, beggers and outcasts. Without doubt their treatment left much to be desired, while the medieval slums of Galway were probably more filthy and brutal than can be imagned.

As for class/caste solidarity? The newly risen can be as oppressive as the highborn and quicker to forget their origins. The *mé féin* principle is medieval and modern because it is so selfishly human. Neither commerical nor political institutions welcome competition or dissent. Threats to the status quo must be co-opted, watered-down, or destroyed. Power kills kindness because it must.

Yet clearly Galway offered some prospects for the lesser families of Gaelic Ireland. Perhaps an enviornment where even the elite actually worked (as opposed to hunting, fighting, consuming, and breeding) created a small society of just slightly better worth or opportunity than the authoritarian lordships all around it. Perhaps. Likely it was the least-worst of few options.

In traditional Irish histories, ethnicity and religion are portrayed as the prime motivators, but that denies the role of class and caste. Though sneered as 'bourgeois' or 'trade', the much-maligned middle-classes generally mediated and created better societies than 'revolutionary' intellectuals or 'absolutist' states. Frightening as it is to leave your home community, adaptation to gain upward mobility is potentially worth a change of location or language, allegiance or identity.

People of economicly disabled backgrounds make incredibles sacrifices for prosperity and their posterity. And just like today, it is rarely achieved in a single lifetime. Two to three generations are often the norm; the break-out generation or individual is noticed, the invisible backers forgotten.

There is never any guarantee of success, but it is a choice people in every generation have chosen to take - within and without Ireland. They understood that change for the better only comes by actively working for it. Even so, *continued* good fortune depends not on 'fate' or 'destiny' but luck, chance, and above all sustained enablement. These women and men did not deny their origins, but neither did they allow themselves to be limited by them. Even fénechas affirmed that

*Is ferr fer a chiniud/A man is better than his birth.* [143]

Remunerative employment, apprenticeships, education *and* critical thinking, fiscal caution, robust political accountability, all fed social innovations that slowly transformed medieval Europe. They may yet do so for modern Ireland.

# CHAPTER FIVE – A TOWN AT THE EDGE OF THE WORLD

## Adversity and Ambitions

In 1998, Kenny's Bookstore on Galway's High Street was extensively renovated. Found within the basement and ground floor walls were thick oak-wood timbers, black with age. No doubt they hailed from the fiodh of Tír Dá Locha. Much of Iar Connacht had extensive woodland and woodland fauna until exploitation by colonist and colonised alike destroyed both in the 1700s. Tests determined the oaks were cut about 1472. [1] *The Annals of Connacht* say little of purely Anglo-Irish affairs. But they do note that in 1473

> Bale na Gallme do loscad do tenid dait isin dara la do mis Iuin, Aine aroi laithe sechtmaine, agus ni soarme are milled ann do maithes amserdo.
> Galway town was set on fire by lightning on the second of June, Friday by the day of the week, and it would be hard to estimate the temporal wealth destroyed. [2]

What this demonstrates is 1) the troubles of the previous century had settled, and 2) with peace had come economic growth and social change. The town's merchants knew how to create wealth. Now they showed they knew how to use it, turning disaster to advantage by creating

> what was virtually a new town. This was the nucleus of that Galway which came to be so well known, a small but compact and extremely well laid out city with many handsome buildings in the beautiful local limestone, those "marble" edifices which were to call forth such admiration from English and Continental visitors in the sixteenth and seventeenth centuries. [3]

The fifteenth-century merchants rebuilt Galway to become as stony as the river, whereas most of urban Europe had wooden buildings well into the 1700s. Notable Galway structures such as Tigh Neachtain, Lynch's Castle, and Blake's Castle, are among the few surviving structures built in those decades and after. The rest were demolished well into the 1900s.

Evidence of the wealth of the town's uppermost class occurs in 1442, when Edmond Lynch fitz Thomas constructed the first *stone* bridge over the Gaillimh to Iar Connacht [4] - presumably the one built before 1424 was made of timber. [5] He was nicknamed *Eamonn a Tuane* ('of the tuns') because of the huge quantities of wine he imported. Edmond's bridge was demolished in 1850. His mansion, that of the Crann Mór Lynchs, was demolished in 1749 for the Shambles Barracks (demolished in turn for what is now St. Patrick's National School). [6] Evidently Edmond thought his profits could be put to practical use and add further lustre to the family. A great-great-grandson of William de Linche, Edmond was Sovereign in 1434 and 1444. [7] His sons *Geffere*, Thomas, and John, became Mayors, as did at least three grandsons. [8] Ambition

*1484 Wardenship Grand of Galway, courtesy of Galway Diocese*

begets ambition, and two long in gestation came into bloom in the years afterwards. One was ecclesiastical, the other political. Both had a single goal: independence.

## The Wardens of Galway

Galway was originally within the diocese of Annaghdown but upon the latter's incorporation to the diocese of Tuam, became subject to its Archbishop. That office remained a Gaelic prerogative, meaning that Gaelic priests administered the rites of the church within Anglo Galway. This was portrayed as a source of antagonism to the parishioners, who described themselves as

> *modest and civil people and that they lived in the said town surrounded with walls, not following the customs of the mountainous and wild people of these parts, and by that reason ... they were so much disturbed that they could not assist at divine service, nor receive the holy sacraments according to the English decency, rite and custom, which the aforesaid inhabitants and their ancestors always used; they being much disquieted therein, and sometimes robbed of their goods, and killed by those unlearned men, and also that they were obliged to sustain many other damages and inconveniences, both in person and substance, from them, and feared to suffer more for the future, if not speedily succoured.* [9]

These actions can be gauged by perpetual vicar of St. Nicholas's, John Riys, who in 1455

> *laid violent hands on and wounded a priest, to the effusion of blood and injury of a limb, thereby incurring sentence of the greater excommunication, and, being under the said sentence, has celebrated masses and other divine offices and taken part therein, ... has committed simony and incurred perjury.* [10]

His successor, Aodh Ó Tighernaigh, was found to be illegitimate, while Fr. Ricard Ó Berra (Berry) illegally detained the office for at least two years. [11] Meanwhile, at Athenry in 1464:

> *Thomas Joy, perpetual vicar of the parish church of Athenry ... made a simoniacal agreement with*

*The faces of Dominick Dubh and one of his wives, Lynch's Castle, Galway*

> *Thomas Bemocham, layman, the true and sole patron.*

Worse, Joy was found to hold the office of archdeacon of Tuam by pretext with the same man, [12] Lord Athenry, Tomás de Bermingham. Such examples were the basis of the Galwegians complaint. Exaggerated perhaps, but nonetheless used for gaining ecclesiastical independence. So in 1484, Archbishop of Tuam Donatus Ó Muireadhaigh, was petitioned by the townspeople

> *to release the town from his own jurisdiction, and create the church of St. Nicholas a Collegiate to be governed by a warden and vicars who were to be presented and solely elected by the inhabitants of the town.* [13]

The inducements made to Archbishop Ó Muireadhaigh (parish priest of St. Nicholas's in the 1440s) must have been persuasive or perhaps he was indeed a man of God, because he supported the creation of the Wardenship of Galway in September 1484. On 8 February 1485 the Pope confirmed a collegiate at St. Nicholas's ruled by a Warden, who was a bishop in all but name. [14] How much or little the issue had to do with ethnic animosity may be judged by the fact that one of the first Wardens of Galway was Reverend Tomás Ó Mocháin (Maughan). [15] In this way, the Church remained a common point of contact across classes and nations in Ireland.

## Dominick Dubh Lynch and the Charter of Mayoralty

Concurrently, the townspeople were pursuing a Charter of Mayoralty to enable de jure (if perhaps not de facto) independence from Clanricard overlordship. The prime mover in the political manoeuvring was Dominick Dubh Lynch fitz John, a grandson of Edmond a Tuane. He is likely the Dominick Lynch of Galway recorded at Lisbon in 1465 with John Lynch (probably his father) and Thomas Font (brother-in-law of John Lynch). He occurs in a petition to the Vatican curia dated 27 January 1481. In it, Dominick Dubh confessed to an irregular sexual relationship with his second cousin, Juliana/Ciliana Dene, admitting that they

> dwell[ed] in the same house ... they have often committed fornication and have had offspring.

He asked that the pope absolve them from being related within prohibited degrees of kinship

> and to dispense them to marry, notwithstanding the said impediments, decreeing past and future offspring legitimate. [16]

Dominick bore the Gaelic nickname *dubh*, denoting that he had very black hair or complexion. His forename was evidently in honour of St Dominick, the Anglo-French patronymic *fitz John* indicated his father's name. His full name is therefore a wonderful mix of cultures and languages. Such combinations were needed to successfully navigate the will-power of one of England's most infamous kings, Richard III. Dominick Dubh must have had flair, because before the unscrupulous king's (valiant) death in battle at Bosworth on 22 August 1485, the charter was approved.

Galway's chief officer or governor under the de Burghs was a *Provost*, selected from among the settlement's burgesses. Originally a military figure, the Provost became an administrator. Both it and the terms *Portreve* (reeve of a port), *Bailiff* and *Seneschal* (steward or chief officer of a lord), underlies the town's subordination to one or other de Burgh. By the 1396 Charter of Richard II, the *burgesses* (town freemen) could elect annually a *Sovereign*. The change of title is significant. Usually understood as the chief citizen of a town, it signifies the *supreme or ruling* person, technically without an overlord. The office of Provost remained as lieutenant to the Sovereign. The Charter of 1484 upgraded matters even further. The practical application of the Mayoralty was

> a landmark in the history of Galway, for politically it completed the edifice of the City State, since henceforth not merely were the Burkes and the native Irish excluded, but the representatives of the King even could not enter the town, except with the consent of the municipal authorities, who were, too, the only agency by which either the decrees of the Government or the laws of Parliament could be enforced. [17]

In matters of trade, law, and order, Galway was now a city-state. Dominick Dubh saw to it that the last Sovereign and Provost - his first cousin once removed, William Lynch, and his own father, John fitz Edmund *a Tuane* - were replaced as first Mayor by his brother, Pierce, with Andrew Lynch fitz Stephen and James Lynch fitz Martin becoming the first bailiffs. [18] In 1486-87 he himself served as Mayor. The office of Mayor of Galway would be held by some eighty-two men surnamed Lynch over the next one hundred and sixty-nine years. [19]

## Strutting, Swaggering, and the Town Statutes

Some of the more interesting statutes passed in the years after the grant are as follows:

1496, Walter Lynch fitz Robert, Mayor: *That all dwellers within this town, as well freemen as unfree, shall from time to time have such reasonable weapon according to their vocation and calling, on pain to forfeit xii.d. Ster.* [20]

1505, Stephen Lynch fitz Dominick Dubh, Mayor: *That no householder of this town be no hostler nor no maintainer of the common whores or harlots, on pain of six shillings eight pence.* [21]

1508, Stephen Lynch fitz Dominick Dubh, Mayor: *Whatsoever man, woman, or child, be found fouling the streets or walls either by night or day to lose two pence.* [22]

1510, James Lynch fitz Stephen, Mayor: *Whatsoever boatmen or master that receives meat, drink and wages for bringing wood or turf, and would convey or bring to his own use any of the said wood or turf, to forfeit four pence.* [23]

1516, Stephen Lynch fitz James, Mayor: *That no leper nor infected pauper or poor shall come or enter within the town to ask their alms, but their clerk or head master for the time being with their bell, on pain their clerk or governor to forfeit twelve pence.* [24]

1517, Stephen Lynch fitz Dominick Dubh, Mayor: *That none of this town shall give nor sell covertly nor openly to no Irish, nor none suspected persons in the way of rebellion, any invention, [such] as hand-guns ... power, lead ... long-bows, crossbows, crossbow strings ... nor no kind of weapon ... on pain to forfeit the same munition and also a hundred shillings. Likewise if any hurt or loss comes to the town through the selling of the same, he that so sells it his body to remain in prison until such time he makes amends of such hurts.* [25]

1518, John Bodkin, Mayor: *That no man of this town shall host nor receive into their house at Christmas, Easter, nor no feast else, any of the Burkes, MacWilliams, the Kellies, nor no sept else, without license of the Mayor and Council for the time being, on pain to forfeit five livres.* [26]

1519, Wylliam Martin, Mayor: *It is ordered that if any man, free or unfree, be found by night time in any man's house to have copulation with or to do with the good man's servant, maid or daughter by way of adultery to lose twenty shillings: And also to the good man in who's house the same person is found with the said fact or crime, to lose so to that good man, twenty shillings: ... If any man of whatever degrees, shall have by copulation or deed with any freeman or merchant's daughter, conceiving or begetting her with child, shall furtherwith marry her, or else to give her such goods as shall be lawful towards her preferment until another may.* [27]

1520, Martin Faunt, Mayor: *It is ordered that no priest, monk, nor canon, nor friar, shall have no whore nor lemon in any man's house within this town, and that man which keeps or hosts the said whore or lemon to forfeit to the officers so being twenty shillings.* [28]

1521, Anthony Lynch, Mayor: *It is ordered, for fear and dread of the pestilence and common diseases, that no man shall go aboard any ship or barque without license of the Mayor and officers for the time being, until further experience be known, to bring any wares or envoys, on pain to forfeit three shillings.* [29]

1530, John Óge Kirwan, Mayor: *It is ordered that whatsoever priest or vicar of the College of the town be found with any fault or crime, or openly known by him, to lose to the officers one hundred shillings, and also to lose their benefice. And also if he or they keep any whore, being with child or bearing children, to pay the above penalty.* [30]

1533, Richard Blake, Mayor: *It is ordered and statuted that whatsoever person or person of this town, of whatsoever degree he or they be of, do begin any strife, debate, or quarrel with any other within this town, to forfeit and pay a hundred shillings; and if he or they should draw out sword, dagger, or knife, the same weapon to be nailed and put up in the pillory; and also to make amends for all such hurts, damages, and losses as he should commit or do with the said weapons.* [31]

The statutes reflect practical concerns with health and safety, for the sake of themselves and their families and to ensure good conditions for business, on which their livelihoods depended. Mayor Bodkin's statute was infamously rewritten as *Neither O nor Mac shall strut nor swagger through the streets of Galway* and so viewed as anti-Gaeil racism (despite including na Búrcaigh, who were Gaill). No doubt some of that is true - there was too much history between the two communities - but the statute was foremost a measure to prevent feuding factions running riot after too much alcohol. Even so, they were allowed in by *license of the Mayor and Council.* Behaviour, not ethnicity, was the issue. Uncontested is that some saw the two as identical.

Mayor Blake's statute was aimed to prevent exactly the same type of incident, but this time expressly aimed at unruly elements (no doubt also young and male) among the townsfolk themselves. Statutes of the Lynch Mayors mirror their preoccupation with defence in the event of attack – a very real fear given Galway's capture and occupation by Clanricards in 1399 and 1504 – as well as controlling access to weapons upon which victory or defeat could swing.

The 1521 statutes were important in an era without a modern concept of hygiene. The town's shambles - where cattle were slaughtered and their hides tanned – was a prime source of everything from ringworm to cattle-pox. And in a port, sailors regularly imported the latest plagues simply by arriving or new venereal diseases via the same-old sexual fads. Epidemics that later devastated the town did in fact originate from highly infectious sailors. That may explain why Mayors passed statutes concerning prostitution. While never an activity that could be allowed on the main streets, they may have being attempts to regulate areas where prostitutes could operate (not to mention 'ordinary' illicit sexual encounters). Within the walls was prohibited. Outside them was probably a different story.

Some events concerning town officials are as intriguing as the statutes. Mayor Arthur Lynch, along with bailiffs *William Josse* and Anthony Lynch, all drowned after falling off the West Bridge or its drawbridge in unknown circumstances on 25 November 1507. [32] Despite the impact the sudden death of the town's top three officers must have had, nothing more is known of this incident.

## The Will of Dominick Dubh Lynch

Written legal accounts of property transactions, articles of trade and charters of incorporation were the tools of the Irish middle class. It is on these that we rely for an overview of life in fifteenth- and sixteenth-century Galway. The best place to start is the will of Dominick Dubh. Dated 12 July 1508, Dominick's will directs that he be buried in St. Nicholas's church with his parents and deceased first wife, *Anastasia Martyn*, naming his executors as his eldest son, Stephen, his cousins Edmund and Walter Lynch, and the *Reverend Thomas Molgan*. The will continues thus:

*I have in a cypress chest in my Writing Room £330 in gold and silver, whereof £94 in silver belongs to my son and heir Stephen Lynch as his share of the provender which Master Waslorianus of the Town of Vella [a town in east-central Switzerland] sent me by the hand of the Prior of Ceratum in Lysperna [the canton or city of Luzern?]*

*I have in my Writing Room and in the room over it 73 hundred-yard rolls of linen and about 15 mantles of russet colour. I have in my office or in the shop under my house, or in my new office, about 5006 ib of wax and 8 ib of sericum of Collona, and 15 ib in serc and 4 ib in Alnie. I have in my cellar at the strand 6 or 8 barrels of salt, and 10 dakers, 5 chores of hides, large and small; the residue of my hides I sent to Clement Servicius of Pisa in the ship of Oliver Luys, the Portuguese, that is, 18 lasts of hides of my own and one last of my sister Margaret Lynch.*

*All the lands and tenements which I bought and acquired and all the pledges I have, will be seen in the Book of Inquisitions of A.D. 1460 in my Writing Room. I call God to witness that my son John Lynch owes me more than 4000 ducats of gold. I order my son Stephan Lynch to finish and complete the new works begun by me in the Collegiate Church, and also to erect an altar to St. James the Apostle, adjoining the nearest column in the Chapel of Blessed Mary in the said Church.*

*I direct my Requiem with daily prayers for the souls of my parents myself and my wife to be said by two priests, one of whom will celebrate in the Chapel of Blessed Mary, and the other at the altar of St. James. I bequeath to the said priests the tenement I acquired from John Slon O'Meolkyllid within the town of Galway, also the house I have acquired from Edmond Blake opposite my tenement, also the house I acquired from Sabina ny-Crywan [Ni Ciordubháin] situate near the house of my brother Peter Lynch, also the lands and tenements I bought in Athenry.*

*I bequeath to my son and heir Stephen Lynch my chief house where I now dwell. I impose on him my Anniversary and those of both my wives to be celebrated perpetually in the said Church. I also bequeath to said Stephen the tenement I acquired from the Reverend Walter Blake and the stone house near it, which I acquired from David Bodkin. I bequeath to each of the seven sons of said Stephen £120.*

*I leave my wife Juliane ... [Dene] to the maintenance and care of the aforesaid Stephen. I bequeath to my son Gabriel Lynch the stone tenement which I acquired from William Lynch fitz Sander, and the stone house where William O'Siredane [Sheridan] lives, and another stone house in front of the other where Fulke now dwells, also the lands of Balleban [Ballyban] and Cecaurewache, mortgaged to me by the said William.*

*I bequeath to my son Peter Lynch the tenement which I acquired from Geoffrey and Peter Blake, and I commit the said Peter Lynch with all his goods, moveable and immoveable, to the protection and guardianship of the aforesaid Stephen. I bequeath all my lands tenements mills and other buildings both within and without the aforesaid town and also the eel weirs and places for netting salmon in the river of the said town, to be equally divided between the said Stephen and Peter when the said Peter comes to full age.*

*If my son John Lynch will come to our town of Galway and settle accounts with the said Stephen and my other sons according to the arbitration of the said Stephen and other executors, he will have his share of my inheritance.*

*I bequeath to my daughter Anastasia 80 hundred-yard rolls of linen or their value. I bequeath to my daughter Agnes 80 hundred-yard rolls of linen or their value.*

*I leave £6 to the Friars Preachers of Athenry. I bequeath 13 shillings 4 pence to every Convent in Ireland. I bequeath £4 to the Convent of the Monastery at Galway. I leave 3 shillings 4 pence to every Convent of the four Mendicant Orders and of the three Orders of Observantines. I leave for the works of the Chapel of Blessed Mary on the hill in the west part of the town £5.*

*I leave £1.13.4. for the poor in the poormens' house in our town. £1 to the house of Lepers in Galway and Athenry: £5 for the repair of the Holy Cross of our Church. I leave £1 to my sister Margaret Lynch and £1 to Margaret daughter of Stephen Lynch. I leave 10 shillings to the wife of John y Kerrawyn [Ó Cíordubháin]*

*I ratify and confirm the gift I made in writing under the hand of William Molgan [Uilliam Ó Mocháin] public notary to said Stephen Lynch my heir, of a certain quantity of lead, sent to Bristol by Gabriel de Radolphus, Merchant of Florence.*

*Will dated at Galway the 12th July 1508. Witnesses: Maurice O'Commain [Muiris Ó Cuimín], expert in medicine, who at the request of the testator wrote the Will; the Reverend Thomas Molgan, Warden of the Collegiate Church in Galway; the Reverend Walter Cussin, canon of the Cathedral Churchs of Tuam and Enaghdune [Annaghdown]; Cornelius McMeoltall .... Andrew Mares [Morris]; Cornelius O'Conan; and many others.* [33]

Dominick Dubh's will is an impressive testament to a medieval life on the Irish west coast. His reference to *my Writing Room* indicates that, if not literate himself, Lynch certainly employed someone who could read, write, and keep accounts. The references to *Master Waslorianus*, the *Prior of Ceratum* and *Clement Servicius* in far-off *Vella, Lysperna* and *Pisa*, demonstrates astonishingly international financial outreach. The provisions show thought was put into the welfare not only of his main heir but younger sons, daughters, grandchildren, siblings, and widow. For all the desire to keep Gaelic clergy and laity out of the town, four out of six of Dominick Dubh's named witnesses bore Gaelic names. *Maurice O'Commain, expert in medicine*, is explicitly stated to have written the will *at the request of the testator.* Obviously there were Gaeil and there were Gaeil.

His provisions for Anastasia and Agnes may indicate a women's role in local textile production. The value of linen could provide a marriage dowry, or the economic basis for an independent life (or indeed allowing some women the ability to choose their own husbands). Their aunt, Margaret Lynch, may have traded in her own right; possibly women had a role in making goods such as the bráta ('15 mantles of russet colour').

In career, wealth, and life-experience, Dominick Dubh was exceptional; it would be a mistake to see his life as a Galway norm. Most townsfolk, even if they bore a prime surname, remained at a more humble economic and political level. All it shows is that given the right economic circumstances, personal talents, and luck, certain people can achieve a great deal. His son Stephen was asked to *complete the new works begun by me in the Collegiate Church ... [and] erect an altar to St. James the Apostle ... in the Chapel of Blessed Mary in the said Church.* Our secular era sees such overt piety as masks for venal demonstrations of wealth. Yet that does not mean their piety was insincere, and like the uninscribed stones that mark many an anonymous grave, it is also a plea to be remembered.

## Fishermen and Fishwives: An Claddagh

Dominick Dubh donated money to the Chapel of Blessed Mary on the Hill. Located across the Gaillimh from an seanceathrú, the village around it has been known since at least 1589 as the Claddagh (*an Cladach*, 'the strand', where fishermen beached their boats). [34] A suburb and a separate village, its inhabitants held to Gaelic custom and language into the early 1900s. Ruled and represented by a nominated king whose ship bore a black sail, among the last kings of the Claddagh were members of the King family. [35] This was an Anglicised version of Mac Con

*Fishwives at the fishmarket, c. 1901, courtesy of Galway City Museum*

Raoi, surname of the long-forgotten kings of Gnó Mór.

Nineteenth-century Claddagh woman wore garments of crimson and maroon; the latter became the county colour. Claddagh men fished Loch Lurgan on boats such as the *gleoteog*, *púcán*, and *húicér*, 'the Galway hooker - though now associated with Connemara, its name denotes its origin in the Claddagh of Galway. Women brought the catch for sale across the bridge into Galway. Yet this was probably an activity that was even then generations old. The economic importance of Galway's fisherfolk is made plain from a statute of 1585:

> *That no seamen or seaman or as I would say fishermen or fisherman do take in hand either the plough, spade, or teithe, that would bar them from fishing, both to serve themselves and the commonwealth with fish, in consideration whereof that the said fishers and their wives and family be reasonably served before others with all necessary sustenance and food of provision as comes to the market, whereby they might be the better able to earn their said livings that way, and have the better hope.* [36]

The availability of fish not only as a source of revenue but as food for locals cannot be underestimated: famines such as *Samradh na Meraithne* ("the Summer of the Aberration") in 1433 devastated inland agricultural communities. Marine and maritime resources enabled coastal folk to better weather such events - though even the Gaillimh dried up in 1462! [37]

Nor was An Claddagh the only such community upon which Galway relied. *Mionlach* (Menlo) was a village four miles up the Gaillimh, who's inhabitants fished both on the river and Loch Orbsen. Both remained interrelated Gaeilgeoir communities well into the 1900s. Other villages with their own relationship to Galway included *Gort an Chlaidh* (Angliham), *Baile an Dulaigh* (Ballindooley), and *Tír Oileán* (Tirellen/Terryland), all on the Gaillimh's east bank. Likewise, the suburbs around *An Faiche* ('the green') and *Boher Mór* ('the great road'). On the west were *Seantallamh*, *Leitreach*, *An Daingean*, *Baile an Bhrúnaigh*, all now vanished under urban sprawl. A clue to their economic role is hinted in the Claddagh placename, Bettystown - *baile biatach*, 'the food-provider's settlement'.

These interdependent communities existed for generations. With this in mind, we can understand the use of Gaelic terms and nicknames among the Galwegians. Though the Anglos Hibernos adopted few formal Gaelic names, epithets such as mór, óge, ballach, dubh, reagh, indicates the language was used at a very personal, deeply familiar level, and dual name-forms in distinct languages. As Gaeilge remained Ireland's dominant spoken language into the 1760s and after, it would be impossible for any but the most xenophobic of colonists to remain uninfluenced.

Except by the 1400s they were not colonists. English, of Ireland, they were native Irish.

## Éireannach

Ethnic divisions of Gaeil and Gaill remained as potent among the Irish as Scot and English did among the British. As recently as 1907, an Irish song of some fame felt the need to address both the "Sons of the Gael! Men of the Pale!" (women, children, and Ulster folk were unaddressed). While Gaelic culture certainly spread, Gaeil territorial re-expansion at the expense of the Anglo-Irish had ceased by the 1420s. The stability of the Anglo-Irish earldoms ensured the ethnic-political survival and immediate regional mastery of the English, especially in the east and south-east. Yet even then, simplistic notions of ethnicity, caste, and class were confounded. De Burgh et Joie became a Búrc agus Seoighe, Ó Chíordhubháin agus Ó Dorchaidhe became Kirwan and Darcy. Like today, the Irish were not a single nation or homogeneous group, but more complex and acted as such.

In the 1470s the term *Éireannach* ('Irishperson') was recorded in Connacht. [38] Notably, it emerged within the Mac Uilliam Íochtar lordship of what became County Mayo, from Gaill Gaeilgoirí. While terms such as Gaeil and Gaill were by their very nature exclusive, Éireannach was intended as "a broader, more inclusive term". [39] It neither denied such ethnicities nor their validity. Instead - by being geographic, not ethnic - it gave all an equal claim on their island home and to their version of Irish identity. It is the term as Gaeilge on Republic of Ireland passports today.

Earlier terms such as *Scotti, Eirugena* (Gaelic-Latin for 'Irish-born'), *fir Érenn*, and *h-Eireannchaibh*, encompassed diverse medieval Irish individuals and groups. As the Érainn, and speakers of Ireland's lost languages could have attested, as the writer of the above English-language song would have grudgingly conceded, 'the Irish' and 'the Gael' were never exactly the same.

Use of the term in the 1470s had more to do with justifying Meic Uilliam lordship than notions of Irish fellowship. After all, they were lords, and lords take; they neither sow or reap. Yet that does not mean that the concept was without merit. It had the virtue of geographic fact, even if its application remained elusive. But tellingly, Éireannach never became a popular term. Unlike Gaeil and Gaill, whose dynastic bearers had power, aristocratic prestige, the seductive weight of their traditions. The cost to their common descendants would be dear.

## An Irish people: Communitas Hibernie

How did the Anglo-Irish see themselves? Meeting at Drogheda in 1460, the Irish parliament declared that laws passed in England's Westminster parliament were invalid in Ireland unless legislated by the Anglo-Irish lords and commons. While subordinate to the Crown, the Irish parliament correctly stated its jurisdictional identity as lawfully separate from and not bound by Westminster legislation. The *communitas Hibernie* stated:

> the land of Ireland is, and at all times has been, corporate of itself by the ancient laws and customs used in the same, freed of the burden of any special law of the realm of England, save only such laws as by the lords spiritual and temporal and the commons of the said land had been in Great Council or Parliament there held, admitted, accepted, affirmed and proclaimed [40]

This assertion of Anglo-Irish rights had being plainly expressed since at least the 1370s, if not significantly earlier. As Parliament represented the commonalty of Anglo Ireland, legislation passed in it bound the *communitas Hibernie* (Anglo-Irish defining themselves as 'the Irish people', exclusive from the Gaelic-Irish). The corollary was they could not be bound by Westminster parliament's legislation as they would not accept legislation without representation – no Irish sat in Westminster. The 1460 Irish parliament was not a revolt, but certainly revolutionary. [41]

Representation meant participation, not just words but deeds. Furthermore, in enfranchising the non-noble merchant class as public representatives, the Anglo-Irish differed from the more autocratic Gaelic view of society. The assertive independence of the Anglo-Irish was demonstrated not only by anointing in Ireland a king of England in 1487, but invading England that year. As equal English, of Ireland, they had every right to so assert themselves. They would do so again.

## Europe's First Americans

> Men of Cathay [China] have come from the west. [Of this] we have seen many signs. And especially in Galway in Ireland, a man and a woman, of extraordinary appearance, have come to land on two tree trunks. [42]

So wrote Christoffa Corombo ('Christopher Columbus') of a visit to Galway in 1477. While the origins and subsequent lives of Galway's presumptive first Americans remains unknown, Corombo's presence shows the routes by which data of Ireland's west coast improved between the early fourteenth and mid-fifteenth centuries (though in 1492 Corombo thought he was approaching India, hence the *West Indies* and the American First Nations have been 'Indians' ever since. Moral of the story; always bring a Navigator). On a map of 1339, Galway is absent while Limerick, Oileáin Árann, Inishbofin, a grossly oversized Cuan Umaill (Clew Bay), and mythical Hy Brazil are depicted. But a map of about 1450 clearly shows Loch Lurgan, Conmhaicne Mara, Galway, and Athenry. [43] Clearly, increased trade with Europe brought this about. According to one writer:

> The hypothesis which would best explain the anomaly of Bristol ships not bringing all Iceland produce direct to Bristol is that they brought their stockfish and oil to the important Irish trading city of Galway and there transferred it to Portuguese vessels. Certainly, Bristol ships sailed down the west coast of Ireland from Iceland at this time (one was wrecked there in 1485). ... This does not entirely exclude the possibility that the Bristol ships carried their cargoes directly to Portugal, merely calling at Galway to dispose of some part and take on Irish exports. [44]

Likewise, Basques and English fished the Grand

*Columbus Monument, Galway Fish Market*

Banks off north America in the 1460s. It is plausible they stopped at Galway on the voyage home, passing on sailor's stories. As for discovering what, if anything, lay west of Árann, Corombo always had his copy of *Navigatio Sancti Brendani Abbatis* to guide and inspire him. In fact it did.

## The Sea Lords of Loch Lurgan

Árann's appearance on such maps reminds us of the thirteenth-century treaty between Galway and the Clan Teige Uí Bhriain, who guarded the bay against pirates. By his will of 1420, John Óge Blake bequeathed to "my two sons 2 coats of mail, 2 shoulder-plates and 2 galleys." [45] Ownership of the latter necessitated use of the former, and in Atlantic Ireland the Gaeil ruled the waves.

Some of the Uí Fhlaithbheartaigh accommodated the Galwegians. Those of Conmhaicne Mara seem to have remained aloof to overtures - one Aodh Mór Ó Flaithbheartaigh was nick-named *nach glacadh airgid* ('he who refused money'). [46] But the Iar Connachta were more amenable. Murchad *na dTuadh* ('of the Battle-axes') Ó Flaithbheartaigh even accepted both a knighthood about 1585 and government appointment of him as chief of the name, a post he held (with opposition) till his death in 1593. [47] The central position of a galley in the Ó Flaithbheartaigh coat of arms recalls their prowess on the sea. No doubt the merchants thought it useful to cultivate alliances with such ferocious near neighbours. Trade, like politics, begins locally.

Ó Loughlin of Boireann and Ó hEidhin of Cenél Guaire were coastal lords happy to trade. Within living memory, boats arrived at Ballyvaughan, Kinvara, Kilcolgan, and Stradbally (Athenry's medieval port [48]), bringing turf from Connemara. Their medieval predecessors returned to Galway with wool, hides, and other commodities the merchants sold further afield. At this time, tower houses appear both within the town and around it - at Ballybane, Barna, Castlegar, Doughiska, Mervue, Oranmore. Further away were Aughanure in Iar Connacht and Dun Guaire on Loch Lurgan. Only partly military, their primary role was as centres of political and economic power by the 'middle-class' under-lords, both Gael and Gall, rural and urban. Some were probably financed and occupied by the merchants; all were created by the wealth generated in property and trade, as each cost a minimum of six to seven hundred pounds. [49]

## The Sea Kings of The West

Greater maritime kings and lords such as Ó Dubhda of Tír Fhiachrach, Ó Máille of Umall ("Terra Marique Potens/Powerful on Land and Sea"), Mac Mathghamhna of Corcu Baiscinn, all did likewise with castles of their own and from similar economies, each outsourced fishing grounds to the Anglo-Irish and foreign multinationals. The cod fish bank known as the Imaireboy ('the yellow ridge'), sixty miles off Connacht, stretched from The North to Munster and was fished by the likes of the Dutch in the 1500s. [50] Marine life escaped destructive predation until the eighteenth century, after which unsustainable exploitation destroyed the economic basis of coastal communities, leading to species extinction and ocean acidification on an imperial scale.

Gaelic kings and lords provided anchorage, protection, and navigational guidance while levying their dues. Maritime "Gaelic lordships were not economically retarded but ... had comprehensive economic management systems." [51] This included Tír Connell, which between the 1460s and 1550s was the most powerful lordship north of the Escir Riada. At its height, Uí Domhnaill kings exercised an imperium over what are now nine modern Irish counties, from Antrim to Mayo, with influence stretching to Scotland, England, and the continent. Aodh Ruadh Ó Domnaill (r. 1461-1505) was the Earl of Kildare's major ally at Knockdoe in 1504, and *de facto* King of The North.

This ensured security for Galway merchants trading on the long route from Iorris (County Mayo) to the Bann (County Antrim), accessing markets at Sligo, Essa Ruadh (Assaroe) on the Erne, and Rath Maoláin (County Donegal). A further benefit was regular communication with other Anglo-Irish enclaves at Carrickfergus (County Antrim), Drogheda (County Louth), and the Irish east coast. It facilitated access to western England, but also Wales, the Isle of Man, Cumbria, Glasgow and Ayr. Indeed the role of Scotland's commercial and military fleets in Irish affairs of the time remains unexamined, despite King James IV (1488-1513) creating Britain's then largest navies.

These ports could be used as secure bases for creating and exploiting new trade networks. Trade deep into otherwise inaccessible areas was created. As Darren Mac Eiteagáin has pointed out

[Tír Connell] was not a depressed economic region in late medieval times. [It was] famous for its vast herds of cattle and flocks of sheep, as well as large unenclosed areas sown with oats. The uplands and the rugged western coastlands were then largely uninhabited, providing its lowland inhabitants with booley pastures, turf banks, large woodlands and extensive reserves of all types of wild game. Rivers and sheltered inlets were also a very valuable natural resource, giving salmon, eel, oyster and seal fisheries. Many sheltered bays attracted large numbers of foreign merchants and fishermen exploiting an immensely valuable salmon and herring fishery, which developed during the course of the early sixteenth century into one of the biggest of its kind in Europe. [It] had long and well-established trading links with ports such as Bristol ... St Malo and Morlaix in Brittany ... Galway and Drogheda. [52]

Similar activities were carried out by the Uí Fhlaithbheartaigh in Iar Connacht and Conmhaicne Mara, the Uí Mháille in Umall and the Meic Uilliam Íochtar in what is now County Mayo. These regions had similar landscapes, largely uninhabited by humans, utilised like Tír Connell. Galway merchants by necessity had personal networks with all sea lords from Tír Connell to Deasmhumha.

We cannot know what less quantifiable effects Gaelic kings and lords had. No doubt they intimidated – sometimes Galway merchants were ill-disposed to Tír Chonaill's kings "and this may have stemmed from Ó Domhnaill military activity in Connacht." [53] Being gaelicised did not necessarily make a Gaeil, no more than anglicisation made someone English. But as regards culture and language, their effect should not be underestimated. Because just as the Gaill were to some degree gaelicised, so too were the Gaeil anglicised. Though distinct nations *to each other*, their borders could be a blur to outsiders. It was in times of stress that distinctions drew blood.

The rural hinterland provided the raw commodities, the urban merchants availed of their legal (king's subjects, lawfully able to trade) and linguistic (fluent speakers of English, Latin, French, Spanish) abilities to market them. This interrelationship benefited both communities. It also mattered far more than the 'national' divide. Frontiers and borders existed, but so too did transitional zones where cultures and nations blended into one another, where English and Gaeilge became diaglossic. Partitions were political, not economic, social, or even entirely ethnic. What evidence survives indicates inter-community relationships existed. No doubt there were social matters of fosterage, god-parenthood, friendship, and marriage that reinforced pragmatic economic ties.

## Lords, pilgrims, and merchant networks

A letter written in Latin between c. 1450 - c. 1467, preserved by the Blake family, addressed John Blake (d. 1468) and his wife Juliane French (fl. 1468). Translated and paraphrased, it says:

> The writer unable to visit them, and requests that they will come with their wine to his town of Roscommon, as they will be able to sell their merchandise there. If they wish the writer to meet them there, let them write by the bearer to fix a day, and the writer will hasten to meet them there, and will have in keeping for them the cloth which he holds for them. If they cannot come to his town, let them write to him to fix a day for his delivery of the cloths to them, and it shall be carried out. [54]

The reference to his *town of Roscommon* indicates the writer may have been a Gaelic merchant - or one of the last *de jure* kings of Connacht, possibly Tadhg Ó Conchobhair Ruadh (reigned 1439-64). Tadhg was buried in Roscommon "with such pomp and dignity as had not been accorded to any king of the line of Cathal Crobderg before him for a very long time", with "offerings to the Church ... of cows and horses and money." [55] Plausibly, these and previous offerings were traded for or included Galway goods. Though viewed as aloof realms of archaic and anarchic 'Celtdom' in modern stereotypes, Gaelic lordships were generally stable and highly ordered. Conflicts were mainly brief and confined to the *derbfine* elite. Otherwise Gaelic kingdoms and lordships could never have created the prosperity needed to trade nor sustain themselves.

Interestingly, it is co-addressed to Blake's wife, Juliane French. As a daughter of Mary Athy - who's family had associations with Roscommon as far back as 1331 - Juliane may have had sustained ties to the region. The two major nations lived in many distinct polities but interacted across them - the anonymous writer stated he had intended to visit them, and communicated not in Gaeilge or English but the language common to both communities, Latin.

Tadhg Ruadh Ó Ceallaigh, King of Uí Maine, was described upon his death in 1410 as "the most bountiful giver of all the Gaels of Ireland and Scotland in his time." A text composed dur-

*Medieval doorways, Kirwan's Lane*

ing his lifetime states his Dál Druithe subjects (their *taoiseach* was surnamed Ó Gabrán, now rendered Smith) "had the carrying of the wine from the harbours of the west of Connaught" to Ó Ceallaigh seat or "storehouses". Certainly the "ten battle-standards" of the Uí Maine had to get their "mhínsróll agus do máethsída"/"fine satin and of soft silk" from somewhere such as Galway or Athenry. Imagery found in Kilconnell Abbey and Clonfert Cathedral - both in Uí Maine - contain El Camino symbolism, a pilgrimage routed through ports such as Galway and Limerick. [56] The histories of merchants such as the Uí Ghabráin within Gaelic lordships remains largely unexamined.

Much as eighteenth-and nineteenth-century County Galway was crammed with gentry of various social degrees, so too was fourteenth and fifteenth-century Connacht full of offshoots of the great and lesser medieval dynasties. Naturally, they purchased the best merchandise available.

Some Gaelic rulers and clergy left Ireland on extended pilgrimages to destinations such as Santiago de Compostela in Castille, or Rome itself, particularly in 1450 and 1462. Tomaltach *an Einigh* ('the Hospitable') Mac Diarmata, King of Maigh Luirg (r. 1421-58), and Margaret, Queen of Ui Falighe (d. 1451), both travelled to Santiago with many others in 1446. [57] Likewise, in 1444 a large group Connacht clergy all went to Rome. They included Bishop Ó hÉidigheáin of Elphin, Abbot Mac Donnnchadha of Boyle, Prior Ó Flannagáin of Roscommon, and Abbot Mac Donnnchadha of Ballysadare. [58] Galway's geographical proximity to those areas makes it all but certain that they and others like them departed Ireland via busy Loch Lurgan. As a source for vestment cloth and sacramental wine, trade links no doubt already existed between these locations. Pilgrimages and/or clerical visitations were capable of been facilitated by the mariners of Galway. While links to exotic Iberia are glamourised and based on actual trade, Galway was as deeply influenced by her immediate neighbours. Trade enhanced links with Gaelic Ireland, and reinforced ones with Anglo Ireland. In 1824, Hely Dutton wrote that

> on my remarking to a gentleman the resemblance of several doors in Athboy, in the county of Meath, to those in Back street [St. Augustine's street since 1858] in Galway, he informed me "they were anciently used as wine vaults by the merchants of Galway, and from whence they supplied Dublin, Drogheda, and several other towns." [59]

## Galwegians on the Atlantic and the Pacific

Galway merchants are not easily traced abroad in these years, but there are glimpses of men who may have been from the town. The tolls of the port of Bridgewater in Somerset lists a

Thomas Jois as master of the *Savyour*, a Wexford ship that arriving in January 1486 carrying salmon, hake, salted fish, and white herring. He departed in March carrying

> *seven weys of beans worth £4, 13s, 4d, upon which he paid a subsidy of 4s 8d; six dozen narrow cloths without grain, paying customs of 21d; a dozen cloths without grain, paying customs of 7d.* [60]

The same accounts refer to a John Blake, master of the *Mari Butston*, which

> *left for Ireland on 20 March 1486 carrying ... eight weys of beans worth 106s 8d, upon which he paid subsidy of 5s 4.* [61]

Trade from Iberia is rarely attested but the *Santa Maria* sailed from Seville to Galway in 1499. Freighted by *Stefano Gentile* and *Gonzalez Suarez*, she carried fifty-five tons of wine and twenty-nine tons of an unknown cargo. [62] The surnames Browne and Martyn appear in this source. [63]

Some Galwegians were even further away. Three named *Guillen*, William, and John (no surnames are given) are listed as serving as cabin boys on Ferdinand Magellan's final voyage. Brothers William and John survived long enough to land in what became Argentina in 1520, among the first Europeans to sail the woefully misnamed El Mar Pacifico. [64] Childhood was a luxury their families could not afford, so they were set to work. What became of them is unknown.

## Maritime traditions of the Lynchs and Martyns

Even today the children of Adam and Aífe respect the sea, if only because it cares nothing for us. Into modern times shipwrecks occurred appallingly often. The knock-on effects of a single death at sea could include poverty, remarriage, fosterage, loss of apprenticeships, all of which upheaved beyond the measure of any balance-sheet. Voyages were a risky business on nature's terms, never mind with the added human menace of piracy. Few felt safe till home was again in sight and land under foot. Only with this in mind can be appreciated two superstitions begun by Richard *Gare* Lynch (Mayor 1529-30) and *Rychard* Martin (Mayor 1526-27).

Lynch fired a gun at the *Black Rock lying in the bay of Gallway* [65] at the start of what proved a prosperous voyage. This began a custom repeated not only by himself and his descendants, but every branch of the Lynch family. Martin, returning from a long and evidently difficult voyage, was so delighted to arrive safely home he *began to shoot at the little castle of Mutton Iland* [Inis Caorach], *which is observed to this day by all the Martins.* [66] Later Martyns aimed at more animated objects, many of whom returned fire.

## Familial insights

Surviving wills of the time preserve familial details that would have otherwise not survived. Dominick Dubh appears to have had a tense relationship with his younger son, John. This may have had much to do with Dominick Dubh's irregular relationship with Juliane Deane. Valentine Blake's will of July 1499 throws light on a problem prevalent in a tightly-knit community, that of consanguinity in marriage. Blake recorded that he, the testator,

> bequeaths to his lawful wife Eveline Lynch the third part of all his goods in Galway and Athenry from the greatest down to a farthing ... on account of her great trouble and expense, and also on account of the redemption of their (marriage) impediment, which she redeemed wholly out of her own goods. [67]

Not quite on par with Dominick Dubh, Blake nevertheless did his best for his surviving family:

> Testator bequeaths to his daughter Anastasia four casks of wine, one pipe of honey, 3 marks in silver and 2,000 bales of lin-cloth, his eldest son John to pay for 1,000 of them, and the other 1,000 to come out of the debts due to testator. Testator bequeaths to his younger sons and the offspring which Evelina has, three casks of wine and a pipe. [68]

The trade in linen was certainly profitable. A *Letter of testimony*, dated August 1492 by Mayor John Skerrett and bailiffs Nicholas French and Walter Blake, gives notice of a reversal by *letters patent from the king* on a judgement they made in favour of *James Adurnus of Genoa*. The Galway court judgement favoured Adurnus, so Lynch sought to overturn it. He successfully "appealed to the Royal Court in Dublin to have said judgement set aside", forcing the Mayor and bailiffs "on pain of our allegiance to seize all the merchandise and goods of said James Adurnus within our jurisdiction" and deliver it to Lynch "until he be fully paid said amount of 6,000 bales of lin-cloth." [69]

Earlier models of the Galway *húicér, gleoteog, púcán* and *currach* were probably active in medieval times. For centuries they were the principal vessels distributing goods in and out of the numerous inlets and havens of the bay. For lengthy voyages, hulks, barges, carracks, galleys, and cogs transported people and goods, with the latter vessel featuring on Galway town seals. Justifiably was Galway's main church dedicated to the patron saint of sailors and merchants (and prostitutes).

## El Camina: Margaret Athy

In the latter, his final resting place, Dominick Dubh wished

> my son Stephen Lynch to finish and complete the new works begun by me in the Collegiate Church, and also to erect an altar to St. James the Apostle, adjoining the nearest column in the Chapel of Blessed Mary in the said Church.

Stephen took an easy-going approach to the task, which were not completed till the lifetime of his son, Nicholas. [70] In addition to serving four times as Mayor, Stephen was a busy merchant, frequently at sea. While returning from a voyage to Spain, circa 1510, he was astonished to see a new monastery on a hill some distance beyond the south wall of the town.

> *He was surprised, on entering the bay, to behold so stately a building in a place where, at his depar-ture, not a stone had been laid; but when, on landing, he found that it had been erected by his own good wife, in honour of St. Augustine, his surprise was converted into joy; and the good man, kneel-ing down on the sea-shore, returned thanks to Heaven for inspiring her with a pious resolution. [71]*

At least that is his recorded reaction. We have no idea what was actually said behind closed doors between the no doubt happily-reunited couple.

Mrs. Lynch, nee Margaret Athy, also funded the construction of Lynch's Aisle in St. Nicholas's. [72] Two of its windows bear her arms and those of her husbands, as well as those of Dominick Dubh and his first wife. [73] The Athys still had some wealth as she apparently paid for the all these works herself. Either that or she freely drew upon her absent husband's re-sources.

The foundation of the abbey marked her introduction of a new order of clergy to the town, the Augustinians. It was no doubt useful to open a new inhumation area as cemeteries associated with ecclesiastical sites within and without the walls were no doubt long since at capacity. Mar-garet may have found some particular practises of the order useful. Plus - as with all other reli-gious foundations in and around the town - the Augustinians did not exist in isolation. They were part of a network to foundations elsewhere in Ireland and beyond, moving personnel and ideas.

Beyond that, we nowadays forget that people had genuine faith, that their activities were based in a sincere beliefs and the necessity of good deeds in a Christian life. Margaret's active piety was mirrored by fellow Irish women Joan Douce (fl. 1381), Queen Maighréad Beán Ó Con-chobhair Failghe (d. 1451), and Máire Ní Mháille (d. 1522/23). [74] These woman made notable use of the church as a means of transforming private wealth into public display:

> Religious observance also fulfilled the important function of affording [women] accept-able reasons to break free of strictures that normally governed their behaviour; for exam-ple, prilgrimages offered one of the few acceptable excuses for women ... to travel beyond their patrionies. ... Like all Christians in western Europe, women in late medieval Ireland were obbsessive about ensuring that they expolited as many options as possible ... in order to maximise their prospects of salvation. [75]

Such acts allowed them to invert gender roles, giving women the opportunity to be the primery actors on stages otherwise reserved for men. Piety was one way by which women could legitimatly claim and express that which they otherwise lacked: power, independence, choice.

Margaret's determination was further displayed by a pilgrimage she subsequently made to San-tiago in Castille, where she would have collected the emblem of *el camino*, a scallop shell. She had intended to travel from there to Jerusalem, probably on the maritime route from Seville to Jaffa (modern-day Tel Aviv), but was prevented by the illness which may have driven her piety. [76]

## The fortunes of Germyn Lynch

Margaret's journey need not have been in strange company. Germyn Lynch (fl. 1437-83), apparently of Galway, ferried pilgrims between Ireland and Santiago de Compostela, where the remains of James the Apostle are said to lie, at the end of *El Camino de Santiago* ('the Way of St. James'). Of Germyn Lynch it has been remarked that

> It is most unusual to be able to trace for over forty years the fate and fortunes of a common man in late medieval Ireland. ... the full life history of Germyn Lynch ... would surely equal the most exciting imaginings of any writer of historical novels. [77]

What is known of Lynch outlines a very active life, perhaps broadly typical of late-medieval Galway merchants. He first appears on record at Bristol in 1437 [78] in a customs account. In 1441 Lynch was sworn into the Worshipful Company of Goldsmiths, London. [79] Over the next twenty years he qualified as a goldsmith, took on apprentices, became a London citizen and a well-established businessman. In August 1461 the newly-crowned Edward IV approved Lynch's appointment as Keeper of the Irish Mints, [80] an office he held on and off till the end of the reign.

By the mid-1400s, the standard of Irish coin, especially silver, was much devalued. Forgeries by the Gaelic-Irish of Meath and Louth brought the valuation down yet further. Edward IV's father had, in exchange for support in his attempt to gain the crown in 1459, struck a deal with the Anglo-Irish, giving them permission to strike coins to a weight lower than in England. These coins stimulated trade in Ireland, but outraged English merchants when circulated in England. Edward IV's subsequent appointment of Lynch

> has to be seen against a political background of Yorkist and Lancastrian faction in a land where central authority was practically non-existent. It was part of an attempt by the king to raise the standard of the coinage and to curtail the large number of semi-legal and illegal mints that had begun producing coins ... while at the same time placating the Anglo-Irish interests involved. [81]

Lynch minted coins in Dublin and Waterford by 1464, and in Galway c. 1470. A silver mine lay across the bay in Ó Loughlin's lordship of Boireann ("in Olouglins country by his castell in borrein, a silver myne xvi myles from Galwey"). Another, owned by *Tirrelaghe obrien*, was at *knock-kylleny* - now Caherglassaun, County Galway. At least one of Lynch's Galway coins survives. [82]

A savvy mint master could make a lucrative profit for himself, and Lynch had no qualms about illegal self-benefit. Lynch was supposed to make one hundred and twenty four penny silver pieces, called *groats*, to the pound, producing ten groats to the ounce. Five of the coins he was allowed to keep for himself. Lynch decided that if he made underweight coins he could get an extra three coins from each ounce. The undermaster discovered his fraud in 1472, but Lynch was pardoned and reappointed, only to be dismissed again in 1474, no doubt for similar reasons. [83]

Not that he lacked for things to do while out of royal employment. In the Holy Year of 1474, he ferried pilgrims to Santiago on his ship, the *Mary Leybourne*. Usually such ships would transport wine, but Holy Year pilgrims from both Ireland and Britain required passage to Santiago. Ships could carry as many as eighty clients, and in good weather reach Spain in five days. [84]

Needing to refit the ship, Lynch obtained a loan from two merchants of Limerick, White and Lewes, via his Limerick servant, Esmond Torger. However, the three men were persuaded into a double-cross scheme, claiming Lynch never repaid them and brought a case against him in Galway. Galwegians John French, John Blake fitz William and Thomas Blake, planned the scheme. [85]

The case was tried in Galway before Sovereign William Lynch fitz Sander, and Germyn Lynch lost. The Sovereign ordered "White and Lewes be given a house and land which Germyn owned in the city worth 200 marks and which brought him an income of £5 per annum." Germyn appealed, and all concerned were summoned to appear before the king. The outcome is unknown. [86]

Documents reveal Lynch's presence in Bristol in March 1478 as master of the *John Evangelist*. She was bound for Iceland, and loaded with "10 tons of salt, 1 1/2 lasts of flour, 9 barrels of butter and lengths of cloth valued at £5 16s 8d, all of which were being shipped by John Pynke of Bristol."

Iceland had rich offshore fishing, and with "a high demand for salt for curing fish and for provisions and cloth, ... the returns were good but the voyage across a dangerous sea was always risky." [87] While ships from Britain and the Baltic regularly visited Iceland, Irish merchants were few. No matter how well he profited from such voyages, Germyn must have lobbied hard to regain lucrative employment on land, especially now that he must have been in his fifties.

Later in 1478 Lynch was made joint Irish mint master but could not resist tampering with the coinage, resulting in his fourth dismissal. [88] Perhaps this is why he is arrived at Bristol in 1480, master of the *Michael of Bristol*, carrying salmon, herring, and cattle hides. He left for Ireland on the *Michael* in March "with a cargo of cloth, salt, honey, alum and old corrupt wine." [89] Incredibly, Lynch secured a fifth appointment to the Irish mint. But all good things come to an end.

In 1483 Germyn Lynch was dismissed for the fifth and final time from his official post as mint worker. By then he must have been well over sixty years of age, an old man by medieval standards but without doubt one who had spent a very full and varied life. Few of his contemporaries in Ireland could look back on a life which had associations not only with state officials and magnates in Ireland, but also with the cream of London's merchant-craftsmen and bankers. Not many could recount stories of life in the sunny ports of Spain and Portugal or describe the difficulties of weathering winter gales off Iceland and of negotiating the sandbanks of the Severn. [90]

## The Hanging Judge?

The most infamous Lynch is known for a terrible act which, apparently, he did not commit. James Lynch fitz Stephen was Mayor for the term 1493-94. [91] He placed stained glass - at the time incredibly expensive - in the windows of St. Nicholas's and erected a choir in St. Mary's, The Claddagh. [92] No town statutes appear to have been issued during his term, and in an apparent editorial blunder, his name is missing from the list of Mayors of Galway published in 2002. [93]   Still, hardly worthy of notice even for ardent historians, except for a story published centuries afterwards by James Hardiman. Despite being laid to rest in the 1900s, the story is re-told every year to new tourists, and will be for years yet.

*Lynch's Window, Market Street, Galway*

Stripped of pages of seafóid, Hardiman's story is as follows. Returning from a successful voyage to Spain with his best friend, Gomez, one Walter Lynch took exception to advances Gomez is supposed to have made to his fiancée. "Urged on by rage" [94] he stabbed Gomez to death at the Spanish Arch (which did not then exist, and is actually Ceann an Bhalla, 'the head of the wall').   Captured and justly tried, the Mayor issued the death sentence upon Walter Lynch. The following morning, Walter stood at an upper-floor window of his house, hands bound behind him and a noose about his neck. With a single push, the Mayor "launched him into eternity!" [95]

According to Hardiman, Mayor James Lynch fitz Stephen was the father of Walter Lynch.

Sadly for lovers of bad romance, Hardiman stole the story almost word-for-word from a novel, *George the III*, written in 1807 by Reverend Edward Mangin. In 1822 Mangin wrote that Hardiman

> quote[s] from a very humble work of fiction which I wrote and published (without my name) fifteen years ago. I <u>invented</u> the story of the heroic Mayor of Galway. [96]

The 'site' of the 'hanging' is still pointed out in Lombard Street. However, it is impossible to hang a fifteenth-century man from a window and wall erected in 1854, cobbled together from different bits of unrelated medieval and modern architecture. [97] Likewise, Ceann an Bhalla was by 1900 renamed 'the Spanish Arch' in commemoration of this unhistorical non-event. But when truth and tourism meet, sell the legend and sell hard.

## At the edge of the world

Historian Maureen Donovan-O'Sullivan wrote of Galway in the 1400s:

If Galway was now confirmed in its loyalty it was also more than ever established in its independence, and this chiefly because of its situation so remote from the seat of Government ... Communication with Dublin was at this stage so precarious that for well nigh half a century Galway was not visited by a King's Deputy ... while the King's Law had long ceased to be administered within its walls ... Clearly, therefore, the protection afforded by the Crown was largely of a nominal character, and Galway was left to a great extent to fend for itself as best it could. In these difficult circumstances it was small wonder it should take on more and more the character of an independent City State. [98]

Though certainly not comparable in opulence or might with city-states such as Florence or Venice, or the Free Imperial Cities such as Hamburg and Bremen, Galway could still be listed with them (links with the Burgundian wine-trading *négociants* of Bruges and Antwerp remain unexplored). This was a real achievement given that Galway was considered to be beyond the periphery of civilization as understood by other urban elites, even in Atlantic Europe.

Even their failures were remarkable. In 1498 Mayor Andrew Lynch fitz Stephen attempted to link the river at Woodquay to the sea at Lough Atalia. Here, ambition outstripped ability, and the uncompleted canal was called *Lynch's Folly*. [99] But no one should have faulted him for trying.

The fifteenth century featured reinvigorated classical investigation ('the Renaissance'), an upsurge of vernacular literature (undiminished in Ireland), and the dawn of globalisation. Irish engagement in this era can be symbolised in musical terms. The *timpán* was a popular Gaelic-Irish instrument yet from the 1460s it was abandoned for an English import first attested in Ireland in 1501, the bagpipes. [100] Future generations likewise adapted the banjo (African) and Bouzuki (Turkish). As now, the Irish could embrace outside influences and make them their own.

## Merchant coats of arms

Achievements need monuments to proclaim their worth, something to show a person has arrived in society. And there was nothing as worthy in the late medieval era as a coat of arms. Few subjects are as popularly misunderstood. Originally borne on shields as a means of identification in battle by knights and nobles, they were later symbols of rank and prestige, introduced to Ireland by the Normans. But the idea that a coat of arms represents all bearers of a given surname is wrong. A coat of arms is property that can legally be used *only* by one person at a time. [101] Most probably date from the fifteenth or sixteenth centuries, as before then few of the families were notable.

The Athy arms may be the personal device of Sir John de Athy, the only certain knight among these families (Thomas de Linche and Walter Husgard are contenders). In heraldic language it is described as *Checky, argent and gules, on a chevron of the last, trois etoiles, or.* [102] This is a checked background of white and red square under an upward-pointing chevron, bearing three gold stars. This device would have continued in use among the Athys as they transitioned from warriors to

*1624 Arms of Martin Darcy ('M.D.')*

merchants. Likewise, the plain Lynch arms may date to when they were marshals of Galway. On a blue background there is an upward pointing white chevron. Below is a shamrock-like device - a trefoil - with two more above it, all coloured gold (*Azure, a chevron between three trefoils, slipped, or*). [103] The Blake arms - *Argent, a fret, gules* - a red fret on a white background, is explicitly stated as been first used by Sheriff Richard Cadel *le blake*. [104]

All three designs are quite spartan. Heraldists say the simpler the arms, the greater its age. Only after the original form of knighthood ceased to exist did arms take on more artistic designs, indicative of social position rather than warlike simplicity. Sir John de Athy, his fellow knights, sheriffs, and marshals would probably have scorned them as effeminate.

That said, none of the merchants arms are overly elaborate. Those of Browne and Joyce might both feature a double-headed eagle, and later generations of all families happily added crests, coronets, supporters and other foliage. But in the original form the arms reflect their origins among the merchant classes as self-identifying (commercial?) logos. They mainly survive carved on fireplaces as 'marriage stones'. Initials, names, and a date were sometimes added. None were then registered with any Herald's Office, and were thus quite illegal in origin and application.

Some arms replaced earlier designs. From the 1700s, the Darcy arms was described as *Azure, semee of cross crosslets, three cinquefoils, argent with a crest of On a chapeau, gules, doubled ermine, a bull passant, sable, corned, unguled, and furnished, or.* [105] Yet as of 1624, the original Darcy arms featured a plain blue shield divided into four quarters by a white cross, with a small cross in each

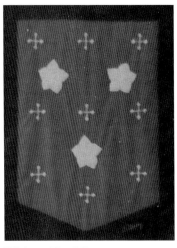

*1752 Arms of Patrick Darcy*

quarter. [106] As the family were of minor importance until the 1590s, these arms were probably created by James Reagh Dorsey, alias Séamus Riabhach Ó Dorchaidhe (d. 1603).

In 1777, James Reagh's descendant, Chevalier Patrick Darcy of Kiltullagh, was ennobled as *Patrice, Comte D'Arci* by King Louis XV of France. This required four-hundred years worth of nobility that his family did not have. Luckily, over twenty years earlier, the Herald's Office in Dublin - no doubt aided by generous 'funding' from the Darcys - concocted a pedigree 'proving' the Ó Dorchaidhe's of Partraighe were descended from the Darcys of Platten in County Meath. The latter, originally from Arci (e.g., de Arci) in France, were an Anglo-Irish family with enough knights and countesses that provided sufficent stolen nobility for Ó Dorchaidhe descendants [107] The surname lost a fada and gained an apostrophe while the motto was rendered *en Francais*, revising the family past for present needs. So it goes. Comte D'Arci's ancestors might have being baffled to find themselves described not as Fir Bolg but French, yet they would have applauded the upwardly-mobile, cute hoor move from the *aithechtuatha* to the aristocracy. So successful was this 'cut and paste' job that some still refuse to believe it is seafóid - proving the best lies are those we want to believe. But DNA tests demonstrate their ancestry lie not in France but Ireland. [108]

The Martyn arms are among the most distinctive of the Tribes, featuring a Calvary cross with a crescent moon on one arm and the shining sun on the other. Hardiman relates that

*Arms of Anastacia Lynch, nee Martin*

> These splendid armorial ensigns, are stated to have been granted by King Richard I to an ancestor of this family, named Oliver Martyn, who accompanied that monarch, as a commanding officer to the holy wars; and distinguished himself in Palestine, but, on his return, he was made prisoner, in Germany, with his master, and died in confinement. [109]

An entirely different story was related by Martyns in the eighteenth and nineteenth centuries:

> In days when the various Irish septs, if they had no common enemy to oppose, were ever engaged in fighting among themselves, the Martins and the O'Flaherties were thus amusing themselves. The O'Flaherties advanced against the Martins in such force, that the utter extirpation of the latter family must have necessarily followed upon their defeat.
>
> The fateful encounter of the opposing parties took place on a Good Friday, and after a fearful struggle the Martins proved victorious, and were enabled to return home safely for the celebration of Easter. In grateful commemoration of this signal deliverance from "ye bloodie O'Flaherties", they (the Martins) adopted thenceforward for the family Arms a Calvary Cross, etc.; with the Motto: Auxilium meum a Domino. [110]

*The 2nd Martyn arms c. 1520*

A seventeenth-century source states "The Martins have the cross with the sun and moon as arms, *and given to William Martin and to his posterity*." [my emphasis] [111] Yet until c. 1500, Martyns bore arms of two horizontal red bars on a plain white background. [112] Versions of this coat of arms are found within St. Nicholas's Church, overlooking Williamsgate Street, and on the mid-seventeenth century map of Galway. They are essentially identical to arms used from the 1130s by individuals surnamed FitzMartin, of England and Wales. The earliest attested bearer was Robert fitz Martin, [113] who once fought alongside Maurice fitz Gerald. So the Martyns could be a junior line of the FitzMartins. Perhaps more likely, some enterprising Martyn assumed them illegally. Sure what was the harm? Heraldic shops have sold 'family coats of arms' on the same basis for decades.

At some point in the early 1500s, the FitzMartin arms were abandoned in favour of the cross, sun, and crescent moon. These decades coincide precisely with the lifetime of *Wylliam Martin* (fl. 1504-47), who is almost certainly the *William Martin* mentioned above. Wylliam's father, *Thomas Martyn*, granted a pardon in 1505 for treason, was later killed in unknown circumstances. In May 1530, Wylliam was granted compensation for Thomas's death. A lawyer in the suit was surnamed *Mac Keegan* (Mac Thadacán, or perhaps Mac Aodhagáin), a family of hereditary *breitheamh* ('judges') who served the likes of the Clann Ricard and Uí Cheallaigh. So the 'battle of Good Friday' and its motto from the Psalms has some factual if misremembered origin. [114]

The Joyce arms was also given a fantastical basis.

Arms of Richard Joyce and Elizabeth Skerrett, courtesty of Finnegan's Restaurant, Market St.

William Joyces, who was married to Agnes Morris, being on his travels from Italy to Greece, he was taken prisoner by the Saracens, and brought to Africa, from whence, after a variety of adventures, and undergoing a captivity of seven years, he escaped to Spain; while here, his exalted virtues were rewarded by heaven, according to the pedigrees of the family, in an extraordinary manner; for, as they relate, an eagle flying over his head, pointed out to him a place, where he discovered vast treasures; with which returning to Galway, he contributed large sums towards building the walls, church and other public edifices of the town, he died, leaving three sons, James, Henry and Robert, and was buried in the Franciscan friary. [115]

A Joyce was indeed "taken prisoner" in north Africa from 1675 to 1689, and this was seemingly backdated into the family history. Yet scallop shell marks on a Joyce arms dated 1589, still in a house on Market Street, hints at time spent at Santiago. Maybe fortune smiled strangely on a Joyce in Castille, and like some Irish emigrants who sojourned abroad, he chose to return home.

A candidate is *Willam Josse*, the first verifiable Joyce in Galway town. He drowned in the Gaillimh while a bailiff in November 1507. Another is his middle son, Henry, Mayor 1542-43, and as such, worthy of a coat of arms. According to the *Geneologia Domini Gregorii Joyes*, Henry's wife, Catherine, was the widow of Thomas Browne of Athenry. The *fess dauncettie* of his Morris grandmother may have become the Joyce's two bars.

My conclusion is Catherine and Henry combined their arms. She took her late husband's double-headed eagle, Henry added his (father's?) two-bar horizontal *fess* with two up, two down, scallop shell marks, and a crescent moon (indicating a younger son?) on its back on the upper bar (misremembered as a single *Fess, Ermine*). Four Brownes of Athenry were made Freeman of Galway just before Henry Joyce became Mayor, and the two events may have some connection.

The Lynch arms would also undergo revision:

> The Lynches obtained their armorial bearings from the following circumstance, one of their name and family, being governor of Lintz (long before the invasion of England by the Conqueror), defended that city with unexampled fortitude, against a powerful enemy; and though from the uncommon length of the siege, all their provisions were consumed, and the garrison reduced to the miserable extremity of subsisting on the common herbage of the fields, he was finally victorious.
>
> His prince, amongst other rewards of his valour, presented him with the trefoil on a field azure, for his arms, and the Lynx, the sharpest sighted of all animals, for his crest, the former, in allusion to the extremity to which he was driven for subsistence during the siege, and the latter, to his foresight and vigilance, and, as a testimonial of his fidelity, he received the motto, *semper fidelis*, which arms, crest and motto are borne by the Lynch family to this day. [116]

Which is a long-winded way of saying the family had probably not a clue about how, where, when, or why the arms were created. So they made it up.

All that is known about the Skerret coat of arms - *squirrel, sejant, proper* - is that they are first attributed to a *John Skerret*, possibly the man alive 1476-84. [117] The alliteration of *Skerrett, squirrel*, might be intentional; perhaps the family dealt in squirrel hides, used for making gloves and purses. The *Iora rua* (red squirrel) thrived in the woods and scrubs of beech and hazel found in abundance on both sides of the Gaillimh, till its apparent extinction in the early 1700s.

The meaning, if any, of each arms was known to the original bearer but over centuries was forgotten, which gave descendants great excuse to invent creative armorial myths. None of the other Tribes preserved any account on why they adopted their arms. Thus we no longer know the basis of *the blue and white wings* of the Deanes, the *lion rampant* of the Fonts and Morris's, the *three shelldrakes* (the cross-bill duck), *sable, beaked and legged, gules* of the Kirwans. Perhaps they indicated some family trait. Perhaps they just liked these animals.

While the arms were the physical logos, mottos were verbal emblems, familial sayings, rallying cries or even brief prayers. In that regard, each motto was a lúireach ('breastplate', literally spiritual armour), words of power to call upon in time of need. Their inventions probably differed wildly in time and circumstance, as hinted in the differing languages. They are mainly in prestigious Latin, with one each in English (French), Gaeilge (Bodkin) and two in French (Darcy, Kirwan). Variously dutiful, pious, even boring, they demonstrate their class origins by the values posed in their rhetoric: *Semper fidelis* ('Always faithful' – Lynch); *Un Dieu, un Roy* ('One God, One King' – Darcy). Blake's *Virtus sola Nobilitat* ('Virtue is the only nobility') is almost a proverb.

The blood-curdling exception is the Bodkin's *Crom aboo!* (Crom a buadaigh!='Crom victorious!' In stealing the FitzGerald motto - in the aftermath of Knockdoe? - they asserted a dubious familial connection. By spelling not *Croome* (a town in County Limerick) but *Crom*, the Bodkins unwittingly made a pre-Gaelic Pagan red god their agent of fortune. But it was memorable, as mottos should be, almost as ominous as *Seo chugainn an Geimhreadh*.

## Rebuilding medieval Galway – and destroying it

The years before and after 1485 were ones of prolonged success. The streets were paved in 1509. [118] That year "the chapel of New Castel ... called St. James's chapel", was built by Stephen Lynch fitz James. [119] In 1511 Walter Lynch fitz Thomas "bestowed on his daughter the house of the poor nuns of the church yard, being now under the name of the Third Order of Saint Francis" [120]

Clearly there had been improvements for the better. Conchobair Mac Con Raoi of Árainn died in 1580, claiming to remember when "there were but 3 stone houses, the [Franciscan] Abbey, the Red Earl's house, and Athy's castle, in Galway; a chapel only where St. Nicholas church stands, and another where St. Mary's chapel [stands]." [121] Allowing for exaggeration (dying aged two hundred and twenty-two and eating implausible amounts of beef), Mac Con Raoi possessed memories inherited from previous generations of Galway before its late-medieval refurbishment. Athy's Castle is the single largest inhabited structure on the c. 1664 map. Probably built by Sovereign John Athy in the 1400s, its height was reminiscent of castellated Tuscan towers, in size de Bermingham's Court/Athenry Castle. [122]

Athy's Castle may have inspired two of medieval Galway's most famous surviving buildings. Blake's Castle and Lynch's Castle are tower houses constructed in the late 1400s as residences of each family's senior line. Lynch's Castle has dominated the town's main street since about 1480, and has become an iconic image of the west. [123] Even so, it is substantially smaller than Athy's Castle. Blake's Castle is located in the seanceathrú at the bottom of Quay Street, and at the time was situated right on the town docks (hence 'quay street'). Like much of medieval Galway, it fared less well. Used as a mill, town jail, and a factory, it came perilously close to demolition in the 1980s. Its restored façade survives as part of the front of Jury's Hotel. [124]

Little else does. Grievously many of Galway's medieval buildings were destroyed into the 1980s. Few of the structures that replaced them, then or since, attempted to harmonise with or re-create Galway's diminishing medieval architecture. Much that was not smashed was stolen or dumped. Often their replacements lacked for nothing except taste, resulting in competing eyesores.

Genuine attempts were made since the 1980s to be sensitive to the medieval form of buildings in the seanceathrú, regenerating local heritage rather than making buildings identical those elsewhere in Europe or north America. Galway's architectural distinctiveness set it apart in the first place.

But too much damage could not, or would not, be undone. The Portmore building at Span-ish Arch overwhelms the latter, the Browne Doorway continues to degrade in public, while a once-beautiful Eyre Square was path-cut and concreted, millions over budget. Old Galway shows Ireland's heritage is valued less than exploitation, not yet as precious in itself.

## William Joy, Archbishop of Tuam

In the spiritual realm, townsmen were being promoted the upper reaches of the church. Wal-ter Blake, previously a canon at Tuam and Annaghdown, became Bishop of Clonmacnoise in March 1487, [125] just missing out on succeeding Donatus Ó Muireadhaigh as Archbishop of Tuam. Ó Muireadhaigh's actual successor was William Joy, alias Uilliam Seóighe. [126] His back-ground is uncertain, perhaps hailing from Tuam or Athenry rather than Galway. He was one of a number of Joys recorded in church documents as clergy for Tuam diocese during the fifteenth century (in these documents, always rendered Joy). Thomas Joy, "skilled in canon law ... lately dispensed by papal authority as the son of unmarried parents, nobles", was in 1440 made vicar of *Killcomayn*, became archdeacon of Tuam, and by 1464 was *perpetual vicar of the parish church of Athenry*. Others gained similar assignments and dispensations, hinting at supporting financial power(s). [127]

Archbishop of Tuam from 1485 to 1501, William Joy was archdeacon of Tuam c. 1479-85. An even-handed modern assessment views medieval archdeacons as "practical men of affairs, in-volved in legal and financial matters ... [being an archdeacon] was a sign that one was progressing up the ladder of ecclesiastical promotion." [128] Yet in their own time they were viewed as spiri-tual zombies, financially corrupt, and sexually incontinent to woeful degrees. Needing a univer-sity education abroad to gain legal knowledge, they started their careers indebted to a sponsor, usually a lord. Thus they came to be seen as venal and political creatures of the upper-classes. [129]

In the 1470s the archdeacon of Tuam was still Thomas Joy, sometime vicar of Athenry. About 1477, a William de Bermingham seized the office for himself. In doing so he "laid violent hands on ... Thomas Joy, priest, and kept him in prison, and treated him so cruelly that he ... died." [130] At the time, William Joy was "perpetual vicar of Chitynglygh in the diocese of Chichester" [131] in England, but heard of the incident and informed Pope Sixtus IV. In a letter of June 1479, Sixtus ordered the diocesan clergy to determine the truth of this, and if Joy's account was true,

> collate and assign the said archdeaconry, a non-major, non-elective dignity with cure, value 16 marks sterling, to the said William Joy. The pope hereby dispenses him to receive it, and to retain with it the said vicarage for life. [132]

The letter noted Joy had been "dispensed by papal authority on account of illegitimacy, as the son of a noble priest, an archdeacon, and an unmarried woman of a race of barons." [133] In all likelihood, Archdeacon Joy and a Bermingham were parents of Archbishop Joy, meaning the de

*West Bridge and Mills plaque, 1562*

Bermingham who murdered the Archdeacon was a maternal relative of Archbishop Joy. In 1486, Archbishop Joy confirmed grants he made to the parishioners of St. Nicholas's, Galway, while in 1501 he added the vicarages of Shrule and Kinlough to that of St. Nicholas's. [134]

## Home improvements

In 1520, the town wall was extended along the docks by Mayor Wylliam Martin, [135] while in the following year, Mayor Andrew Lynch oversaw the slating of the roofs of all houses situated near the town gates and walls. [136] This was exceptional, as thatched roofs were the norm in Ireland well into the 1900s. During his mayoral year of 1538-39, Seán an tSalainn French erected

> the north body of the St. Nicholas's church from the north pinnacle to the chapel of the sacrament. He also built the great chapel which lieth in the south side of St. Francis's Abbey in the north of Gallway together with the stone house that stands over the river annexed to the said west pinnacle of the said Abbey, called John French's chamber. [137]

The provincial chapter of the Franciscans was held at Galway in 1562, possibly in this chapel. [138] *Tigh Brigd* ('St Bridget's House [Hospital]') was founded in 1543, in time to deal with an epidemic of the sweating sickness. [139] A further town Charter was granted in 1545. [140] The West Bridge saw the addition in 1558-62 of the West Gate and Mills (demolished 1800), financed by husband and wife Thomas Óge Martin and Evelin Linche. [141] Their arms and a commemorative Latin inscription adorned the Gate; it now overlooks the junction of Shop Street, the Mainguard, and High Street, and reads THOMAS.MARTIN:ET:EVELIN LINCHE : HOC: OP MVLINONVO3 FIERI FE??ERVT:AD 1562 (*"Thomas Martin and Eveline Linche caused this work and mill to be made AD 1562"*) In popular accounts this Latin script became an English phrase - From the ferocious O'Flaherties deliver us oh lord. As a myth always does, it grew bigger than the truth.

In 1566 Dominick Lynch proposed a Free School be formed in the town. [142] Even the town's capture in 1504 by Uilleag Fionn a Búrc was offset by his defeat at Knockdoe by his father-in-law, the 8th Earl of Kildare. [143] In the latter's honour, the Lynchs sculpted an elaborate FitzGerald arms on Lynch's Castle, displaying symbols of the Earls of Kildare. [144] More immediately, in thanks for expelling a Búrc and his followers, Mayor Edmond Deane awarded FitzGerald and his army thirty tuns of wine. [145] They didn't think it too many.

## Maire Lynch, Countess Clanricard

Galway's Corporation Book A demonstrates that *fénechas* was sometimes used in arbitration. It's system of fines instead of physical punishment such as execution or mutilation under English law, may

*Blake's Castle, Quay Lane*

have influenced Galway's town statutes. Some were of the opinion that Galway was too familiar with its Gaelic neighbours. King Henry VIII's 1536 *Ordinances for Galway* exhorted the townspeople to cut their hair in English fashion, wear English garments, and speak English. Apparently, too many townsmen were growing long hair and the *crombeal* moustache, wearing bráta and speaking the king's English in Irish accents (or was it *vise versa?*). The *Ordinances* ended with a barely veiled threat: "See that we hear no further complaint in this behalf, or in any of the premises, upon you, as you intend our favours, and avoiding the contrary." [146]

What may have been at the back of this was a *rapprochement* reached between Galway and the new Clanricard, Uilleag na gCeann a Búrc. Perhaps it helped that he was a grandnephew of Anabel de Burgh, wife of Mayor John Blake (d. 1489). Yet even by Clanricard standards, Uilleag was "a man of wild governance in those parts where he dwelled" (Loughrea). [147] His nickname, *na gCeann* ('of the heads'), alluded to his habit of decapitating foes, including his first cousins and would-be Clanricard's John Dubh and Redmond Ruadh. [148]

The merchants believed they had secured permanent peace when Uilleag sought marriage to one of their own, Marie Lynch. She must have been a formidable person in her own right; not only was she marrying one of the most powerful Gaeilgeoir warlords in Connacht, Marie was tasked with teaching him English, the king's laws, correct forms of Anglo-Irish dress, and table manners, all marks of English civility. [149] Like many women before and after, she may nevertheless felt she was marrying beneath her station, especially as Irish men still struggle with these concepts.

Yet the marriage was a success; when in London in June 1543, they had an audience with King Henry VIII. [150] There, in exchange for allowing Galway to be removed from his jurisdiction, [151] Uilleag was ennobled as 1st Earl of Clanricard. The hope was that Marie Lynch's son would follow Uilleag as Earl, be the king's loyal subject and Galway's good friend.

Alas, on his death in October 1544, it was discovered Uilleag was already married to Gráinne Ní Chearrbhaill of Éile. This invalidated his marriage to Marie, her son could not succeed as Earl, and she was technically guilty of adultery. She contented herself with marriage to Pierce Martin and three hundred sterling in damages from the 2nd Earl. More grimly, the ensuing four years of dynastic war saw various a Búrcaigh kill "the men, women, and children" of freehold lords such as Mac Cooge, Mac Hubert, Ó hEidhin, Ó Seachnasaigh, and others. [152]

## Boon Times, Boom Town

Annals, state papers, and town statutes record violence increasing in the early-to-mid 1500s, hazarding travel. Stephen Lynch fitz Arthur, Nicholas Blake, and Andrew Browne, all forfeited a financial bond for missing an 1556 appointment at Dublin with the Chancellor of Ireland. They explained that were unable to travel across the country due to "the fears they had ... if they should have travelled through Irishman's country's ... [of] been taken and spoiled."[153] The surface impression is Ireland was economically undeveloped because of endemic warfare, that modernisation only occurred as a result of New English conquest and colonisation.

Yet "by the 1540s, the majority of Ireland's export trade to England consisted not of fish and hides, as generally assumed, but of manufactured goods, a state of affairs that Ireland would not enjoy again until modern times." [154] Nor was this because of New English colonists (almost non-existent until the 1570s); "the factors driving these changes were rooted in the [already-existing] Irish economy and society." [155] So "despite the fragmented nature of their societies, economies, and the geographical isolation of their more western communities" [156] Anglo-Irish *communitas* was reinforced by sharing a material culture produced by this economy.

But these materials were in turn traded to the Gaelic-Irish whose goods often enabled Anglo-Irish economies in the first place. Inter-community trade had further knock-on effects, without and within Galway. Men surnamed Mág Fhloinn (McGlynn), Ó Bruadair (Broderick), le Poer (Power), Ó Coinne (Quinn), Lawless, Nolan, Moore, Ó Fallamhain (Fallon), Meskey, Begge (Small), appear in the town between the 1490s and 1550s. They are specified as becoming freemen, or noted as Galway merchants which implies being freemen. Eight surnames are Gaelic, all ten are of sub-lordship families. Between 1543-1554, Edmund Ó Bruadair, Cornell [Conchobair] Mesky, Nicholas Power, Denis [Donnchad?] Mág Fhloinn were sent to Bristol for apprenticeships, enabled because their fathers were Galway merchants. [155] How many others did so? As surviving records hint, as further research may demonstrate, in that era Galwegians ranged all over Atlantic Europe.

29 August 1539. *Deposition of Thomas Lynche of Ratcliffe in the parish of Stepney, mariner, born in Galway, aged about 36. This deponent has been a governor and master of ships for ten years, and has served in voyages from England to France, Flanders and Spain.*
14 March 1554. *Commission from William Howard, lord admiral, concerning certain goods claimed by Peter Marten, James Linche and Patrick Marten of Galway, merchants.*
30 April 1562. *Deposition of Diego de Galway of Galway, mariner, now living in Portugalete, born at Galway, aged about 23. That this deponent was hired for a voyage in the Sta Crux from Portugalete to London.* [157]

During the term of Mayor Dominick French (1568-69), there came an Italian traveller

> *to this town of Galway who observing the situation of the said town, the cut and manner of the building, and he being at mass in some house or other in the first year of the suppression who observing the sacrament as he was sitting at a window and boats coming and going on the river, and on the other side a ship coming with full sails, a salmon killed with a lance or spear and saw hunters chasing a deer, observing these things, alone, instantly said, in good faith, I travelled the best part of Christendom, and never saw such a sight as this is.* [158]

It was the best of times. And like any boon it could never last.

*Irish heads and English soldiers from John Derricke's 'The Image of Ireland', 1581, courtesy of Wikipedia Commons*

*Ceithern attacking a house from John Derricke's 'The Image of Ireland', 1581, courtesy of Wikipedia Commons*

# CHAPTER SIX – THE LONG WAR

## A Town of War

In April 1567, Lord Deputy of Ireland Sir Henry Sidney crossed the Shannon at Limerick and led a military force through Thomond into Connacht, reaching one of its few towns. Magnificent stone walls were from a distance impressive, giving the illusion of a prosperous community.

But within was devastation. Entire streets of houses and buildings were burned to the ground. Gardens and orchards were uprooted, destroyed. Even the friary and parish church had been deliberately desecrated, windows smashed, altars profaned. Remaining inhabitants looked like animals, beseeching him for salvation. Sir Henry was deeply shaken by the experience. In a letter written shortly after for the personal attention of Queen Elizabeth I, he described what he saw:

> I was offered a pitiful and lamentable present, namely the keys of the town, not as to receive them of me again as all others acustumably do, but for me still to keep, or otherwise dispose at my pleasure, in as much as they were so impoverished by the extortion of the lords about them, as they were no longer able to keep that town.
>
> The town is large and well walled, and it appears by matter of record there had been in it three hundred good householders, and since I knew this land, there was twenty, and now I find but fewer, and they poor, and, as I write, ready to leave the place. The cry and lamentation of the poor people was great and pitiful, and nothing but thus "succour, succour, succour. [1]

This was Athenry. It was what the Galwegians feared their own town would yet be. Galway had held out, so far, but the previously busy merchant town now

> resemble[d] a town of war frontiering upon an enemy ... They watch their walls nightly, and guard their gates daily with armed men. They complained much of the wars of Mac William Íochtar, and Ó Flaithbertaigh, against the Earl of Clanricard, but, most of all, of the Earl of Clanricard's two sons, which he hath by two wives, and both alive, and these two young boys in the life of their father, yet likely long to live, do strive who shall be their father's heir, and in the same strife, commit no small spoils and damage to the country. [2]

## An age of atrocity

Four hundred years later, historians view early sixteenth-century Ireland as the crucible to an age of atrocity. [3] Despite thousands of casualties at Knockdoe in 1504, such large-scale battles were exceptional. Skirmishes, raids, and short-term guerilla warfare were the Irish norm, violence no more endemic to Ireland than any other region in late medieval/early modern Europe. The advent of the Tudor dynasty coincided with the apex of the FitzGerald earls of Kildare, who dominated fifteenth and early sixteenth century Ireland. A mutually beneficial relationship ensured a politically stable era from 1496, leading to an economic boon. So what went so wrong?

One reason given is the deaths, c. 1511-20, of long-reigned rulers in both major Irish nations, succeeded by *too many Caesars*. It's an attractive idea; too many wrathful globes in a single orbit, against which the centre could not hold. It has a historical basis and played a role.

Another was the ever-increasing availability of artillery, firearms, and cheap Scots 'Redshank' mercenaries during the 1520s (Scottish emigration to Ireland was continuous and distinct from English enterprises). Larger private armies funded by the greater lords - Kildare, Ormond, Desmond, Mac Carthaigh, Ó Briain, Ó Domhnaill, Ó Neill - threatened to recreate *ina fód crithaigh* of the 1140s. Men who needed few lessons in coercion, their brutality should not be underestimated, nor the responses they provoked. This too played its part.

Yet the decisive factor was King Henry VIII's introduction of large, well-armed military forces from England, Cornwall, and Wales to conquer Ireland and make it English.

Unable to act on a wider European stage because England was barely a second-rate power, Henry indulged in fickle schemes and personal extravagances that regularly beggared it. Glorious in retrospect he was a living terror to his subjects, despised by many, feared by all.

Inheriting a realm with great fiscal wealth in 1509, on his death in 1547 England and Wales was politically unstable, religiously traumatised, and bankrupt (again). Coinage was debased, inflation high, the middle-classes forced into austerity, the lower-classes starved. A pariah realm on course for failed state status, Henry's legacy was judicial abuse, social destruction, inconsistent internal and external policies, topped off with staggering economic and military incompetence.

All in all King Henry VIII was one of England's worst monarchs ever.

One view holds that as his physical health worsened, Henry became more brutal in his exercise of power; indeed royal *tighearnais* remained an undiminished prerogative. Trapped in a severely deteriorating body that from 1528 caused ever-increasing physical and mental anguish, he vented in the only way left to him. But this is an excuse; he was ever a tyrant, driven by impulse and ego.

Because ambitions of making France English were no longer practical, more attention was paid to less glamorous local lordships. The notion that all Britain was under English high-kingship dated at least to Athelred's claim in 927 to be *rex totius Britanniae* ('King of all Britain'), while in the 980s ealdorman Athelweard claimed that Britain was merely Greater England ("ideoque Brittania nunc Anglia appelatur, assumens nomen victorum/in this way Britannia was now known as Anglia, as it took the name of the victors"). These House of Wessex ideas - of kingship if not kingdoms - were inherited by their various successors, actively so by Édouard I. It was made explicit in 1417 when, confusing geography with ethnicity, the English specifically included the Britons and Wales as "part of the English nation, alias British" ('inclyta natio Anglicana alias Brytannica'). They also stated on the same basis that Ireland's "four provinces ... are recognized parts of the English nation." [4]

Thus the English political realm was Britain, the English *The* British, and as the English were in Ireland then all the isles were British.

If France could no longer be the jewel in an English crown, as Scotland remained fiercely independent, then needs must fashion an imperial sceptre from the Irish isle. So this Catholic king and his dynasty imposed its grip on Ireland like none before it. As David Edwards remarked:

> [In 1534 King Henry VIII] abandoned his dependence on the great rival Anglo-Irish affinities and despatched a force of 2,300 English soldiers ... it was the harbinger of more than a century of direct rule from Whitehall ... and signalled the establishment of a permanent English garrison, or army of occupation, something that was destined to become a key component of English rule in Ireland ... [5]

On 18 June 1541 at Dublin, in a bill presented as Gaeilge and English, King Henry VIII upgraded his status from Lord of Ireland to King of Ireland (remaining VIII, not I). For the first time, the Gaelic-Irish were enabled under English law. [6]

But in removing power from regional and local lords, civilized men such as Sir Henry Sidney used methods that were barbaric. Sanctioned state terror saw "prisoners ... routinely executed, torture ... widely used, civilians [including women, children, and infants] routinely murdered", and the almost casual use of massacres. [7] Social restraints that held within England were unbound outside it. English aggression, amid already serious destabilisation, kept escalating violence to levels previously unknown in either isle. Deliberate English tactics included ethnic cleansing and mass head-hunting that decapitated "fathers, brothers, children, kinfolk and friends".[8]

And for the first time in centuries, religion was divisive. Divisions between Christian denominations of Protestant and Catholic, uncomprehended in Ireland into the 1540s, acquired importance by the 1560s. This trend accelerated in successive decades as Reformation and Counter-Reformation split Irish political, ethnic, and familial identities. [9]

Not only the people suffered. Ireland had an architectural and literate heritage that thrived after the destruction of the Roman Empire, survived wars of vikings, Irish, Normans, Scots. But in acts of deliberate cultural vandalism, they were targeted and destroyed by "the ruthless and systematic assault on Irish societ[ies] and culture[s] by the English government in the sixteenth and seventeenth centuries." [10]

Ireland was underdeveloped and its peoples crude - so was every region and folk in Europe. But while persuasive cases have been made for Irish barbarity none have demonstrated it was perpetual. Irish history shows otherwise. All human cultures become similar civilizations, with 'barbarian' cultures every bit as complex as 'civil' societies. But for about the fourth time in a thousand years, Ireland underwent tremendous cultural shift, and a political enforcement which constrained her nations' abilities to set their own pace of development.

Differences of identity based on ethnicity, denominations, languages, cultures, and geographies, all enhanced hostilities. Irish alliances with anti-English Catholic powers such as France and Spain fostered hate - Henry's European pretensions and papal disputes meant the French and Spanish were willing to assist such Irishmen. This in turn had a further knock-on effect on English policy. All combined to make the English view the Irish as their 'primitive' *Other* and had a huge impact on the subsequent creation of the Anglo-British nation-state.

This was the bleakest of ironies, given the Irish role in making the Angelcynn literate Christians. But it excused viewing the Irish as savages akin to the American First Nations. Understandably, some historians see Ireland as imperial ground zero as several colonizers in English America first saw service in Ireland and its Plantations. Yet this can be a superficial view. The model was used far more sharply by colonial states in the Americas; English colonists were much more acculturated by Irish contacts than with Americans; the Irish and their cultures survived. [11]

And English military units always had fighting Irish. Numbering at least a third to as much as half of England's forces in Ireland during the sixteenth-century, they were an absolute necessity as then English, Cornish, and Welsh populations - some two millions - never had enough professional mercenaries or conscripted musket fodder for any Charley's war. Bonds of comradeship by military companies in victory and adversity, and ties of loyalty to their lord, all over-rode national sentiments. Future imperial armies were overwhelmingly of non-English, non-British peoples. Irish served from beginning to end. [12]

Like all brutally powerful men, Henry VIII ruled through tyranny. No slight to his authority could go unpunished; *oft sceall eorl monig anes willan wraec adreogan*. In 1536 the English commons revolted against his repression in Lincolnshire, Yorkshire, and Cumbria. Two hundred died fighting in Yorkshire, while hundreds were massacred at Carlisle. To discourage others, over seventy Cumbrians were hung in chains, dying cruelly slow. [13]

Yet it was in Ireland that King Henry VIII truly unleashed his wardogs, treating it as a 'strange realm'. The 1534-35 FitzGerald rebellion - which included some New English ethnic cleansing - was met with scorched earth tactics and indiscriminate mass murder. Calculated massacres occurred not only of prisoners who surrendered in good faith, but servants, peasants, women, and children, resulting in several hundred civilian deaths alone. Against the English-speaking *Anglo-Irish*.

Obedience in Ireland was to be enforced through state-sponsored terrorism and tyranny. It set English policy in Ireland for the next four centuries. [14]

Foreign adventures in exploitation always have horrific results, imperialism no more than ruling stupidly at home and brutally abroad. Henry's VIII's intervention began decades-long wars of terror in an on-going, mismanaged, blundering conquest. English, Cornish, and Welsh butchery begat Irish brutality. Caught in between were non-combatants who cared little for either but were devoured by both. 'Lesser' crimes such as rape and cruelty to children certainly increased, as they always do. Entire regions were abandoned, left to raiders and the wolves.

And in successive generations matters went from bad, to worse, to horror. By 1560, warfare replaced the plague as the prime morbidity factor, English scorched-earth tactics creating famines even in the heart of the Pale. Violence maimed victims and brutalised perpetrators. Generations went from the cradle to the grave without knowing sustained civic peace, only the troubled norm of extreme violence. It was this environment, which had no parallel in the two realms of the British isle, that saw Athenry destroyed and Galway threatened, time and time again.

## Cogaigh meic an Iarla

The Galway region was from c. 1565 to 1583 dominated by the meic an Iarla wars. The *meic an Iarla* ('sons of the Earl') were the half-brothers Uilleag and John a Búrc, sons of Ricárd *Sassanach* ('the Saxon [English]'), 2nd Earl of Clanricard. It was they that Sir Henry described as striving to "be their father's heir, and in the same strife, commit no small spoils and damage to the country." [15]

The cause was the succession to the earldom. John was the product of a valid marriage under Gaelic law, and his father's choice of heir. But the earldom was an English grant and under English law the marriage of John's parents was illegal, making him illegitimate and so ineligible to become earl. John refused to recognise this or cede any ground to Uilleag, who likewise used any means necessary to undermine his brother. Thus the two were as likely to fight each other as their enemies.

The conflict occurred against a backdrop of ever encroaching English government over the entire island. The meic an Iarla used the conflicts of loyalist versus rebel, Gaeil versus Gaill, Irish versus English, Catholic verses Protestant, purely for their own ends. Events proved neither faith nor fatherland mattered to them, only personal power. And power has no ethics.

## "A perpetrator of destruction": William Óge Martyn

By January 1570, Sir Edward Fitton had been appointed Lord President of Connacht, and a large swathe of land either side of the Gaillimh was for the first time designated *County Galway*. A letter in the Irish State Papers describes Connacht at the time:

> *quiet, but not as civil as might be desired. The common people now desire justice against the great. There have been sessions, assemblies and good appearances of freeholders and jurors. There is now no want of justice. Some notorious rebels have been executed and others have been saved by benefit of clergy.*
> *Everyone in Connacht is now afraid of the laws, and they are submitting to Fitton, sending over great sums of money and keeping the peace. They are ready to answer when called for, and they have made lists of all the men under them. A provost-marshal has been appointed to capture those who will not submit.* [16]

The provost marshal was William Óge Martyn, named after his grandfather Wylliam, Mayor 1519-20. His parents, Thomas Óge Martin and Evelin Linche, built the West Mills and West Gate in 1562. [17] It was a sign of the times that their son did no such worthy civic labours. Instead - uniquely among the Galwegians - Martyn was a brutal paramilitary enforcer of English martial law.

Unlike a sheriff, tied to the rule of law and trial by jury, a provost marshal could terrorise a population into obedience and not be held lawfully accountable. A blunt instrument, Martyn was a feared appointee of the President of Connacht, whose broad discretionary powers allowed such agents useful leeway in 'dispatching' rebels and lawbreakers, or people simply suspected of such.   The marshal was responsible for the welfare of hostages, was granted financial aid from trade in hides, and from cattle seized from the town's enemies. All incentives to prosecute his terms of office to the fullest extent. [18]

All available evidence indicates William Óge Martyn was very good at his job.

## Warfare

On 21 December 1569 Athenry was again attacked, by Mathghamhain Ó Briain who took five hundred kine and two prisoners into Thomond. [19] On 18 January 1570, Martyn, his force of four horsemen and a *ceithearn* ('battle-troop', anglicised as 'kern') of fifty to sixty *ceithearnach*, accompanied Sir Edward Fitton, the 2nd Earl of Clanricard, and their forces to meet the 3rd Earl of Thomond "to seek restitution." They arrived in Ennis on 22 January, greeted by Sir Domnaill Ó Briain, but not Thomond. [20]

No provision had been made for their arrival, joined there by a Captain Apsley and "36 horsemen from Munster" [21] so the large group foraged and cessed upon locals. The following day the Earl of Thomond arrived but "would not remain." [22] Martyn "was sent after him, but Thomond said he would not come unless Clanricard came to fetch him, which they would not agree to." [23]   Instead, Thomond killed a man and kidnapped Martyn, Sir Domnaill, and Captain Apsley. [24] Fitton and his men had to retreat, skirmishing with and harried by "about 300 of Thomond's ceithearnach and gallóclaigh, and about 30 horsemen" [25] all the way back to Galway. Thomond refused to exchange Martyn, instead sending a letter to the Mayor and burgesses of Galway, inciting "them to mislike Fitton." [26]

Due to the forceful intercession of the 10th Earl of Ormond, Thomond "set at liberty ... the President's prisoners", [27] including Martyn. During the summer, Martyn accompanied a large force led by Fitton across the county to fight Mac William Íochtar. They were joined, in a show of support, by Clanricard himself, "although many of Clanricard's men deserted." [28] On 8 July 1570 Fitton brought his forces to Shrule, "the key to Íochtar Connacht." An initial attack before duskus was unsuccessful, the only result being the loss of some men. During the night, the castle garrison attempted to escape but were caught and killed. "The rebels ... attempted to regain the castle but in a hard fight were defeated ... about 400 of them [were killed] including Walter Burke, and 10 or 11 of their chief leaders ...", with Fitton losing some seventy-two men. [29]

## Athenry 'desolate and destroyed'

Amid this warfare, no one appeared to be concerned for the people of Athenry except Gregory Bodkin, brother of the Archbishop of Tuam. A list of *Extraordinary payments* in March-June 1572 by Lord Deputy Fitzwilliam notes that the then considerable sum of twenty pounds was awarded to Bodkin. [30] Fitzwilliam noted underneath that "This was given upon his offer to keep Athenry's walls from razing after the earl of Clanricard's sons had been in the town." [31]

How many of Athenry's population were still alive to benefit from the aid is not recorded. The *duibhchíos* ([extortion or illegal] 'tax') and years of violence by the Clanricards had forced the meic Fheorais (de Berminghams) to leave Athenry and relocate to their Miltown and Dunmore estates. To add injury to injury, Athenry had again been raided that February by septs of the Uí

Bhriain (O'Brians) and Meic Suibhne (MacSweeneys), Clanricard allowing them unhindered access across his lands. [32] Gregory Bodkin did not confine his solicitations to the Lord Deputy. The President of Connacht found himself moved by his efforts, describing him as

> Gregory Bodkin, late alderman and freeman of the now desolate and destroyed town of Athenry ... He is entrusted by his neighbours of that corporation (dispersed in several places) to follow their complaint against the rebels and destroyers of the town. He has been in Dublin since before I last came to England and yet tells me he has had small comfort. ... He has moved me to commend him to you. A more charitable deed could not be done than to refresh those miserable souls in the recovery of their right, not only of goods but to their dwellings in the ancient walled town. [33]

His efforts brought him to Dublin, only for him to be caught up in a murder trial when one of Fitton's servants was stabbed to death in Castle Street. [34] Yet it did result in the likes of the Bishop of Meath aiding Bodkin to rebuild Athenry:

> Hugh Brady, bishop of Meath and John Garvey to Burghley 26 March 1574. In favour of the suits of this poor man, Gregory Bodkin, factor for the desolate town of Athenry for himself and for Athenry so that these few of so great a number that famine and misery has not consumed may by your good means be relieved. The earl and his sons are so far off from helping them as rather is their whole care and bent to bring the town of Galway to the same state of Athenry ... we fear great mischief to follow. [35]

However, Bodkin's efforts only resulted in personal impoverishment, being forced in Dublin to "beg alms and charity of good people." [36] Another letter by Fitton to Burghley (dated 27 March 1574) stated that Bodkin "has moved me and indeed, my own conscience moves me to do my best to further the restoration of that corporation." [37] But nothing could be done while conflict continued, leading Fitton to ominously conclude that "There is no way to man any part of Ireland but one which is force and extremity." [38]

## Intrigues, losses, appeals

Nor were some Galwegians helping matters. Some were too close to local warlords. Nicholas Lynch was a foster-brother of Clanricard, and arranged for the meic an Iarla to break out from internment at Galway jail; for this he was censured by the furious town council. [39] His father, Stephen fitz Arthur, was given custody of their sister Mary a Búrc, only for her to escape and join her brother John. [40] President Fitton confined Stephen and his daughter-in-law, Juliana Martin, "to the custody of the Mayor"; another Lynch son was held by Provost Marshal Martyn. [41]

For others, friendship with the great was unrewarding. Dominick Browne of Athenry was admitted as a freeman of Galway on 29 July 1541, and was Mayor 1575-76. [42] He made a home at Barna, indicative of his relationship with Murchad na dTuagh Ó Flaithbeartaigh - Browne's wife, Onora, was said to be a daughter of Ó Flaithbertaigh. [43] One of Galway's richest merchants,

Browne had cultivated a close friendship with Clanricard, but during his term as Mayor, grimly related its bitter fruits:

> The loss I sustained by the spoil of Athenry for the whole is generally destroyed and spoiled. For all my good will towards the earl, my poor tenants and servants were more extremely used than others. Not one penny was saved of all I had in Athenry. Our marchers and neighbours from the highest to the lowest do spoil our poor tenants almost within a quarter of a mile of the town [Galway] so as we can have no manner of provision out of the country and must live like a ward except you prevent this mischief. [44]

Such seige-like conditions did not abate. Mayor Piers Lynch wrote on 13 November 1573:

> A merchant named Geoffrey Fonnt was murdered within a mile of Galway by Johnocke and Redmund Reagh of the wood hard beside them. They being followers and servants to the earl of Clanricard and two more of our men were apprehended and taken also. So that no kind of victuals, provision nor wares can come or pass from Galway but it is spoiled and taken by the highway by the inhabitants of Clanricard. The most part of our tithes and provision detained and kept from us. What avails it to send men without victuals or munition since we have no store for ourselves? [45]

Lynch wrote that the Munster rebels, James Fitzmaurice and Sir John of Desmond had, along with lords such as Murchad na dTuadh and the Mac William Íochtar, all conferred with Clanricard. "What their intent was we know not but we are sure it was for no goodness." In a later letter he appealed to Fitzwilliam and the Irish Privy council, complaining of their "great want of grain, powder, munition", stating that

> No town nor place in Ireland endures more sufferance of our neighbours. On all sides we are tossed and turmoiled by them in such sort that none dares to resort to and from us. We see no hope of quietness whereby there is no mean in us to send any money with our agent for corn. We, therefore, beseech you to tender our urgent need and to provide for us speedily either by corn itself or by money for having the same in England. [46]

As appeals for charity clearly did not suffice, Mayor Lynch invoked political realism:

> We trust you will consider how we and our ancestors have done hitherto in defending this place. The loss of Galway would be more in the prince's way that of Knockfergus [Carrickfergus] and divers other places which you daily furnish with great sums of victuals, money and munition. Galway is the only stay, fortress and chamber the queen has in the province of Connacht. [47]

## The Lord Deputy revisits

In March 1576 Sir Henry Sidney, reappointed Lord Deputy, reached Galway and found it worse than his previous visit nearly ten years earlier:

> The town of Galway [was] much decayed, both in number of expert sage men of years, and younger men of war, in respect of that I have seen, which great decay has grown through the horrible spoil done upon them by the sons of the Earl of Clanricard, in so much as it was evidently proved before me, that fifty householders of the town do now inhabit under Mac William Íochtar. And it seems, they have not only lost their wealth, but with it their wits and harts; surely it may well seem they were in point to have given up all, and almost to have forgotten that they are received any corporation of the Crown. [48]

Sidney suborned the meic an Iarla, who endured a fierce sermon in St. Nicholas's by Reverend Roland Lynch, a Protestant *preacher in three tongues, Irish, English, and Latin*. [49] But in June they attacked and burned what was left of Athenry, and seized Claregalway. [50] Matters grew so dire within Galway that Mayor Dominick Browne wrote to Lord Deputy Sidney for "license to obtain some [grain] from the rebels." [51] Clanricard asked Browne to send Nicholas and Dominick Lynch, "to the Deputy to induce him to a reconciliation." But the meic an Iarla escaped east over the Shannon, having "set the new gates of Athenry on fire, and beaten away the masons." [52]

Clanricard met Lord Deputy Sidney who arrested him and seized his castle of Loughrea. Sidney saw Clanricard as his sons' aider, and implored Queen Elizabeth to seize the dynasty, else there would never be peace. [53] News of their father's imprisonment enraged and induced the sons to rise all Connacht. A terrible war of fire and sword ensued, in which neither side spared anyone. Not until September 1578 was Connacht re-pacified, only to see warfare re-erupt in the summer of 1579 with the Desmond Rebellion in Munster. The meic an Iarla happily joined in. When the rebellion faltered, the meic an Iarla cut their losses and arrived in Galway to submit. [54]

## The Dread Pirate Ní Mháille

William Óge Martyn was by then dealing with a truly notorious rebel, the pirate Gráinne Ní Mháille, aka *Granuaile*. Astonishingly for a chauvinistic society, she gained tighearnais of the Fir Umall. Tellingly, she is invisible in 'official' Gaelic sources, recalled only in folklore and English sources. Lethally independent, a storm-seasoned sailor and mother of three, Ní Mháille

> was so determined and persevering in her hostility to the English, and committed so many acts of depredation, that it was found necessary, in 1579, to send a body of troops from Galway, under the command of Capt. William Martin, to besiege her romantic and impregnable castle of Carrick a Uile, near Newport, in the county of Mayo.
> This expedition sailed from Galway on the 8th March, but so spirited was the defence made by this extraordinary woman, that they were obliged to retreat on the 26th of the same month, and very narrowly escaped being made prisoners – a circumstance which

*The Gallows Pole on the Green, now Eyre Square, Courtesy of NUI, Galway*

would have attended with the instant death of the entire. [55]

Predators such as Ní Mháille and her comrade in crime, the Afro-Iberian corsair Don Alonzo Bosco, regularly hijacked ships departing from or sailing to Galway. Their long-time naval allies, Clann Teige Uí Briain of Árann, had been overthrown by Murchad na dTuadh. While he was personally friendly to the merchants - more or less - many other Uí Fhlaithbeartaigh remained utterly ferocious. [56]

## Gallows pole

In summer 1580, the meic an Iarla were at peace with the government but at war with each other. John forced terms on Uilleag by kidnapping his eldest surviving son, six-year old Ricárd, and

> They first demolished the castle of Loughrea, the principal fortress of the territory; and they scarcely left a castle from Clonfert-Brendan, in the east of the territory of Síl-Anmchadha, to Kilmacduagh, in the north of Cinel-Aedha-na-hEchtge, and from Uaran to Cluain-da-damh, which they did not demolish. [57]

Uilleag withdrew in October only for John to be joined by their teenage brother, Uilliam, who wished to soak his hands in Protestant blood. [58] They proclaimed themselves "the Pope's men", saying "that all priests shall say mass or lose their heads, and that the churches shall be burned." [59]   A long winter's terrorism ensued. By March 1581, the meic an Iarla were "ready to starve" and so tried to make terms, Uilliam Búrc excusing his actions on his "youthfulness". [60] In April, Búrc, his foster-father Shane Wall, and Toirdhealbhach Ó Briain of Fomerla (a brother of the 3rd Earl of Thomond), submitted but were captured by William Óge Martyn. Nine of Búrc's men were hanged. [61] Búrc, Wall, and Ó Briain were tried. By June they were found guilty and sentenced to be hanged, but Mayor Dominick Lynch, Clanricard's friend, effected their reprieve. The town archives tell what happened next:

> William Burke younger son to Richard earl of Clanricard, and the earl of Thomond's younger son being apprehended near Galway were hanged by the King's wall by one William Martin marshal as being rebels against the crown. In the time the mayor brought home their pardons; notwithstanding this this William did prevent its coming. [62]

The contemporary entry in the Annala Loch Cé contains more detail:

> The Earl of Clann-Rickard's son, i.e. William Burk, went to Gaillimh to make peace with the Foreigners, on the engagement and guarantees of the Mayor, and of the town besides; and there was within before him a perpetrator of injury and destruction upon the Clann-Rickard, i.e. William Og Martin ("ocus do bí roimhe astigh fer uilc ocus urbhuidhe do dhenamh ar cloinn Ricaird .i. Uilliam Og Mairtín"), and two bands of soldiers along with him.
> And after the Earl's son went in, William Martin and the Saxons acted treacherously towards him; and they apprehended himself; and nine of his people were hanged, and he himself was put in prison, in despite of the mayor, and of the town. And not long after that the Earl's son, and Toirdhelbhach, the son of Donnchadh O'Briain, were hanged; and on Corpus Christi the Earl's son was hanged, O'Briain's son was hanged on the morrow. [63]

Within Galway there was outrage, both at the illegality of the hangings and by those who had guaranteed their safety. Yet Martyn appears unrepentant, while his superior, Sir Nicholas Malby, openly acknowledged his refusal of a thousand pounds for Ó Briain's life. [64] *Wm. Martyn of Gallaway*, gent[leman], was granted a pardon in July 1581 "upon the recommendation of Sir N. Malby." [65] The following year, a commission was given to "William Martene, sheriff of the County Galway ... to execute marital law in the county." [66] He must have been terrorisingly thorough because in April 1584 he was one of over eighteen state officers pardoned for offences committed in the course of their duties. [67] Even an accusation "Against William Martyn Oage merchant of Galway and gaoler of certain prisoners" by government agent, Barnaby Gooche, achieved nothing. Certainly it didn't prevent Martyn being granted lands in recognition of his government service. [68]

Given his association with Sir Richard Bingham, Martyn may have had some role in Bingham's January 1586 session at Galway, which saw the executions of "Seventy men and women." Martyn may have likewise participated in Bingham's notorious activities that year, which included the massacres of "women, boys, peasants, and decrepit persons" in Iar Connacht, and the mass slaughter of all the defenders of Cluain Dubhain Castle in Thomond, who surrendered in good faith.

He certainly had a role in a Galway session of December 1586, where "many women and men were put to death." [69] Because in September, William Óge reached the peak of civic achievement when he was elected Mayor of Galway. His signature - *William Martyn, Mayor* - appears in the Corporation Book more often than any other first citizen of Galway, before or after. [70]

## Grey merchants, black markets

Both the town in general, and the merchants in particular, were penurized by this near-ceaseless warfare. The grey merchant network could no longer easily access the raw materials needed both to live and to export. Wealthy families got by, lesser ones were squeezed out. When any community is unable to access general commerce, they will create their own, licit or otherwise. Some turned to black market trade in guns and munitions with the Gaelic-Irish, specifically forbidden by the 1517 statutes. The English were unhappy about this, but the merchants justified it by 'whataboutery', noting the English illegally profited from their posts (their irregular pay was partly to blame). [71] Galway's troubles went on, and on.

## Political and fraternal settlements

On the death of their father in July 1582, John and Uilleag "impugn[ed] and oppose[d] each other." [72] As a consolation for not becoming Earl, the title and barony of Leitrim was awarded to John on 30 April 1583. [73] The 3rd Earl of Clanricard and Lord Leitrim were described as having "Their other lands, towns, and church livings, ... accordingly divided between them, so that they were publicly at peace, but privately at strife." [74] The fraternal hate ended on 11 November 1583. Earl Uilleag led an night assault on Ballyfintan Castle, seven miles east of Loughrea, murdering John. Irony of ironies, Lord Leitrim was buried in Athenry friary, which he had once burned when his mother was newly buried in it. [75] Fifty years later, the *Annals of the*

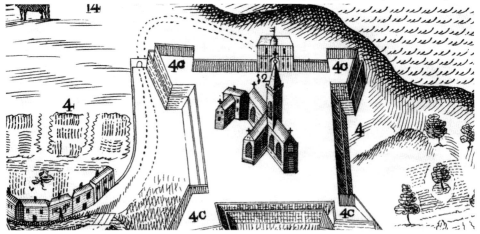

*St. Augustine's on the Hill, now Fort Hill, Courtesy of NUI, Galway*

*Four Masters* treated him as a patriot, improbably lamenting

> The death of this good man ... on account of his good sense, his personal form, his noble birth, his hospitality, his nobleness, and his renowned achievements. [76]

A contemporary, more cynical commentator, wrote of John that

> He ... did ever thirst after blood. He was a common haunter of women, and men say he had a child by his own sister, and a great maintainer of thieves he was. [77]

His family went to exile as mercenaries, eventually disappearing into obscurity in the Spanish Netherlands. [78] Few within Athenry or Galway could have been sorry to see them go. Having got what he wanted, Earl Uilleag mac an Iarla a Búrc remained the Queen's loyal subject, successfully transitioning from rebel warlord to loyal landlord. For the rest of his life, he willingly slaughtered and executed her Majesty's enemies, even (especially?) other Búrca. His heir, Ricárd, Lord Dunkellin, was educated and raised at Queen Elizabeth's court. The family's pragmatic conversion is illuminated by a letter of 1599, in which Dunkellin wrote:

> Ireland shall not long lodge me. All the fortune this land can afford me cannot make me disloyal to Her Majesty, nor a stranger to my worthy friends in England. [79]

## Executions at St. Augustine's

For a time, there was peace. But it was just a ceasefire between battles. In 1585, war broke out between England and Spain. In 1588, Felipe II King of Spain (d. 1598) sent a great armada to conquer England and re-instate the Catholic faith. Events conspired to send it around the coasts of Britain and Ireland. At least twenty ships were wrecked, some six thousand men drowned.

Survivors met varied fates. The dreaded Uí Mháille stripped and killed dozens, [80] while the English foster-brothers of the Protestant 2nd Earl of Tyrone massacred over three hundred. [81] One hundred and fifty Spanish who escaped were humanely sheltered by Bishop of Derry Réamonn Ó Gallchobhair, who arranged their passage to Scotland (proving the gods let no good deed go unpunished, Ó Gallchobhair was murdered in 1601, possibly with Ó Domhnaill connivance). [82]

Hearing of survivors in coastal Connacht, Lord Deputy Fitzwilliam made his way to Galway, arriving in June 1589. [83] He demanded that Mayor Andrew Morris, the recently-knighted Murchad na dTuadh, and Mac Uilliam Íochtar, hand over all Armada survivors. Said to be some two hundred in number, they were taken to St. Augustine's monastery and beheaded. The women of the town carefully wrapped the bodies in fine linen before burial in the monastic cemetery. Only two, hidden in the town, eventually escaped. [84]

## In secret service: James Blake

In Cuan Umhaill (Clew Bay), one Armada ship was wrecked in mid-September. It was plundered by *James Blake and others*, who took "a boat-full of treasure out of the ship." [85]

Thus does Galway's own international man of mystery enter the stage. Blake was a younger brother of Valentine Blake, with a wife and family of his own. [86] In the years ahead, his bewildering shift of alliances made many a spymaster's head ache, precisely because he was not a dedicated spy but a free agent. It is difficult to discern any political or religious motives behind his intrigues; as with so many, the great game was the thrill. Like his contemporaries in secret service, Blake lived most intensely in the shadow theatre. What sets him apart from many, including the handful of other known Galway intelligencers, was the scale and quality of high-level contacts he had - or claimed to have - on all sides. Apparently a very charismatic geidimín, he was described by one who knew him as

> *a traveller the most part of his life, and professes arms, having had charge both by land and sea ...*
> *he is a good linguist, witty and courageous enough to preform anything that he takes in hand,*
> *though utterly without any grounds of art, saving what he has gotten by long experience abroad.*
> [87]

Blake charmed Don Alonzo de Leva, whose ship, the *Duquesa Santa Ana*, was stranded off Tir Connell. Don Alonzo gave Blake letters of recommendation for King Felipe. When Blake turned up at court (Don Alonzo drowned in the interim), Felipe received him cordially, as "the Spaniards have great hopes to get the town of Galway through the means of the said James Blake." [88]

## Men of War, Men of Peace

While Blake was diverting himself in Spain, Galway's communities were strained by further disturbances within and without. Everything from victualling to religion created tension between the garrison and the townspeople, who were ostensibly on the same side. Winter 1589/90 saw the rebellion of Meic Uilliam Íochtar Búrca, Clann Seoige, Uí Fhlaithbeartaigh, Uí Mháille, Meic Muiris, and other septs. [89] In order to end the disturbances, a commission travelled west comprising of the Protestant bishops of Meath and Kilmore, Sir Robert Dillon, Sir Nicholas White, and Sir Thomas Lestrange. They were greeted at Galway by the Chief Commissioner and former Governor of Connacht, Sir Richard Bingham, who had much to say of the perfidious Gael. [90] The commissioners, however, learned all was not as black and white as Bingham had portrayed:

> *Great complaints were made of the abuses of the soldiers, that ordinarily they took meat, drink, and*
> *money, notwithstanding the covenants of the late composition. Sir Richard was very impatient in*
> *the matter, defended the soldiers, and said it could not be otherwise.* [91]

The commissioners principal source was Galway merchant, Robuck French. A son of Seán an tSalainn, he was elected Mayor for the term 1582-83 and responsible for a serious corporation quarrel that year. Apparently, he wished to see one of his sons, Edmond, made a bailiff. Several aldermen vehemently disagreed with this, to the point that Sir Nicholas Malby had to bind all concerned to the peace, and station sixty of the garrison about the town to ensure they kept it. [92]

In May 1586, French was one of two Galwaymen who refused to ratify the Act of Attainder on the 15th Earl of Desmond, till certain legal matters were attended. [93] That same month, state correspondence observed that French was attempting to sue Clanricard for "such losses as by the late wars of the said Earl and his brother, the town of Galway sustained." [94] However, Clanricard was now such a valued subject that it was deemed best not to support such an action, as it might "thrust the said Earl into bad action." Previous crimes went unpunished for political expediency, Galwegian loyalty was sacrificed for the process of peace.

French was frank with Meath and Dillon, who lodged at his house, and gave them an account that differed greatly from Bingham's. According to French, Sir Murchad na dTuadh had swore

> by a solemn oath that his purpose never was to rebel against Her Majesty or to hurt any good subject, but that he had sustained great wrongs from the governor of the province, and therefore he desired a protection from the mayor and aldermen that he might come into the town and declare his griefs, that they might be signified to the Lord Deputy. [95]

But Gerald Comerford, an attorney and ally of Sir Richard Bingham

> dissuaded the Mayor from granting any such protection ... whereupon Sir Morough departed because he could not get a protection, which the mayor and aldermen durst not give for fear of Mr. Gerald Comerford. [96]

French's account was backed by the town recorder, Dominick Martin (like French, a Protestant), who said that the Mayor and aldermen feared that "if they had done so Sir Richard would have taken him out of their hands, and so they should have lost their credits."[97] Clearly, the prospect of Galway's principal Gaelic ally being imprisoned or even executed by Bingham was too unnerving to contemplate. The commissioners likewise found Comerford intolerant of the Irish, and "a man wholly addicted to feed Sir Richard's humour in all things, especially for prosecution of wars."[98]

Just how addicted was soon revealed. The rebels Uilleag a Búrc, Báitéar ne Mully a Búrc, and Robert Ó Máille, came to the town and lodged with French. Meath and Dillon departed for a conference with Bingham when members of the garrison attacked French's house

> forcibly striving to break open the door ... with their weapons prepared for their assistance. The door was kept within by Edmond French, son to Robuck, and the servants of the house. They that were in the hall above, especially Robuck himself ... looked out of the window, wherein there was no glass, and demanded the cause of that uproar, but they were by the soldiers in the street forced to

*shut the windows' ... the soldiers throwing great stones, so as they dared not look out. Ulick Burke,*
*Walter Ne Mully and Robert O'Malley, dismayed with this assault, prepared themselves with their*
*weapons to keep the hall.* [99]

Bloodshed was only averted when the soldiers, unable to break open the door, became bored and left. Bingham responded to the outrage by briefly imprisoning his brother Francis, and made excuses for the rest of the men instead of punishing them.

Na Búrcaigh and Ó Máille then revealed the real reason behind the recent turmoil. Sheriff of Mayo, John Brown of the Neal (from County Westmeath, unrelated to the Galway Brownes) and his deputy, Domnaill Ó Dálaigh, had committed "depredations and homicides" in Iorris. Killed by the meic Uilliam Íochtar Búrca, Brown was found to be carrying a "commission to prosecute them with fire and sword. Bingham and others wished to provoke them, start a war." [100]

Na Búrcaigh, Ó Máille, and French volunteered to bring in the principal leaders, namely Sir Murchad na dTuadh, Mac William Íochtar, and others. Nicholas Lynch, Clanricard's foster-brother, was ordered to accompany them, but failed to do so. [101] The rebels agreed to meet the commissioners, but utterly refused to come anywhere near Bingham. So the commissioners arranged to travel by boat a quarter of a mile up the Gaillimh to Martyn Lynch's 'new castle', where the peace conference would be held. Robuck French went before them "with 20 shot of his kinsfolk and some of our own trusty servants to hold the castle for us." [102]

The Newcastle conference was fraught with mistrust and angry accusations, yet mainly thanks to French, peace was secured. Bingham was furious at the outcome, most especially at French "for levying forces, as he termed it" but in actuality for preventing the war the English wanted. [103] The commissioners were fulsome in French's praise, stating "This Robuck we found a very good instrument to procure and further peace." [104] French knew Galway could not exist aloof from its neighbours. As a report said of Sir Murchad "We find him a very good neighbour and friend to Galway and without whose friendship indeed they could hardly live, both for fire and grass." [105]

As in all conflicts, what worth existed was found not on one side or the other but in between. Men like French and Sir Murchad, flawed as they were, were needed to cultivate relationships without which normal day-to-day life could not continue. Yet without conflict and war, Bingham and tyrants like him had no means to create the personal fortunes or tighearnais they desired. Therefore such relationships and communities had to be suborned, or destroyed.

## *"Ireland's Great Hurt": The Nine Year's War*

All local affairs paled upon the outbreak of what was later termed the Nine Year's War. Responding in kind to English aggression Aodh Mag Uidhir (Hugh McGuire) and Aodh Ruadh Ó Domhnaill (Red Hugh O'Donnell), lords of Fir Managh and Tir Connell, began the war in 1594. In 1595, they were publicly joined by its architect and supreme leader, 2nd Earl of Tyrone Aodh Ó Neill (Hugh O'Neill, 'the Great O'Neill'). Like other Gaelic-Irish and Anglo-Irish during the 1500s, the Ulster lords sought aid from the Empire of Spain on the grounds of a shared religious denomination and a common political enemy. England's foe was Ulster's friend.

The implications of the Spanish Inquisition in Ireland was unconsidered, as was the fact that Ireland would still be colonised. Anglicisation would be swapped for Castilisation - Gaelic culture was doomed to be Basqued amid Greater Spain. The alliance was opportunistic and expedient, dressed up by ideals and 'tradition'. Similarly unconsidered were the European consequences of making Ireland Spanish. As it was in her vital interests to prevent Spain becoming Europe's supreme power, France would have invaded Ireland. Not only would this in turn invite a massive English troop-surge, it would oblige Scotland, the Netherlands, Denmark and the German states to intervene in an escalating international domino effect. Such a conflict, involving multiple superpowers all fighting for various ends, would have utterly devastated Ireland. The Irish would have no independent exit strategy.

The Spanish viewed the Irish as pawns in a greater game. Like the Bruces, they used its insurgency as a quagmire to exhaust England, constraining English interventions in the Netherlands and their tentative expansion in the Americas, areas Spain saw as her 'backyard'.

Nor were the Ulster lords advocating Irish independence; unrestricted autonomous lordship was the issue. All they wanted was a monarch who barely interfered in their affairs and/or granted them more land and privileges. Like many Irish rulers, the Ulster lords wanted their monarch to be like the Pope - near in heart, but far away. To that end Ó Neill offered Ireland not only to Catholic Spain but to Protestant Scotland, and regularly negotiated with the English for terms during the war.

What was at first an orchestrated local rebellion spread nationally, till it became a serious action gaining intense attention all over Europe. It pushed England into financial ruin, saw successive Irish victories coupled with devastating English defeats, the complete destruction of the New English colony in Munster, and became alarmingly critical to England's already debatable survival as an independent Protestant state.

Never noted for any personal faith, Ó Neill (raised a Protestant) exploited Catholicism to gain support. Coercive tactics included pretending that Pope Pius VIII - who remained deeply suspicious of Ó Neill – would excommunicate those who did not join him. However the war was not seen in religious terms by all the Irish, plus Ó Neill's 'faith and fatherland' rhetoric fell very flat on Anglo-Irish and Gaelic-Irish penalised for active Catholicism when he had being safely Protestant.

Traditional Irish histories - often written by their partisans - portrays these lords as unselfish patriots fighting for faith, freedom, and Ireland. Given the terrible persecution the Irish had by then endured from the English - and would long continue to endure - such paragons were direly needed.

Yet the Ulster lords were aristocrats who held lordships via tyranny, and were personally hostile to each other. Those they should have protected they abused. To demonstrate his new-found piety, Ó Neill enforced celibacy among priests by whipping, branding, or mutilating their wives (the priests themselves were untouched). Each murdered and betrayed when expedient. Ó Neill used his wives and children as dynastic tools, disposed and derided when no longer useful. Ó Domhnaill murdered a four-year old nephew by beating his brains out. [106]

The Ulster lords most certainly did fight for Ireland - they craved it. But they cared little for the Irish. For them, 'Ireland'='Ulster'. Their world-view was aristocratic, in which their house of lords treated with each other and kept the commons firmly in their place. Contrary to popular belief and contemporary rhetoric, the lords had no concept of *res publica* ('the common good') towards Ireland's communities, only *mé féin*, only *ofermód*. Nobles at the apex of their society, they were autocrats as much as the meic an Iarla. And exactly like them, they were willing to use all means necessary to preserve and enhance their status. If that included the coercion and murder of their 'fellow' Irish, so be it. They would not be the last.

## The desolation of Athenry

It was at this point that James Blake, alias *Caddell*, alias *Blackcaddell*, reappears in official correspondence. A letter dated 13 August 1595 dryly comments "The matter of Captain Cadell of Galway may put the Spaniards out of taste with trusting to the Irish." [107] We can only wonder what devilment lay behind this comment; like every other industry, espionage generates its own inflation, at which Blake apparently excelled. By then he had made the acquaintance of Ó Neill, carrying his letters back and forth from abroad. Blake used this access to propose to the English "designs ... to take or cut off O Donnell, McWilliam, O Rourke, or O Neill himself."[108]

Ó Domhnaill was someone with whom much of Connacht had dealings, as he claimed overlordship of its northern districts. In January 1597, he led an army from Bréifne with his vassal, Mac Uilliam Íochtar (Ní Mháille's son, Tibbott ne Long a Búrc), till they arrived at Ballinasloe, from where

*he sent forth swift-moving marauding parties through the district of Caladh, and the upper part of*

St. Bridget's Hospital, Prospect Hill, Courtesy of NUI, Galway

the territory; and they carried off many herds of cows and other preys to O'Donnell, to the town of Athenry. [109]

The town warders defended their town, but gangs of Ó Domhnaill's followers fired the gates and climbed the walls with long ladders, leaping into the streets and opening the gates from within:

> They then proceeded to demolish the storehouses and the strong habitations; and they carried away all the goods and valuables that were in them. They remained that night in the town. It was not easy to enumerate or reckon the quantities of copper, iron, clothes, and habiliments, which they carried away from the town on the following day. From the same town he sent forth marauding parties. [110]

*Restored Shoemakers Tower, Eyre Square Centre*

Ó Domhnaill's marauders did their work well, plundering from Laragh to Moycola to Rathgorgin (areas held by Clanricard's Ó Dálaigh, Mac Suibhne, a Búrc, and Dolfin vassal lords), before moving west from Athenry - which they burned - to Maree and Rinville. [111] Everywhere they went they raided, raped, plundered, and burned, right up to the gates of Galway itself. Clanricard wrote from Loughrea that Ó Domhnaill's marauders "... will not leave any corn or cottage, within three days unburnt within the whole country." [112] In the middle of winter, destruction of food and shelter amounted to outright terrorism, and it succeeded.

## Galway stands

Galway became packed with refugees. Despite the hospital's military insignificance, Ó Domhnaill burned Tigh Brigde on Boher Mór, camping that night at Clogh an Lingsigh ('Lynch's rock') beside Loch an tSaile (Lough Atalia, 'saltwater lake'). The next day he rode to the town to parley. [113] Mayor Oliver Óge French heard Ó Domhnaill's 'requests'; entry to the town, "traffic and sale of their various wares and rich raiment for some of the preys" stolen from Athenry. French refused, upon which Ó Domhnaill began burning the east suburbs around An Fhaiche and Boher Mór, endangering the entire town and destroying homes of those who could least afford it. His forces grouped around St. Augustine's to attack Galway. [114]

Mayor French was having none of it, and gave leave to the garrison to open fire. From the top of the rampart about Shoemaker's Tower, cannon fire roared. An armed group issued forth from a postern gate, making straight for St. Augustine's and engaged with the northerners. Suffering casualties from the cannon fire, this attack demoralised Ó Domhnaill's forces, who withdrew with several dead and many wounded. Mayor French surely felt it nowhere near enough.

Ó Domhnaill retreated and destroyed every village in his path, stealing vast numbers of cattle and other goods. Observing the effects, Mayor French wrote to that Ó Domhnaill had "destroyed almost the whole county of Galway." [115] Winter was made that much harsher, and as a result many in counties Galway, Mayo, and Roscommon did not live to see spring.

Ó Domhnaill returned in late summer 1599. He sent a section of his army off to devastate County Mayo, killing several Meic Oisdealbhaigh (Costellos), Uí Mháille, and Meic Ghiobúin (Gibbons's). Travelling across County Galway to County Clare - attacking Athenry *en route* - he raided territories of the Uí Fhlannchadha (Flannerys), Uí Lochlainn (O'Lochlainns), Uí Chonchobair (O'Conors), Uí Dheádhaidh (O'Deas), Uí Ógáin (Hogans), Uí Ghríobhta (Griffins), and Uí Bhriain (O'Briens). Ó Domhnaill returned to north "with many preys, and spoils, and booty." [116]

## Hearts and Mines

By then, the situation within Galway was so bad the townsfolk sent their factor, John Lynch, to London seeking financial aid and food. Lynch had a blunt message for Lord Burghley; support Galway, or "The greatest part of the inhabitants will both starve and abandon the town." [117]

The longer the war lasted, the less likely victory seemed for the English, fighting on the cheap. Their treasury simply did not have the finances, which the often indecisive Queen in any case usually refused to spend. Yet Ó Neill could not secure all Ireland or continue the fight indefinitely even within Ulster - his lack of navy and an urban base was crucial. Only with considerable foreign aid could military victory be imposed, whereas Ó Neill wanted a political deal sealing his lordship.

But Spain had broader vital interests, European and global, such as securing the Netherlands, keeping the French and English out of the Americas, and conquering England - Felipe II had being King of England in the 1550s and wished to return it to the Catholic church. Ireland was never an end in itself to the Spanish but a tool in a greater game. Thus the Irish could be used, or sacrificed, as best suited Spanish needs. Ó Neill was given enough tactical support to continue fighting, but never enough for a decisive, strategic victory. [118]

Ó Neill understood many southern Irish were disaffected with English rule as enforced by tyrants like Bingham. He thought the rebellion and his own personal charisma would unite them, under his command. So he was genuinely shocked when Gael and Gall alike refused. [119]

Unlike Ó Néill, who owed his position in life to (a very dubious) aristocratic pedigree, Galway's merchants had to work for a living. They supported the crown not only because it was their communal tradition, but because it offered some protection against extortionate lords like Ó Néill. Few conflicts have a 'side' worth fighting for. Most chose self-interest over the 'right' or 'wrong' one. Ó Néill's war threatened to destroy their livelihoods, beggar their families, ruin their town. In ravaging Catholic communities in Ulster, Leinster, and Munster as Ó Domhnaill had in Connacht, both men made themselves 'great' on other folk's wounds. How then could support

*Tribes of Galway 1124-1642*

be expected?

The Galwegians had experienced generations of tyrants, and struggled to be independent of them all. Galway was a trade nexus between economic units, always open to predation. It had taken lifetimes to build up their town, businesses, and community. If they would not surrender to an Ó Flaithbheartaigh lord or a Clanricard earl, they would not do so for Ó Néill. He was appealing to hearts already burned.

Infuriated, a wrothful Ó Neill's sent James Blake to Spain, asking Felipe II for "great artillery, powder, and men to batter the towns." [120] They who could not be cajoled would be coerced.

## Infernal disputes

By September 1600, various Uí Mháille and Uí Fhlaithbheartaigh pirates seized Galway ships "which they have not only rifled to the utter overthrow of the owners and merchants, but also have most wickedly murdered divers of our young men, to the great terror of such as would willingly traffic." [121] This drove outgoing Mayor, Michael Lynch, to ask Sir Robert Cecil to have Captain James Blackcaddell, alias Blake, command two hundred foot-soldiers on land and sea

> to suppress ... these roving rebels, as also to prosecute the Joys [Clann Seoige] and other bad members, that keep upon Lough Corrib, where they let and hinder our town from firing timber and other necessaries. [122]

Lynch had evidently been very taken with Blake, who had retrieved - or being allowed to retrieve? - a ship laden with wine, stolen by some Uí Mháille the previous month. Captain Henry Clare of the town garrison was however distinctly unimpressed, describing Blake to the Privy Council as "a very dangerous man, having served the King of Spain, and been in rebellion with the said MacWilliam." [123] Worse, he was a Catholic, and very great in the town with the "most obstinate of that sort". [124] The new Mayor, Francis Martin, was Protestant, but his wife, Marie Lynch, was Catholic and so suspect to Clare. The Mayor in turn castigated Clare for bringing

> in amongst us certain Irish soldiers, people suspected, seized upon Her Highness's keys of this place, marched with his men in arms to our .... Townhouse .... five of his soldiers by direction from the said Clare ... have assaulted myself in person, bending their pikes to my breast, so as I escaped in great danger of my life, with a thousand other mischiefs and outrages committed by his solders. [125]

To "prevent all further mischief " Martin wanted Clare gone and Blake instead, he being "a man of experience, sufficiency, and wisdom." [126] This implied Clare had none of these qualities. A scandalised Captain Clare hit back in a letter dated 25 June 1601. Mayor Martin had misinformed the Privy Council, he said, and allowed into the town Ruaidrí mac Teige Ó Flaithbheartaigh, "a notable rebel" [127] with a body of men on condition that they "should be of dutiful behaviour." [128] These conditions were promptly broken. Mayor Martin subsequently conveyed Ó Flaithbheartaigh out a postern gate, in advance of his arrest, all without the consent of any aldermen. Clare reacted by

> *advising with the Recorder* [Dominick Martin] *and some of the best Aldermen of the town, purposed to have entreated the Corporation to take some order for the more safe keeping of the keys, because that the rebels of Iar Connacht (whom I found the Mayor to favour) were able to bring five hundred men within three hours to any gate of the town, and that myself had but mine own company only to keep the same;* [129]

Clare's letter described the Mayor as "mortally hating me", his wife being chief of the recusants, and "he himself a Protestant in show." [130] Appended was a Testament in Clare's favour from some townsmen and Aldermen, apparently including James Reagh Dorsey. It stated Clare's company had seized Moycullen and banished from it the Iar Connacht rebels, who prior to his arrival "were wont daily to spoil them at their very gates, to stay their fuel, and took their lives, goods and prey at pleasure." [131] Thus Mayor Martin had to account for himself at the next Galway Assizes.

## A Spanish Armada for Galway

Far from such local malices, the Spanish fleet was set to sail. Years of strife left Connacht wide-open for attack; invasion would be virtually unopposed. Sir Geoffrey Fenton wrote to Sir Robert Cecil in June that an attack was imminent, especially advising the Lord Deputy to

> *be careful of the safety of Galway, for that the Spaniards will sooner strike at that town than any port town in Ireland, both for the seat of the place lying open upon Spain, and for other commodities and hopes in some of the inhabitants, some of whom have Spanish hearts.* [132]

Fenton was correct; some did. In August 1601, the fleet departed and made for Ireland.

## Spanish hearts, Irish blood

On the 10 October, the Mayor and aldermen of Galway interviewed two locals who had travelled with the fleet, "Andrew Lynch fitz John fitz Harry, merchant, of Galway, aged 52 or thereabouts" and "Thomas Lynch fitznicholas, doctor of physic, aged about 32 years, having lived in Portugal for the most part of 18 years." [133] It was from them the Galwegians learned the fate of the fleet.

Andrew Lynch said he and four other passengers left Galway in mid-May, arriving in Lisbon fourteen days later (Portugal had been annexed by Spain in 1580). Promptly arrested, with the ship and its cargo of "ashen poles and salt hides" seized, they were not allowed to depart "lest they should bring news of the army so coming". [134] Oddly, instead of remaining detained, Lynch was brought abroad the *Crucifix*, one of the King's ships. He stated that there were thirty-nine ships in the fleet, mainly Spanish, but also 'biscans' [Basques], Flemish, Scots, and Irish. His crucial piece of information was the following:

*Whilst he was on board the Spanish ship, deponent heard from one of the pilots of the Admiral that if the wind should hold they had come for Limerick or Galway, but that owing to the wind they were driven southward and so put into Kinsale.* [135]

Now this was not the whole truth, but Andrew Lynch had his own reasons for an economical version. Meanwhile, the Mayor and aldermen were curious why Dr. Lynch had chosen this of all times to travel. While he too may have had other motives, the doctor cited personal events:

*Asked why he now came to Ireland when he had lived so long abroad and had married there, he said that his mother [Juliana Martin] wrote him a letter of the death of his elder brother and desired him to repair home to her. He did so the more willingly because his wife had died abroad a year ago.* [136]

A letter of October 1601 from Fenton to Cecil agreed with the Lynchs account:

*All the examinations taken concur in saying the enemy set out from Lisbon 4,000 strong or a little less. They were well appointed with munitions for Limerick and Galway, but were driven into Kinsale by contrary weather.* [137]

None of this was fully true. In Spain, General Juan del Águila wanted to land in The North, but was opposed by Irish expatriates and Spanish clerics (!) who pushed for Munster. In Ireland, Ó Neill and Ó Domhnaill gave contradictory suggestions, including Galway. Or Limerick. Or Carlingford Lough. The actual decision was made at sea by Admiral Brochero, directing the fleet to Kinsale.

Under-resourced, incompetently supported, the Spanish endured a horrific hundred-day winter siege under the tenacious leadership of del Águila. Ó Neill delayed his arrival to plunder Louth and Meath mercilessly. Squabbles between the Ulster lords handed victory to Lord Lieutenant Mountjoy's forces in battle on 24 December 1601. With total siege losses of six thousand men and as demoralised as the Spanish, the English were astonished to find they had won. [138]

## An assassination at Simancas?

Suffering a mental breakdown, Ó Domhnaill fled to Spain on 27 December 1601. En route, he was joined by James Blake. At Simancas on 10 September 1602, Aodh Ruadh Ó Domhnaill died. Within the Irish State Papers is a copy of a letter, originally encrypted in several places, containing incendiary news (words underlined denotes ciphered text. Deciphered, it reads):

*O Donnell is dead ... and I do think it will fall out that he is <u>poisoned</u> by <u>James Blake</u>, of whom your lordship has been formerly acquainted. At his coming <u>into Spain</u>, he was suspected by <u>O Donnell</u>, because he was <u>embarqued</u> at <u>Cork</u>, but afterwards he insinuated his access and <u>O Donnell is</u>*

*dead. He never told the President [Sir George Carew] in what manner he would kill him, but he did assure him it should be effected. It will not be many days before the truth will appear.* [139]

At the time of Ó Domhnaill's death no foul play was suspected. Either Blake was supremely careful, or claimed credit for a happenstance. An ambiguity perfect for those who preform in such shadows, into which he subsequently disappeared.

## A peace without consensus

Kinsale ended Spain's interventions in Ireland and England, and her status as an unchallenged global superpower. In negotiating the 1604 Treaty of London, the Spanish abandoned their Irish allies, excluding them from the protection of its provisions. To end the war, during the fifteen months after Kinsale Mountjoy deployed on Ulster the same tactics its lords used all over Ireland - calculated massacres and induced famines, to horrific effect. It was terrorism and it succeeded.

Those Irish forced into exile often went to Spain, who's rulers found them useful material for their military agendas. In the centuries to come, such exiles were likewise used in Europe and the Americas by other imperial powers. None did anything useful for the Irish in Ireland.

Queen Elizabeth I died in March 1603 and was succeeded by her Stewart cousin, King James VI of Scotland. He had remained neutral during the conflict so as not to jeopardise his succession to the Crowns of England and Ireland, only to find the Irish wars left England all but bankrupt. James's personal union of the three crowns did not result in 'Great Britain' (created 1707), a 'British nation' (created c.1790s-c.1820s), nor even 'the British Isles' (extant 1801-1922); that was all in the unknown future. The Stewarts ruled the three kingdoms, on and off and with opposition, till 1714. England's London-based elite remained mostly dominant in this and subsequent unions, whatever the monarchy's changing ethnic origins, and so survived to blunder many another day. [140]

Spain's overstretch necessitated better mutual relations. From 1604 James VI/I and Felipe III allied against their common foe, France, resurgent under Henri IV. The great game went on.

With the Irish and Spanish neutralised, English aspirations widened. "Peace in the Atlantic gave the English freedom to colonise America, and particularly Virginia." [141] These commercially successful English colonies in the Americas acheived in decades what centuries of conflict failed to do - the creation of Great Britain in 1707. An empire beckoned.

In December 1602, Aodh Ruadh's younger brother Rudhraighe Ó Domhnaill submitted and was pardoned. Rehabilitated, he received the English title of 1st Earl of Tyrconnell and regained his estates entirely. But in 1607 his continued dealings with Spain, amid a land-dispute with his tenants, compromised him and his senior confederate into a hasty, ill-judged exile.

Abandoned by his major vassals and close to capture, Ó Neill was instead allowed to negotiate his surrender in March 1603, officially ending the war. His most zealous supporter was none other than Lord Lieutenant Mountjoy (d. 1606), with whom he enjoyed a warm, mutually collusive friendship. Likewise pardoned and rehabilitated, retaining his earldom, estates, and marital law commission, Ó Neill offered his loyalty and services to King James in person, accepted amid great ceremony in London. "On the collapse of the Ulster rebellion in 1603 ... for the first time in Irish history, all the inhabitants of the island were made subject to a single government." [142]

Perhaps in all conflicts, someone must win else all shall lose. Yet that is dependent on what happens in a subsequent peace, on ignoring the causes, forgetting the casualties. Establishing England's first modern colony outside Britain came at a terrible human cost, British and Irish. If victors write history, they also forget it - because they can. Losers too forget their roles in their defeat, yet brood in its poison. Meanwhile, those most abused are locked-in, unable to forget, forgive, or 'move on'. Violent childhoods portend nightmares. Sooner or later, they erupt. [143]

By 1610 territorial units in Ireland were reconstituted in line with English models - Ireland's thirty-two counties remain to this day. Fénechas was replaced by English common law. At the war's conclusion, Galway seemed a ghost town. The population was reduced, their wealth impoverished. Only the most vigorous trade could regenerate its fortunes. [144]

But now a religious divide had definitively opened up between the Anglo-Irish and the English, who lumped all Irish Catholics together, as if they were one group. From 1594 each Mayor of Galway had to take the Oath of Supremacy or be dismissed from office, but enforcing such acts upon loyal Catholics was stupidly counterproductive (few English policies in Ireland have ever being called 'brilliant'). In freeing themselves from oppressive local Catholic lords, they found successive Protestant kings not only disfavoured them religiously, but from 1632 wished to confiscate their properties. Over the next four decades, this forced a new identity on Gael and Gall, both now seeing themselves not only as common Irish, but Catholic Europeans. Scots and English, already aware of themselves as European Protestants, began seeing themselves as common British.

Over the next two centuries, these painfully formed the modern basis of the main national identities of Ireland and Britain - a nation in search of a state, and a state in search of a nation. As it was in the beginning and always shall be, each identity fed upon an Other.

James Blake returned to Galway sometime after September 1602. His later life is obscure; a letter of April 1618 by the 4th Earl of Clanricard complains that he was *infinitely troublesome*. Termed by an Ó Domhnaill partisan as *this wretched individual*, Blake died in February 1635 and was buried in St Francis's. He was survived by two known children; Geoffrey (married to Julian Martin) and Jennett (married to John Browne and Ruaidrí Ó Flaithbheartaigh, successively). [145]

His elder brother Valentine, merchant and occasional intelligencer, was elected Mayor in 1611 but was forced out of office for refusing the Oath of Supremacy. He was MP for the town of Galway in 1613, and nominated for a baronetcy in July 1623. His first wife was Margaret French, daughter of Robuck. His second wife was Annabel Lynch, daughter of his factor, James. Re-elected Mayor in 1630, he took the Oath. He died in January 1634 and was also buried in St Francis's Abbey. [146]

Gregory Bodkin does not appear in any official correspondence after 1574. One son, *Thomas Bodkin fitz Gregory of Galway, merchant*, is mentioned in a Blake deed of 1599. A grandson, Gregory, was born in 1590 to Leo Bodkin and Isabel Lynch, eventually becoming a Jesuit. [147]

Writing in 1820, James Hardiman considered "Since that time Athenry has been entirely neglected, and, although once esteemed of so much importance, it is at present reduced to the state of an inconsiderable village." [148]

Dominick Browne was accused of diverting £1700 awarded to Athenry and stealing money meant for billeting soldiers. He denied it, but after his death his heirs cleared the debts. His children included Geoffrey, Oliver, Edward, and Margery (wife of James Blake). He died in 1596. [149]

Robuck French's known children were Walter, Edmond (Mayor 1606-07), and Margaret, first wife of Sir Valentine Blake. He died in 1602. [150]

Sir Murchad na dTuadh Ó Flaithbhcartaigh died in 1593. His will directed that strife among his family "to be ordered and discided by my deere friends Robuck Frenche fitz John and Anthony Linche" [151] His senior descendants remained landlords at Oughterard into the 1900s.

Dr. Thomas Lynch fitz Nicholas was granted a "General Pardon" in May 1603, serving as Mayor 1625-26. In 1640 he owned a dwelling house of three stories "with a back side; and a thatched house, one story." He was recently "deceased", possibly of the plague, by 8 January 1650. [152]

Research published in 2004 revealed Andrew Lynch fitz John fitz Harry was one of those Galwegians with "Spanish hearts". At Lisbon he "gave an encouraging report to the authorities about Ireland being ripe for a full-scale Catholic insurrection in the event of a Spanish landing", possibly guiding the armada to Kinsale. What became of him is unknown. [153]

William Óge Martyn "in consideration of his service diversely done to the state" received lands in Clanricard and Iar Connacht in 1585. He was removed from his position as jailer of Galway, but reinstated in 1590 at the insistence of Sir Richard Bingham. By Elizabeth Lynch he had at least two children, John (alive 1593) and Richard (died 1622). Martyn died in spring 1593. [154]

His brother, Francis Martin, died in 1602. He was one of a number of Galwegians pardoned in May 1603. He was survived by his wife Mary Lynch and at least one child, Stephen. Descendants owned an estate north of Gort called Coole Park till the 1760s. [155]

Vice-President of Connacht in 1597, whatever role James Reagh Dorsey played opposing Francis Martin may have had some effect as he became Mayor in September 1602, dying in office on 12 June 1603. He was survived by ten children from two marriages and his widow Elizabeth Martin, grandaughter of William Óge Martyn. Darcy's Protestant faith was obliviated by his descendants, just as they revised his ancestry. [156]

Andrew Morris was a town master from 1589 to 1593, but was dead by September 1594. His senior descendants are believed to be the Barons Kilanainn. [157]

Uilleag mac an Iarla died in 1601, succeeded as 4th Earl Clanricard by his son. Ricárd a Búrc fought bravely at Kinsale, his personal actions decisive in containing the Spanish and defeating the Ulster lords. For this he was knighted on the battlefield. In doing so Clanricard and his a Búrc, Ó Dálaigh, Mac Suibhne, Ó Madadháin and other followers changed the course of Irish and British history. He lived and died a firm English loyalist and a deeply committed Irish

Catholic. [158]

Sir Richard Bingham's aggressive governance led to disgrace, and imprisonment in London. He had returned as Marshal of Ireland upon his death in 1599. His brother's descendants became major Irish landowners, were briefly Catholic in the 1640s, later ennobled as Earls of Lucan. [159]

The Pope is said to have forgiven the Galwegians for executing the Spanish sailors. [160]

In 1607, Mag Uidhir, Ó Domhnaill, and Ó Neill fled Ireland. They never returned. [161]

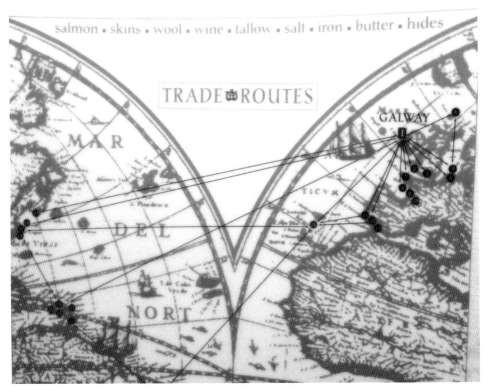

salmon ▪ skins ▪ wool ▪ wine ▪ tallow ▪ salt ▪ iron ▪ butter ▪ hides

TRADE ROUTES

*Galway's trade networks in the early 1600s, courtesy of Galway City Museum*

# CHAPTER SEVEN – A GOLDEN AGE

## Bulimid an Bothar

The post-conquest population was reduced to perhaps under half-a-million. [1] The environment was devastated from decades of warfare. For Ireland the only way was up. Galway made its name by trade and by sea trade it survived the war-induced recession that near strangled it. An early seventeenth-century account described it thus:

> This town is situated in a bay. Country about it, very rocky and barren, trade great, chiefly in transporting hides, yarn, woolfells, beef, furs, &c., returns wine, iron, salt, and some commodities out of England which may amount unto per annum 20,000l. [2]

Dated 1623, A Rutter for Ireland describes the route ships sailed from the mouth of Loch Lurgan, north of Inishmore, till they anchored offshore from the town:

> E.N.E. - If you go before the town of Galway you must bear up from Saint Gregorie's Sound E.N.E. 7 leagues. Moreover if you go by Galway's Head bear on N.E. till you see Motton Island, then go far to the south side of this island before you come to 7 fathoms, and then anchor. You shall not keep the north too much before you see this island, for a ledge of rocks ½ a league off is seen at the last quarter tide. [3]

For generations, the route in and out of Galway's harbour has been known as The Roads. Seventeenth-century evidence shows Bealach na Gaillimhe was a maritime super highway.

Thomas French unloaded wine from Calais valued at £13 17s 6d (£13 17 shillings and 6 pence) in December 1614, while in early March, William Skerritt brought in French wine from Nantes valued at £2 5s. Days later, Robuck French came in from St Malo with *1 ton iii hogsheads sacke* (casks of fortified white wine) valued at £2 12s 6d. [4] Outdoing them the following month was Robert Blake, from the Canaries on the *Phoenix* of Barnstaple carrying *xvi tons sacke* valued at £23. John Bodkin, John Streitch, Nicholas Blake, John Font, Martin French and Peter Lynch all arrived in Galway on the 23 April on the *Hopewell* with cargoes of various values. Lynch's *ij ton demi sacke* was valued at £6, which compared badly to Font's *xx ton sacke*, valued at £30. [5]

Surpassing all was Jasper Martin's *xxiij demi sacke*, brought in on the *St John* from Calais, valued at £47 on 26 June 1615. The *Francis* of Galway arrived on the same day, carrying wine by Thomas Blake, Dominick Skerrett, Richard Barrett, Thomas Martin, and Martin Browne, none less than £30 in value. [6] Perhaps seeing an early, lone fáinleog off Gran Canaria gave hope to such Galwegians that, after years of recession, an economic spring was in season. Galway saw wine valued at £341 7s 6d unloaded that year - official figures that take no account of smuggling. Evidently the hinterland still had a thirst for good wine and the means to purchase it. [7] This is born out in a license dated 18 February 1621, which granted

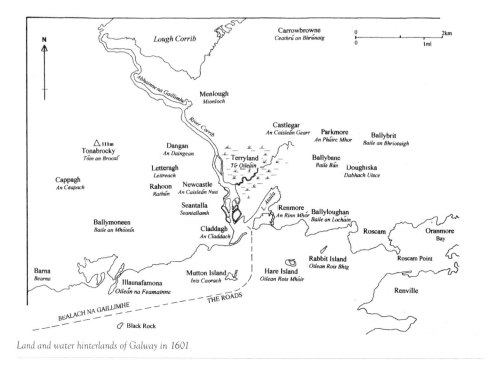

*Land and water hinterlands of Galway in 1601*

Robert Blake, Jeffry Linch Fitz Dominick, Nicholas Martin, John Bodkin Fitz Dominick and Edmond Kerwane, of Galway, merchant, during the natural lives of Richard Blake and Peter French and the survivor of them, to sell good and wholesome wine, to be drunk as well on the premises as elsewhere within the liberties of the town, and in the town of Galway ...

A similar license to Martin Darcy, Richard Darcy, James Darcy and Peter Darcy, of Athenry, to make and sell aqua vite or usquebagh, in the abbeys, towns and parishes of Ardnary and Moyne, in the barony of Tirrawley and county of Mayo. [8]

Some sought short-cuts to a quick profit. In 1625, *Marquisious* [Marcus?] *Linch Fitz John of Galway* stole "a boat riding on the harbour of Galway, with packs of wool" valued £20. He successfully exported the cargo but was forced to pay a fine of forty shillings. [9]

## From St. Malo to Algiers

Galway merchants had long been living abroad. Thomas Lynch, a mariner born in Galway about 1503, was by August 1539 living at Ratcliffe in the parish of Stepney, London. Resident there since 1529, he worked as "a governor and master of ships", serving "in voyages from England to France, Flanders and Spain." [10] No doubt there were many others like him, lost to history.

It is from the disturbed years of the mid-sixteenth century that entire Galway families emigrated. Spain and the Isle of Madeira became destinations for the Frenches, Cadiz for the Fonts, Southampton for Lynches and Bodkins. Surnames such as Martyn, Lynch, and Kirwan appear in the archives and parish registrars of St. Malo in Brittany from the 1560s. Close relationships are demonstrated by Galwegians standing as godparents for Malouin relatives, [11] while trade mainatined contacts. "Stephen French of Galway, merchant" was at St. Malo in September 1586, delivering Galway hides on the *Spritt*. He continued to

*17th century wine bottles found during excavations in Galway, Courtesy of Galway City Museum*

Spain where he loaded "20 tuns of sack and 15 tuns of aquavitae" for his own use. But the *Spritt* was taken by the *Bark Burre*, a pirate or privateer ship. French was lucky to escape with his life, being put ashore at Falmouth. [12]

He was not the only Galwayman to so suffer. In 1588 'Peers Martin' and 'Dorhan Nollen', both aged twenty-two, loaded goods from England bound for Galway. But the ship and cargo "were spoiled and carried away by Cooke and his company, pirates." [13]

There was no assurance that life ashore was any less hazardous. In 1583, 'James Skirrott, of Galway' was brought out of Spain to England where "he was condemned for high treason against her majesty." The Englishman who carried him was accused in Lisbon of betraying Skerrett, and forced "to keep himself secret ... And he had not dared to trade in any part of the king of Spain's dominions since." [14] Skerrett's fate is uncertain, but he may have been executed.

About 1603, Francis Martyn was one of three men held captive at Salé, Morocco, "as prisoners in pawn with the Moors, until £100 was paid." This ransom was paid by John Muckell of England. The three "promised to repay Muckell when they came to England, saying they would be as slaves to him until the money was paid." [15]

A letter dated "Galway, 4 April, 1616" from Nicholas Blake to his son, John, said that he received his letter of 23 February, which arrived

*Galway was as busy a port as the Arsenal de Rochefort as depicted by Joseph Vernet, courtesy Wikipedia Commons*

in Galway on 14 March. Nicholas reminded John that he and his cousins, Richard and Andrew Martin, had directed him to Lisbon for a cargo of salt. If he should meet the bearer of the letter, Charles Nolan, the two should go into partnership for merchandise. Nicholas recommended John lay out all his money in indigo. Mindful of the distractions available for a young man abroad, Nicholas instructed John "to shun bad company at all heeds, and to fix his mind wholly on the Almighty God." It is uncertain if these pious instructions were heeded. As confession is pointless without something sinful to confess, John doubtless solved this troubling dilemma by being a bad boy and making a good confession.

Lastly, Nicholas prayed for John's safe return to Galway, relating the sober news that "There happened great losses here both of men and goods this winter, as you shall learn of the bearer." [16] The dreadful winter storms that afflict the west of Ireland drew a toll on many balance sheets, not all financial. Little wonder that in 1622, "being whole in body and mind, being ready to go to sea for the Canaries, and doubting what might happen" [17] John Blake wrote his will. Just in case.

## Adam Fonte and the Young Prince

Adam Fonte (alias Faunt) was a merchant and former town sheriff married to Juliane Browne, and a son-in-law of Sir Valentine. Born in 1575 and coming of age in the turbulent late 1500s, he was aged fifty-two in November 1627 when he witnessed a high seas misadventure that began for him as a passenger aboard the Young Prince of Amsterdam, at Ile de Ré.

Thirty-four year old Edward Browne and Andrew Martyn left Galway for France in November 1627. The two were joint owners of a cargo of Irish butter, while Martyn owned staves and pilchards taken on at Kenmare and sold at La Rochelle. Browne and Martyn undertook to certify the butter they loaded at Galway was sold in either La Rochelle or England. At Kenmare, Martyn undertook a similar bond for the staves and pilchards. Browne later said the reason for these certificates was because no Irish customs official would suffer "any goods to be exported from thence without such bonds given, since the wars began." [18] The Young Prince put in at Ile de Ré, where Fonte came aboard. But the ship could not travel to La Rochelle due to the ongoing siege by Cardinal Richelieu. Martyn and the ship's master, Nicholas Janson, decided if another ship could carry his goods elsewhere or sell them at Ré within eight days, then Martyn would pay Janson £650 for his freight. If not, then Janson would sail for Plymouth with the king's fleet.

Instead, Janson stayed behind while the fleet set sail. When the Young Prince did eventually leave port and approach Plymouth, Janson had a second change of mind and abruptly stated that they would go to Holland to avoid wintering in England. At this, an already anxious Martyn lost his temper, telling Janson "he might as well carry him to Algiers, and sell him for a slave there, as to carry him to Holland where his goods would yield him nothing." [19] The Young Prince put in at the Isle of Wight, where Martyn had the ship arrested and her sails taken ashore. No doubt feeling too old for this, Fonte related his version of the tale in an official interview. Martyn went on to other adventures. His descendants named the eldest son in each generation after him; the last of whom was Andrew the Eleventh of Duniry, County Galway, who died in 1932 aged eighty.

## Losses and lost at sea

The oldest, most lethal foe, was nature. Twenty-four year old William Linche was a passenger on the *Peter* when she left Gothenburg, Sweden, for London on 1 October 1639, but the ship was driven upon the sands through extremity of weather. Charles Athy was one of three men who freighted the *Fortune* of Kirkcaldy in 1632, "for a voyage from Ireland to Bilbao. And the ship was laden with Irish pilchards, cow hides and butter." But the *Fortune* disappeared without trace. [20]

In December 1634, twenty-eight year old Oliver Kirwan loaded the *Margaret* of Le Croisic at Galway. Her cargo was "10 butts and 27 barrels of beef, 9 barrels of tallow, 12 stone of old butter, about 280 salt hides, and 13 packs of frieze and rugs" for Dominick Lynch, Edmond Bodkin, and Martin Kirwan. "These goods, with all charges clear aboard, cost this deponent and the rest of the merchants £500 and upwards. And they were assured, by the said policy, for £400. " [21] On 28 January 1635, the *Margaret* experienced "tempestuous weather"[22] and was driven onto the rocks close to Port Luney, Cornwall. The *Margaret* was wrecked, the cargo "cast away", and "about four of her company were drowned." [23] Oliver Kirwan and five others survived. His account skips grief and post-traumatic stress, delving straight back to the matter at hand:

> And the following goods were also saved, vizt. 140 hides, 2 packs of frieze, containing 1,306 yards, 2 barrels of tallow, 4 barrels of beef, and 15 small rugs. And all these goods were sold, upon public notice thereof, at the following rates, vizt. The hides for 5s. each, every 100 yards of frieze for 40s., the tallow (weighing 525 lb.) for 30 s. per hundred, the beef at 17s. per barrel, and the rugs for £5. And this deponent laid out £4 16s. in the selling of the said goods. [24]

Kirwan's tale of woes was not unique even in a port as small as Galway. In December 1639 the *Elizabeth of London* was loaded at Galway with "salt, sack, aquavitae, madder, and some other

*Ships Running Aground in a Storm by Ludolf Bakhuizen, courtesy Wikipedia Commons*

goods" [25] freighted by Andrew Blake. She sailed north, with some of the goods unloaded at Killybegs, County Donegal. The *Elizabeth* then made for St Malo. On 9 January 1640 it experienced "foul weather", an "extreme storm which lasted for fourteen or fifteen days" [26] forcing it well out into the Atlantic. The storm destroyed nearly all the *Elizabeth's* sails, forcing the exhausted crew to cut the main mast. The *Elizabeth* then had "to run in a gut between two islands on the west coast of Scotland", [27] before the pilot let her run aground on the Isle of Rhum. The crew took to a boat to save themselves, but three men and all the goods were lost.

The survivors included three Galwaymen - Thomas King and William Duff, mariners, and William Martin, pilot. The storm refused to abate, trapping them on the island for another two weeks but retrieving any cargo washed ashore trí na chéile. Once on the mainland they made to the court of the 8th Earl of Argyll, Archibald Campbell. Duff and Martin asked for and received of Argyll a pass to aid their passage home, but still had to travel some sixty miles before they found a port with a ship bound for Ireland. "They took shipping at Greenock and landed at Londonderry. The master gave them £3 to get home which he raised from the sale of some of the goods." [28] Duff and Martin docked at Galway on Saint Patrick's day.

## New Worlds

From 1492 Iberian colonies were established in the Americas. Major nations and empire states were destroyed, millions of Americans dispossessed or exterminated. Danes, Dutch, English, French, Germans, and Swedes were by the 1620s pushing out the Spanish, Portuguese, and each other. West Indies (Caribbean) colonies opened up new markets for Galway and Ireland.

Barbados was settled by the English in 1627. In May 1630, the *Jane* of London sailed from the island to Galway with eight hogsheads of tobacco. [29] A new merchandise with an already huge market in Ireland and Britain, it enabled survival of England's struggling American colonies. It was one of many American imports such as coffee, cotton, sugar, upon which many a fortune was made. The tomato was rapidly naturalised, as had *an Spáinneach Geal*/the potato (in north America via Ulster Presbyterians by the 1720s), fallow deer, rabbits, pheasants, centuries before. They were welcome additions to a wholesome, if bland diet of meat and dairy products, fruit, fish, and bread - the latter full of grit which wore away teeth. [30]

Some Galwegians were living on the islands by then. In 1630, Gregory French was brought before a

*Tobacco Inn by Adriaen Brouwer 1630-32, Courtesy of Wikipedia Commons.*

court on the island of St Christopher - settled in 1623 - for "certain speeches spoken ... tending to the dishonour of"[31] King Charles. He may, or may not, be identical with a Mr. French of Galway who appeared at Kinsale some years later, concerning the *Dolphin* of Southampton.

The *Dolphin* anchored at Kenmare, County Cork, in August 1634. Once ashore, its captain was "sorely beaten and wounded", some of the ship's company kidnapped and imprisoned, the Dolphin's rudder was removed "then cut and mangled and made utterly unserviceable." [32] Finally, a warrant for piracy was issued against the captain, the ship was driven onto the rocks, and sunk. The *Dolphin's* company later heard "general speech" that "one French, a merchant of Galway" [33] was responsible for all these acts. It was later ascertained that the ship was detained by French and his associates because she voyaged a valuable run to St Christopher and the West Indies that

> would yield £600 or £700. And there were many passengers who offered themselves ready to go in the said ship to the West Indies ... the said ship could have carried 150 passengers thence, for which passage there is commonly paid £6 per head ... and the freight of goods from Ireland to St Christopher, or other parts of the West Indies, is £3 to £4 per ton. [34]

While the *Dolphin* was sunk, "two small ships, laden with goods and passengers, left Kinsale and Youghal bound for St Christopher, and from thence to Virginia." [35] The *Dolphin's* company said the passengers should have been on their ship.Among those mentioned in evidence was one *Martyn of Kinsale* who was "put in possession of the ship", and *Clements Blake of Kinsale, aged about 60.* [36] A plausible conclusion is that French, supported by Galwaymen based at Kinsale, was trying to eliminate competition on the lucrative trans-Atlantic route. By any means necessary.

It may not be coincidence that in the 1630s a Richard Blake lived on St Christopher as a resident planter, and traded tobacco to London, Plymouth, and Kinsale. Blake's wife is recorded as sailing from St Christopher on the *Plough* of London, in April 1637 to Kinsale. She had forty-five rolls of tobacco from Blake's plantation, all of which were sold in London. [37]

In the generations to come, Galway merchants and other Irish created great personal wealth from exploiting West Indies commerce. French's actions at Kinsale reveal how ruthless some of these enterprising Irish could be, if the gains could justify the means. For many, they always do. More ominously, it portended the moral vacuum upon which, from the 1660s, some West Indies Irish created personal fortunes from tobacco and sugar, all harvested by African chattel slaves.

## Economic emigration

The seventeenth-century saw about one hundred thousand Irish emirate to Iberia, France, England, and their colonies. But others sailed to the sub-tropical islands of the Americas. Irish communities in the early 1600s were marked by colonisation, rising populations, and environmental exploitation. Yet they were also marked positively by increased international links and opportunities, as much 'pull' as 'push'. Because Britain alone could not meet its needs, demand for

*The Joyce family home, now Finnegan's Restaurant, Market Street.*

labour in the tobacco plantations drew droves of adventurous Irish emigrants. So, an lucht mbochtán 'a bótharín Connacht agus Mumha, the poor of rural Devon and urban London, and elsewhere, all went west over an tAigéan Mór.

They were overwhelmingly indentured servants, who signed on for a set period as contract labourers. Two-thirds of the seventeenth and eighteenth-century emigrants from Ireland, Britain, the German states, went to England's American colonies as indentured servants. Indenture was a legal contract with mutual obligations and courts of appeal for the indentured. For their labour they received a cash payment or a property grant - the latter an especial incentive among land-hungry Irish, British, and German commoners alike. They often bought the contracts of incoming indentures which were hired out in turn, harvesting tobacco in the fields or sugar in the mills. Others laboured to clear their own lands for further tobacco and sugar production.

It was not a perfect world for emigrants - it still isn't. They were often grossly exploited - emigrants still are. Unused to the searing heat of tropical labour, plagued by its humidity, diseases and vermin, Europeans died in huge numbers each year so turnovers of fresh labourers were frequent. Masters were harsh as a matter of course, brutal when they could get away with it. Social divides were similar to those experienced by Irish emigrants in 19th-century USA or Irish navvies in 20th-century Britain. West Indies indentured servitude was for the brave, the desperate, or both.

People make the best of their lives through available options. Often the only choices available are different degress of harsh. People without trades or education have nothing but their physical labour to enable themselves, extreme forms being military service and prostitution. Yet still people choose because they want to make a go of their lives. In this predatory world the ability to make even narrow choices matters and should never be slighted. They can be life-changing and life-affirming. "Life is worthless without freedom, without dignity." [38] Is ferr lucht a chiniud.

These Irish were in the heart of darkness and light that created the modern world. Coffee, tobacco, and sugar are addictive luxury drugs like modern products of the same regions, marijuana and cocaine. The financial capital generated by the former partly stimulated European expansions and the Industrial Revolution - not to mention industrial imperialism and the Anthropocene - but at the horrific cost of black slavery and its continuing after-effects.

## The 'Irish slaves' myth

Deliberate misrepresentation has led to the popular belief that seventeenth-century Irish in the West Indies and north America were chattel slaves. [39] While some genuinely misunderstand the issue, the belief is actively propagated by US white supremacists. The argument goes "My Irish ancestors [sic] were slaves [sic], yet they did okay so blacks should get over it too." This attempts to claim a 'similar' 'ancestral' 'victimhood' to African-Americans and so excuse the appalling social/economic status many black citizens of the USA still endure. The ignorance this shows towards the very different conditions of Irish and Africans in the Americas is wilful [40] It denies Irish emigrants to the West Indies and north America were capable of active decisions, instead dismissing them as passive and their life-choices as worthless.

A house of the French family , now Cooke's Restaurant, Abbeygate Street.

Worst of all, Irish writers deliberately sensationalised the issue via factually untroubled books such as *To Hell or Barbados* (by Sean O'Callaghan, 2000) and *White Cargo* (by Don Jordan and Michael Walsh, 2007). Despite these severe handicaps both sold and misinformed widely.

It's understandable - though not excusable - that some US citizens stoop to racism to fudge issues of 'racial' inequality and oppression, past and present. But as natives of Ireland, which never experienced modern slavery, the above authors lack even that excuse.

The 'Irish slaves' myth is exactly that, a deliberate fiction. It is not supported by evidence nor by historians, Irish or otherwise, because historians deal with factual events not fiction. What gives it traction is England's appalling treatment of the Irish in that era, and because Irish history was long taught with a religious certainty that cast the Irish as perpetual victims who harmed none. This makes it difficult for some to understand the Irish actively victimised Others in turn. Plus, because Ireland has no history of modern slavery, many Irish have genuine difficulty grasping its horrific nature, that what African slaves endured was a whole other world of bad compared to the lot of our ancestors. The Irish had choices. Slaves had none.

Unlike the Irish, Africans were not allowed to keep their names, languages, or cultures. Rape, flogging, castration, mutilation, deliberate familial destruction, and sheer terrorism were a *daily* experience for generations of African-Americans. For the most minor of offences they were tortured, burned alive or starved to death. Into the twentieth-century their free descendants were lynched with impunity. The likes of this was never the common Irish-American experience - at least not on the receiving end. Dehumanised as an Other 'race' meant lynching was a common African-American experience. Social disablement, disproportionate imprisonment, and judicial murders are its continuing expressions.

Up to the 1600s, Irish and other Europeans distinguished between each other on the basis of ethnicity, not skin colour. But encountering black-skinned humans created 'white' identity in the 17th-century. Purely by accident, the Irish found themselves on the white side of this skin-colour barrier, one which they were happy to remain. Kept in their caste for centuries by white suprema-cist laws, African-American slaves had no prospect of liberty, only death. Though they made sometimes successful efforts to escape or rebel, active resistance was met with fearful brutality. Because they were black they could be enslaved, and because they were slaves they were not legally human. They were livestock. And livestock have no choices. There is no parallel in the Irish experience anywhere in the Americas.

Outnumbered by blacks from the 1660s and correctly fearing for their lives in the event of a successful slave rebellion, white communities of English and Irish co-operated in securing their positions and keeping the blacks in theirs. Why fight the system when you can profit from it? The Irish received wages, travelled freely, had access to education, became socially mobile, prac-tised their faiths and purchased property. Including African slaves. "[T]he Irish did not make common cause with the slaves ... they were white and wished to exercise the advantage it con-ferred." [41]

At least twelve million Africans were enslaved in the Americas into the 1800s, some three million others dying en route. Black skin was the mark of a slave. To be white was to be free.

But whites in the West Indies were susceptible to tropical disease. So many British and Irish indentures died before completing their service that planters regularly bought new contracts. The problem was indentures demanded payment - quite rightly, given the brutality of the labour and the prospect of a mortal disease or injury. Fortunes are made by cutting labour costs, so planters ceased hiring expensive white Europeans. Americans were nearly wiped out by disease and exter-mination so they were not an option as a labour force. Instead, from the 1660s vast numbers of enslaved Africans were transported. They had a better resistance to tropical diseases than Euro-peans and as livestock (chattel=property), they could be worked all their lives, till death.

Indentured servitude was abandoned when indentures found it unrewarding and employers found it expensive. Atlantic black slavery was created because it was cost-effective. Its malign ef-fects included vast human suffering, its rationalization, and institutional racism. The Atlantic slave trade began the end of indenture boom, most Irish indentures went elsewhere in the West Indies or north America, but others returned to Ireland like the bradán to the Gaillimh. Those that remained as estate owners or Plantation agents sired children on African slave women, all too often by rape. It is these descendants who were Irish slaves - except they were not white but black. And because the Irish embraced a white Anglo identity, "black Irish Americans [have] re-ceived limited attention from historians of the Irish diaspora." [42] 'White' is not a skin colour but an ethnos for domination.

Irish emigrants could transform themselves from labourers or artisans into merchants, estate managers, or colonial administrators. The luckiest gained extensive property. Caribbean sojourn-ers like the Frenches, Blakes, and Lynches went west to make enough money to return to Ireland and buy estates. Other lower-class Irish did the same on a more humble scale (five of my great-grandparents likewise worked for some years in the USA then returned home to purchase farms, a fairly common activity even then). They had the potential to achieve this because their servitude was limited and remunerated. And because they were white.

Slaves were purchased precisely because they did not need to be paid, and could go on being not paid for life - in the case of their descendants, for generations. Because they were black.

As late as 1857 African-Americans were denied citizenship and legal rights in the USA because their "ancestors were imported into this country and sold as slaves". [43] Whereas servitude was never inherited, slavery by its very nature was perpetual and multi-generational. Even when free, upward mobility was long denied because of racism. Little wonder they remained oppressed and marginalised while the Irish generally flourished and assimilated. The actual colour line of slavery was made bluntly clear in sexual and reproductive terms:

> many black women who were normally partnered to black men ... preferred to be impregnated by white men in the knowledge that any mulatto children born to them had a much better chance than their black children of advancing within the system, and might even have their freedom purchased for them by their white fathers. [44]

This, and the practise of 'crossing-over' by light-skinned African-Americans, drives home how obscene the wilfully ignorant notions of 'Irish/white slavery' truly are.

## The Imperial Irish

By 1670, at least ten percent of the seven hundred and seventeen property-owners in Jamaica were either Irish-born or ethnic Irish. [45] Others assimilated so well they were considered entirely English in origin by their descendants, their ancestry forgotten. Other Irish rose through the ranks of the colonial administration to be employed as governors and attorney-generals (unlike any black African). [46] England's empire succeeded in part because of its Irish helpers, as did those of Portugal, Spain, France. Had Toirdhealbhach created a United Kingdom of Éire, some form of external imperialism would have followed. If the Gaeil ran an Irish empire it would have being a very British one.

Three thousand Irish resided in the Leeward Islands, including Barbados, in 1637. By 1669 some twelve thousand Irish lived in the English West Indies, which by then included Jamaica. Smaller numbers of Irish inhabited Danish, Dutch, French, Portuguese and Spanish colonies. [47] Their numbers were small compared with the masses who in the 1600s emigrated to Britain, Iberia, France, and elsewhere in Europe, but were notable for the distances involved. Women had more reason to go. With pitiful economic opportunities in Ireland, they welcomed the emancipating possibilities of emigration; not all emigrants are sorrowful! As most married, changing from (say) Grainne Ní Ceallaigh to Mrs. John Smith, their stories are less visible and still await comprehensive research, Irish emigration too often seen as purely masculine or familial.

Galway surnames like Burke, Daly, Lynch, Kirwan, Fahy, Fallon, French, Madden, Murphy,

Skerrett, Quin, are recorded among the West Indies Irish in the 1600s, both in English and Spanish colonies. They were convicts, farmers, fishwives, labourers, maid-servants, merchants, landlords, pirates, priests, prisoners of war, privateers, prostitutes, rebels, sailors, smiths, soldiers, spies. None were slaves. Like present Irish emigrants, they had clear ideas about their economic self-interest and were well capable of active life-choices. At Kinsale in 1636, Captain Thomas Anthony was forced by his Irish passengers to change his destination:

> Irish labourers were well informed about comparative wage rates and knew that they would be better paid in the West Indies than in Virginia. So Captain Anthony was forced to change his plans and to make St. Christopher his destination; this is where most of them wanted to go ... their contracts were sold for between 450 and 500 pounds of tobacco apiece [48]

Contrary to racist stereotypes, Irish emigrants were not passive victims but decisive and bold. This remains the case today.

English north American colonies deliberately admitted few Irish or Catholics. Settlements with a more tolerant ethos such as Nieuw Amsterdam (from 1664, New York) seem to have being outside the Irish world-view, then. But Bodkin is recorded in Boston from 1672, [49] and where one Galway family went, others followed. In any case, very little of European north America was English. The Dutch had Manhattan island and the vast Hudson Valley region. Florida, Louisiana and Canada, were claimed by Spain and France respectively; the Galwegians had long-term ties to both.

None of which ever healed the pain of exile. A seventeenth-century east Galway native wrote:

> Mar éirighim gach aon mhaidin moch-thrátha
> Dhul d'fhéachaim sean-mhacha mong-Mháine
> For daily at the dawn I rise up sadly
> look forth in hope to see grass-grown Uí Mhaine [50]

The lot of returning emigrants too could be heart-wrenching, like Oisín finding Ireland unfamiliar after too long an absence, strangers to family and freinds. Only the Gaillimh seemed unchanged. So it goes. But then as now "To a large extent, the Irish found abroad opportunities denied them at home." [51] It was an emigration pattern repeated in successive generations the world over. In a brilliant summation of the era, Alexandra Hartnett wrote:

> Galway was a moderately sized and relatively isolated port that existed on a periphery until the discovery of the Americas and the expansion of the Atlantic economy ... The opening of the Americas expanded Galway's mercantile opportunities by allowing it to act briefly as the chief exporter of provisions to the English-speaking Caribbean islands until Cork and Dublin surpassed it in the 1650s while Galway was in the midst of extreme political turmoil.

Before it was eclipsed, Galway exported everything from salted beef and beer to woollen items, leather shoes and, undoubtedly, emigrants. This allowed Galway to enter a New World economy based largely on the tobacco trade that was forced underground in Ireland by increasingly punitive navigation acts and is apparent in the presence of many clay pipes among the finds from the Galway city [archaeological] investigations.

During the seventeenth century the children of Galway's merchant community were planted in trading houses from London to Bordeaux, and from the West Indies to Boston, in order to facilitate trade. ... The merchant community of Galway saw the sea as a link rather than an obstacle; it was the means by which its authority was locally enabled through the establishment of by-laws that allowed it to create and maintain a mercantile oligopoly. The turbulent happenings of the second half of the seventeenth century displaced that power, but, to the best of their capabilities, the 'Tribes' encouraged trade on their own terms. [52]

Mr. French's brutal actions at Kinsale demonstrates the ability of some Galwegians to make good on the demand for passage. Galway surely served its hinterlands in a similar fashion in these years, bringing Connacht natives to the Americas direct from Loch Lurgan/Galway Bay. This idea is supported by the actions of Archbishop of Tuam Mael Eachlainn Ó Caollaidhe (1630-45), who in 1638 sent two priests to St. Kitts "where a great number of Irish live." [53] Ó Caollaidhe later stated that the priests had accompanied "six hundred Irish of both sexes [who] came to those parts, thanks to a safe and functional communication line, recently established." [54] Those six hundred, their predecessors and successors, were from the diocese of Tuam and by implication from Galway.

In contrast to many emigrants, Galwegians could read and write, add and subtract, were apprenticed and multilingual. This placed them one or two steps higher up the job market ladder, thanks to the efforts of their ancestors. Helpful was the self-assured charisma that can come from being raised at a certain level in society, or indeed the go-for-it brashness of those who were not. None of which guaranteed they would thrive further, but it gave them a damn good start.

And the West Indies emigrants were just a part of a global Irish diaspora that by the 1640s already stretched from Flanders to La Coruna, from the Philippines to Fort Taurege on the Amazon, Nieuw Amsterdam to the Rzeczpospolita of Poland-Lithuania. So broad are these largely forgotten early modern Irish diasporas that they have yet to be fully examined or understood.

## Upward mobility

The profits of such voyages were for the first time spent in purchasing extensive property far beyond the town walls. While merchant families owned property outside Galway for generations, this was proprietorship on a vastly different scale. In 1574, Blakes, Lynchs, and Skerretts owned castles in the hinterlands of Galway and on Inishmore. [55] The 1585 Composition of Connacht

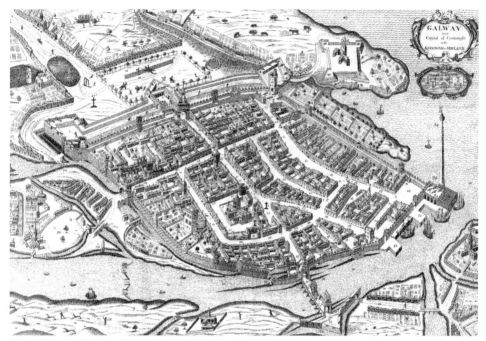

The c. 1664 map of Galway, Courtesy of NUI, Galway

lists Dominick Browne, James Reagh Dorsey, and William Óge Martyn as holding land in Clanricard, while in Iar Connacht seven men are listed:

> Dominick Lynch of the Ballagh gen, Dominick Browne of the Barny gen, William Martin of
> gortetleua gen, Richard Martin of Ballyertir gen, Anthony Lynch of the dengine gen, Marcus Lynch
> fitz Nicholas for furlagh gen, and Pattrick Ffrench of Curchollen gen, [56]

Each of these areas lay within just a few miles of Galway, further demonstration of how unwise it was to venture too far from walled security in such troubled times. There was no change early in King James VI and I's reign. Of forty-one Galwegians granted a General Pardon in 1603, only eight were living beyond the walls, mostly in the environs of Athenry and Loughrea. The one Galwegian listed afield was "Stephen Linch of Galway, merchant, now of Ardneglas" [57] in County Sligo.

But by the reign of Charles I they were purchasing land all over Connacht, in the 1640s owning small to substantial properties in each Connacht county, save Leitrim. Some were straightforward transactions; others were gained from landowners who could not repay mortgages. These formed the basis of estates such as Rinville (Athy), Ardfry, Menlo (Blake), Kilcluny, Annagh (Bodkin), Castlemacgarrett, Kilskeagh (Browne), Kiltullagh, Gorteen, New Forest (Darcy), Balrobuck, Castlemoyle (Deane), Frenchpark, Monivea (French), Rahoon, Merview (Joyce), Blindwell, Castlehackett, Cregg (Kirwan), Barna, Lavally, Partry (Lynch), Ross, Curraghmore, Dunguire (Martyn), An Spiddeal, Ballinboy (Morris), Ballinduff, Dangan, Finvarra (Skerrett). [58]

# A rising people

Further down the social scale, the break-up or subordination of independent lordships by the early 1600s led to some enablement opportunities for their long-suppressed peasant and serf castes. Families long obliged to "tillage and hard labour for the nobles and aristocracy" [59] now had some surplus wealth entirely for their own use. Property was leased or purchased, sons were apprenticed, indentured, and educated, while daughters married better or learned "silk-work and sampler making." [60] Some changed denomination, or migrated; others chanced their luck outside Ireland.

Lords and poets hated the rising lower-classes because the processes that were enabling *both-ach, fuidir, sen chléithe* (even the word *mogh* is used) were impoverishing lords and poets alike. Collectively termed c.1608-11 as the *Chloinne Tomáis*, the Gaelic upper class sneered at "each beggerwoman's son", "each churl or his son" [61] now dressing as good as or finer than the better sort, and making the unGaelic economic choice to learn English to further enable themselves: "a churl in each house that is owned by a speaker of nasty English and no one paying any heed to a man of the poetic company, but for "Piss off with you and your precious Gaeilge!" [62]

The so-called Chloinne Tomáis were following adaptation patterns set by the Galwegians and other Irish communities. Only lack of opportunities held them back. Tradition had bound them to lords for whom loyalism was a one-way service, so they unbound themselves of tradition.

## Irish economic sovereignty

In these decades, the Kingdom of Ireland experienced rapid economic growth, yet remained poor and underdeveloped, despite "this time of so well settled a peace". To Galway merchant, Peter Óge French (later Sir Peter), there were a number of reasons for this; unfavourable balance of trade, inefficient marketing, underemployment, above all a lack of credit creation. Despite being a legally sovereign kingdom, Ireland lacked a distinct coinage because unlike Scotland and England, it was a colonial creation whose economy (and much else) was directed from, and limited by, London.

Yet this could be countered by devaluing coinage and establishing an independent Irish mint. Devaluation would stop imports of "bad wine, tobacco" which were "unnecessary commodities" because unlike currency they could not be converted into coin. Merchants would have to "bring in bullion of all sorts, viz. Old plate, ingots of gold and silver, Spanish ryals, pistolletts [pistole coins] in great plenty". These would be converted into bullion and Irish coin upon which the economy could literally pay for itself. French argued this would increase the common wealth of the kingdom as "no edict or politic institution that the invention of man can devise will so soon reclaim an uncivil, barbarous people as riches where all commerce and famous industry proceed, which course in time without further instigation will banish idleness, the bane of that commonwealth."

Politically incorrect though it was phrased, French's proposal made economic sense. He furthermore believed it made excellent social sense, as it would give monetised remunerative employment to the underemployed. This would in turn enable families to "repair their children to learning and other employments at home and so many will not wander about the world at the devotion of foreign princes as now they do out of all parts of that kingdom." Perhaps only someone whose family and community experienced recession and emigration could have written this.

Government schemes such as coinage debasement, copper coin tokens, or compelling merchants to repatriate foreign profits, ended in calamity or were stupidly unworkable. Whereas being a merchant from a merchant community, "The approach Peter French outlined ... was a much more realistic one ... he proposed an effective devaluation of the Irish currency which would boost exports and curb imports, the net effect of which would be an increase of coin and bullion brought into the country, which would then be processed through the newly established mint." For whatever reasons - apparently inertia rather than malice - the project was never realised. Its absence was detrimental from 1636, as economic slow-down played a direct role in fuelling the conspiracy that led to the 1641 rebellion, and its consequent atrocities. [63]

Before his death in February 1632, French surely outlined aloud his thoughts on Irish economic sovereignty. Listeners may have included two of his sons-in-law, first-cousins and law colleagues Patrick Darcy and Richard Óge Martin, who were in Irish government during the 1640s.

## *"so well settled a peace"?*

In one respect, Peter Óge French was wrong. Ireland's peace was an unsettled one. Despite declining numbers of rebels (as opposed to rising numbers of dislocated poor), marital law commissions and provost marshals continued long after the end of the Nine Year's War. Several who held peace-time commissions gained them during the war and earned well their dreaded reputations. Since 1603, occasional "political fallout ... persuad[ed] the government to give it a somewhat lower profile than it had previously enjoyed." Somewhat. Yet from 1606 summery use of provisional law increased resentment among Catholics, against whom it was aimed. Its use in post-war Ireland bore no relationship to peacetime practise in either realm on the British isle. Planters used marshals as hired thugs, guarding and enforcing their wealth, from which they too drew profit.

"Why, despite the commitment of so many people of influence to rational argument, [was] Ireland's historical experience during the early modern centuries" [64] so immoderate, so bloody, so violent? Because moderates are rarely so influential. Because people are not rational. Because the response to violence is violence, especially when societies give great stór to hatred. Beneath all our civil veneers lies a monster that comes out roaring. And what is sown, is reaped, unto generations.

In the aftermath of the atrocities inflicted upon them during the terrible winter of 1641-42, English and Scot alike were truly bewildered by what, to them, were unprovoked attacks in a time that was peaceful and prosperous. While genuine, these views were one-sided. The atrocities arose not from 'nowhere' but as responses to confiscations, plantations, and persecution, not only historic but on-going (especial targets in south Ulster were Protestant clergy made wealthy from money-lending and tithes). Refusing to acknowledge these factors made the insurrection of

1641-42 seem unprovoked and so peculiarly reprehensible. Indicative of how profound religious divisions were, the Irish loathed Scots Presbyterians though many were Gaeil and Gaeilgeoirí, while Irish Catholics made common cause with Ireland's English Catholics against English and Irish Protestants. [65]

Demonstrating how wrongs only further wrongs, the 'unprovoked' belief conditioned responses enacted by men named St Ledger, Coote, O'Brien, Jones, Ireton, Cromwell. [66]

## National Constitutionalism

Even the wealthiest of Galway's main families remained working merchants, while the humblest bearers of the surnames were smiths, sailors, tanners, labourers, economic emigrants. But trade and property-ownership enabled some of them to advance financial credit by which further properties were purchased, with ownership of substantial lands propelling some into the gentry class. And as the 4th Earl of Clanricard made clear to Henry Lynch in 1624, gentlemen did not work:

> Now for your [eldest] son [Robuck], in my opinion plainly and briefly I think you shall do best not to think to make him a lawyer, for it will require a great deal of time, in which your eldest son is not necessarily to be expected ... send him over [to England] for some two years, one in the university [Oxford] ... and then one more about London where he may learn qualities fit for a gentleman ... Your second son [Nicholas] may do well to prepare for the law, and let him toil out for his living. [67]

Yet both Robuck and Nicholas became lawyers. Perhaps the family were not yet secure enough to afford leisured gentlemen – their father only became a baronet in 1623, by purchase. Records for the first half of the 1600s demonstrate that apart from a few knights and esquires, the majority of town freemen were middle-class of various degrees, some quite humble. In a reveal of how an actual aristocrat viewed them, Earl Ricárd insisted Henry Lynch deal with such people on his behalf - I will have no meddling or wrangling with the merchants, that is fitter amongst themselves. [68]

The Lynch brothers, cousins Anthony and Richard Óge Martin, Geoffrey, Dominick, and Francis Browne, Geoffrey and Valentine Blake, nephew and uncle James Óge and Patrick Darcy, Jasper and Nicholas Kirwan, Dominick fitz John Bodkin, and Stephen French, all made the law their profession. So crucial were their skills that within years they would find themselves propelled into the heart of matters of inter-national importance. [69]

## An independent Irish state: Confederate Ireland

Renaissance humanism, common in their backgrounds and education, cumulated in the national constitutional of Patrick Darcy's Argument. Delivered at Dublin Castle on 9 June 1641, it was a devastating rebuttal of oppressive measures by the Protestant castle administration and illegal impositions from London. Darcy's ideas had an impact now all but forgotten, though they stated and anticipated ones thought unique to 1649, 1774/89/98, 1867, 1912/16/98.

While acknowledging the monarch - none then considered a state legitimate without one - Darcy correctly demonstrated Ireland was a separate, *sovereign* kingdom from England - not yet 'Britain' - and that the Irish parliament had always been independent of Westminster, something expressed at least as far back as 1460. [70] Practical application came in 1642 with the creation of the first modern independent Irish state, Confederate Ireland (Darcy joined its Supreme Council).

With the moderation that can only come with maturity and/or bitter experience, their most inclusive civic measure - opposed by hard-line Catholics - was that "Place of birth, rather than blood, now provided the essential criterion for membership of the Irish nation." [71]

This was clarified by statements made in 1644. Sectarianism was disavowed by the Irish state: "Protestant [and] Roman Catholic [can] enjoy their freedom of their own religion, and peaceably and quietly enjoy their own estates, so far forth as they or any of them shall join with us." [72]

Ethnicity too was treated positively: "he that is born in Ireland, though his parents and all his ancestors were aliens, nay if his parents are Indians [American First Nations] or Turks [Muslims], ... is an Irishman. ... Such marks of distinction, being the insteps to trouble and war, are incompatible with peace and quiet."

Confederate insistence that the Crown's Irish subjects were all lawfully equal was reflected in their motto in which Gaeil and Gaill nationalism were for the first time superseded by a common *Irish* patriotism: *Hiberni unaimes pro Deo Rege et Patria* ("Irish of one mind for God, King, and Country"). [73] Confederate Ireland was to be an inclusive commonwealth, respectful of denomination and ethnicity yet with an emphasis on the common bonds of the homeland or *patria* (hence '*patriotism*'). In finding common ground between ethnic and civic nationality and other matters, Galwegians had "a hugely disproportionate influence on confederate politics." [74]

Of course there were qualifications. Their patriotism was that of the Irish *Catholic* Confederation. Because of this and their own anti-'papism', understandably few Protestants saw any reason to join. Different peoples loving the same landmass rarely results in a common patriotism, only different nationalisms. Had any 'Indians' or 'Turks' ventured to so do, they would have had to be "converted to Christianity" [Catholicism] before being allowed to call themselves Irish.

And increasingly upward social mobility by the lower castes and classes alarmed enabled Catholic Irish and Protestant British alike. The social order would be conserved; the Chloinne Tomáis and other dubhtúatha would remember their places and keep to them. As ever, matters pertaining to women and children were unconsidered and unaddressed. As future Irish revolutionaries demonstrated, rethoric is a fine thing except in practise – the true test of all grand designs is when they are placed under stress. Most shatter.

But that is not to say that even such qualified concepts were without merit. Once stated, they cannot be readily withdrawn and are open to continual transformation - what a much later, similarly conservative, Irish Catholic rebel termed 'the freedom to achieve [further] freedom'. Adaptation, not strict adherence to withering tradition, has been the key to successful civic states, commonwealths, even empires. Disabling only delays what becomes inevitable, with frequently woeful results.

Remarkably, this new Irish identity of Éireannach had by 1644 achieved a fragile solidarity across ethnicity, caste, and class (if not denomination), perhaps a first in the island's history. Inclusive moderation reflected the real distaste shared by confederates for intransigent positions – religious or legal, Irish or British.

Like the Irish as a whole, Darcy had diverse inheritances and multiple identities. He was a Gaeilgeoir and English-speaker, son of a Protestant 'Fir Bolg' father and a Catholic 'Old English' mother. A Crown subject he nevertheless sought religious, legislative and political independence, public accountability and legal enablement. The principal achievement of the confederates was an independent Irish state from 1642 to 1649, not seen again till January 1919. The tragedy of Confederate Ireland was being beset by too many uncompromising hard-liners; some within, mostly without. Confederate wisdom was hard-won and seldom heeded.

Embarrassingly, while its principal destroyer, English Republican Oliver Cromwell, is actively recalled, Confederate Ireland is totally absent from Irish popular 'memory'. Its ideas of *res publica* would be later claimed by others as their own, often espoused, rarely practised or understood. If their definitions sound too contemporary to be true, it demonstrates how little traditional Irish notions have adapted that the same ideas need repeating, nearly four hundred years later. It shows the power of traditions, but also their frequent futility. The Confederation's core principles were based on consent and moderation. Too many within and without would not abide.

## Conscience and Civil Rights

Part of the reason many middle-class Irish Catholics in the early 1600s became lawyers was because of defective land titles. Long ago, Sir Murchad na dTuadh expressed the situation when his counsellor, Dominick Lynch, urged him to legally make out his title to his lands. "Why man I got it with the sword, what title should I say else?"[75]

Ever greedy for cash in hand, the first two Stewart kings were unscrupulously eager to exploit such defects, and proposed to confiscate such lands, which they would then sell for their personal profit. Naturally this was opposed by a merchant class who had spent a great time of time and trouble gaining these properties by sometimes similarly dubious means.

But being learned in the law was also a way of defending Irish Catholic civil rights. King James was deeply prejudiced against his Catholic subjects, Irish and British - especially if Gaelic. He persecuted clerics for preforming their religious duties, schoolmasters for teaching, and officials who refused to swear the Oath of Supremacy (recognising him as the head of the church).

From 1609, King James rigorously enforced the Oath. Thus the officers elected that year - Oliver Browne, Nicholas French, Dominick Browne - were dismissed for refusing to swear it. Thomas Browne fitz Dominick was elected to serve as Mayor instead, only for him to likewise refuse. This resulted in a fine and Browne being made ineligible to ever after become Mayor "by reason of his contempt in despising and putting off the office". [76] Other likewise refused and paid the fines. While some of the corporation were Protestant - and sincerely so - most were Catholic. Loyalty persuaded many to grit their teeth and take the Oath. Such Crown extortion aided a new political consciousness. In precisely these years, the Catholic IHS symbol is first found on Galwegian coats of arms. The result was not compliance but the creation of common ground between Ireland's two principal nations, pushed together in opposition to crown policy and Britain's Protestant identities.

## Anthony Lynch – merchant, Dominican, captive

Not all members of the families found themselves cut out for the secular world. Anthony Lynch was born about 1574 to Juliana Martin and Nicholas Lynch fitz Stephen (foster-brother to 2nd Earl of Clanricard). A working merchant, he was one of twelve brothers including Mayor Marcus (1595-96), Doctor Thomas, Sir Henry, and Nicholas, OP. Early in the 1590s, he found he had a calling for a more spiritual life. He emigrated to Lisbon (where his brother, Thomas, had been resident since 1583) and studied at St. Patrick's College, graduating as a Master in Sacred Theology. [77] He was made a sub-deacon in December 1599, before moving to the Irish College of Salamanca, Spain, in 1602. He returned to Lisbon in September 1606, taking vows as a brother of the Dominican order. In 1615 he was on board a Spanish ship bound for Ireland when it was attacked by Barbary corsairs, who took Lynch and the crew as captives to Morocco. [78]

The Barbary corsairs of Salé and other west African cities - a mixture of Andalusian moriscos, Arab north Africans, and white European converso pirates - had a well-earned notorious reputation as pirates and enslavers. Long the scourge of Iberia and the Mediterranean, corsairs made captive some eight thousand British and some Irish in the 1600s. [79] Their treatment was savage.

While many were enslaved, another motivation was ransom. This seems to have been the case with men like Francis Martyn, held at Salé in 1603 as a financial hostage. European rulers and religious groups sent embassies redeeming captives and slaves as early as 1579. [80] Anthony Lynch's brother, friar Nicholas OP, travelled to Spain in 1621 with ransom money to pay for his release, which was secured by 1623. [81] Very few were so lucky. Lynch's life after liberation is recorded mainly in church documents; due to religious persecution, he lived in obscure locations. He was recommended as bishop of Achonry in the early 1630s. In 1634 it was reported that he supplied false information that secured a papal brief naming him as vicar apostolic for Killala. [82] There are no references to him after that year.

## Religious Orders

Friar Nicholas Lynch (c. 1590-1634) was described as the "chief father" of the Dominican order, as "a very learned man and of great estimation among them." [83] He is said to have arrived back from Spain with money to support a Spanish invasion of Galway, but it is far more likely that any money Nicholas had was spent on paying his brother Anthony's ransom.

From c. 1625, Nicholas was associated with Dominican eduction in Galway, possibly instigating it. While prior of Galway 1626-27, he and his fellow Dominicans - Peter Martin, Stephen Lynch, Dominick Lynch and Richard Bermingham - ratified the establishment and status of Galway's Dominican schools. He succeeded Ross MacGeoghegan as provincial of Ireland in June 1627. [84]

In February 1629, he presided over a provincial chapter held at Athenry. After this he left for Rome to attend the general chapter of the Irish province to be held there that June. During the chapter, he was named a Master of Theology. Nicholas left Rome for Ireland, arriving at Louvain in September. But persecution made his return unwise, forcing him to stay on the continent. [85]

In March 1630 Nicholas was in Brussels, receiving 100 crowns from Felipe IV of Spain for himself and his two companions, impoverished after their journey. His term of office was extended that year by Pope Urban VIII. Aodh Ó Domnaill, the exiled 2nd Earl of Tyrconnell, nominated him for the see of Achonry that year. [86] Nicholas next travelled to Lisbon, arriving in January 1632, en route to a never-convened Dominican chapter in Seville. Over the next two years he lived in Spain and Portugal, his term of office further extended. He petitioned Felipe IV for help to restore the Dominican province in Ireland, and presided over a chapter of the Portuguese province. [87]

Nicholas departed from Portugal for Rome, where on 1 March 1634 he was named prior of San Sisto Vecchio. While prior, he was nominated for Killala or Achonry, but died in July; he was buried in Santa Maria Sopra Minerva, the Dominican order's principal church in Rome at the time. [88]

Others who followed such callings may have included Michael Morris, SJ. Born in 1590, he studied in Lisbon and became a Jesuit, aged seventeen. He was ordained in 1615 or 1616, after which he was Minister for the Irish College at Seville. Morris returned to Ireland but for unknown reasons was dismissed from the Jesuits in 1630. Morris is last heard of en route to Rome, where he planned to issue complaints against the Jesuits and Ireland's regular clergy. [89]

Gregory Bodkin was born in Galway the same year as Morris, to Isabel Lynch and Leo Bodkin. Bodkin studied at St Patrick's College, Seville, from 1610 to June 1615, being ordained on the latter date. He served as proctor of the College in 1627. A Charles Kirwan is noted as receiving the *viaticum* (the royal contribution) of *four milreis* to return to Ireland in March 1625, while a Gregory Skerrett had by 1633 sufficient Portuguese to hear confessions. [90] Walter Lynch was another Seville graduate, ordained there sometime prior to 1625. In 1647 he became Bishop of Clonfert but was exiled the following year, dying in Gyor, Hungary, in 1663. [91]

The character of Irish Catholicism, both Gaeil and Gaill, changed during the 1600s. Religious repression resulted in clerical students being schooled in Counter-Reformation seminaries of Iberia and France. Their strident orthodoxy made Irish Catholicism less Gaelic - no more wives, concubines, children, or divorce - and more fundamentalist. It was a much interrupted, drawn-out process, but by the late 1800s created one of the most observant Catholic national congregations in Europe. And to be Catholic in Ireland was to be *Éireannach*.

## Creating the nation: Cine Éireannach

Valentine Browne, OFM, is thought to have been a younger brother of Sir Dominick Browne (c.1588-1668). His first cousin, Andrew Browne, was dismissed from the office of Mayor in 1632 for refusing to take the Oath of Supremacy. Andrew's father, Oliver fitz Dominick, had done the same in 1609. Of Andrew's children, his eldest son Francis joined the Franciscans while his daughters Mary and Catherine became members of the Poor Clares. [92] Religion was now a highly divisive issue with otherwise loyal subjects sacrificing civic roles for spiritual reasons. With at least four closely related family members in Catholic orders as well as a father, son, and cousin who refused the town's highest office for spiritual reasons, the Brownes were seen as staunch Catholics. Why this was so, in a town who's leading citizens usually conformed to the Crown's religious policy, has been directly attributed to the behind-the-scenes role of urban women in those years:

> Female adherence to the Church of Rome was to have significant implications for the failure of Protestant Reformation. ... The familial pressure exerted by women whose consciences had been activated by Counter-Reformation clergy undoubtedly acted as a growing barrier to the continued conformity of many male heads of households. ... Even if husband proved immune to wifely persuasion, they often proved unwilling or unable to prevent their wives from transmitting their religious culture to their children and the tightly linked marriage patterns of the Old English community resulted in its rapid diffusion. [93]

The religious stance of the Brownes might be best understood if the *bean an tí* was, as family tradition insists, Onora Ní Flaithbertaigh. Fathers may head the house, but mothers rule the heart(h).

Such opposition to the state religion drove Catholics into closer association. The term revived by intellectuals for this new *cine* or nation of merging Gael and Gall was *Éireannach* ('Irishperson'). Its most vigorous preacher was Seathrún Céitinn, who's *Foras Feasa ar Éireinn* (1634) revised *Lebor Gabála Érenn's* medieval themes for modern circumstances. The past is never neutral - it is constantly reused for the shifting needs of the present. As had being the case exactly a thousand years before, identity in Ireland was regenerated from older materials into something new. But what had once been inclusive was now exclusive. Éireannach's key component was membership of the Catholic denomination, something that would last as long as the Irish nation wished to be Catholic. Up to the 1960s other religious affiliations were not regarded as part of the 'true Irish nation', demeaned as 'foreign faiths' - as if Catholicism wasn't.

This demonstrates that conceptions of 'the Irish nation' - *Scotti, Goídil, fer n-Erenn, communitas Hibernie, cine Éireannach* - were frequently politically-driven. Consequently, any natural commonality ignored many internal fault-lines. But without such evasions, a united Catholic cine Éireannach could never be realised. And by the 1630s the need was urgent.

The single greatest difference between the Irish and the British in the 1600s was their experience of imperialism. For the British nation, it was a positive participatory process, 'benevolent'. For the Irish nation, it was generally negative, exploitative, malevolent. Even when ruled from London, neither Scotland nor Wales experienced land theft as did the Irish. The Scots, Welsh, and English were partners in the British imperial project. Ireland was their first colony, the Irish the first to refuse being British. The multi-lingual Cornish, English, Scot (hence Ulster-Scotch in Norlin Airlann), and Welsh Planter communities in Ireland grew "from virtually nothing [in 1601] to over one quarter" of the total population by 1701. [94] Only for such numbers ceaseing by the 1720s and their continious emigration across the Atlantic from the 1680s, Ireland would have become as ethnically British as its American colonies.

Termed 'New English' after the dominent group - in distinction to the 'Old English' (Anglo-Irish) - these British and various Continentals ran a Protestant kingdom in a Catholic country. They held major political and judicial posts along with more and more land. [95] Such enablements gave power out of all proportion to their numbers. Co-existence with or assimilation by the Irish was first attempted, not warfare or outright confiscation - if only because "we cannot, without too great an effusion of blood, avoid their [the Irish!] presence here." [96] Yet they could not seem to grasp that such agressive cultural enforcement would cause conflicts, whose wounds heal uneasily.

During the 1700s the English and Scots created a new island state, the Kingdom of Great Britain, and from it an entirely new nation, the British. The unions succeded because Scot and Welsh had an integrated status akin to English, so into the 1960s Scot and Welsh nationalisms were proudly unionist and imperialist. It would continue until the English no longer wished to be British.

The same could work in Ireland if the Irish nations likewise merged by consent. Events proved even Catholic New English became Irish Confederates because Catholicism was their unifying identity. And unlike Gaeilge or English, Catholicism had European and therefore global dimensions – just like Protestantism. Éireannach/Irish Catholic and Anglo/British Protestant evolved as a result of each Other. Both had a long gestation in the seventeenth century before becoming national identities in the eighteenth. And some fell in-between and outside such neat categories.

This is the point in time when Gaeilge began to lose ground among the Irish. When the Kingdom of Ireland was proclaimed at Dublin in 1541, only one peer understood English. When the Confederation was created in 1642, all Irish state business was conducted in English. By the 1720s it replaced Latin as the language of Irish Catholic church. The pivotal decades were the 1750s-60s, after which majority Gaelic monolingualism gave way to bilingual diaglossia, and from that to majority English monolingualism. The 17th- and 18th-centuries saw Gaeilge become not just a European but an American community language, in Talamh Éisc (Irish of Munster), Cape Breton (Scots Presbyterians), and Montserrat (African slaves). Yet by 1800 only 45% of the Irish population were Gaeilgeoirí, perhaps a third of whom were bilingual. Popular perception is the Great Famine was the breaking point, but vast swathes of Ireland had monolingual English-speaking communities by the 1820s, so post-Famine emigrants were increasingly Anglophone. Wanting to get on in a world where English was a language of economic success, Gaeilgeoirí viewed its decline with regretful pragmatism. The Irish are now almost as far removed from the Gael as the English are from the Anglecynn. It is the way of things. [97]

Instead of language, Catholicism became the prime factor in *Gael+Gall=Irish* identity, as did Protestantism for *English+Scot=British*. That each new island identity adopted their labels from vanquished or subordinate folk (Érainn, Brythoniad) was an unacknowleged irony. That each embraced different forms of imperialism - Catholicism, Britishness - was another. Groups who would have being ethnically and linguistically unpalatable were included on a religious basis; New English Catholics by the Irish, Protestant Cymraeg by the British. Each remained viable until forced to regenerate in the 1960s. They had a good run.

Creating this new national identity may explain Browne's enthusiastic support of an extraordinary project conceived by Irish Franciscans, to compile a huge, multi-volume chronicle of Ireland from the prehistoric past to recent times. It would help create the Irish Catholic nation.

Gaelic political independence ended with the advent of the Stewarts, yet Gaelic culture outlasted them by a very healthy margin. Inspired by other European national histories - Virgil's *Anglica historia* (1534), Prise's *Historiae Brytannicae defensio* (1573), de Mariana's *Historia general de Espana* (1592), and Du Chesne's *Les antiquitez ... des roys de France* (1609) – its compilers wished to dignify and propagate Ireland's history with a like-minded, fully-modern account. After all, in Gaelic-Irish civilization they had possibly the best vernacular material in all Europe. To that end and advertising its modern political nature, it was given a deliberately revisionist title, *Annála ríoghachta Éireann/The Annals of the Kingdom of Ireland*. But in commemoration of it compilers, since the 1640s it has been justly known as *The Annals of the Four Masters*. [98] Unremarked even today is the patron of this Irish Catholic work, Fergal Ó Gara, was Protestant.

In a letter dated 15 May 1632, Valentine Browne gave an important letter of support to Míchéal Ó Cléirigh, OFM, leader of the project. It was an assurance that Ó Cléirigh had Browne's support, and that of the Franciscan order, in his national antiquarian efforts:

> *you have purposed to compile from the ancient and almost obliterated Irish records whatever concerns the annals of our kings, and relates to the state, both ecclesiastical and civil, of this kingdom; lest we might not appear to second your work, which is so virtuous, and fills such a long-felt want, we command you by the merit of holy obedience to persevere until the end, if God shall give you life, in this laborious work of the Annals which you have already begun, and to submit all that you shall compile to the judgement of men skilful in the Irish tongue, as you have done in the case of the smaller works.* [99]

This was an extraordinary recommendation from an Anglo-Irishman, especially for a caste who were avowed partisans of Ó Domnaill and Ó Neill. Yet Browne's efforts were to be matched if not superseded by his first cousin-once removed, Mary Bonaventure Browne, a nun of the Poor Clares.

The Poor Clares were established in Ireland at Dublin in June 1629, but were banished by the authorities in October 1630. By then a new settlement, Bethlehem, was founded on the east shore of Lough Ree, the community numbering sixty nuns. Between then and October 1636, abbess Mother Cicely Dillon gave fathers Aodh Ó Raghailligh and Séamus Ó Siaghail the task of translating *The Rule of our Holy Mother S. Clare* into Gaeilge. [100] Despite mostly being Anglo-Irish, they chose Gaeilge as the daily language of their religious observations. When Míchéal Ó Cléirigh stopped at Bethlehem, Mother Cicely induced him to make a copy. Evidently, even among some Anglo-Irish, Gaeilge was then seen as a component of the Catholic *cine/náision Éire-annach*, just as English language and culture was deemed essential to the later Protestant British nation.

Mary and Catherine Browne joined the Poor Clares in 1632. Use of Gaeilge within the community, and *saoi* such as Ó Cléirigh, must have created a deep impression. When Mary became third abbess of a new foundation, situated a little further west, she would commission one of the greatest Irish scribes of the age, and later still, create her own utterly unique work. [101]

## Secular lives and legal disputes

But just as Anthony Lynch was unsuited to trade, not everyone found themselves liking the religious life. In March 1637, Francis Blake,

> *a youth of Tuam diocese … who put aside the religious habit and rejected the catholic faith a year after he had made his profession as a Friar Minor, now wishes to be reconciled to the Church but not to be bound by his religious profession, which he alleges was invalid.* [102]

Not all of the dealings of the merchants were bloodless. Andrew Blake was murdered in his Galway house on 15 July 1610 by one *John Griffyn*, solicitor. The motive is unknown but Griffyn (Ó Gríobhta?) was found guilty of "wilful murther by a jury of xij men of the said Towne". Because the trial was carried out illegally, Mayor Stephen Kirwan and diverse aldermen were summoned to "the Star Chamber at Dublin … to answer for contempt and misdemeanour." [103] Principal councillor Walter French was fined two hundred pounds, while James Óge Darcy was fined forty pounds and given a prison sentence. The case against Valentine Blake was dismissed "for that appeared no sufficient proof to find him guilty of the said misdemeanour." As for Mayor Kirwan, "his death hath freed him" from the court's judgement. [104]

Walter French soon returned to the Star Chamber where he "exhibited information that… Dominick Browne … Ambrose Bodkyne …" [105] and others, gathered at French's property at *Cowlrahan* in late October 1611. They "did put upon the same four score cows and oxen of the said Dominick Browne and there riotously and forcibly kept upon the said land", [106] and other misdemeanour's. Browne was summoned, found guilty, and being the principal actor behind the intimidation, was fined one hundred pounds and imprisoned. Presumably indifferent justice was visited on Lawrence Bodkin of *Farhgar* in 1617, after he and fellow jurors found James Evers and Ann Janes not guilty of Henry Spratt's murder. This despite several witnesses demonstrating "that Evers did murder Sprat and that Ann Janes was the plotter and procurer of Evers." Bound for contempt and offence, Bodkin was fined forty pounds. [107] Even attempting to be an honest broker could backfire, as Anthony Lynch found out. He acted as

> *an umpire between John McJonyn and Feagh McJonyn [Jennings], two brothers of Ballycusen, Co. Mayo, who had a dispute about the meares of some lands. John had attacked petitioner and, in self-defence, petitioner struck him with the hilt of his dagger. John died a few days after, but chiefly from*

*The three Arms of Galway; 1361, 1396, 1485, Courtesy of NUI, Galway*

being careless about his wound. [108]

McJonyn's family rounded on Lynch, forcing him abroad "to escape the vengeance of John's relatives". In absentia, he was tried for murder, "condemned and outlawed." In 1629, Lynch petitioned Charles I for a pardon as he "is now getting old and is poor ... a widower with six children". The king directed a pardon be drawn up for Lynch. [109] What sounds like a barring order was obtained in April 1636, protecting Lady Sara Ó Conchobhair Sligo "daughter to the Earl of Antrim, and wife of Donnchadh Ó Conchobhair Sligo ... against Patrick John French, from whose unconscionable devices they have suffered much." [110]

The most serious of these legal affairs occurred in 1620, when Dominick Browne fitz Geoffrey killed Henry Rany, a Galway stonemason, in unknown circumstances. Browne was tried at Athenry in July, and found guilty of felony and homicide. Perhaps there were mitigating factors or perhaps money talks, because for the sum of £5.00 Browne was pardoned. [111] The incident seems to have done him no long-term harm, as he was elected M.P. for Athenry in 1634, and as Mayor of Galway that September. He was knighted in 1635. [112]

## Senatus Populusque Galvianus - SPQG

In the early 1600s Galway's economy slowly improved, as evidenced by works created by the prime families. Under 1601-02, *An Account of the Town of Galway* states "Margaret Joyce fitz John", wife to Oliver Óge French, "built upon her own expenses all or the most part of the bridges of Conaght."[113] However garbled, this tradition highlights another Galwegian who, like Margaret Ballach Lenche and Margaret Athy before her, was of some service to her community. Sir Henry Lynch willed "£300 for the building of a college and £500 the use thereof to be paid yearly towards the preferment of orphans of the natives of the town." [114] Perhaps too ambitious was "the new work [which in 1618] was begun by consent of merchants of this town, intending to make a more commodious town thereof for trading." £35,000 was offered by forty families from Holland, who undertook to "to finish the whole work in 15 years time, yet this work fell for want of prosecution." [115] There were other reverses; on 1 May 1619

*this town was burnt. Upon Monday it took fire in the east suburbs occasioned by a musket shot,*

*Tribes of Galway 1124-1642*

*being a usual day for a game for the youths and tradesmen of the town. ... [it] did consume 400 houses, and utterly defaced the Abbey [St. Francis's] being so vehement that the bodyes of the dead lying in vaults were consumed to ashes. [116]*

But on the whole, progress moved onward and upward. Galway was praised as "the Windsor of Ireland.", counted as Ireland's second city, next to Dublin and ahead of Waterford, Limerick, Cork and [London]Derry. [117] Galway stood at the crossroads of European and American markets. A driver of economic growth, its potential was not fully realised, but potentially vast. Ports such as Glasgow and Liverpool had or soon would. Why not Galway? Why not indeed. Some of the projects the merchants undertook in those years were the following:

1624-25: *This year the fort of Balenamanagh was built at the King's Charge.* [118]

1630-31: *... rails of timber [were] put around the green ... with a row of ashtrees.* [119]

1631-32: *Robert Kirwan sheriff left £10 sterling per annum to relieve the poor prisoners of Gallway.* [120]

1633-34: *Patrick French fitz George being mayor, the streets from the outside of the great gate to the cross was paved.* [121]

1637-38: *... Sir Thomas Blake being mayor the east tower gate of the hour clock was built upon the cost of the corporation.* [122] (the SPQR flag flew above this).

1638-39: *In the year of Sir Robuck Lynch Baronet the market house was built upon the cost of the corporation.* [123]

1639-40: *In the year that Walter Brown was mayor, the great and strong bulwork about Shoemaker's tower was begun, but not finished in his time.* [124]

1642-43: *Mayor Richard Óge Martin continued the old works, which is the outer wall, and brought to a considerable height. He left £800 for the building of two chapels, the one at St. Francis abbey and the other at St. Nicholas church within the town and left legacies to all the convents and abbeys in Conaght.* [125]

Some knew more about consuming wealth than creating it, but the pursuit of wealth is not shameful, only the means, and ends. Summing them up, Maureen Donovan-O'Sullivan wrote:

if they were hard task-masters and accumulated their wealth sometimes by questionable means, [the Galway merchants] had an excellent sense of the responsibilities which affluence brings – *noblesse oblige* was no empty motto to these merchant princes. [126]

But how did *noblesse oblige* square with the *res publica* implied in *SPQR*? Were Galwegians emulating a phrase because it evoked prestigious Rome? Potent terms are often profoundly misapplied but the prime families probably knew its then sense perfectly. The *publica Galvia* were not the general population, no more than in Rome. They were the freemen property-owners who held actual commercial and political power, like the *Féni* of a *túath*. Understandably, such Galwegians soon saw themselves as "superior lords and masters" [127] - all power groups do.

Everything *avant-garde* becomes *passé*, hence the brand-loyalty of 'tradition', religious/political faith, even songs. It can be entrenched if the wider public believe they have a say, no matter how delusional. Because power is ever held by a very few, who guard it well. Subjects may become citi-

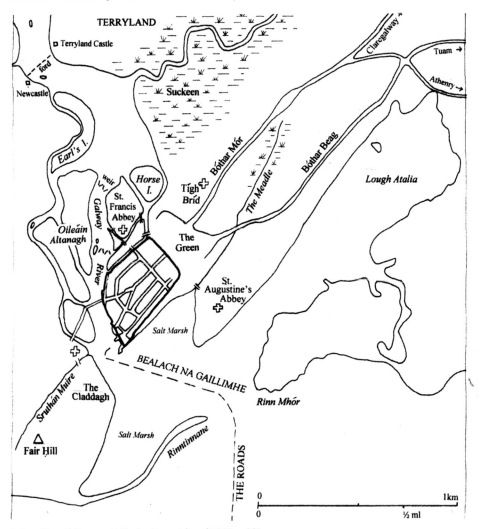

*Galway Town & Environs 1642 after Fitzpatrick et al 2007, p. 291*

zens but the grip on and exercise of power has not changed and probably never will.

None of which matters a damn to most folk, even now. Life goes on as normal until life is no longer normal. Dissatisfaction only transforms into action by guided coordination, often taking advantage of unexpected popular outbursts. People everywhere are otherwise immersed in personal issues - happiness and unhappiness generally derive from people and matters which are less than a footnote in any history. In that regard, our ancestors were probably no more happy or unhappy than ourselves. Most human needs come down to having a home and a family, a community and a job, to love and be loved. It is these from which folk everywhere derive their greatest joys, deepest sorrows, and whatever meanings may be in life. Differences between humans are not values, which are similar and almost irrelevant, but identities, which are different and thus crucial. Someone must rule and few care who do - until things fall apart.

Change is constant, and the *comunitatis Galvia/túath Gaillimhe* made room for newcomers: men surnamed Barrett, Bermingham, Bourke, Butler, Gowna [Smith?], Flynne, Hynes, Nolan, Royne [Rooney? Ryan?], Tarpy are all listed as town freemen and proprietors in the 1640s. [128] Whatever their ancestry, they obeyed the civic rules and loyalties by which the town operated. Few wish to overthrow or reform establishments; they either want to join up or replace its officers ('elite displacement'/'transfer of power'), keeping its functions intact. None of the above were then numerous or wealthy - no more than the Lynches, once upon a time.

None of this should underestimate the challenges any underclass faces to 'get out from under'. Economic wealth enables political power. Neither are willingly shared. They accrue within power groups (dynasties, institutions, political parties, criminal gangs – all of which overlap) who go to extraordinary degrees to retain them. They are only gained for a wider public by great pains, often at terrible, unapologetic cost - swiftly forgotten.

Like today, *noblesse oblige*, alias philanthropy, are mixed acts of genuine altruism and personal prestige. At worst they are occasional charities instead of civic obligations - no society is human-proof. Among European and global cultures, aristocratic notions of 'blood', 'race', class, and caste, were then supreme, privileging mé féin entitlement. Egalitarian implications in *SPQR* - *"Senatus Populusque Romanus"* - were utterly fantastic among *Senatus Populusque Galvianus, Hiberni, Europa*. Indeed a case can be made that contrary to 'rebel' stereotypes, Irish society is conformist and conservative, even its dissidents dogmatically traditional. The *res publica* concept is often mouthed but mostly unpractised, fundamentally misunderstood by those who claim it most. Greece via Rome bequeathed a concept of *res publica* but like the Roman, most favour *imperium*. And those considered outside a *túath* ('community', 'publica') can go walk. Yet having the opportunity to live in better conditions than which you were born was an aspiration demonstrated by the Tribes. Proportional economic representation enables individuals and society as a whole. That continuously enabled power groups have reciprocal responsibilities to those they rule was as vivid an issue then as now. Failure to understand this caused conflicts which consumed seventeenth-century Ireland, Britain, and Europe, with repercussions entirely alive today.

## Messers Lynch and Lynch

Back on the high seas, Galwaymen continued their trade, some less honestly than others. Richard and Simon Lynch were owners of the *St. Patrick* of Galway, which they freighted in March 1627 for a voyage from St. Malo to Malaga. To evade an embargo, Simon Lynch, a burgess of St. Malo, arranged to conceal her nationality by engaging a French crew. Lynch also underwrote the cost of readying her for the voyage, providing her with "sails, anchors, ... a small armament and a crew of nine men and a [cabin] boy." [129] So far, so swimmingly.

The voyage to Malaga was uneventful, with the St. Patrick taking on a cargo of wine and raisins and escaping detection. But the rough weather that brought the armada to grief in 1601 did exactly the same in 1627, driving the *St. Patrick* right into Kinsale. She was seized on the reasonable assumption that she was a French ship, only for the authorities to discover *au contraire*. Upon which Messrs. Lynch and Lynch had some explaining to do. Yet with the testicular fortitude of certain species of entrepreneurs and politicians, the Lynchs sent a petition documenting the illegal arrangements made at St. Malo, in the belief that this would get the ship restored to them. The response is unknown, but must have been worth hearing. [130]

## Christopher Kirwan and the Alice

Perseverance brought Christopher Kirwan reward after substantial loss. His ship, the *Alice* of Ipswich, had been at Killybegs in November 1637 when she was forcibly impressed into the navy. Kirwan only retained his cargo by loading it on another ship, costing a prohibitive £91.00. Kirwan "lost much by the hindrance of his voyage" [131] and was deprived of the ship by which he made a living. Compensation was slow in coming, but worth the wait. Written at Westminster and addressed to the Lords Justice and Vice Treasurer, it directed them to "pay him the £91 and an additional sum of £300, he giving a discharge from himself and all the other merchants who have lost." Directing the compensation was King Charles I. [132] Dated January 1641, Kirwan's compensation was timely, as great waves wrecked many affairs that year.

## Blowback effects

The Alice may have been seized in the build-up to the Bishop's Wars of 1638-40, when as a result of religious conflict Scotland declared war on England. However, King Charles was unable to put down the rebellion because England's Westminster parliament refused to grant him the taxes he needed to raise an army. [133] King Charles proposed to get around this by promising to grant Irish Catholics full civil and religious rights, if they mobilised an Irish army to put down the Scots. Scots, Welsh, and English Protestants, variously denominated, were horrified at the prospect of an army of Irish Catholics anywhere in pre-united Britain. So early in 1641, some urged an invasion of Ireland to pre-emptively prevent the army assembling.

Domino-like, the prospect of a British invasion frightened a small group of Irishmen - all facing financial ruin due to economic recession and bad harvests since 1636 - to conspire to seize control of the Irish government. Dublin Castle and a number of important garrisons would be captured in what was planned as a bloodless *coup d'etat*. When Catholic Ireland rose up to support them, their position would be secure, bargaining from a position of strength until King Charles granted their demands. Then they'd fight wherever the king wished. The rising was set for 23 October 1641, Feast of Saint Ignatius of Loyola. What could possibly go wrong?

In what came to be the grand tradition of subsequent Irish rebellions, matters went awry before the start. A conspirator talked, an informer alerted Dublin Castle. Popular revolt in south Ulster unleashed decades of bile while brutal government reactions pushed Catholics into insurrection. Sectarian massacres ensued on all sides, and anger destroyed their world. Some four thousand Protestant Scots, English, Welsh, Cornish, and Irish either died from exposure to winter conditions after being thrown out of their homes, or were murdered by their Catholic neighbours. How many Irish and English Catholics died is uncertain, but in one incident in April 1642 unknown numbers were burned alive on a hill of furze between Naas and Celbridge. Catholics and Protestants who tried to moderate events or remain neutral found few Catholics or Protestants respected moderation or neutrality, forcing them to join up or be against them. Ulster Scots Presbyterians refused to stand with Ulster's English Anglicans, allowing the old enemy to be picked off by the Catholic Irish until they became targets. New English Catholic's enthusiastically joined the insurgent Gaelic-Irish and Anglo-Irish against Protestant English and Scot.

Over Christmas, insurrection spread from Ulster to north Connacht, targeting the province's tiny Protestant communities. Thirty-eight of the forty Protestants of Sligo were murdered in the town jail on 13 January 1642. On 12 February, fifty-five Protestant refugees from Sligo and Mayo en route to Galway were murdered at the bridge of Shrule. News of such massacres spread to Scotland then Wales and England, alarming enough for emergency measures to be introduced by the English House of Commons amidst it own civil strife. In south Wales, the mayors of Haverfordwest and Pembroke received commands to stay all goods, ships, and commodities from or belonging to a native of Ireland. In February 1642 they detained a barque on which travelled

> certain Irishmen that were landed at Pill within the port of Milford and bound for Ireland, viz, Dominick Bodkin, Joseph Everard, John Lynch, Turough Obryan, Patrick Poore [Power] and Robert Harrold, all of Galloway in the realm of Ireland. Who being examined before us did confess themselves to be Roman Catholics, and some of them do refuse to take the oath of supremacy and allegiance, ... they are stayed and committed to the sheriff of the town of Haverfordwest, there to remain until we shall receive directions from the said noble house of Commons for their enlargement. [134]

Nothing more incriminating that a saddle of Spanish leather (belonging to Bodkin) and certain law books" was found. [135] The good men of Haverfordwest and Pembroke were just doing their duty, following orders to detain "any person of the towns of Ireland ... which are in rebellion." [136] But Galway was not rebelling. Its people had stood by the Crown and English government for over three hundred years, in times when many thought it smart to do otherwise. They were merchants, not rebels. Until ...

*1646 Galway arms from the Lion Tower (courtesy of Paul Walsh)*

# EPILOUGE –
## "THE WEIGHTIEST BUSINESS THAT EVER WAS."

About nine a.m. on 19 March 1642, Captain Anthony Willoughby sat in the captain's lodging by the drawbridge of St. Augustine's Fort, Galway, finishing a letter to the 5th Earl of Clanricard. Willoughby's father, Sir Francis, the fort's governor since 1636, had departed for Dublin in October. Captain Willoughby commanded two companies armed with pikes, firelocks, and cannon in a well-provisioned fort on a highly defensible position, surrounded on three sides by the sea and overlooking Galway. It had a double wall of stone, three sally ports and a drawbridge.

Less than a century after Margaret Athy built St Augustine's abbey, the prospect of an armada in Loch Lurgan/Galway Bay frightened the government into action. By 1603 the friars were expelled and the abbey housed a garrison lodged alongside the church, which held stores and munitions. Its governor held authority over the fort - and the town. That clipped Galway's cherished independence, forever transforming its relationship with the Crown. Even yet, though its people were no longer English and barely Protestant, the Galwegians were still loyal. The Crown remained at the core of Galwegian identity, the relationship seen as almost a sacred partnership.

But the prospects of a Connacht Plantation since 1632 eroded that tradition. Galwegians now understood the relationship was neither sacred nor a partnership, but that of subjects to a power who would confiscate their properties and destroy their religious identities. In England, king and parliament were in a conflict that in August would erupt into civil war. If the English were at war with themselves, and the Scots, on a continent enflamed, where stood the Irish? Where indeed.

Few conflicts have a side worth fighting for. The community of Galway supported the Crown and English government because it had offered some protection against extortionate local lords. Now it extorted them all. In power relationships, the disabled understand the way the world is run better than the self-justifying enabled ever do, because it is they who the enabled run over. [1] The strong brutalise and dominate the weak while claiming the allegiance not of citizens but subjects.

And now the price of that allegiance had proved too dear.

A ship had recently arrived in the bay, and lay at anchor in The Roads. On board were twelve pieces of cannon, a dozen muskets, plus several barrels of gunpowder. The ship's master had taken a small boat to the fort, where he and his men were taking on ballast stones to make up for the loss in weight when the supplies were offloaded.

Suddenly, Captain Willoughby was alerted by shouts from the sentries. A small boat from the town had pulled alongside the ship, and a number of young townsmen – their leaders later identified as Brian Ruadh Mac Mathghamhna Mór, Stephen Lynch, Dominick Kirwan, Walter Óge Martin - armed with pistols, swords and sceana, leapt aboard like pirates. High above on the south wall of the fort, Willoughby could see the crew being attacked, wounded, and killed.

The townsmen imprisoned the surviving crew below decks, lowered the sails and weighed anchor, preparing to bring the ship in The Roads to the town. To prevent the munitions being brought to the town, Captain Willoughby ordered the garrison to open fire and sink the ship. Several cannonballs were fired as it sailed by the fort to Bun Gaillimhe. None struck.

Before long, the ship was lost to sight behind Ceann an Bhalla, where it docked and had its munitions taken ashore. Before the offloading was finished the town gates were shut, while any English within the town were disarmed. This done, the townspeople made ready to besiege the fort. That night, an utterly unnerved Captain Willoughby added a postscript to his letter describing the day's events, rightly remarking that this was "the weightiest business that ever was." [2] This news had to be communicated post-haste. Galway, one of the most consistently loyal communities in the Kingdom of Ireland, was in rebellion.

And nothing would ever again be the same.

*To Be Continued*

*The 1652 West Gate and Mills, the 1442 Bridge and John Ffrench's chamber of 1539
with Terryland Castle in the background. Courtesy of the British Library*

# AFTERWORD

From February 1996 I researched the Martyn 'Tribe'. *Martyn: People and Places* was to be published in 1999; I regret not doing so. My eighty-page chapbook *The Tribes of Galway* (June 2001) was intended as a forerunner to a larger work to be published about 2003. But by then I was very seriously ill. Only in summer 2010 did writing commence on this volume, with many tedious delays before completion. Volume II (1642-?) will follow, should the gods spare me the health.

For some, 'history' - Irish and otherwise - is a fixed tradition not subject to criticism or revision. I disagree. Traditions are often prejudiced versions of past events which crumble under scrutiny (different from a local folk or family tradition, which are generally sincere). Often they are believed with religious intensity, so dissent is blasphemous. Such traditions are called history, but are myths which involve not only selective remembrance but a great oblivion. History is far more gritty, troublesome, and interesting.

A myth can be defined as a belief that a certain version of past events is true (e.g., historic). Such beliefs always have some factual basis - everything is 'based on a true story.' Yet unlike history, myths are dramas and need heroes, so certain people and actions are dramatised while others are demeaned or excluded. This legitimises and ingrains loyalty to actors of the dramas, their genealogical/political descendants and their tradition, their 'memory', their myth. Unless myths are investigated, the actual course of events is lost in time.

As facts uncovered by research into the shadows of Irish history are bound to upset tradition, they must be attacked, derided, and dismissed; 'revisionist', 'academic', even 'historian', become slurs. Often they succeed. Little wonder the practise and teaching of history, and history itself, is so profoundly misunderstood, while the romantic drama of myth grows bigger than truth. The arts and politics make fiction real; historians strive to make reality understood. Tellingly, 'myth' is glossed as *fiction, fable, fancy, fantasy*. This makes 'traditional history' [sic] doubly unhistorical - something that cannot withstand investigative scrutiny - and dangerous.

Dangerous? Surely an extreme choice of word! Yet no one of my generation in Ireland can be unaware of the power of our indoctrinated traditions, nor the horrific cost of dumb loyalty to them.

Beliefs influence our views, our views affect our choices, our choices drive our decisions. But what if our beliefs are biased? What if what we believe to be truth is false? Decisions reverberate far and wide through time and space, long after our present becomes the past and gives way to the future. Futures all too often created by deeply flawed decisions, all with consequences. Bias and reality are splintered doors of perception and like love, sometimes a terrible thing.

History can be defined as an attempt to establish the actual course of events in a particular space in time. It derives from Greek *historia*, "[knowledge from] 'enquiry', 'research'". The Greek-derived term in Modern Gaeilge, *stair*, means just that. *Seanchas* is the older term as Gaeilge, meaning 'lore'. Its glosses include *learning, facts, tradition*. So I enquired, I researched, learned traditions and facts, not only to see but observe and therefore to understand. This book is the result. I consider it worthwhile. The research and vocation must generally be its own reward.

There was no 'Author's Grand Design'. Various themes arose during research and are included as contextual *agusína*. Some can be argued as having no connection to the Tribes, but I felt the backgrounds and contexts they provided were important. In seeking to avoid contentious issues, I painfully arrived at the same conclusion many others have before me - that no history can be free of contention. So the issues were embraced and dealt with evidentially. Others must pursue topics to which I could only allude. In the meantime, I draw attention to the many fine works listed in the bibliography that should reach a far wider audience - though sadly unlikely to do so.

There is an impertinence in summing up entire lives in a few words, and I hope readers will be mindful of this. The passing of time since I began this work has certainly made me so.

Adrian Martyn
Radharc na Caoille
April 2016.

# ABBREVIATIONS, ORTHOGRAPHY, STYLES

Primary documentation has being the evidential foundation for this book. The *New History of Ireland* series and other such works have being my scholarly guides, their authors my role-models. The distinct yet overlapping disciplines (from archaeology to linguistics, genealogy to economics, politics to historiography) made writing this book infinitely easier. For that I owe much to those who wrote and published them

Names as Gaeilge are generally in the standard orthography of Classical Modern Gaeilge, derived principally from Ó Muraíle's *Great Book of Irish Genealogies*, itself an edition and translation of Mac Fhirbhisgh's *Leabhar na nGenealach*. However quoting from different texts has made the end result more *trí na chéile* than intended! For further linguistic flavour in some cases Édouard not Edward, Felipe not Phillip, usv. I have not attempted to give a pronunciation guide, instead relying on Anglicised forms quoted in the text to guide the reader. Some words and phrases have been left untranslated to reflect the almost vanished speech of the community in which I grew up.

Where individuals are concerned I have generally rendered their names as found in the documentation concerned; so Ó Dorchaidhe or Dorsey not Darcy, de Linche or Lenche not Lynch. When referring to the families as a whole, however, Browne rather than Brun, Martyn rather than Martin. Similarly with geographies and polities, so Britain (an island) rather than Great Britain (a state created in 1707), Iberia rather than Spain, and so forth.

While scholarly best practise and consistency has been attempted, eagle-eyed readers will spot my undoubted eff-ups. At least the underlying reasons can be understood.

| | | | |
|---|---|---|---|
| ADdR | - Annales Dominicani de Roscoman | JIFHS | - Journal of the Irish Family History Society |
| AFM | - Annals of the Four Masters | JRSAI | - Journal of the Royal Society of Antiquarians of |
| AClon | - Annals of Clonmacnoise | | Ireland |
| AC | - Annals of Connacht | GBIG | - The Great Book of Irish Genealogies |
| AI | - Annals of Inisfallen. | Grace's Annals | - Annales Hiberniae |
| ALCé | - Annals of Loch Cé | IEP | - Irish Exchequer Payments 1270-1446 |
| ATig | - Annals of Tigernach | IHS | - Irish Historical Studies |
| AU | - Annals of Ulster | IPRJI | - Irish Patent Rolls of James I |
| BFR | - Blake Family Records | JGAHS | - Journal of the Galway Archaeological and |
| BBCS | - Bulletin of the Board of Celtic Studies | | Historical Society |
| CCMI, I, 1515-74 | - Calendar of Carew Manuscripts, Ireland I, | McCB | - Mac Carthaigh's Book |
| | 1515-74. | NHI | - A New History of Ireland |
| CDI | - Calendar of Documents relating to Ireland | ODNB | - Oxford Dictionary of National Biography |
| CJRI | - Calendar of Justicary Rolls of Ireland | PHCC | - Proceedings of the Harvard Celtic Colloquium |
| CMCS | - Cambridge Medieval Celtic Studies | PRIA | - Proceedings of the Royal Irish Academy |
| Compossicion | - Compossicion Booke of Conought | Seanchus Burcach | - Seanchus Burcach: historia et |
| CSPI | - Calendar of State Papers of Ireland | | genealogia familae de Burgo |
| DoIB | - Dictionary of Irish Biography | Regestum | - Regestum Monasterii Fratrum Praedicatorum de |
| Clyn's Annals | - The Annals of Ireland by Friar John Clyn | | Athenry |
| CS | - Chronicum Scotorum | RSAIJ | - Royal Society of Antiquarians of Ireland Journal |
| FAI | - Fragmentary Annals of Ireland | TJIA | - The Journal of Irish Archaeology |
| fiants | - The Irish Fiants of the Tudor Sovereigns | TNA | - The National Archives |
| JGSI | - Journal of the Genealogical Society of Ireland | | |

# GENEALOGIES – A NOTE AND A KEY

Except where stated, the genealogies are my own work, generally derived from strictly contemporary documents listed under *Primary Sources* in the bibliography. Any particular document that has provided the main frame of the genealogy is so listed, but even they will be supplemented by stray family members found in other sources. Obviously I could not list all sources on the pages concerned, though an attempt has been made. They can be found by checking the relevant parts of the text and their notes. The years noted indicates their chronological location within the sources.

I chose to do this because as I rapidly found in early 1996, many Tribes genealogies created in the eighteenth and nineteenth centuries were, for the early generations, fictions. Those who compiled them evidently did not have the slightest clue of their actual origins, or if they did, chose to corrupt them. The Lynch genealogies are perhaps the most risible example, but they are by no means the only ones. The Darcys in the 1700s suppressed their actual Irish origins in favour of a French one, becoming D'Arcy.

For whatever reason, little serious medieval genealogical research has been undertaken on any of these families. Since modern descendants have nothing else on the subject, their views of their early ancestors are highly inaccurate. In mitigation, the genealogies are generally reliable from the 1600s, but that still leaves earlier generations lost in fiction (I cannot get over the feeling that for eighteenth and nineteenth century descendants, the medieval era was too distant to be real, fit only for clichés, stereotypes, and other fantasy. But then almost none of them were historians and all wished to inflate their ancestry for social reasons. For why see Chapter Two, note 6, but also for comparison Chapter One, notes 13, 16, 18, 19, 79, 80, 131). Alone of all the Tribes, the Blakes have almost complete family trees, though only because successive generations troubled themselves to preserve the day-to-day working documents and important legal papers. But even here luck played a role in their preservation and publication. Time otherwise destroys all.

So rightly or wrongly I have chosen to present the genealogies in this manner, following the method I used to create the Martyn genealogies from early 1996 onwards. The genealogical outlines (they cannot all be called genealogies) compiled from contemporary documents act as a control. Printed or unpublished family trees were treated to critical scrutiny. Some family trees are presented both for comparison, and because they represent family traditions found nowhere else which may be authentic, even if transmitted clumsily. The 1766 pedigree of Mark Kirwan was an especially interesting case in point. Many women can only be rendred as "?". However even this advertises their existence, so has better gynatic value than purely agnatic genealogies or pedigrees.

Nevertheless, it must be emphasised that further critical research needs to be done. Though an attempt has being made, I do not pretend that any of these genealogies are comprehensive. Because illness prevented much travel outside of Galway, resources such as the Heraldic Office and the National Archives (both in Dublin), were largely unused aside from notes made on research trips back in the 1990s. Research was confined to the era covered by this book; for later times I relied on previously published work. Subsequent researchers will certainly improve on what I have presented here, as well as other aspects of these families. Indeed I look forward to it.

The sources for the pedigree of the Uí hAllmhuráin of Clann Fhearghaile, and the genealogies of the Muintir Murchadha and Uí Fhlaithbheartaigh, Uí Chonchobair, and de Burghs, are stated under the headings. I am thankful to Anne Connon (formerly of National University of Ireland, Galway) for useful direction on the first four. Most of the Gaelic-Irish men concerned had multiple wives and this should be borne in mind.

*fl.=flourit*, meaning the person concerned is documented as alive in the year cited.
*c.=circa*, 'about'. *d.*=died. *af.*='after'. *bef.*='before'.
Broken lines '_ _ _' denotes 'uncertain relationship'. Dotted lines '.....' denotes illegitimacy.
?='name unknown'. Equal sign ('=') denotes 'married'. Plus sign ('+') denotes 'unmarried relationship'
Question mark after name (e.g., *Mary Athy?*) denotes 'name uncertain', only stated in family tradition.
M= Mayor     Blf. = Bailiff  mas. = Master
OP = Order of Preachers (Dominicans)
OFM = Order of Francican Missionaries

# Athy, 1253-1709

Sources: *CDI*; Connolly, 1998; Dryburgh and Smith, 2005; *CIRCLE*; *BFR*; *IEP*; Corporation Book A; *BSD*.
*John's descendants derived from Athy, 1999.

William de Athy, *fl.* 1253.

Peter, *fl.* 1275-80.    Henry of *Cathyr*, *fl.* 1275-76.

John, *fl.* 1270, d. by 1281.
=?

William, *fl.* 1278-82.    Nicholas, *fl.* 1281.    Sir William, *fl.* 1290s-1305    Robert, *fl.* 1297

Richard    Thomas
=?    =?

John    William, *fl.* 1302.
[Sir William?]

Sir John de Athy, *fl.* 1310 - *c.*1344

William, *fl.* 1320-42.  Mary?=Thomas Lynch fitz William.  Elias, *fl.* 1342

William de Athy, Treasurer of Connacht, *fl.* 1388.  Elias, *fl.* 1398-1424.

Ms. Athy =William Blake

William [*fl.* 1388?] =?

John Athy, *fl.* 1404-44; Soverign of Galway =Margaret, *fl.* 1428.

Edmund, *fl.* 1440-44.  Thomas, *fl.* 1440.

Walter, *fl.* 1440-45.  Richard, *fl.* 1424-40.  Nicholas, *fl.* 1424-40/72?

William, Bailiff 1511-12.

Nicholas, *fl.* 1535 =Katiline Kyrwayn, *fl.* 1535

Walter, *fl.* 1440.  dau=Walter French (issue)

Nicholas Athy, *fl.* 1472 (Nicholas son of William, *fl.* 1424-40?)

Edmond, Blf 1505-06, 1514-15.

John, Master, *fl.* 1497-1511.  Richard son of Walter Athy, *fl.* 1505. =?

Margaret, *fl. c.* 1508 =Stephen Lynch fitz Dominick Dubh

Marcus, *fl.* 1586 [=Mark, *fl.* 1603?]

Livinia, *fl.* 1604=Andrew French of Barcelona.

John Athy, *fl.* 1568* =?

Mark, *fl.* 1603.  James, *fl.* 1621.

Walter, *fl.* 1591 =dau. of Francis Martin?  ?Edmund =Margaret Lynch

Charles, *fl.* 1640.  Walter, *fl.* 1641.  Nicholas, *fl.* 1652.  Jennock, *fl.* 1657.  Giles, *fl.* 1657.

Walter of Oranmore, *fl. c.* 1673 =sister of Peter Kirwin?

Francis, fl. 1634, Sheriff 1639-40. =dau. of George Martyn?

Edmond, *fl.* 1692. of Limerick City

Captain Andrew, *fl.* 1686-91. (issue)

Mary Athy, dau and heiress, m. 1693 =Walter Blake fitz And. fitz Wal. of Dunmacrina, d. 1740 (issue)

John =? (issue)

Captain George of Maryland, 1642-1709. (issue)

# Blake of Galway and Athenry, 1278-1680

Source: *BFR*, pp. 138-148, vol. I.

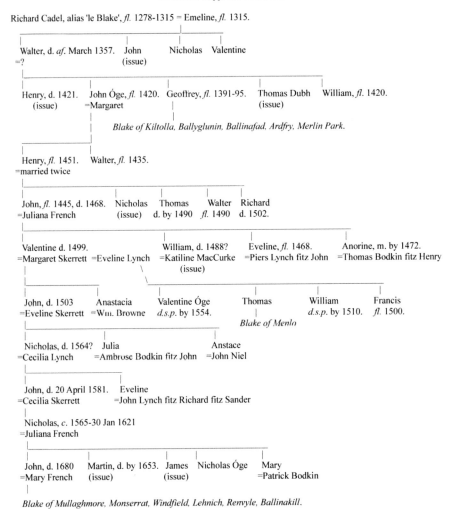

Richard Cadel, alias 'le Blake', *fl.* 1278-1315 = Emeline, *fl.* 1315.

Walter, d. *af.* March 1357.    John    Nicholas   Valentine
=?                  (issue)

Henry, d. 1421.   John Óge, *fl.* 1420.   Geoffrey, *fl.* 1391-95.   Thomas Dubh   William, *fl.* 1420.
(issue)       =Margaret                                 (issue)

                  *Blake of Kiltolla, Ballyglunin, Ballinafad, Ardfry, Merlin Park.*

Henry, *fl.* 1451.   Walter, *fl.* 1435.
=married twice

John, *fl.* 1445, d. 1468.   Nicholas   Thomas   Walter   Richard
=Juliana French         (issue)   d. by 1490   *fl.* 1490   d. 1502.

Valentine d. 1499.           William, d. 1488?   Eveline, *fl.* 1468.    Anorine, m. by 1472.
=Margaret Skerrett   =Eveline Lynch   =Katiline MacCurke   =Piers Lynch fitz John   =Thomas Bodkin fitz Henry
                                  (issue)

John, d. 1503    Anastacia    Valentine Óge    Thomas     William      Francis
=Eveline Skerrett   =Wm. Browne   *d.s.p.* by 1554.              *d.s.p.* by 1510.   *fl.* 1500.
                                   *Blake of Menlo*

Nicholas, d. 1564?   Julia                Anstace
=Cecilia Lynch     =Ambrose Bodkin fitz John   =John Niel

John, d. 20 April 1581.   Eveline
=Cecilia Skerrett        =John Lynch fitz Richard fitz Sander

Nicholas, *c.* 1565-30 Jan 1621
=Juliana French

John, d. 1680    Martin, d. by 1653.   James   Nicholas Óge   Mary
=Mary French    (issue)           (issue)                 =Patrick Bodkin

*Blake of Mullaghmore, Monserrat, Windfield, Lehnich, Renvyle, Ballinakill.*

# Bodkin, 1343-1737

Sources: Regestum; BFR; Corporation Book A; Wardenship; PRJI; Blake, 1915-16; *Irish in Europe website *** Cunningham, 2004 #Mulveen, 1994.
** The London Gazette, number 534, Monday December 26-Thursday December 29 1670, recieved courtesy of Matt Bodkin, Rocky Point, NY, January 2014.

Thomas son of Richard of Athenry = ?    Ysybel Bodkyn of Athenry = Wyllyn Wallys, d. 1343
(issue)

Nicholas fitz Thomas, fl. 1380-84.    John Baudekyn, clerk, fl. 1375-80.    Henry, fl. 1398-1420, Provost of Athenry 1428?

Thomas Bodykyn, fl. 1429=Silma, fl. 1429.

Richard Clerk, alias Bawdekyn, fl. 1407, d. by 1421.
=?

Walter, fl. 1421-51.    Edmond, fl. 1444.    Richard, Provost of Athenry 1454.    Robert, provost Athenry 1450.    James, Bailiff of Athenry 1450, fl. 1454.    Walter, fl. 1450.    Henry, fl. 1457.
=?    Edmond =Eveling Kyruan, fl. 1500.

Thomas, fl. 1472-99=Anorine Blake, m. by 1472.    John, Blf, 1499, M. 1518, d. 1523.    Janet, fl. 1499.    Stephen, fl. 1507.    Thomas, fl. 1507, M. 1508.    David, fl. bef. 1508.    Ambrose, Blf. 1570-71.
=?

James, fl. 1523-27.    Henry, fl. 1527.

Christopher, Archbishop of Tuam, 1505-72.    Gregory, Bl. 1569, fl. 1572-74.    Janetta    Bridget    Mary    Margaret    Mt. Bodkin =Julian, sis. of Nich. Blake d. 1568.

Edmund, Bl. 1543.    David, Blf. 1550-51.
=?

Anastace dau of Marcus fitz Laurence

John of Limerick, fl. 1592-95.
=?

Leo =Isabel Lynch    Thomas, fl. 1597-99.    Dominick =?    Jonocke, fl. 1597.    Harry, fl. 1599.

Richard, fl. 1610.
=?    David =?    Nicholas, Blf. 1646-47, fl. Dublin 1663-64.

Gregory, SJ, b. 1590, fl. 1627.    Christopher, Bl. 1610, fl. 1618.    John, fl. 1621, M. 1639.

F. [Francis?]
=?    Christopher, fl. 1614-20.    Ambrose, fl. 1620. =?    Michael and brother, fl. 1663.    Ambrose, and John, fl. 1663.    Augustin, ingreso en la orden de Calatrava, Madrid, 1673*

John, fl. 1686.    Anthony, fl. 1686.

Arthur, fl. 1645 =Mary French? (fl. 1638#)    Patrick, fl. 1645.    Edmund, fl. 1645.    ? =John Blake    Captain Francis, pirate, fl. 1670**

Edmond b. 1626, alive 1686.

Nell Bodkin, husband Michael Lynch, and son, fl. 1721#    Julia(n) Bodkin and her husband, James Browne, fl. 1722. #
Widow Bodkin, and Nicholas, Abbeygate Street; Jon, Thomas, and Jon, Flood Street; Anthony, and Anthony Jr., Middle Street; Ambrose, Lawrence, [Councillor?] John, Shop Street; all fl. 1724.***
Anthony Bodkin and his wife Catherine Browne, fl. 1737.#

## Browne of Athenry and Galway 1286-1647

Sources: Holland, 1997; *Regestum*; *BFR*; *PRJI*; Corporation Book A. *Blake, 1910.

John Brun, fl. 1286.

Geoffrey le Broun/Brun, fl. 1289.　Walter Brun of Balyduf, fl. 1289.　Adam Bruen of Balyduf, fl. 1289.　Friar Galfridus Brown of Athenry, OP, fl. c. 1300.

Tancard Brun of Balyduf, fl. 1321.　Walter Brun of Ballymacorthan, fl. 1333.

Thomas, fl. 1404.

John of Athenry, fl. 1424.

Denis =?

Friar Gilbert Bron, d. London 1451.　John Brun, fl. 1449-51.

Stephen =?

William, fl. 1499.

James, fl. 1523.

William, fl. 1523-27 =Anastasia Blake

Richard, fl. 1542-89. =?　John　Walter, fl. 1603.　Hubert of Loughrea, fl. 1584.　Jasper of Tooloobaun, fl. 1603.

Jasper of Athenry fl. 1588.　Michael, fl. 1603.　Robert of Newcastle, fl. 1618.　Walter fitz Thomas, fl. 1618.

Jasper of Athenry. fl. 1588. =Patrick Kirwan　Martin, fl. 1613　Andrew, Stephen, Nicholas, of Athenry, fl. 1618.　Oliver, fl. 1620.

John, OFM, 1594-9 September 1623, died Franciscan convent, San Lucar, Spain*

Dominick Browne of Galway and Barna, fl. 1542-96. =Onora, dau. Sir Murrough na dTuadh Ó Flaithbertaigh

Jane =Patrick Kirwan　Onora =Walter French　dau. =Anthony Lynch　Andrew fitz Dominick, fl. 1620.

Andrew, fl. 1539-74.　Nicholas, fl. 1542-66.　Robert, fl. 1542.　Margery =James Blake (issue)　James (issue) =?　Thomas (issue)

James of Galway, fl. 1619-20.　Peter, fl. 1647.

Geoffrey, d. 1596. (issue)　Oliver, d. 1619. (issue)　Edward fl. 1571.　Marcus

Agnes, fl. 1640.

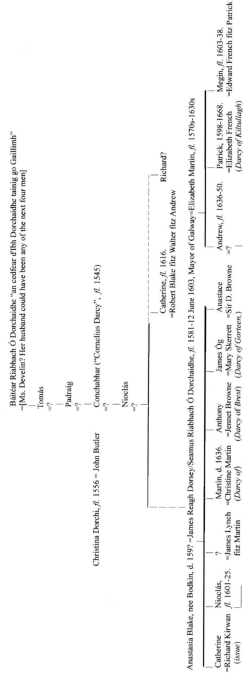

## Uí Dhorchaidhe Gaillimhe, 1417-1668.

Sources: *Leabhar na nGenealach*; Betham Abstracts; *BFR*; *Wardenship*; *State Papers.

Ó Dorchaidhe "taoisioch Partraighe", 1417.

Báitéar Riabhach Ó Dorchaidhe "an cedfear d'Íbh Dorchaidhe tainig go Gaillimh"
=[Ms. Develin? Her husband could have been any of the next four men]

Tomás
=?

Padraig
=?

Conchabhar ("Cornelius Darcy", *fl.* 1545)
=?

Nioclás
=?

Christina Dorchi, *fl.* 1556 = John Butler

Catherine, *fl.* 1616.
=Robert Blake fitz Walter fitz Andrew

Richard?

Anastasia Blake, nee Bodkin, d. 1591 =James Reagh Dorsey/Seamus Riabhach Ó Dorchaidhe, *fl.* 1581-12 June 1603, Mayor of Galway=Elizabeth Martin, *fl.* 1570s-1630s

Catherine
=Richard Kirwan
(issue)

Nioclás, *fl.* 1601-25.
=James Lynch
fitz Martin

James Dominick
both *d.s.p.*

?
Martin, d. 1636.
=Christine Martin
(*Darcy of*)
(*New Forest*)

Anthony
=Jennet Browne
(*Darcy of Brest*)

James Óg
=Mary Skerrett
(*Darcy of Gorteen,*)
(*Housnbwood, Tuam,*)
(*Stanmore in Middlesex*)

Anastace
=Sir D. Browne

Andrew, *fl.* 1636-50.
=?

Elizabeth
=Patrick French

Patrick, 1598-1668.
=Elizabeth French
(*Darcy of Kiltullagh*)

Megin, *fl.* 1603-38.
=Edward French fitz Patrick

Marcus, *fl.* 1648-65, "a younger brother …hath eight sons" "*

## Deane, 1446-1792

Sources: Hardiman, 1820; Corporation Book A. * Cunningham, 2004. *Tuam Herald*, 21 Dec 1918.
** Mulkeen, 1994. √Talon, 2006. vv. Crossle, 1931-33. *** Flavin and Evans, 2009, p. "37.

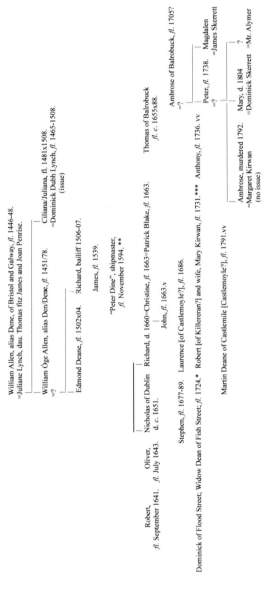

William Allen, alias Dene, of Bristol and Galway, *fl.* 1446-48.
=Juliane Lynch, dau. Thomas fitz James and Joan Penrise.

William Óge Allen, alias Den/Dene, *fl.* 1451/78.
=?

Ciliana/Juliana, fl. 1481x1508.
=Dominick Dubh Lynch, *fl.* 1465-1508.
(issue)

Edmond Deane, *fl.* 1502x04.

Richard, bailiff 1506-07.

James, *fl.* 1539.

"Peter Dine", shipmaster, *fl.* November 1594. **

Robert, *fl.* September 1641.

Oliver, *fl.* July 1643.

Nicholas of Dublin d. c. 1651.

Richard, d. 1660=Christine, *fl.* 1663=Patrick Blake, *fl.* 1663.

John, *fl.* 1663.v

Thomas of Balrobuck *fl. c.* 1655x88.

Stephen, *fl.* 1677-89.

Laurence [of Castlemoyle?], *fl.* 1686.

Dominick of Flood Street; Widow Dean of Fish Street; *fl.* 1724.*

Robert [of Killereran?] and wife, Mary Kirwan, *fl.* 1731.***

Anthony, *fl.* 1736. vv

Ambrose of Balrobuck, *fl.* 1705?
=?

Peter, *fl.* 1738.
=?

Magdalen
=James Skerrett

Martin Deane of Castlemile [Castlemoyle?], *fl.* 1791.vv

Ambrose, murdered 1792.
=Margaret Kirwan
(no issue)

Mary, d. 1804
=Dominick Skerrett

?
=Mr. Alymer

Thomas Deane was granted over 1500 acres mainly in Clare, Dunmore, and Kilmaine baronies by patent 2 June 1677. Stephen Deane was granted lands in Loughrea, Moycullen, Athenry, Carra, in May 1677. Circa Griffith's Evaluation, Edward H. Deane held land at Cummer, Clare barony. Edward Deane was agent to Chris. McManus of Barlyhill. He married Esmy O'Flaherty of Lisdonagh, Headford, emigrated to USA to escape creditors, with a brother and sister marrying the McDermotts of Coolavin in Sligo. Castlemoyle is in Killererin parish, near Tuam.

## Fonte, 1409-1814

Main sources: Hardiman, 1820, p. 13; Corporation Book A; *BFR*; *PRJI*
*Ó Floinn, pp. 94-96. ***Irish in Europe* website *** Cunningham, 2004

William de Font, *fl.* 1409.
=?
|
Thomas, *fl.* 1437 [relationship to the following uncertain]


Walter, Provost of Galway 1443.
=Evelyn Kirwan
|_____
|                   |
Thomas Fonte (Faute), *fl.* 1465.   dau.           John, portreeve of Galway 1472.
=Elenor French            = Geoffrey Lynch, *fl.* 1465-1501.
|                           (*issue*)                   Richard=Joanne French, both *fl.* 1498.
Martin, *fl.* 1498-1520.
=Juliana Lynch of Skreene.                    Adam, *fl.* 1509-27.
|
|                                                                  Bartholomew,    Richard,
Stephen, *fl.* 1543-47.    James, fl. 1546-70?              Givane, fl. 1549-70.    *fl.* 1518-29.   *fl.* 1524-25.
=Juliana Kirwan                          Geoffrey, murdered 1573.
|
? *missing generation?*    Patrick, *fl.* 1586-87.              Magdalen Font, dau. of Francis=Valentine French
=?                                    Bartholomew, *fl.* 1602.
|                                                          Adam, b. 1577, Blf. 1612-14, *fl.* 1627
Francis, married 1626.    Martin, *fl.* 1604/05-21=Elizabeth Butler.*   John, *fl.* 1613.   =Juliane Blake
=Maria, dau. John Athy
|                        Thomas, *fl.* 1620.   Anthony, *fl.* 1620.   Simon Frens [y] de la Fuente, *fl.* Madrid, 1622**   James, *fl.* bef. 1631.
Dominick, *fl.* 1641-after 1660.                             *ingreso en la orden de Santiago*
=Anna Dillon of Loughlin                                                        Geoffrey, *fl.* 1636-41.
|                        Bonaventure, OFM, *fl.* 1639-5?*    Gaspar, OFM, *fl.* 1645-48*
Francis de Fonte of Boyle
=Margaret, dau. John Blake of Dromorenagh
|
Edward de Fonte of Boyle, m. 1690          John, merchant of Galway *fl.* 1696.
=Maria Gibbons
|                                    Geo., Abbeygate Steet, *fl.* 1724.***
Bridget, sole heiress.
=Peter Bath of Knightstown, Meath, d. 1778.
                         Geoffrey Font of Galway, *c.* 1709-1814.

# French, 1420-1648

Main Source: Blake 1905-06; 1917-18; 1920-21; NLI Ms. 13, 650. * Archives", 1992, pp. 447-48.
** PRJI *** PRJI ****Irish in Europe website *****State Papers, 1665. vv Blake, 1910.

Walter French, fl. 1420-53.
={Mary?}, daughter of John Athy

Nicholas
=Elizabeth Browne, dau. of Thomas

James

John, fl. 1474.

Robert
=?

Juliane=John Blake, d. 1468.

Joanne = Richard Font
fl. 1498.

Valentine
=Helen, dau of Gregory Joyce

Walter    Alexander    Oliver
                       Blf. 1520-21

Peter, Blf. 1499-1500
Blf. 1499-1500 =?

Nicholas, Blf. 1500-01.  Edmond, Blf. 1509-10.  Stephen,
                                                Blf. 1511-12.

Edmund,*
fl. 1577.

Seán an tSalainn, 1489-1545.
(issue)

Peter, M. 1565
=Julian, dau. Dominick Lynch

Andrew   Agnes   Anstace

Walter, fl. 1572.   Jonick, fl. 1575.

Patrick fitz George, fl. 1603.   Walter, Dominick, Nicholas, Dareghan, of Turlough, County Mayo, fl.1604. **

Valentine
=Magdalen, dau. Francis Font

Ellis   Jennet   Mary   Nicholas, fl. 1619-20.

Robert of Athenry, Patrick fitz Robert of Galway, fl. 1618.***

Walter of Galway, fl. 1618.   George
=?                            =?

Sir Peter Óge, d. 1628   Jeffrey,   Thomas   Mary   Magdalen   Julian   Catherine
=Mary Browne            fl. 1587.

John
=Anne, dau. John Bermingham

Nicholas, fl. 1619-20.   Dominick, fl. 1620.   Patrick, fl. 1619-20.

James and John
of Sligo, fl. 1621.

Simon Frens [y] de la Fuente****   ?
fl. 1622, Madrid
ingreso en la orden de Santiago

Joan, fl. 1634.

Gregory, OFM,
fl. 1634. vv

Maggaret/Megan   Ellis
=Richard Óge Martyn   =Sir Robuck Lynch
(issue)              (issue)

Elizabeth
=Patrick Darcy
(issue)

Gennett
=Maurice Lynch
(issue)

Dominick
=Mary Crean

Juliane

Patrick, killed in swordfight in St. Nicholas's, 1648. *****

Peter   John   Valentine
=Mary Bodkin

# Joyce of Galway town, c. 1500-1725

*fireplace coat of arms, Finnegan's Resturant, Market Street. ** captive in North Africa, 1675-89; see Hardiman, pp. 15-16.
*** See Joyce of Merview. **** Cunningham, 2004. *v Mulveen, 1994. vv GO MS 64-79 Funeral Entries Vol. 6, 17. +Fahey, 2013.

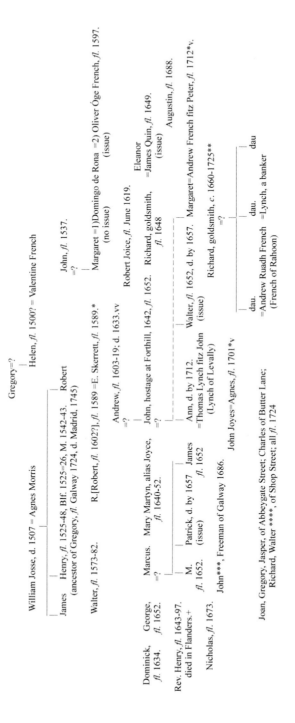

Gregory=?

Helen, *fl.* 1500? = Valentine French

William Josse, d. 1507 = Agnes Morris

James    Henry, *fl.* 1525-48, Blf. 1525=26, M. 1542-43.    Robert          John, *fl.* 1537.
         (ancestor of Gregory, *fl.* Galway 1724, d. Madrid, 1745)                =?

Walter, *fl.* 1573-82.    R.[Robert, *fl.* 1602?], *fl.* 1589 =E. Skerrett, *fl.* 1589.*    Margaret =1)Domingo de Rona =2) Oliver Óge French, *fl.* 1597.
                                                                                    (no issue)       (issue)

                          Andrew, *fl.* 1603-19; d. 1633.vv                         Robert Joice, *fl.* June 1619.
                             =?

Dominick,   George,   Marcus.   Mary Martyn, alias Joyce,   John, hostage at Forthill, 1642, *fl.* 1652.   Richard, goldsmith,    Eleanor
*fl.* 1634.  *fl.* 1652.   =?      *fl.* 1640-52.                     =?                                      *fl.* 1648            =James Quin, *fl.* 1649.
                                                                                                                                       (issue)

Rev. Henry, *fl.* 1643-97.      M.      Patrick, d. by 1657    James        Ann, d. by 1712.          Walter, *fl.* 1652, d. by 1657.   Margaret=Andrew French fitz Peter, *fl.* 1712*v.   Augustin, *fl.* 1688.
died in Flanders.+           *fl.* 1652.  (issue)          *fl.* 1652     =Thomas Lynch fitz John    (issue)
                                                                          (Lynch of Levally)

Nicholas, *fl.* 1673.         John***, Freeman of Galway 1686.                                       Richard, goldsmith, c. 1660-1725**
                                                                          John Joyes=Agnes, *fl.* 1701*v                =?

                             Joan, Gregory, Jasper, of Abbeygate Street; Charles of Butter Lane;      dau.                  dau.                    dau.
                             Richard, Walter ****, of Shop Street; all *fl.* 1724                     =Andrew Ruadh French  =Lynch, a banker
                                                                                                       (French of Rahoon)

# Ó Ciardubháin/Kirwan, 1420-1689

Main sources: *BFR*; Wardenship; Corporation Book A; *PRJI*.

* *Iar Connacht*, p. 392. ** *Life of Bishop Kirwan*. *** *Irish in Europe* website ****Mulveen, 1994.

Dermot O Kyrvayn, *fl.* 1420.     Walter Kervyk, King's Justice, *fl.* 1432.

Thomas O'Kervyke of Athenry, *fl.* 1439, Provost of Athenry 1465 [=Thomas O'Kyrruan, *fl.* 1482?]     Evelyn = Walter Font, *fl. c.* 1440.

Uilliam, *fl.* 1488, Blf. 1503-04, 1510-11 = Anastacia Lynch

Úna, *fl.* after 1488 = Tomás Óg de Bermingham

Eveling Kyruan, *fl.* 1500. = Edmond Bodkin

David, Blf. 1501-02.     Edward, *fl.* 1505.     Sabina, *fl.* pre-1508.

Tomás Caoch/Mór, *fl.* 1517-46.

Patrick, *fl.* 1551.

Jonock [John Óge?], Blf. 15?3-14, M. 1530-31. =?, alive 1508.

James, *fl.* 1541-75; M. 1566-67, 74-75.

Edmond, Blf. 1543-44.

Stephen, *fl.* 1522.     Tomás Óge, d. 1542. = Catherine Lynch

Richard, Blf. 1528-29.

Katiline, *fl.* 1535= Nicholas Athy

Evelin * = Murchad Ó Flaithbheartaigh (Uí Flaithbertaigh of Gnobeg)

Helena, *fl.* 1573=Thomas Birmingham****

Denis, Blf. 1550-51, M. =?

Davy, Blf. 1554-55.

Anastace, *fl.* 1571=William Lynch fitz Martin (issue)

Rob, *fl.* 1603.     Janet, *fl.* 1603=MacSuibhne of Rathglass

Matthew, *fl.* 1603 =Juliana Lynch

Martin, Blf. 1568-69.

Thomas, Blf. 1576-77.

Richard, *al.* 1581 [=Richard of Ringitan, *fl.* 1620?].

John of Tuam, *fl.* 1612. =?

Piers Ballagh, *fl.* 1597 =?

Bp. Francis, 1589-1661***

Nicholas, Blf. 1574-74. =dau. of Robuck Martin

Patrick, Blf. 1588-89 [*fl.* 1637?] =?

Oliver, Blf. 1589-90

William, *fl.* 1597.

David, *fl.* 1603.

Oliver, *fl.* 1652.

James, *fl.* 1637 =?

M[atthew?], *fl.* 1652.

Denis, *fl.* 1594.

John of Galway, *fl.* 1620.

Andrew, *fl.* 1620-37 =?

Richard, Blf. 1630-31, M. 1650-51. =?

Thomas alias Francis, *fl.* 1640.

Marcus, *fl.* 1621-37

Edmond, Blf. 1627-28, M. 1645-46.

Martin, Blf. 1645-46.

Thomas Reagh, *fl.* 1640.

Stephen, *fl.* 1637-52.

Christopher, *fl.* 1637-41/Cristobal Quiroban, *ingreso en la orden de Santiago de Simon Frens, Madrid*, 1650***

Robert, Blf. 1630-31.

Marcus fitz Dominick *fl.* 1652.

James, *fl.* 1652.

Peter, *fl.* 1670-73 [sister married to Walter Athy?]

Captain Dominick of Nantes *fl.* 1652-63.

Patrick,  Andrew, *fl.* 1689.

John, Martin, Marcus, Robert, *fl.* 1686.

## The early Lynchs 1257-1507

Main sources: "Account", 1913-14; Blake, 1915-16. *Who's Who in Medieval Limerick.*
Relationships in early generations may be beyond recovery. This reconstruction is evidential.

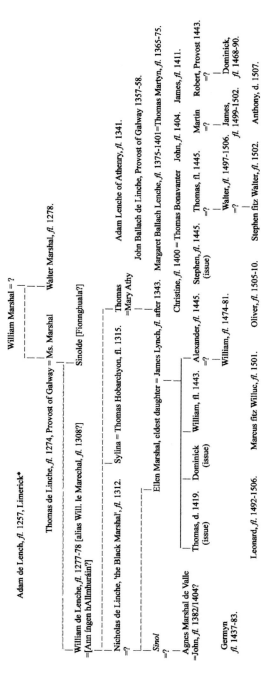

# The Lynch baronets

Sources: Corporation Book A; Wardenship; State papers; "Account" 1913-14; Blake 1915-16.
Descendants of Sir Henry (d. 1634) mainly derived from *Burke's Peerage and Baronetage*, vol. II, 106th edition, Switzerland, 1999.

Andrew Lynch, fl. 1498.
=Eleanor Martin

Arthur, fl. 1539. =?
John, fl. 1528. (issue)
Dame Maire Lynch, fl. 1543-47.
=1) Uilleag, 1st Earl Clarricard, d. 1544. (issue)
=2) Pierce Martin, fl. 1547-65. (issue?)

Stephen, d. 1579. =?
James, fl. 1585.

Nicholas, fl. 1572-99. =Juliane Martin, fl. 1572-af.1601.
Dominick, fl. 1580-99. =?
Michael, Blf. 1575.
Marcus, B. 1578. M. 1603, fl. 1608. =?
dau. =O Flaitbertaigh
Thomas, fl. 1608.
Geoffrey, fl. 1610.

Ms. Lynch =John Skerrett, brother of Robert.

Marcus, fl. 1579-1602.
son d. 1601.
Dr. Thomas, c.1574-1634.
Anthony, OP, 1568-1650 =Elizabeth Martin.
Sir Henry, d. 1634.
Ms. Lynch =Geof. Browne, d. 1596.
Nicholas, OP c.1590-1634.
William, fl. 1623.
Johneg fl. 1621.
Andrew, fl. 1624.
? ? ?

Maurice =Gennett French
Nicholas fl. 1634.
Elizabeth =Thomas Lynch (Lynch of Drimcong)
Mary, d. 1671. =Geoffrey Browne (Oranmore and Browne)
Ellinor, m. 1632, d. 1692. =Sir Valentine Blake, 3rd Bt.

Sir Robuck, d. c. 1667. =Ellis French
Arthur (Lynch of) (Partry)
Peter
Mary =Stephen Lynch fitz Johr fitz Stephen of Lavally (Lynch of Carrunrane and Antigua)

Sir Henry, d. 1691.

## Martyn, 1365-1663

Sources: *BFR*; Wardenship: *Corporation Book A*; *CIRCLE*; State Papers: *fiants*; *PR.II.*

Thomas Martyn, *fl.* 1365-1375 =Margaret Balach de Lenche, *fl.* 1375-1401

- Thomas, *fl.* 1387.
- William, *fl.* 1398-1407/1444?
  - William, *fl.* [1407?] 1444.
    - Richard, *fl.* 1424-1440.
    - Anastacia, d. by 1481=Dominick Dubh Lynch, *fl.* 1465, d. 1507
      - William, *fl.* [1444?] 1490.
      - Peter, *fl.* 1498.
      - Joan, *fl.* 1499=Andrew Lynch. (issue)
      - Eleanor, *fl.* 1502.
      - Emeline, *fl.* 1502.
      - Walter, *fl.* 1505

- Thomas, *fl.* 1505, dead by 1530. =?
  - Wylliam, *fl.* 1504-47. =?
    - Rychard, *fl.* 1519-37. =?
      - Dame Maire Lynch =Pierce, fl. 1547-65 [Peter, *fl.* 1554?]
      - Patrick, *fl.* 1554-63.
        - Juliana, *fl.* 1572-af.1601=Nicholas Lynch (issue)
        - Thomas, *fl.* 1573. =?
          - Julian =Jeffery Blake
        - Robuck, d. 1594. =Margaret Lynch (issue)
        - Sisley =Mr. Bodkin
        - Christina, *fl.* 1591.
        - John, *fl.* 1590-1602 (issue)
      - heirs 1560.

- Thomas Óge, *fl.* 1533-77. =Eveline Linche, *fl.* 1562.
  - William Óge, d. 1593. =Mary Lynch (issue)
  - Francis, d. 1603. =Elizabeth Lynch
    - Mary =Peter French
    - Stephen, *fl.* 1642. (issue)

- Allin, *fl.* 1582-94. (four daughters)
- Edmund, *fl.* 1574-85.
- Jasper, murdered 1586. *fl.* 1587-1620. (issue)
- Walter,
- Ellin, *fl.* 1591.
- Marcus, *fl.* 1602.
  - Thomas, born 1603, *fl.* 1663.

- Piers, born 1562, *fl.* 1588. (issue?)
- Dominick, *fl.* 1568-1611.
- Thomas, *fl.* 1615.
  - Elizabeth, *fl.* 1645=Peter Darcy.

## The family of William Óge Martyn, 1566-1722

Sources: Betham Abstracts; Corporation Book A; *PRJI*; Heraldic Office; Tallon, 2006.

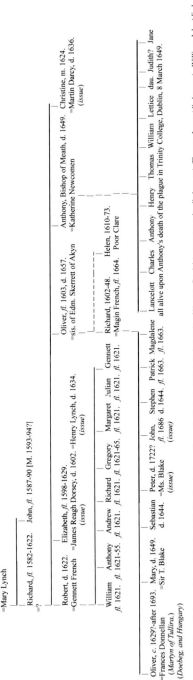

William Óge, *fl.* 1566, died Spring 1593.
=Mary Lynch

Richard, *fl.* 1582-1622.    John, *fl.* 1587-90 [M. 1593-94?]
=?.

Robert, d. 1622.    Elizabeth, *fl.* 1598-1629.    Oliver, *fl.* 1603, d. 1657.    Anthony, Bishop of Meath, d. 1649.    Christine, m. 1624,
=Gennett French    =James Reagh Dorsey, d. 1602.    =sis. of Edm. Skerrett of Akyn    =Katherine Newcomen    =Martin Darcy, d. 1636.
  (*issue*)    =Henry Lynch, d. 1634.    (*issue*)    (*issue*)
    (*issue*)

William    Anthony    Andrew    Richard    Gregory    Margaret    Julian    Gennett    Richard, 1602-48.    Helen, 1610-73.
*fl.* 1621.    *fl.* 1621-55.    *fl.* 1621.    *fl.* 1621.    *fl.* 1621.    *fl.* 1621.    *fl.* 1621.    *fl.* 1621.    =Magin French, *fl.* 1664.    Poor Clare

Oliver, c. 1629?-after 1693.    Mary, d. 1649.    Sebastian    Peter, d. 1722?    John,    Stephen    Patrick    Magdalene    Lancelott    Charles    Anthony    Henry    Thomas    William    Lettice    dau.    Judith?    Jane
=Frances Donnellan    =Sir T. Blake    d. 1644.    =Ms. Blake    *fl.* 1686    d. 1644. *fl.* 1663.    *fl.* 1663.    *fl.* 1663.    all alive upon Anthony's death of the plague in Trinity College, Dublin, 8 March 1649.
(*Martyn of Tullira*,)    (*issue*)    (*issue*)
(*Doebeg, and Hungary*)

*Robert (died young), Lancelott, alive 1649; Charles, Anthony, Henry, Benhamyne (died an infant, twin of Henry), Daniel (name uncertain, died young), Thomas, James (died young), William, John (died young) [all survivors unmarried 1649], Lettice (married to Laurence Dowdall of Monkstown?, Meath), Anne (died young), a daughter, Judith?, Jane. Source: Funeral Entries, Heraldic Office, Kildare Street, Dublin, 1997.

## The family of Nicholas Martin fitz John, 1582-1702

Sources: Betham abstracts, *Kilfenora Ms.*, National Archives; Corporation Book A, *BFR.*
*Robert, c. 1620-1700, is the first Martin known to have lived at Ross.

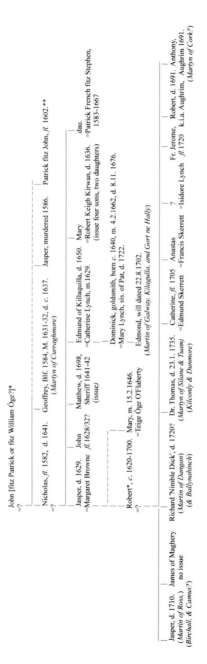

John [fitz Patrick or fitz William Óge?]*
=?

Nicholas, *fl.* 1582, d. 1641.
=?

Geoffrey, Bl/f. 1584, M. 1631-32, d. c. 1637.
(*Martyn of Curraghmore*)

Jasper, murdered 1586.

Patrick fitz John, *fl.* 1602.**

Edmund of Killaquilla, d. 1650.
=Catherine Lynch, m.1629.

Mary
=Robert Keigh Kirwan, d. 1636.
(issue four sons, two daughters)

dau.
=Patrick French fitz Stephen, 1583-1667

Jasper, d. 1629.
=Margaret Browne

John
*fl.*1628/32?

Matthew, d. 1698,
Sheriff 1641-42
(issue)

Dominick, goldsmith, born c. 1640, m. 4.2.1662, d. 8.11.1676.
=Mary Lynch, sis. of Pat, d. 1722.

Robert*, c. 1620-1700.
=?
=Teige Óge O'Flaherty

Mary, m. 15.2.1646.

Edmond, will dated 22.8.1702.
(*Martin of Galway, Killaquilla, and Gort ne Hally*)

Richard 'Nimble Dick', d. 1720?
(*Martin of Dangan*)
(*& Ballynahinch*)

Dr. Thomas, d. 23.1. 1735.
(*Martyn of Silane & Tuam*)
(*Kilconly & Dunmore*)

Catherine, *fl.* 1705
=Edmund Skerret

Anastas
=Francis Skerrett

?
=Isidore Lynch

Fr. Jerome,
*fl.*1720

Robert, d. 1691.
k.i.a. Aughrim,

Anthony,
Aughrim 1691.
(*Martyn of Cork?*)

Jasper, d. 1710.
(*Martin of Ross,*)
(*Birchall, & Camus?*)

James of Maghery
no issue

*The exact identity of the progenitor of this branch of the family remains uncertain. He may to have been a son of Patrick or Wiliam Óge. Patrick may also have been a son of John, son of Thomas Martin of 'Rahone'. Nicholas (fl. 1582-41) may be the unnamed son of John Martin, who he refers to in a letter of "Galway, July 2, 1580" to Captain William Collier ("for his friendly letter to England in behalf of his son the bearer, who is determined to go forward in his learning."). Source: *CSPI*, II, 1574-85, p. 230.

** See *Descendants of Patrick and Thomas Martin*.

# The family of Walter Martyn, 1498-1840

Sources: Corporation Book A; State Papers; *Admiralty*; Blake, 1928*

Peter, *fl.* 1498.    Walter, *fl.*1505.

Maire Lynch, *fl.* 1543-47 = Pierce/Peter Martin, *fl.* 1547-1565.

Walter, *fl.* 1587-1620.    Piers, b. 1562, *fl.* 1588

=?

Pierce (aka Peter?), *fl.* 1619-33. | George, d. 1637? = Ms. Bodkin | William | Francis | Patrick, d. 1641. | Julian, *fl.* 1630 =Andrew Blake fitz Patrick, d. 1624. | Agnes =Thomas Nolan, d. 1628. (son, Gregory)

=?

Julian =Dr. Thady FitzPatrick, d. 1674.

George of Kilannin, *fl.* 1654.

dau. =Francis Athy, *fl.* 1639. (issue)

Alice =Turlough Ó Loughlin

Christina =Robuck French fitz John

George Óge of Moycullen and Gregans, *fl.* 1650s. =Julian?

Walter Óge, *fl.* 1642, d. by 1654 =Elizabeth Lynch, *fl.* Liskeevy, 1654.

George Óge | William | Francis | Friar Peter | Sibil | Patrick, k. 1691, Aughrim.

Katherine, marr. 10th March 1678, *fl.* 1706. =Richard 'Nimble Dick' Martin, d. c. 1720. (*Martin of Ballynahinch*)

Gregory, *fl.*1677** =Ms. Bodkin

George, d. 1741=Elizabeth Bodkin

Alice | Gregory=Julia Blake (*no issue*) | John, died in a duel. | George, died in Brazil. | Francis=Mary McNamara

George Óge***=? | Gregory | Walter | John ***

George=Elizabeth Browne | William, emigrated to USA in 1828.

Francis, d. 1840+Bridget FitzPatrick. | George | John | Gregory=Mary Lynch (*Martyn of Gregans*)

Patrick [of Dublin? illigitimate]

*Blake, 1928, in his genealogy of the Martyn family of Gregans Castle, Ballyvaughan, County Clare. The senior legitimate representative as of 2015 is Agnes Martyn O'Loughlin of Gregans Valley and her children David and Gillian; Agnes is gr-gr-granddaughter of Gregory Martyn and Mary Lynch. Her father was Cyril Martyn, 1927-2003 ***"Gregory Marten of Galway, merchant, aged 32" was examined on 28 November 1655 (Murphy, 2011, p. 145). He described himself as "a bachelor and merchant and lived for a while in Holland, Spain, England, and France." It is possible that he is the Gregory Martyn who was alive in 1677. I hope Blake did not confused him with a son of Robert fitz Richard, d. 1622! ***Blake states George Óge and John were poisoned by their foster family, the Blakes, et Menlo.

# Morris of Galway 1477-1912

Main sources: *BFR*; Corporation Book A; Hardiman, 1820.

*Burke's Peerage*, vol. II, 2003, pp. 2150. ** Cunningham, 2004. ***Villiers-Tuthill, 1986, pp. 146-149.

John Mares, *fl.* 1477.
= Christina Lynch

Richard Mares, Blf. 1486-87.

Janet = John Bodkin, d. 1523.

John Maris, Blf. 1501-02, 1515-16; *fl.* 1518.

William Jose, d. 1507. = Agnes [Browne, nee ?]

Andrew, *fl.* 1508.

William Maryse, Blf. 1508-09, M. 1527-28.

Thomas Mares, *fl.* 1548.

Andrew, M. 1587-88, *fl.* 1555-94.

George, *fl.* 1588-1605.

William, *fl.* 1640.

Andrew, and Andrew, *fl.* 1652.

George (son of James?), lived in "west suburbs of Galway"; gained An Spiddeal 1709.*
= Catherine FitzPatrick, m. 1684.

Andrew
= Monica Browne

Widow Morris of Shop Street, *fl.* 1724**

James Morris, 1710-1791***
= Mary Lynch

George
= Joanna Kilkelly, m. 1770.

James, 1732-1813
= Deborah Lynch

Capt. Anthony, b. 1763
=?

Mary
= John Staunton

James Morris, 1790-1840=Elinor Staunton

Capt. Edmond
d. Borneo 1813.

Mary, d. 26 November 1856.
= Maj. Tho. Macan=Chris Oldfield
(issue)

Catherine, m. 1798
= William Towers Smith
(issue)

Moncia
= Andrew Blake

son    son

Martin, 1784-1862
= Julia Blake

Anthony of Ballinboy, 1822-1898
= Elizabeth Hanly

dau.    dau.    Michael, 1st Baron Killanin, 1826-1901.
= Ann Hughes
(issue)

Sir George, 1833-1921
(issue extinct)

James 1844-1914.    son    son    son
= Anna Maria Stacy
(issue)

# Huscarl, Scared, Skerrett, 1042-1800

Main sources: Turner, 1981; *Regestum*; Holland, 1997; *BFR*; Corporation Book A; PRJI; *coat of arms and initials in Finnegan's Resturant, Market Street. **O'Connell, 2004. ***Irish in Europe website. ****Cunningham, 2004. *v Mulveen, 1994.

Huscarl of Eastrip, Somerset, *fl.* 1042-66.

[several generations]

Rainbald Huscarl    son
*fl.* 1124.
Richard, *fl.* 1124.

Roger Huscarl of Somerset and Dublin, *fl.* 1222-27.

Robert Huscard of Connacht, *fl.* 1242.

Edmund Huskald, *fl.* 1289.    Robert Huscard of Dublin *fl.* 1280.

Walter Husgard=Joanna    Richard Huskard, *fl.* 1333.

Richard Scared, Provost of Athenry 1378-79.

Walter Skeret, Provost, 1414-15, 1417-18, *fl.* 1443.

John Skeret, *fl.* 1476-84.    Margaret, *fl.* 1494 =Valentine Blake

James and Walter, *fl* 1533.    William, *fl* 1542.    Henry, *fl.* 1545.
=?

James, *fl.* 1583.    John fitz William, *fl.* 1596.

E[lizabeth?], *fl.* 1589=R. Joyce,*.    Stephen, *fl.* 1596 [and 1620?]    M., *fl.* 1603 = M. Lynch, *fl.* 1603.    James fitz Richard, *fl.* 1603.

    ?    Edmund of Akyn
    =Oliver Martin

Edmund of Cahirmorish,    Nicholas,    Stephen,    Francis,    James, SJ/Diogo Scarbet,    Martin,
*fl.* 1619.    *fl.* 1618-29.    *fl.* 1620.    *fl.* 1623    of Evora university, *fl.* 1619-23**    *fl.* 1629.

Francis fitz William, *fl.* (1623?) 1637.

Dominick, *fl.* 1645.    Raimundo Esqueret, *fl.* 1650, Madrid***    'John', OSA.
=?    *de la orden de Santiago de … Planqueto*

Edmund, born 1626, alive 1686.    Elis and Elizabeth, *fl.* 1696*v

Stephen and wife Maire Blake, *fl.* 1707 *v   Patt, Abbeygate Street; Walter, Middle Street; William, Shop Street; Widow Skerrett, Francis, Lombard Street, all *fl.* 1724.****
Mother Mary Gabriel, and her nephew Fr. Mark, *fl.* 1732*v   Thomas and wife Mary Lynch, early 1700s *   Nicholas and Jane of Creagh, *fl.* 1800. *v

# CHAPTER NOTES:

## Chapter One: Stony River

1 - For an overview I am relying on Byrne, 1973; Richter, 1985; Simms, 1987; Ó Cróinín, 1995, and 2005 (*NHI*, vol. I); Charles-Edwards, 2000; Jaski, 2000; Johnson, 2003; Duffy, 2005; Mallory, 2013; Bhreathnach, 2014. For Gaillimh see Ó Máille, 1954, p. 28, agus Ó Máille, 1985, pp. 51-52. For 1762, see Larn, 2002 ("*Royal Charlotte*, master Sinclair, from Quebec for London, sprung a leak at Sea and in going into Galway river in Ireland ran ashore and is full of water": Lloyd's *List* 2,808, Friday 10 December 1762). For 1178, see *AnnTig*; for 1190, see *ADdR*; for 1462 see AC and O'Donovan, 1846, p. 249; for 1647, and 1683-84, see Ó Flaithbheartaigh, 1684, p. 29. An instance of the river freezing occoured in 1174, when "desiciatur Galvia et lacus fuit meabiles propter gelu./The Galvia [sic] river may be crossed and the lakes have been made traversable by the frost." (*ADdR*). See also *AFM* and *ALCé* under the above years. The settlement's name varied in contempoary sources. *AnnTig* terms it 'caistél Gaillme' in 1124, 'Caislén Gaillme' in 1132. CS calls it 'caislen Duin Gaillme' in 1124, 'Bun Gaillme' in 1125, and 'Bona Gaillme' in 1132. McCB calls it "Caislen Buna Gaillmh" in 1132, while in 1230 a hosting by de Burgh goes into Connacht, "gu rangadur an Gaillim" ("and they reached Galway"), fighting Ó Flaithbheartaigh at "Atha na Gaillme" ("the ford(s?) of [the] Galway"). AI for 1315 calls it "Galbhi", so the prefixes *bun, dun,* and *caislen* were dropped by then. I use *Dún Gaillimhe* in recognition of the settlement, *Bun Gaillimhe* for the physical landsape. Storms and tide-surges of spring 2013 exposed prehistoric material along the shores of Galway Bay, including an oak trackway between An Furbo and An Spiddal; see Siggins, August 2014.

2 - Hardiman, 1820, p. 2, quoting Ó Cléirigh's *Beatha Aodha Ruaidh Uí Dhomhnaill.*

3 - For Sogca, see GBIG, vol. I, 2003, pp. 232-33. For suicín, see Ó Máille, 1985, pp. 59-62. The medieval Irish adduced placenames from people, real or mythical, as that was their way of making sense of the world. We merely have more scientific means – the underlying need to know remains.

4 - *GBIG*, vol. I, 2003, pp. 252-53. For the possible depositions, see Rynne, 1983-4.

5 - Ó Flaithbheartaigh, 1684, pp. 19-20.

6 - op. cit., p. 27, 68, pp. 95-97. This may reflect a taboo, whose meaning became obscured. Seals were slaughtered yearly into the 1680s on Oilean da Branoge, just west of Aran (op. cit., p. 68).

7 - See Viney, 2015. Dowd (2015) puts human presence in Ireland at 12,500 before present.

8 - Gilbert, 1882, pp. 96-97. I have regularised the spelling.

9 - CS, pp. 169-70. "Gabáil for Loch Oirbsen do Gallaibh Luimnigh & innsi an locha d'argain doibh." For viking use of portage techniques, see Ferguson, 2009, p. 125.

10 - op. cit., pp. 169-70. "Ar na n-Gáll ro battur for Loch Oirbsen do chur la Connachtaibh."

11 - For the explanation of this and other placenames in this chapter, I am indebted to an email of Professor Nollaig Ó Muraíle, Arus na Gaeilge, NUI Galway, received 29 September 2012 (hereafter cited as NÓM 2012).

12 - See Ó Cróinín, 1995, pp. 41-47; and Mallory, 2013, pp. 201-14. Warner (1990) and Ballie (2009) have drawn attention to a remarkable concordance between catastrophic environmental events recorded in tree-ring dates, and prehistoric events written in *AFM* during the 1630s. See also note 1, above. Such concordances apparently demonstrates significant population continuity, a point expressed by O'Brien, 2012, p. 249, but implicitly rejected in Mallory, 2016.

13 - For this section I draw principally upon the following: Tolkien, 1955 [1983]; Tierney, 1960; Greene, 1960, 1964 (quoted in Renfrew, 1987); Caulfield, 1981; Renfrew, 1987; Hill, 1989; Cooney and Grogan, 1994; Raftery, 1991, 1994; Warner, 1994, 1995, 1996, 2002, 2009; Waddell, 1995; Sims-Williams, 1998, 1998, 2012; Waddell and Conroy, 1999; Ó Donnabháin, 2000 (I am grateful to Professor Ó Donnabháin for sending this article to me); Carey, 2001; Duffy, Edwards, FitzPatrick, 2001, pp. 35-39; Collis, 2003, 2010, 2013; Bridgman, 2005; Deitler, 2006; Newton, 2006; Becker, 2009; Campbell, 2009; Defente, 2009; O'Brien, 2009, 2013 (and 2016, forthcoming); Mallory, 2013; Legett, 2011; Frehan, 2012 – an especially useful text from which I draw the story of Edward Mainn; Carew, 2012, 2013; Mallory, 2013, 2016; Foster, 2014; O'Sullivan, McCormick, Kerr, Harney, 2014; Pope, 2015; Chapple, 2015; Hughes, 2016.

14 - Schrijver, 2015, pp. 198-200, 200-203.

15 - "But it is essential that we do not transfer the definition in the modern world, where the modern Celts are defined by their language, to the ancient world as it causes considerable confusion in our attempts to interpret what was going on - in the Classical world Celtic was an ethnic concept, and possibly in some cases geographical or

administrative (e.g., the Roman name of the province). When ancient authors use the term *celtice*, they are referring to the language spoken by ethnic Celts, not a language belonging to the Celtic language group as we do today." (Collis, 2010, p. 35). See also Fraser, *Pictish Progress*, p. 37: "Links between ethnicity and language seem generally not to have been as fundamental to early medieval conceptions of identity as they have since become."

16 - Campbell, 2009.

17 - "'The Isles' ... *Vanished Kingdoms: The History of Half-Forgotten Europe*, 2011, p. 42; "though few ..." *The Isles: A History*, 1999, p. xxii, both by Norman Davies. Davies is exasperating as he is clearly sympathetic to non-English histories, but all his work on Ireland have maddening errors that undermine their usefulness.

18 - Carew, 2012, p. 38.

19 - Frehan, 2012.

20 - For O'Donovan, see Boyne, 1987, and MacDonagh, 2014. For Tolkien, see Tolkien 1955 [1983], pp. 171-172.

21 - For the 'Irish kilt', see H., 1954.

22 - Mac Neill, 1919, p. 4, 9.

23 - Collis, 2009, p. 239. See also Herrlott, 2005. While non-national scholars and TV presenters continue to apply the terms quite freely to the Irish and Ireland, Irish scholars and academics use the terms Celt and Celtic rarely, carefully, and in context. See O'Sullivan et al, eds, 2014, p. 14, 16, 34-36; Duffy et al, 2001, pp. 35-38.

24 - "ludicrous", Mallory, 2016, p. 279. For genetics see Røyrvik, 2010; McEvoy, Richards, Forster, Bradley, 2004; Jaski, 2013, p. 5; Wilson et al, 2001; MacEvoy and Bradley, 2010; "the notion", Duffy et al, 2001, p. 36.

25 - Schrijver, 2014, p. 75.

26 - Raftery, 1994, p. 228; Caulfield, 1981. For Britain, see Francis Pryor's *Britain BC* (2003) and *Britain AD* (2004).

27 - Waddell, 1995, p. 158; "a bogus historiography", p. 166.

28 - Ó Donnabháin, 2000.

29 - http://etc.ancient.eu/2012/05/16/interview-linking-ancient-rome-and-ireland/ As to when Ireland's medieval era ended, c. 1600 is preferred by Duffy, Edwards, and FitzPatrick (2001), while Irish archaeologists such as Martin Jope, Kieran O'Conor, and Tom E. McNeill incline towards c. 1650.

30 - O'Brien, 2012, p. 249, though Dowd and Carden (2016) attest pre-glacial humans 12, 500 bp.

31 - Schrijver, 2005; Mac Eoin, 2007; Broderick, 2013. See Ó Donnchadha, 2004, pp. 47-48; Mallory, 2013; Forsyth, 1997, p. 15, 22, 23-25; Ó Muraíle, 2001, pp. 223-224. See also Schrijver, 2014, pp. 195-196, on an north European 'language of geminates' between Finland and Ireland and its effects on both IE and Uralic language groups. Mallory, Schrijver, and Mac Eoin all believe that "the language which later became Irish ... was introduced ... from Britain." (Mac Eoin, 2007, p. 123). Dublin antiquarian, Sir James Ware (1594-1666), wondered in 1654 if "lingua Hibernorum veterum ... eadem fuerit cum Britannica." (see Leerssen, p. 248). 32 - For an overview, see Carey, 1994. See also notes 128, 131, below. For *coimgne*, see Ó Cróinín, 2013, p. 200.

33 - Carey, 2001; Mallory, 2013, pp. 201-14. For Gaeilge and Greek, see Moran, 2014, especially pp. 505-509.

34 - Kinsella, 1969, p. l:

35 - Carey, 1994, p. 13,20, 24).

36 - Jaski, 1996, p. 176.

37 - Based on the first line of the song *Myth*, from the album *pages* by Julie Feeney, 2009. Myths work best not only when when people have a reason to want to believe them, but when a motivated power group enforces them. History is more inconvenient.

38 - Tribes ... 1843; Ni Mhaonaigh, 2000, pp. 362-381; Russell, 2000, pp. 527-551. Richard Warner (pers. comm. 11 January 2016) described an earlier draft of this section as "very dodgy. The Fir Bolg cannot be called a 'genuine' ethnic group as we know nothing about them historically or archaeologically." So I hope to have made clear now that my conclusion is they were not a genuine Iron Age group - at least not by that name - but were medieval groups – including Erainn descendants - recategorised during the eleventh and twelfth centuries by the Gael.

39 - 1029.2, *GBIG*, pp. 362-363, vol. III, 2003. See also 1007.5-1032, pp. 334-365, op. cit. See also 11.3-14.2, pp. 176 -181, 43.1-68.6, pp. 206-247, vol. I, 2003. *Lucht* seems to be a term that came into use in the 11th and 12th centuries, firstly in the sense of a military company on sea or land. This is why I think the term and concept of an Lucht Siúl (first attested in the 1500s) dates from after this period, as hinted by the presence of Norman surnames such as Barrett and Joyce among present-day Travellers.

40 - See Carey, 1988, pp. 78-79; O'Rahilly, 1946, p. 16, 33, 42-56, 75-84, 99-101, 155, 313, 388; Byrne, 1973, p. 9, 55, 193; *NHI* I, p. 183, 461, 463, 465. MacNeill states "That **Fir Bolg**, commonly used as a name for the older subjugated race or races, was an extension of the genuine name of an historical people may be judged from the instances of **Bolgthuath** and **Bolgraige** in *Onomasticon Godelicum*." Furthermore, "It is evident that **Fir Bolg** (=Bolgthuath, Bolgraige) was the name of a known historical population existing in various parts of Connacht and in north-western **Ulster**. Its location and its vassal status, importing early conquest, as well as the traditions of

its existence in Ireland before the **Góedil,** show clearly that the Fir Bolg must not be equated with the historical Belgae. The name was extended in the Irish history-legend at an early period so as to denote the whole or main population of Ireland before the **Góedil.**" (MacNeill, 1911, pp. 99-100). *Nosa Uí Maine* states: "d'Feraib Bolc ... lucht freasdail ocus fir duchais"/"the Fir Bolg ... are serfs and hereditary followers" (*Tribes and Customs*, 1843, pp. 84-86). Campbell (2013, pp. 123-130) is almost alone in discussing Mac Fhirbhisigh's treatment of the Fir Bolg. My own belief is that Fir Bolg was to the Érainn what Milesian was to the Góedil; terms which came to be applied and used interchagably, not the original group name but derived from some aspect of their identity.

41 - Carey, 1988, p. 83. It is also the root of the term *Belgae* of northern Gaul. However the two groups were not otherwise connected, as pointed out by MacNeill in 1911 (see note 34). Compare with Old English '*gebolgen*'.

42 - *GBIG*, vol. I, 2003, pp. 244-45.

43 - NÓM 2012. Melia, 2000, p. 11, glosses *Ol n-Echtmacht* as "beyond the fastness".

44 - Map 14 ("Ptolmey's Map of Ireland, c. 160 AD") and Map 15 ("Ireland 1st-5th century from Roman Evidence"), *NHI*, IX, p. 16.

45 - Mallory, 2013, p. 269; Warner 2013, p. 23.

46 - O'Brien, 2012, p. 236. Or ominously, like the 'peace walls' that have proliferated since 1998 in Belfast. David McGuinness's *The Prehistoric Burial Mounds and Related Monuments of County Westmeath*, 2012, lists a possible unrecorded monument of this type north-east, and south-west, of Lough Owel (p. 20).

47 - Mac Niocaill, 1972, p. 1.

48 - Schrijver, 2015, pp. 206-207.

49 - Mac Giolla Easpaig, 1996, p. 810.

50 - Ó Riain, 2011, pp. 374-75.

51 - op. cit., p. 810.

52 - *GBIG*, vol. III, pp. 272-73 (946.2). AnnTig, 1135.3 "Muircheartach **Ó Cadhla** was killed by men of Munster." 1139.5 "Aedh Ó Cadhla, king of Conmaicne Mara, was treacherously killed by his own people." *Leabhar Oiris* places "Muircheartach Ó Ceallaigh [sic], rí Chonmhaicne Mara" at the 1014 battle of Clontarf (Best, 1904, p. 86). The AI record in 1016 both "Ár n-Arne diaro marbad h-Ua Lochlaind, rígdamna Corcu Mruad, h-i Purt Chiarain i n-Árainn, Conmacne rod marb./The slaughter of Ára, in which Ua Lochlainn, royal heir of Corcu Modruad, was killed in Port Ciaráin in Ára. It was the Conmaicne who slew him." and the subsequent "Bás Muirethaich m. Cadlai. rí Conmacne Mara./Death of Muiredach son of Cadla, king of Conmaicne Mara."

53 - *GBIG*, vol. I, 2003, pp. 612-13 (271.4). Noted as "Ó Gormghail" op. cit., pp. 630-3 (278.3). For the placenames cited at 271.2, 3, and 4, see the section on placenames, *GBIG*, vol. IV, 2004, pp. 409-489.

54 - NÓM 2012. See also Zotov, Maynooth, 2011 (see also note 19).

55 - *GBIG*, vol. II, 2003, pp. 636-37 (655.7, 656.3). Some descendants of the Meic Chon Raoi are rendered King, in the mistaken but understandable belief that *raoi* is a form of *rí* ('king'). While aware of this discrepency I had no idea what raoi actually represented. Therefore I an indebted to Luke McInerney for explaining to me that it denotes a plain, so Mac Con Raoi can be rendered as 'son of the hound of the plain'. Zotov (see note 43, above) equates the Dealbhna with Ptolomey's *Eblana*, which he reconstructs as '(people) from the plain'. Interestingly, the Dealbhna were all located from the Irish Sea to the Atlantic Ocean, spanning Ireland's central plain.

56 - *GBIG*, vol. I, 2003, pp. 450-51 (204.11).

57 - op. cit., pp. 448-49 (204.6). MacLysaght (1978, p. 143) glosses O'Halloran from "*allmhurach*, pirate or stranger from overseas."

58 - My thanks to Dr. Tyrone Bowes, who informed of this on 25 October 2013

59 - *GBIG*, vol. I, 2003, pp. 448-49, (204.7). Meadhraighe (Ballynacourty) was incorporated into Clann Fhearghaile.

60 - Comber, 2001, p. 75, 79, 82, 85, 86, 89.

61 - ATig, 993.4. See also *GBIG*, vol. I, 2003, pp. 442-43 (201.2, 3, 4, 5, 6), and pp. 444-45 (202.6).

62 - MacCotter, 2008, pp. 134-35. For Ua Thaidg an Teaglaig see ATig, 1048.13, 1159.6, AU 1188.9, AC, 1225.9, 18, 24; 1226.4, 1251.9, 1256.5, 1342.5, 1408.7, 1476.10. For the unrelated clerical family of Killaloe, see ATig, 1083.3. For the epynom of the Ui Con Cheanainn, see ATig, 992.4.

63 - For the extent of the constituent parts of Uí Maine, see MacCotter, 2008, pp. 140-41, 147-48, as well as 134-35. For Ua Ceallaigh and Ua Madadháin, see op. cit. p. 141 and 147-48, and MacLysaght, 1978, p. 178 and 208. For the Dál Druithe, see *GBIG* vol. I, pp. 222-23 (54.3); for Catraighe, op. cit., pp. 222-23 (54.2).

64 - For Soghain surnames of County Galway, see Mannion, 2004, p.37-38.
*Contra* MacCotter (2008), Dr. Mannion does not believe the Meig Oireachtaig had any involvement in the Athenry area, and that the Cenél nDéigill rulers of Sogain (with their ruling line, Ua Mannain) resided there till c. 1135-52. 2-3, 8. Dr. Mannion and myself believe Kingland townland east of Athenry represents some demesne lands of the Ua Mannain kings.

65 - According to Sproule (1984, pp. 31-32, ) "It does not seem that the word *Connacht* can originally have meant 'the descendants of Conn': it may have meant 'headship' or 'supremacy' from *cond* or *conn* 'head' and later have being derived from the word Connacht rather than *vice versa*." He further notes that the names *Éoganacht* and *Ciannacht* "were formed in imitation ..." These three were the only groups to use the -acht suffix, which Thurneysen (1946, p. 168) suggested originally denoted a collective. MacNeill wrote that the name Connachta was, "though plural, is the plural not of a word denoting an individual, but of a collective noun." (1911, p. 60)

66 - Bryne (1973, p. 132 ) notes this etymology derives from their confederates, the Gailenga or Gáileóin=the 'spearmen', not the Laigin themselves.

67 - Ford, 2006, pp. 68-70, 73.

68 - O'Rahilly, 1946, p. 10, 455-56.

69 - Thompson, 1985, pp. 126-143 (also 109-113).

70 - Byrne, 1973, p. 11. For these traditions, see Byrne, 1973, p. 8 (Érainn), p. 108 (Cruithin), p. 132-33 (Laigin). See Duffy, 2005, pp. 155-56l; and Johnston, 2013.

71 - Patterson, 1994, pp. 47-53. However Katharine Simms takes great issue with some of her ideas (see her review of Patterson in *Irish Historical Studies*, vol. 31, no. 121, May 1998, pp. 125-127). O'Brien (2014, pp. 233-261, especially pp. 233-235, 235-236, 249) demonstrated that late prehistoric/early historic archaeology of County Cork has a distinctiveness that ties in with regional resistance to a new, incoming culture.

72 - *NHI*, vol. VIII, 1982, pp. 14-16. Also Raftery, 2005, p. 174-81.

73 - NÓM 2012. Ó Muraíle (2001, p. 223) carefully states Ériu's non-Celtic roots are deeply contested but Schrijver (2014, p. 78) boldly states it is not originally Celtic, (2015, p. 206) that "*Ériu* ... is probably non-Indo-European." (see also Schrijver 2014, p. 78). Nina Zhivlova is researching non-IE name-types in medieval Ireland.

74 - "Introduction", MacLysaght, Dublin, 1978, pp. ix-x; Adams, 1979, pp. 83-84; Ó Cuív, 1986, pp. 31-36. According to F. J. Byrne, even they were not the first, as some Gaelic ecclesiastical families appear to have used surnames in the ninth century. See Byrne, 2001, pp. xxxiii-xxxiv, and MacNeill, 1911, p. 64 ('raige', earlier 'rige' denoting a group ruled by a king; 'na', earlier 'ne', denoted a collective, a people).

75 - Adams, 1979, pp. 83-84. See also Charles-Edwards, 2000, pp. 630-31; and GBIG, vol. I, 2003, p. xiv.

76 - Jaski, 2000, p. 355. See also Byrne, 1973, p. 119, 122-23; O'Donovan, 2003, pp. 27-30 et al.

77 - MacCotter, 2008, pp. 22-23, 89-91, 108.

78 - For a translation and explanation of these terms, see Mulligan, 2005, pp. 21-22, 35-36, 54-55, 56-57, 74. See also Naessens and O'Conor, 2012.

79 - O'Sullivan et al, 2010, pp. 52-53; O'Sullivan and Nicholl, 2010, p. 64, 66. Also Fitzpatrick, 2009, p. 271, 303.

80 - I owe this insight to Paul Gosling, GMIT, delivered at an Ireland Reaching Out talk at Loughrea about 2009.

81 - O'Sullivan, 2000, p. 5, 8-9, 11, 19, 31, 32, 42, 44-45.

82 - Mulligan, 2005, p. 74. Fitzpatrick, 2009, p. 271-75, 281-84, 303. Naessens and O'Conor, 2012, p. 115, 118, 120-21.

83 - MacCotter, 2008, p. 88.

84 - Byrne, 1973, p. 58, 106-107, 113-114, 254, for Ulaid; p. 58, 142, 255, for Laigin.

85 - Jaski, 2000, p. 214-18. Tara is not the only place of the name in Ireland. See Ó Muraíle, 2005, pp. 449-477.

86 - Byrne, 1973, p. 168, 202. For c. 737, see Jaski, 1995, pp. 311-312.

87 - Geissel, 2006.

88 - Jaski, 2000, p. 227.

89 - AU 1126.8, AFM, 1145.13.

90 - Duffy, 2003, p. 425. "**Gall** (derived from 'Gaul'), translated 'foreigner' and an antonym (opposite in meaning) of Gael (from the Old Irish 'Goídel'). Since the defining characteristic of the latter was use of the IRISH LANGUAGE, to the early Irish the world was composed of those who spoke Irish, Goídel, and those who did not, Gaill. The name became attached to the VIKINGS who settled in Ireland in the ninth century ... the descendants of the Anglo-Normans, ... were termed Sean-Ghaill ('Old Foreigners')." Charles-Edwards (2000, p. 222), remarks "One term, apparently for the exile from overseas, typically an *Albanach* 'Briton' or *Gall* 'Gaul', was *cú glas*, 'grey wolf'. The wolf was the characteristic outsider, both as hapless alien and as the dedicated raider and pirate, the *díbergach* or *féinnid*." Up to the seventh century, the term for foreigner as Gaeilge was murchoirthe ('sea-borne person'). See also O'Brien, 2012, pp. 229-230.

91 - NÓM 2012. Sims-Williams (1998, p. 22, note 83) states Goídil "is thought to derive from the Welsh Gwyddyl, originally meaning 'wild men' from Welsh *gwydd* 'wild' (not *gwydd*, 'forest', ...". Koch disagrees, stating that it derives from the same root as *Féni*, going back to a root term comon to Old Irish, Old Breton and Middle Welsh that denote "'wild, feral, uncultivated'", which in turn go back to *weidh(e)l*, *weidh-n-* 'forest people'" (p. 13). Perhaps 'feral' would be the best expression of all terms? See also Byrne, 1973, p. 8; and Sim-Williams, 1998, p. 14, 22. The latter comments "In the Middle Ages and beyond, the Welsh generally disliked the Irish

, the term *Guyddel* 'Irishman' being used alongside Sais and  *Iddew*, 'Englishman' and 'Jew', as a term of abuse. The native names for their languages were quite distinct, and no  umbrella term like 'Celtic' was in use. The two nations gave themselves very distinct ancestries; while the Britons came from Troy via Greece, the Irish came from Scythia via Egypt and Spain." (p. 14)

92 - Campbell (2001, p. 286) "To the classical authors of late antiquity, the peoples of Ireland were *Scotti,* **probably a derogatory term** [my emphasis] meaning something like 'pirates'. The name was used by early medieval writers in Latin for all speakers of Gaelic, whether in Ireland or Scotland. Much later the usage became associated exclusively with the peoples of Scotland, whether speaking Gaelic or not." It suggests a sense of 'feral' applies here too. The Brythonic and Gaelic terms for the English, *Sacain, Sasanach,* might reflect original application of the terms. English originated as a *Christian* identity thanks to Bede (d. 735), and a *political* ethnicity due to King Alfred of Wessex (d. 899)

93 - Byrne, 1973, p. 8. This places the term on a par with 'Indian' (as applied to the First Nations of the Americas) or 'Gypsy' (as applied to the Roma of Europe). See "The Rootless Roma", *The American Interest*, March/April 2011.

94 - Byrne, 1973, p. 106 ("Batar trí prímcheinéla i nHére .i. Féni 7 Ulaith 7 Gáilni .i. Laigin"/"There were three principal races in Ireland; the Féni, the Ulaid and the Gáilni, i.e., the Laigin." Compare Féni with Gothic *Widugauja,* 'wood-dweller'.

95 - Sherratt, 2005, p. 31; Smith, 1986, pp. 22-31.

96 - Byrne, 1973, p. 8, 9. However, MacNeill believed that the term was once "an ancient people-name, not the name of a class as has been supposed." (1911, p. 61) David O'Brien wrote "That *Féni,* though applied technically as a general name to the landowning classes ... and *Fir Féne,* which does not seem to have been so applied, denoted one of the 'population-groups' of ancient Ireland, hardly admits of doubt." "[They] were a dominant people distinct from the Ulaid and Laigin ... Their territory lay, partly at least, to the south of the Ulaid ... there is a suggestion that they occupied the outskirts of a wooded region on the Meath-Gabrán border." He thought they "denoted the dominant people of the Old Connacht and Uisnech monarchy and its offshoots ..." suggesting that the term arose from an unrecorded word denoting 'warriors,' "applied as a general non-committal, complimentary term to the *airig* attending the national assemblies, at which those of the Féni in the restricted sense would have increasingly preponderated." (1932, pp. 182-83).

97 - Byrne, 1973, pp. 45-56. MacNeill (1911, p. 93) agrees, stating "The genealogical doctrine, however, must be taken as often expressing political status rather than racial origin." The identification of the Aithechthuatha with the *Attacotti* of late-Roman Britain is uncertain, but see Rance, 2001, who believes they are identical - my own suggestion is the Attacotti were the vassal folk of Munster, some of whom later became the Eoghnachta. MacNeill (1911, p. 60) wrote "The names **Scotti** and **Atecotti,** known through Latin writings of the fourth century, are probably of a general application, not designative of special groups." For perceived racial distinctions between Gael and Fir Bolg, see 11.4-12.8, pp. 176-177, *GBIG,* vol. I. Rather like settlers and travellers in modern Ireland, these distinctions have more to do with the wealth/poverty divide than genes.

98 - Bhreathnach, 2014, p. 78.

99 - See note 28, this chapter; O'Rahilly, 1946, 85-92; Warner 1994 (especially p. 26), 1995, 2009.

100 - Schrivjer, 2014, p. 81. See Schrijver, 2015, p. 206.

101 - *AnnTig,* 1124.3 - "Tri caisdeoil la Connachtaib .i. caistél Gaillme & Caistél Cul Maile & Castél Dúin Leódha." CS describes it as *caislen Duin Gaillme* (see note 90). **Dún** Leódha is attested in 1114 so some form of fort existed at Ballinasloe prior to the construction of the *caistél* in 1124. Perhaps likewise Galway. 1124 features as Galway's foundation date on t-shirts and hoodies since about 2012. My guess is that it derives from Wikipedia's "History of Galway" and "Galway" articles, which due to my edits on 1 May 2005 and 30 September 2005 respectively, included the date 1124 for the first time (user id 213.202.156.45, and 83.71.162.221, later Fergananim). Previously, 1232 was seen as the 'proper' foundation date, entirely because of the arrival of the Normans. Absence of Gaelic material in the otherwise excellent *Galway:History and Society* (1996) led me to redress the balance.

102 - Perros-Walton, 2013, p. 291, who also states: "the terminology used in the annals for some of [Toirdhealbhach]'s fortifications shows that he was influenced by European as well as by Irish developments. ... the European term 'castle' ... debuted in the Irish annals to describe the fortresses that [he] built in Connacht at Galway, Collooney, and Dunlo in 1124, at Athlone in 1129, and at Loch Carrigan by 1136." See also Fitzpatrick, 2009.

103 - Naessens and O'Conor, 2012, p. 121. The *caistél's* exact situation however is unknown and it is only assumed that it was situated on the same general site as de Burgh's castle. O'Keffe (1998, p. 188) holds that "The elevation of Castél Duín Leódha and Dún Mór would have made their defence easier and would have allowed those within a better view of what lay outside". Perhaps the site of St. Nicholas's church would be a better candidate for Toirdhealbhach's Castél Duín Gaillimhe? I regard the *dún* and *caistél* as related yet distinct structures.

104 - NHI, IX, p. 192. Also ATig, 1119. Helen Perros-Walton notes that Tairrdelbach "must have been the king of

Ireland who in 1121 notified Henry I that Gregorius had been chosen as bishop of Dublin and sent to the archbishop of Canterbury for consecration, his colleague-like approach to Henry evident in Henry's own writ to the archbishop informing him that '[m]andavit mihi rex Hibernia per breve suum, et burgenses Dublinae, quod elegerunt hunc Gergorium in episcopum, et eum tibi mittunt consecrandum'" (2013, pp. 291-92). Flanagan (1989) believed the king to have been either Toirdhealbhach "or Énna mac Donnchada Mac Murchada, king of Leinster." (p. 30). Toirdhealbhach's reign as King of Ireland can be said to have ended in 1150, when the hostages of Connaught were delivered to Muircheartach Mac Lochlainn (see AFM, 1150).

105 - CS, 1124 - "Tri caistel la Connacht .i. caislen Duin Gaillme et Dun Leoda & Cul Maile."

106 - ATig. 1154; AFM 1154.

107 - CS, 1124; ATig, 1127.3, 4, 1130.1. CS, 1131; ATig, 1132.1.

108 - Miscellaneous Irish Annals, 1132.1 – Breandán Mac Gabhann of Galway City Museum pointed out to me that while An Claddagh denotes a sea-strand (where the Claddagh fishermen beached their boats), An Cloidhe denotes a ditch. Thus this identification with An Claddagh (not otherwise attested till 1589; see note 34, Chapter Five) is problematic. Paul Walsh notes that TCD MS 886 records that Stephen Lynch fitz Dominick Dubh "removed the ditch from Leam Teig near the town walls and the corporation gave him the lands near the same." (1992, p. 62) In the same note he records that Richard Bellings noted a "a large drye ditch" east of the town in the 1600s (note 74, pp. 91-92). Further research is required.

109 - ATig, 1051.4.

110 - ATig, 1092.1.

111 - "Ua Conchobair, Tairrdelbach (1088-1156)", Duffy, ed., 2005, pp. 471-74. See also DoIB.

112 - For Toirdhealbhach's known daughters see ATig, 1134.12; Atig,1153.3; AU, 1190.3. His known sons are listed at GBIG, vol. I, 2003, pp. 486-89 (219.16).

113 - ATig, 1139.4

114 - Duffy, ed., 2005, p. 472; Harbison, 2000, p. 2, 10; Etchingham, 2000, pp. 22-25, 27.

115 - Claffey, 2000, p. 5.

116 - ATig, 1136.7; AFM 1136.14.

117 - Hardiman, 1820, pp. 47-48.

118 - FitzPatrick, O'Brien, Walsh, eds., 2004, p. 297."What distinguished a town from a village was economic functionality. A genuine town inhabited by craftworkers and traders existed primarily to produce and distrubute artefacts made locally and imported from elsewhere, with a support system derived from the rural economy." (Howard Clarke's review of Patrick Wallace's Viking Dublin: The Wood Quay Excavations, in The Irish Times, Saturday 30 January 2016. Bristol existed by the 1050s, and traded with Ireland from that decade.

119 - CDI, 1171-1251. "1201. 153. ... to Richard Tirel – Dungalue. [Chart, of April.] 2 John, m. 8 dors.]" Tirel may have been related to Hugh Tyrell, custos of Trim Castle, abandoned to an Ui Chonchobair onslaught in 1174.

120 - Bhreathnach, 2014, pp. 14-15.

121 - Quiggin, 1912, p. 169, 174. Toirdhealbhach's Ui Briain kindred held lordship over Limerick (founded about 922) from c. 967 to at least the 1300s. Did their city inspire Galway?

122 - Kelly, 2010, p. 176.

123 - op. cit, p. 186. A more sceptical view has been expressed by Gibbons, JGAHS vol. 59, 2007, pp. 190-93.

124 - See Bhreathnach, 2014, pp. 13-17. "islands were important strategic stopping points for navigation and for gaining a foothold in a territory. Iona and the Aran Islands are classic examples of islands that were at the centre of seafaring communications, and the excavations at the great stone fort of Dun Aonghasa on Aran confirmed that this apparently remote island was a centre of activity from the late Bronze Age to the late medieval period." (p.16)

125 - NHI, 2005, p. 168. The Atlantic 'fringe' is only so if viewed from 'darkest Mummerset', or perhaps Westminster.

126 - op. cit., p. 152.

127 - "297 First mention of Picts: attack Roman Britain in conjunction with Irish (Hiberni)" "297 – c. 450 Irish raids on Roman Britain" "367-70 Assault on Britain by Picts, Irish (Scotti), and Saxons; Hadrian's wall breached for third time; restored by Theodosius" NHI, vol. VIII, 1982 (2002 reprint), p. 15; "Scotti in 314", Rance, 2012, p. 228, 229. For Patrick, see Thompson, 1985, and Warner, 1995. In an online exchange on 16 December 2015, historian and former Lecturer University of Edinburgh Alex Woolf informed me that contra Rance, the 'Attacotti=aithech tuatha' "simply doesn't work linguistically". All that can be said is they were certainly from beyond the frontier, subsequently forming four Roman army units stationed in Illyricum, Italia, and Gaul.

128 - Duffy, 2005, p. 369. See also Holm, 2005, pp. 430-31, and Gillingham, 2011 and 2012.

129 - op. cit., p. 122, 155, 421. For the 'Ichtian sea'/the English channel, see Byrne, 1973, p. 77.

130 - Byrne, 1973, p, 110.

131 - op. cit., pp. 8-9, 39, 108, 109, 110.

132 - McManus, 1991, and Swift, 1997.

133 - Slavin, 2010. For continuity of Pagan culture into at least the 12th century, see "Continuity, cult and contest" by John Waddell, in Landscapes of Cult and Kingship, Roseanne Schot, Conor Newman & Edel Breathnach, editors, Four Courts Press, 2011, pp.203-05.

134 - Sharpe, 1995, p. 201 (also pp. 132, 188-193, 196-98).

135 - Comber, 2001, p. 82. According to the La Vita of Filiberti (Gascon monk, founder of Noirmoutier, d. 684): "Nec multum post scothorum navis diver siis mercinmoniis plena ad litus adfuit ..." (Book Five, p. 42).

136 - Duffy, 2005, pp. 128-29, 420; and Ó Cróinín, 2005, pp. 394-95, 624.

137 - For the section on Brendan, I have relied upon Ó Donnchadha, 2004, and Ó Cróinín, 1995 (see below).

138 - Ó Cróinín, 1995, p. 220, 229-30. See also Ó Donnchadha, 2004.

139 - AI, 1166.9.

140 - See "The synod of Cashel, 1101: conservative or innovation?" by Donnchadh Ó Corráin, in Regions and Rulers in Ireland 1100-1650: Essays for Kenneth Nicholls, ed. David Edwards, 2004, pp. 13-19; Ireland and Europe in the Twelfth Century: Reform and Renewal, eds. Damian Bracken and Dagmar Ó Riain-Raedel, Dublin, 2006; The Transformation of the Irish Church in the Twelfth Century, Maire Therese Flanagan, Woodbridge, 2010; "Irish Hagiographical Lives in the Twelfth Century: Church Reform before the Anglo-Norman Invasion", Roel Joris, Master's Thesis, Radboud University Nijmegen, 2014.

141 - Duffy, 2005, pp. 312-14; and Hazard, 2006, pp. 212-29, but also Zumbhul, 2005, pp. 269-284. For catha marcshluaigh see AT 1000.7; formna fer, AI 999.4; daingne, AI 1012.5.

142 - See Flannagan. 2005; Jaski, 2011; Mac Niocaill, 1990; Simms, 1987.

143 - Hazard, 2006, pp. 21-46, 109-122; Holm, 1986, pp. 317-45. Also Holm, 2005, and Gillingham, 2011 and 2012.

144 - For Gryffud, see Hazard, 2006, pp. 95-97 and Ó Cróinín, 2005, pp. 863-64. For Gofraid, see Ó Cróinín, 2005, p. 864. For Echmarcach, see Ó Cróinín, 2005, p. 890. For Dagobert, see NHI, IX, p. 25, 26.

145 - For the Irish role in the conversion of the English see Ó Cróinín, 2004; Grimmer, 2008;Graham-Campbell and Ryan, 2009; Carella, 2011. Bede (d. 735) praises the Irish contribution to English Christian civilization.

146 - For Queen Emma, see Tyler, pp. 183-184. For St. Bride's see Hazard, 2006, p. 51.

147 - Hudson, 2006, pp. 100-107.

148 - McManus, 2004, pp. 107-134, esp. 126-130.

149 - Byrne, 1973, p. 9. "The course of Irish history as outlined in ... Lebor Gabála Érenn ... was the result of efforts to harmonise different political and genealogical traditions and to weave the various strands into a unified whole." (Ó Cróinín, 2005, p. 183) "The story of Mil ... seems to have been cooked up in the eighth century ... and the whole story nothing more than a learned fiction ... which tells us nothing about Irish prehistory." (op. cit., pp. 185-86) "The Ulaid ... never acknowledged the claims to sovereignty made by the Ui Neill, and hence had to be fitted into the scheme by the addition of Ir son of Mil ... Later again other dynasties ... were grafted on to the scheme." (op. cit., p. 186) "If there ever was a popular native tradition concerning the origins of the Irish people, it did not survive." (op. cit., p. 186) "The dynasties ... have their origin legends, but they tell us nothing about the ethnic roots of these people.." (op. cit., p. 186). All this alludes to the role elites have played in influencing/dictating Irish identities, be they medieval dynasties or modern political parties.

150 - FAI, 265-266, pp. 106-107. Elizabeth Boyle (2013, p. 17, 22) notes a tenth-century use of the form "do feraib Herend" as a "geographic identifier" in very early Middle Irish. In another case, written in the Middle Irish period but reworked in the Early Modern Irish period, "the linguistic/ethnic identifier Goidil" is used instead.

151 - "Although they held a common 'nation' consciousness against others ... there was no unified soverignty amongst the Irish and consequently 'nation' consciousness was also limited at that time." (Tanaka, 2010, p. 13) The equation 'medieval dynasty'='modern political party' and associated notions of lordship seems sadly apt.

152 - Ni Bhrolcháin, 1980, p. 302, 416, verse 554. For Ua Ruairc and MacMurchada's attempts to suborn Mide, see Byrne, 1973, p. 273. For Ua Ruairc's military intents see Veach, 2007.

153 - Expugnatio, pp. 93-97, 312-13; NHI, VIII, p. 77; AU, ATig, both 1171; Frame, 1981 (2012); Flanagan, 1989 (1998). See also CDI, 1171-1251, no. 38, where Pope Alexander III addresses "the Kings and Princes of Ireland. Has learnt with joy that they have taken Henry King of England for their King, and sworn fealty to him, whereby great advantage would accrue to them, to the church, and the Irish people. Exhorts them to persevere in their fealty." See also anxieties over Hugh de Lacy in Veach, 2009. " None of the other Irish kings"; this is entirely my own suggestion, though with some support from Gervase of Canterbury (see Crooks, 2005, pp. 272-273).

# Chapter Two: Dungulae

1 - The official definition of *linch* is "A bank formed at the end of a field by soil which, loosened by the plough, gradually moves down slope through a combination of gravity and erosion." See http://thesaurus.english heritage.org.uk/thesaurus_term.asp?thes_no=1&term_no=68626 For Linces et al, see Williams and Martin, 1992. Peter Crooks, in the Glossary for his invaluable *A Calendar of Irish Chancery Letters, c. 1244-1509* (see chancery.tcd.ie), notes that the Latin term for a measure of tin, *lincia*, is rendered linch in English. I however greatly doubt that this term has anything to do with the surname in any form! I have used his Glossary to explain the terms avoirdupois, [cask], livery, messuage, novel disseisin, tun, valettus, both in the main text and footnotes. For an overview, see *NHI* I and II; Frame,1981 (2012 reprint); O'Bryne, 2003; Crooks, ed., 2008.

2 - Williams and Martin, 2002, p. 56. For Urse de Linces and the de Stopham family, see http://www.british -history.ac.uk/report.aspx?compid=41701.

3 - In Gaeilge, '*mór*' denotes '*senior*' and '[the] great'. William de Burgh has often and wrongly been identified with Henri II's prominent official, William fitz Aldelin/FitzAldelin (fl. 1160-89), a son of Aldelin de Aldefeld of Hampshire and Juliana daughter of Robert Doisnell. But de Burgh was an elder son of Alice and [Walter?] de Burgh of Burgh Castle, Suffolk (in Norfolk since 1974). Another son was Hubert, earl of Kent (d. 1243). For fitz Aldelin see Martin and Scott, 1978, p. 317 n. 189, and p. 331 n. 294; for de Burgh see *NHI*, IX, 1984, p. 170.

4 - I am very grateful to Dr. Freya Verstraten-Veach for correcting my initial errors in this family tree, and enlightening me on the manner in which Walter de Burgh became Earl of Ulster. *NHI* volume IX states that Hugh de Lacy was created Earl of Ulster on 29 May 1205, forfeited it in 1210, and had it restored on 20 April 1227 (pp. 234-235). According to family trees 38 and 41 (op. cit., p. 170, 173), Egidia was a daughter of Hugh de Lacy and it was from her that Walter de Burgh inherited the earldom. Dr. Verstraten writes "This is stated in many good books (and follows a statement in some late fourteenth-century annals), but is in fact incorrect. Egidia was the daughter of Walter de Lacy, who was never Earl of Ulster." (email, 3 December 2012). See also Curtis, 1923, p. 150; and Orpen, 1911-20, p. 266. For the invasion and settlement of Connacht, see also Crooks, 1995.

5 - Hardiman, 1820, p. 198. "Richard White and William de Lench" were "collectors of the custom of the vill of Galuy [Galway], from May 24, a.r. 5 [1277], until Michaelmas in the same year - [£]24 15[s] 2[d]". On p. 197, Hardiman states "The earliest magistrates of Galway of whom any account remains extant, were provosts or portreves, (called also bailiffs or seneschals,) appointed by the earls of Ulster, and the family of de Burgo until 1396. These were succeeded by sovereigns and provosts, elected under the charter of Richard II until 1485."

6 - op. cit., p. 17. See also Melville, 2012, p. 375, 361, 367, 377, 382, 383.

7 - *CJRI 1303-1305*, 1914, p. 12. An inquisition held at Claregalway on 8 December 1333 records that the Brown Earl had purchased a house in the town of Galway from "William Marescall", once valued at nine shillings but by then of no value. That there were at first two distinct families named Lynch and Marshal is proven by an inquisition held at "Aneri" ('A-ne-ri', *Ath na Rí*, Athenry, wrongly cited in the text as Ardnaree, County Sligo) on Thursday 20 October 1278, which lists "the following jurors, namely: - **Walter Marshal**, Richard le Blund, Thomas Applegard, Elias le Keu, John Traherne, Alexander Bastard, William le Wite, of Foran [Oranmore?], Robert Fitz Peter, Hugh de Mortimer, Adam Lathred, **William de Lenche**, and Nicholas Miauth ..." (*CDI 1252-1284*, 1877, p. 280).

8 - Hardiman, 1820, p. 55.

9 - op. cit., p. 53

10 - Hanks and Hodges, 1988, p. 349. For Marshal, see Crouch, 2002 (second edition).

11 - Blake, 1913-14, pp. 85-86. 'Linceus' is risible. "Sr. Hugo de Lynch" is fiction. "Andrew Lynch" is unattested. His supposed youngest son, "John Lynch", cannot have come to Connacht "in the Viceroyship of John Lackland" because on neither of his two Irish visits (1185 and 1210) did John venture west of the Shannon. See note 6.

12 - op. cit., p. 86. For further details, see "Leinster Lordships" *NHI*, IX, 1984, p. 174.

13 - Blake, 1915-16, p. 97. See also Hardiman, 1820, p. 17.

14 - *Fiants-Henry VIII* , p. 11; "Deposition of William Lynche, of the Knock, in the County of Meath, Gent.", Christchurch, Dublin, 21 January 1535.

15 - See Hodgekinson's "Who's Who in Medieval Limerick", online; and *Blake Family Records*, vol. I.

16 - Blake, 1915-16, pp. 91-92. For Lynch seizure of O'Halloran estates, see Ó Flaithbheartaigh, 1684, pp. 253-261.

17 - For 1277, see *CDI*, 1252-84, London, 1877, p. 415. For 1278, op. cit., p. 280.

18 - Curtis, 1940, pp. 288-89.

19 - See *The Norman Conquest*, Marc Morris, 2013. Useful are Tom Shippey's *J.R.R. Tolkien: Author of the Century* (2001), and *The Road to Middle Earth* (2005) and works by Elizabeth Tyler and Carter Revard. See also Duffy et al, 2001 (paperback edition, 2004), especially its introductory essay, "Recovering Gaelic Ireland, c. 1250-c.1650",

pp. 21-73, by the editors.

20 - *Grace's Annals*, 1341. See also "The middle nation", Lydon, 1984, pp. 1-26; NHI II, 1987, pp. 303-351; Clarke, 2000, pp. 15-27; Campbell, 2013, pp. 1-23. See also *Great Deeds* ..., 2013, pp. 106-111, where Stanihurst in 1584 describes his own nation as *Anglo-Hiberni*, 'Anglo-Irish' (pp. 108-109). Lydon notes **To thus emphasise their Englishness did not mean that the Anglo-Irish identified less with Ireland** [my emphasis]. (Lydon, "The middle nation", 1984, p. 23). "Frenchmen, Flemings and Normans"; *La Geste* ..., line 2645, p. 121.

21 - Campbell, 2008, pp. 181-220. See also Campbell, 2014.

22 - Lydon, 1984, pp. 8-9.

23 - Hardiman, 1820, p. 50.

24 - *CDI 1285-1292*, p. 419. The Landes peninsula is in Gascony.

25 - AC, 1247.7 – See op. cit. 1233.6; Curtis, 1940, p. 288 for le Bret lands at Shrule and in Conmhaicne Cúile Toland; Rice, 2001, pp. 33-37. Their identification with Ballybrit is my suggestion.

26 - Holland, 1997, p. 190, where "Roger Francys" is listed as holding "Balydondehyny" in 1289, as did "Roger Franceys" in 1321. "Domengun le Fraunceys, Gascon merchant", is cited in *CDI 1282-1285*, p. 419, as delivering wine to Ireland in 1284, and to Galway in 1281 by Westropp, 1912-13, p. 384. **Francis** is associated with Menlo.

27 - "Alexander Bastard" - CDI, 1252-1284, p. 280.

28 - "Geoffrey de la Vale" - Holland, 1997, p. 185, 190; "Walter Hosee" - op. cit., p. 185; "Bonaventure" - BFR); "Talun" - CDI 1285-1292, p. 102.

29 - *"Loinges na fFlémendach"*; AFM, 1169.9.

30 - Hardiman, 1820, p. 60; and Hanks and Hodges, 1988, p. 11.

31 - Hardiman, 1820, p. 52. Fletcher, 2002, page 158, notes that it was a common name in eleventh-century Northumbria The surname is now rendered **Dolphin** but the element *dolf* derives from Old Norse *úlfr*, 'wolf'.

32 - "Adam Lathred", *CDI 1252-1284*, p. 280. "Peter Hereward", *CDI 1252-1284*, p. 417, 419; *CDI 1285-1292*, p. 102; *BFR* no. 4. "William Wodelond", CDI 1252-1284, p. 419. **Kent** derives from the shire in south-east England. Hugh of Kent was in 1282 "keeper of the new custom of Galway" (*CDI 1255-1282*, p. 419), having served with Peter Hereward from Michaelmas 1280 to Easter 1282 as "collectors of the new custom in the vill of Galway" (op. cit, p. 417); For **Lawless** see Martyn, 2011. The earlies treference I have found to them in Connacht is in ALCé 1242.11, as *Loghbhais*, rendered "Lewis" in translation. The surname **White** appears to have been Latinised as *Albus* in the thirteenth and fourteenth centuries (see Hardiman, 1820, p. 49, and BFR). Are they *le Blund?*

33 - ""Peter Breythnok", Inquisitions, 2007, p. 102. Found as **Breathnach**, or **Walsh**. "Griffin Cradok, of Bradach", op. cit., p. 102. "Hostig" This is the epynom of the surname **Hosty**, found in counties Galway and Mayo. "Meurig" This is the epynom of the surname **Merrick**, found in small numbers in counties Galway and Mayo. "Philip le Walyes" (*'Phillip the Welshman'*). This surname is now rendered **Wallace** or **Walsh**.
     **Penrise** derives from Penrose, near Porthleven in Cornwall, or Penrice on the Gower peninsula in south Wales. I am indebted to David Etheridge (University of Bristol), for a discussion on this section. For *Ywerddon*, see Issac, 2009. For the Welsh as a nation to c. AD 1200, see Stokes, 2001.

34 - *BFR*, vol. I, 1902, p. 14.

35 - *BFR no. 12*, 1902, pp. 11-12. For Mac Catharnaigh, see *GBIG*, vol. I, 2003, pp. 448-49 (204.7).

36 - Hardiman, 1820, p. 198, and n101, C4. For Ó Docomláin (now **Dolan?**) of Rinn na hEdhnighe, see Russell, 2000.

37 - *NHI II*, 1987, pp. 301-02, 395, 553-5.

38 - **Begge** – A statute of 1500 states that "Richard Begge made free, on condition of his keeping a common house or ynne for victualling and lodgeing strangers."
     **Boland** – A family surnamed Mac Beolláin were erenaghs of Killower, Knockmaa, hereditary keepers of the Clogh Dubh Pátraic/Black Bell of St. Patrick c. 1100 (*Ordnance*, 2009, p. 90).
     **Branegan** - "Sir Henry Branegan was warden in 1497 (Hardiman, 1820, p. 6).
     **Carr** - "Edmund Kar" was bequeathed "a half *dosselum* of cloth, together with 2 quarters of salt;" in the 1420 will of John Óge Blake (BFR 19, 1902, p. 20).
     **Colman** – The will of Valentine Blake, dated 12 July 1499, bequeaths "To the two daughters of Thomas y'Colman a cask of wine." (*BFR 69*, 1902, pp. 47-49).
     **Curran** - "Sir Henry Curryn, warden of the Collegiate Church of St. Nicholas, Galway", is named in a "Sentence" dated 2 December 1525 (*Wardenship*, 1944, p. 11). "Sir" in this context was an honorific used by churchmen.
     **Cunningham** - "Jacobus Cunningham, mercator [merchant], made Freeman July 1600 (*Archives*, 1992, p. 458).
     **Dermody** - "John O'Dermode" was Warden of Galway about 1528 (Hardiman, 1820, p. 238).
     **Duff** - A man surnamed Ó Duibh was one of the minor lords of Ui Briuin Eola c. 1100.
     **Fallon** – In 1500, "Andraue Ffallon" requested Galway Corporation grant the freedom of the town to his son-in-law, "Donill Oge Ovolloghan [O'Nolan?]", who was married to his daughter, Julian Fallon. This was granted.

**Flynn** - "Thomas O'Floyn" was a witness to the will of John Óge Blake, made at Galway on 7 September 1420 (*BFR* 19, 1902, p. 20). "Richard Flynne" is listed as a townsman in April 1652 (Hardiman, 1820, p. xxxiii)

**Folan** - "Donald McFolan" is mentioned as living in a house in Galway in a decree dated 10 February 1506 (*BFR* 76, 1902, pp. 56-57). "Dermott mcffollane ... brogmakere" was a member of a Galway jury in 1609 (*IC*, p. 237).

**Halloran** - "Teige Holleran" is stated as dwelling in a house mentioned in a "Bond" dated 28 March 1561 (*Wardenship*, 1944, p. 13).

**Hannon** - "Deed of grant in fee simple by Katherine Hannyn, daughter and heiress of John, son of Phillip Hannyn, burgess of Galway" (*BFR* no. 10, dated 1394).

**Higgins** - "the chamber of the late Sir Philip ihiggin, priest, on the east" is mentioned in a "Lease, for twenty years", dated 23 May 1569 (*Wardenship*, 1944, p. 10).

**Keane** - "Catherine ny Cahan of Galway" is mentioned in a "General Pardon" dated 2t July 1610 (*PRJI*, p. 143).

**Kenny** - "Turlough O'Keynay of Galway, an Irish priest, taken as a fugitive, doth give information of matters of danger that may happen in Connaught." (*CSPI 1588-1592, p. 455*). "

**Larkin** – John Óge Blake's will of September 1420 notes that he left one hourse and two measures of oats to "John O'Lorchayn." "Matheue Lurcan" was town clerk in 1529 ("Archives", 1992, p. 389).

**Moore** – In 1529, "the said Thomas Moore and his heires shall have the liberties of this town as fre as anny man of the same had or hath, within and withoute, in bu[y]ing and selling, acording as the Mayor" ("Archives", 1992, p. 389). "Thomas Moore" was a witness to deed dated at Galway on 1 May 1602 (*BFR*, 1905, pp. 1-2).

**Mullen** - A family surnamed Ó Maoilin were erenaghs of Kilkilvery c. 1100 (Ordnance, 2009, p. 90). "Thomas Omvylen, mercator [merchant]" was made a Freeman of Galway in February 1596 ("Archives", 1992, pp. 455-56).

**Molgan** – Father Thomas Molgan (Tomás Ó Mocháin) was Warden of Galway in 1488. William Molgan was public notary for Galway Corporation in 1492, as was Nicholas Molgan in the mid-1500s (possibly the latter man exemplified earlier records!). Now rendered **Maughan**, or **Mongan**.

**Nolan** - "Donatus Niger [Domnall Dubh] O'Nolyn" is mentioned as dwelling in a building on Galway's main street in a deed dated 20 April 1535 (*BFR* 88, 1902, p. 68).

**Quin** – Thomas Quin was a tailor living in Galway in 1581. The family had a monument in the graveyard of St. Francis's Abbey, which read "This tomb was first erected in the year 1649, by James Quin, of Galway, merchant, and Eleanor Joyes, his wife. In memory of whom, James Quin, of Galway, aforesaid, merchant, one of the descendants of said James, caused the same to be entirely repaired and ornamented, the year 1762. Requiesant in pace." (Hardiman, 1820, p. 269).

**Quirke** – "Cateline ny Curke" was executor of the 1488 will of her husband, William Blake of Galway.

The preeeding list is not exaustive.

For other surnames of early modern Galway town, I am grateful to Niall O'Brien for allowing me to read a first draft of his article, *Galway apprentices at Bristol in the sixteenth-century*. "On 29 July 1543 Dennis **Makglyn**, son of Dennis Makglyn, merchant of Galway, was enrolled as apprentice to Phillip Dawkyn, dyer, and Anne his wife for seven years." (p. 1) "On 30 August 1548 Edmund **Brother**, son of David Brother, merchant of Galway, was enrolled as apprentice to Thomas Lukes, dyer, and Elizabeth his wife for seven years." (p. 2) "On 19 June 1554 Cornell **Mesky**, son of Thomas Mesky, husbandman of Galway, was enrolled as apprentice to Richard Mathew, smith and Katherine his wife." (p. 2) "On 25 September 1554 Nicholas **Poyer,** son of John Poyer, mercer of Galway, was made apprentice to Robert Salesbury, dyer and Elizabeth his wife." (p. 3) I would identify three of the surnames as follows: Mag Fhloinn, now rendered **Flynn, Glynn, McGlynn**. Ó Bruadair, later Broder, now incorrectly rendered **Broderick**. Le Poher, now **Power**. I cannot place Meskey, unless it is a form of Miskelly, Mescal, or indeed an entirely different surname. See Hewer, 2015, for a recent overview on the free Gael in Anglo-Ireland.

39 - Ó Madagáin, 1986, p. 17. Verstraten's (2006, pp. 52-53) thoughts on the process driving the adoption, or not, of new names is well worth reading, and possibly the most insightful to date on the subject.

40 - For French as a late medieval maritime *lingua franca* in Ireland and the British islands, see Rothwell, 1999, and Kowaleski, 2007. At Kinsale in 1518, Laurent Vital "made the acquainteance of an honest old man, a native of there, because he spoke good French." (Covery, 2012, p. 283). For the Statutes of Kilkenny, see Picard, 2003.

41 - *CDI, 1285-1292*, p. 103.

42 - "Italian traders in Ireland came chiefly from Lucca, Florence, and Lombardy." Donovan-O'Sullivan, 1942, p. 27. See also Donovan-O'Sullivan, 1949 and 1962.

43 - Bell, 1988 (1997 reprint), p. 23.

44 - Hardiman, 1820, p. 10.

45 - Hardiman, 1820, p. 10.

46 - Hoare, 1901, pp. 34-43, 57, 58.

47 - Colfer, 1987, pp. 65-101; Browne and Whelan, 1987, pp. 467.

48 - Browne and Whelan, 1987, p. 467; See also Colfer, 1987, op. cit. Hoare, 1906, p. 414,

49 - *CDI 1285-1295*, p. 102.

50 - *CDI 1285-1295*, p. 103.

51 - *CDI 1285-1295*, p. 370.

52 - *Walter Brun*, Holland, 1997, p. 190; *Walter Broun*, op. cit., p. 185; *Adam Bruen*, op. cit., p. 190; *Tancard Brun*, op. cit., p. 190. Another Brun with an unusual forename was Fromund le Brun (p. 954, *DoIB*).

53 - Curtis, 1940, p. 291.

54 - For *Do Bhreathnuibh*, see *GBIG III*, 2003, 841.1, 2, pp. 184-185.

55 - Oranmore and Browne, 1907-08, p. 49 ("Sir David le Brun or Browne, obtained a large property near Athenry, which ... is known to this day as David's Castle. I am afraid I have not up to this identified the spot."). The identification with Ballydavid is my suggestion.

56 - For *John son of Denis, see BFR no. 48, Fifteenth Century*, 1902, p. 33. For *John Brun*, op cit., p. 34.

57 - Brother Colman Ó Clabaigh, O.P., kindly made his unfinished translation of the *Regestum Monasterii Fratrum Praedicatorum de Athenry* available for me. It is referred to as Ó Clabaigh's *Regestum*. 'para' denotes the paragraph translated by Brother Colman, 'p.' denotes the corresponding page of the Latin text as published by Ambrose Colman, O.P,. in the first volume of *Archivum Hibernicum* in 1912. Untranslated sections are in **bold italics**. Thus for this note, see Ó Clabaigh's Regestum, para 131, p. 216.

58 - William Brown, 1499, BFR, 1902, p. 48. *William Brun, BFR no. 82* (op. cit., p. 62). For *John Broun* of 1424, see Peter Crooks (ed.), *A Calendar of Irish Chancery Letters*, c. 1244-1509, Patent Roll 2, Henry VI §60 (hereafter chancery.tcd.ie/document/2-henry-vi/60). "This year Andrew Browne of Attenry was made freeman of this town the 22nd of October 1539", p. 63, and "This year Nicholas Brown, Robert Brown and Dominick Brown fitz William were made freemen of this town the 19th of January" 1542, (Walsh, 1992, p. 64).

59 - Holland, 1997, p. 189. Hodkinson (2012) lists "Hugh Joye" (*fl.* 1286), "Gilbert Joye" (*fl.* 1298), "Richard Joye" (fl. 1300), and a monk named "Simon Joy" (*fl.* 1376; see note 46, below). I wish to thank the writer James Martyn Joyce of Ballyloughan, Galway City, and especially Brian Anton of Boston, Mass., USA (gr-gr-gr grandson of Walter Joyce of Cloonmaghaura, Glenamaddy, c. 1800-c.1848) for discussions which I hope have clarified my thoughts on all matters Joyce in this book.

60 - Holland, 1997, p. 189.

61 - Knox, 1911-12, p. 81.

62 - Holland, 1997, p. 189.

63 - Curtis, 1940, p. 292

64 - "Simon Óge Joy" in Holland, 1997. "John Joy, Provost ... 1392", *BFR*, 1902, p. 10.

65 - Ó Clabaigh's *Regestum*, para 32, p. 209 ("Item Symo Seoy fuit amicus fratrum et dedit eis parcellam terrarum quae terria Mic vocatur portus de Halatun"/"Symo Seoy (Simon Joyce?) was a friend of the friars and gave a parcel of land to them which is called the land Mic gate of Halatun." See also paragraph 94, p. 215. Paragraph 4, p. 204 mentions *Semonis Sey*.

66 - Stanley, 2000, p. 178. The words in brackets are my own sense of the word caher as understood locally.

67 - Knox, 1902, pp. 101-02; Curtis, 1934-35, p. 69.

68 - "Genealach Seóigheach: Sliocht Risderd/The genealogy of the Joyces. The lineage of Risteard", GBIG, vol. III, 2003, pp. 168-69 (832.5).

69 - Knox, 1902, p. 324.

70 - The *Oxford Dictionary of Saints*, Oxford Univeristy Press, 1997, p. 278.

71 - Hardiman, 1820, p. 19. See also O'Brien, 2014, and the online Fine Rolls Project.

72 - Hanks and Hodges, 1988, p. 284.

73 - Knox, 1902, p. 324. For land Thomas Ruadh donated to Cong Abbey, see Blake, 1905.

74 - Hardiman, 1820, pp. 14-15.

75 - In his notes to Ó Flaithbheartaigh's *Iar-Connacht* (ed. 1846, pp. 247-250), Hardiman disscuses and quotes untranslated from *Genealogia Domini Gregorii Joyes*, still held in the Heraldic Office, Kildare Street, Dublin. A Gregory Joyce is attested at Galway in 1724; Hardiman states he died at Madrid in 1745. In *History of Galway* (1820), he summerised it without comment but by 1846 derides its hyperbole. I now believe even the early sections may contain genuine historic facts. Hence the need for critical comparative research.

76 - Holland, 1997, p. 177.

77 - See O'Brien, 2014, and the online Fine Rolls Project.

78 - *CDI 1255-1282*, p. 335. Otway-Ruthven, 1968, pp. 159-60

79 - *CDI 1252-1284*, London, 1877, p. 103.

80 - See R.V. Turner, 'Roger Huscarl: professional lawyer in England and royal justice in Ireland, c. 1199-1230', *Irish*

*Jurist* vol. 16, 1981, pp. 290-98. See also http://www.british-history.ac.uk/report.aspx?compid=18731.

81 - Hardiman, 1820, p. 51; and Holland, 1997, p. 156, 178. For *Richard Huskard*, see Holland, 1997, p. 169, 187.

82 - Ó Clabaigh's *Regestum*, para 31, p. 209

83 - Hardiman, 1820, p. 19. For knights, see Williams, 2007, pp. 103-110.

84 - Mac Lysaght, 1978, p. 275, where it is described as "*Huscarle* (house care)". In *Beowulf*, the term '*hós(e)*' denotes a retinue, a band of people connected by mutual oaths. It is the root of the Old High German word *hansa*, as in The Hanseatic League (see Shippey, 2005, p. 15).

85 - "in 1414 and again in 1417", "after 1476 and before 1484", Hardiman, 1820, p. 198.

86 - *BFR*, No. 1, etc; Blake, 1902. The meic Ruadh may be anglicised as **Crowe**, a surname found in Galway town.

87 - MacLysaght, 1978, p. 19, 32.

88 - *FAI*, pp. 167-168 (FA 426). The man concerned, Cadell ap Rhodri, was king of Deheubarth (south-west Wales).

89 - Hardiman, 1820, p. 8. Hodkinson (2012) lists thirteen Blacks/Blakes in Limerick between c. 1240x1400. A note to *BFR* no. 1 alludes to a connection between Richard *le Blake* Cadel of Galway and the Cadel/Caddells of Meath. MacLysaght (1978, p. 19) notes Blakes "settled in Co. Kildare where their name is perpetuated in three townlands called Blakestown." For Sir William Cadel, see Hartland, 2007, pp. 335-336, 337; 200, 215-216.

90 - Martin Joseph Blake published *Blake Family Records* in two volumes, 1902 and 1905. Neither have been reprinted.

91 - Westropp, 1912-13, p. 399.

92 - Hoare, 2008, p. 96, 97.

93 - op. cit., p. 399.

94 - Hardiman, 1820, p. 58.

95 - op. cit., p. 58.

96 - op. cit., p. 58; and FitzPatrick et al, 2004, p. 305.

97 - Dunlevy, 1989, p. 39. For Irish dress in the early 1600s, see *A Discourse ... 1620*, pp. 356-359. For Irish merchants in Cambridge in the 960s, see *Liber Eliensis*, ed. by E. O. Blake, London, 1962, II.32, p. 107.

98 - op. cit. , p. 40.

99 - Baldwin, 2013, p. 34.

100 - op. cit., p. 40.

101 - Broderick, 2011, p. 7.

102 - Hardiman, 1820, p. 29.

103 - op. cit.

104 - Hardiman, 1820. p. 58.

105 - op. cit., p. 58.

106 - Doherty, 2015, pp. 21-30.

107 - Comber, 2001, p. 80.

108 - *ATig*, 1135.

109 - See O'Flaherty, 2013.

110 - As a painting by William J. Bond (dated 1870) shows, this commerce continued long after the 1200s, ceasing mid -1900s. For "the normal method of transport", "some of those", and the Irish cott, see Nicholls, 2001, pp. 188-189.

111 - Regularly seen by my father while a county council roadworker in Connemara and Inis Mór in the 1960s. Swimming is still used to get stock to and from islands along the Shannon.

112 - Paine, 2013, p. 3. "nemforcendach"; Stokes, 1888 and 1889, ed., p. 463.

113 - FitzPatrick et al, 2004, Figure 5.2:1, p. 295.

114 - *Calendar Carew Ms.*, Ireland 6, 1873 (reprinted 1974), p. 206.

115 - FitzPatrick et al, 2004, p. 295; and O'Neill, 1987, p. 39.

116 - Ward, 2009, p. 73.

117 - Daly, 2006, pp. 75-76.

118 - Hardiman, 1820, pp. 51-52. For a pirate attack on a merchant ship, see AC, 1258.6-8.

119 - Ó Flaithbheartaigh, 1684, p. 91, 92.

120 - AFM, 1565.3.

121 - Chapple, 1996, p. 5. Hardiman,1820, p. 54, states "The church of Saint Nicholas was founded in 1320" but gives no source for this statement. However, in a papal taxation of Annagdown diocese in 1302-06, the bishop's revenue included twenty-two shillings from Galway church (*CDI*, vol. 5, pp. 234-236). See especially McKeon, 2009. If only for this book, I have coined the term *seanceathrú* ('old quarter') in opposition to "The Latin Quarter", used since the 1990s, as unhistorical as "Spanish Arch" or "Spanish Parade" yet just as likely to endure.

122 – McKeon, 2009, p. 111, winner of the JIA Postgraduate Prize.

123 - See Higgins and Heringklee, 1991.

124 - Ward, 2009, p. 127.

125 - AC, 1310.10. An area of coastal County Sligo, north-west of Benbulin, once called *Magh Cétni na Fomoraige*.

126 - *Tairired na Désse* copied from Swift, 2004, p. 2.

127 - Hardiman, 1820, p. 51.

128 - op. cit., p. 51.

129 - op. cit.

# Chapter Three: A Game of Thrones

1 - Lydon, 1972, p. 103. For a contrary view see Hartland, May 2004, pp. 161-177. However she conceeds that "these links were not retained by royal effort. [For] Edward I ... Ireland was a relatively low priority and he played no active part in the recruitment of many of these men into the Dublin administration and other posts." (p. 177). For an overview, see NHI, II; Nicholls, 1972; Frame, 1981 (2012 reprint); Simms, 1987; Duffy, 2002; Lydon, 2003; O'Bryne, 2003; Crooks, ed., 2008.

2 - Prestwich, 1988, p. 353.

3 - op. cit., p. 14. Consequent on reading Kelly and Ó Gráda 2010, I removed all references to the European Warm Period c. 950-c.1250, and the 'subsequent' European Little Ice Age. As a ten-year old attempting to save hay during the wet summer of 1985, what astonished me was that pitchforked haycocks – not used on our farm since we built a hayshed and began making mechanised bales of hay – weathered the rain better than the innovation.

4 - op. cit., p. 103. For Gascony, "Ireland in 1297: 'At peace after its manner'", Lydon (ed.), 1997, p. 15-16.

5 - "some half-a-dozen famines between 1270 and 1300."Grace's Annals, 1294 - "A great scarcity in Ireland for three years continually, and pestilence." See Clyn's Annals, p. 148, 156-67; AI 1272.2, 1281.2, 1281.8, 1282.2, 1284.2, 1296.7, 1296.2. ALCé 1270.6.

6 - Clyn's Annals, p. 200.

7 - See AI, 1281.2, 1296.7, 1296.2, 1321.3; AU 1298.5, 1318.7, 1321. 2, 1324.5; AC 1286.3, 1302.7, 1308.11, 1318.11, 1321.5, 1324.4; ALCé 1286.2, 1302.6, 1321.4, 1324.3, 1325.6.

8 - Clyn's Annals, p. 200.

9 - AI, 1272.2.

10 - I owe this quotable soundbite to Toby D. Griffin's "The Great Famine and the Collapse of the Pax Britannica"

11 - See Simms, "Relations with the Irish", pp. 66-86, in Lydon (ed.), 1997. For County Galway, see Holland, 1997.

12 - Hartland, 2007, p. 323.

13 - The hostility of this generation of Gaelic leaders towards the Anglo-Irish has been remarked upon by Verstraten, 2003. See also Frame, 1981, p. 49.

14 - Nicholls, 1972, p. 159.

15 - See O'Byrne, 2003, pp. 58-86. Also Nicholls, 1972, pp. 170-74.

16 - Nicholls, 1972, pp. 174-77, 141-53, 127-40.

17 - Marsden, 2003, p.2, 22, 25, 65, 72; NHI II, p. 11.

18 - Lydon, 1972, pp. 131-35.

19 - op. cit., pp. 131-35.

20 - Lydon (ed.), 1997, p. 13.

21 - Ó Rian, Ó Murchadha, Murray, 2003, p. 36. See also MacLysaght, 1978, p. 8; Joyce, 1870, p. 89.

22 - CDI 1255-1282, p. 147, 402. The earliest reference I have thus far recovered on a bearer of the surname is for William de Athy, fifth on a list of jurors on an "Inquisition into the lands late of Geoffrey de Costantin, their true value, and into his nearest heir" held at Dublin on 3 February 1253 (Inquisitions, 2007, p. 8). For John de Athy of 1270, see Connolly, 1998, p. 102. The debt was incurred during de Audlye's term of 1270-1272, so the man referred to was probably John of Athy (fl. 1270), who was possibly the grandfather of Sir John.

23 - CDI 1255-1282, p. 430. For Dunbrody Abbey, see p. 274, 305, op. cit.

24 - CJRI 1295-1303, p. 399.

25 - De Athy (alias de Ascy) was sheriff of Limerick in 1310, constable of Limerick castle from 1310-12, stood as pledge in 1311, and again sheriff in 1315. See Hodkinson, 2012.

26 - Connolly, 1998, p. 272. Crooks glosses valettus as "A term designating social status: translated 'yeoman'.

27 - Lydon, 1973, p. 114.

28 - op. cit., p. 114.

29 - Duffy, 2002, pp. 2-13.

30 - Grace's Annals, pp. 67-68. The same source (pp. 64-65) says the battle of Connor was fought on 10 September.

Duffy 2002, p. 18, states "one of its veterans soon afterwards gives the date as 1 September."

31 - Nowhere is it stated that de Athy was constable or keeper during the siege of Carrickfergus castle, so my placing him there is educated guesswork. John de Athy's term as Sheriff of Limerick ended sometime in 1315. He is absent from official records until winter 1316-17, when made Admiral of the Irish navy. I believe this, and subsequent appointments, were due to his role in the fourteen-month siege.

32 - Duffy, 2002, p. 29; Lydon, 1987, pp. 290-92.

33 - *Grace's Annals*, pp. 65-66; ALCé, 1315.1.

34 - See Lucas,1930, pp. 343-77; Jordan, 1996. Kelly, 2001, pp. 39-40, draws attention to generational chronic malnutrition caused by successive famines from the 1270s, as a morbidity factor in the plagues of 1349 and 1361.

35 - See *Annals of Loch Cé 1315.7*, and AI 1315.2.

36 - ALCé, 1315.9.

37 - ALCé 1315.17. Tadhg deposed his brother Gilbert.

38 - ALCé , 1315.18.

39 - ALCé, 1315.19.

40 - ALCé 1316.3.

41 - *Seanchus Burcach*, pp. 134-35: ALCé, 1316. 3; *Grace's Annals*, p. 72-73.

42 - *Grace's Annals*, pp. 66-67.

43 - *Annals of Loch Cé*, 1315.19.

44 - ALCé 1315.20.

45 - *Grace's Annals*, p. 93.

46 - ALCé, 1315.13.

47 - *Grace's Annals*, pp. 70-71.

48 - *Grace's Annals*, pp. 72-73.

49 - *Holinshed*, 1979, p. 214. See also *Grace's Annals*, pp. 76-77.

50 - *Grace's Annals.*, pp. 72-73.

51 - *Grace's Annals*, pp. 72-73.

52 - *Grace's Annals*, pp. 74-75.

53 - ALCé 1316.3. *Grace's Annals*, pp.76-77; see note 86, below.

54 - AC, 1316.4.

55 - op. cit.

56 - op. cit. , 1316.5.

57 - op cit.

58 - "granted to the bailiffs and good men of *Athenry*, dated 13 Oct. 1312" Hardiman, 1820, p. 49. For Templetogher, see AU, 1313.1." For *Robuc Mac Feorais*", see ALCé, 1316.3.

59 - AC, 1316.5.

60 - *Seanchus Burcach*, p. 135.

61 - AC, 1316.3

62 - AU, 1313.2

63 - Ó Clabaigh's *Regestum*, para 13, p. 205 ("in quo bello fuerunt interfecti de Hibernis tria millia"). *Grace's Annals* for 15 September, reads "On the day of the Exaltation of the Cross O'Conor is killed and Mac Kelly with five hundred Irish, by William de Burgh and Richard Birmingham, in Connaught." If about Athenry, then this figure is the most plausible we are likely to get. Notable Gael dead are listed in ALCé at 1316.3.

64 - *Clyn's Annals*, pp. 164-66. For a much abbreviated overview of the aftermath of Athenry, see my article "One King To Rule Them All: Fedlimid O Conochobair, the Battle of Athenry, and the Kingship of Ireland." (available online). I intend to return to this subject in much more depth when circumstances allows.

65 - *Grace's Annals*, pp. 76-77.

66 - It is only after this point that de Athy is again referenced in documents of the time; see note 27, above.

67 - Connolly,  1998, p. 244.

68 - Grace's Annals, pp. 168-69.

69 - *Clyn's Annals*, pp. 170-71; *Grace's Annals*, p. 95.

70 - AC, 1318.8.

71 - *Clyn's Annals*, pp. 184-86.

72 - Blake, 1913-14, p. 81.

73 - Connolly, 1998, p. 256, 261, 272, 276, 281, 288, 291, 294, 297, 301, 306, 310, 314. "Trim Castle" - op. cit., p. 314. "... after September ... June 1328" - p. 319, 324, 328, 333.

74 - op. cit., p. 333, 356, 363, 368, 613, 620.

75 - op. cit., p. 379.

76 - op. cit., p. 623. See also chancery.tcd./document/close/9-edward-iii/33.

77 - Dryburgh and Smith, 2005, p. 395.

78 - op. cit., p. 148.

79 - Connolly, 1998, p. 404.

80 - op. cit., p. 413. Joe Athy of Renville, Oranmore, murdered 1921, was among the last of the name in the area.

81 - *Inquisitions*, 2007, p. 150. *BFR* no. 5 (dated at Athenry, Monday 25 December 1342) describes William de Athy as having a "tenement" (a residential building), implying that he had being living in the area for some time. An Elias de Athy in attested in Athenry in that year in a Blake deed.

82 - chancery.tcd.ie/document/patent/12-richard-ii/85 - " Mentioned as such on p. 7, Hardiman, 1820, who states the appointment came "with the fee of £10 yearly."

83 - Dryburgh and Smith, 2005, p. 292. "John Athy" was issued a licence dated 13 April 1404 "for goods shipped on the *Trinite* of Poole", namely "for three lasts, a dicker and four hides." "John Athy, of the diocese of Annadown, and Margaret his wife" are mentioned in a Papal document dated 2 April 1428 (*Papal Letters, vol. V, 1396-1404*, p. 40).

84 - Williams, 2007, p. 206, 208. See also biographies of Sir William Liath and Earl William Donn, in DoIB, 2009.

85 - Williams, 2007, p. 210. See also Connolly, 1995, p. 152, which notes there was a reward of 100 marks for the capture of Richard and Gyles (Jill) de Mandeville.

86 - AFM, 1335.4; ALCé, 1335.4. Sir Edmund Albanach de Burgh (died 1375), the first Mac William Íochtar.

87 - ALCé, 1338.3.

88 - Roscommon last appears in Irish exchequer records in 1343, when "Richard Sprot, burgess of the town of Roscommon, [was] assigned to provide victuals for the castle there:£3." See Connolly, 1998, p. 413. Rindoon castle was last referenced in 1335 when John de Fontayne was granted custody of it but surrendered it to the king shortly afterwards. See Harbison, 1995. I am thankful to the late Dr. Sheelagh Harbison who gave me a copy of her 1995 article on Rindoon at Trinity College, Dublin, in January 1997.

89 - MacCotter, 2008, note 85, p. 142.

90 - Simms, 1987.

91- In his otherwise excellent Slionnte *Uile Éireann/All Ireland Surnames*, Séan de Bhulbh (born 1922) explicitly uses the term **The Resistance**, defining it as "the 800-year long struggle [sic]to reverse the effect of the Invasion." He defines the latter as "the Anglo-Norman invasion of 1170 [sic], which remains the basic turning point of Irish history [sic]." (2002, p. 146). "800 years of oppression" it takes no notice whatsoever of the events of c. 1260-1541, nor indeed 1642-49, or the 13th, 15th, 18th,19th and 20th centuries, during which no major war was fought in Ireland, despite claims of "relentless and unremitting warefare that has last [since 1169] down to this very day".

92 -Verstraten, 2011, p. 2. The verse is from Davies's A *discovery of the true causes*, which is in turn quoted from the lost *Liber Albus Scaccarii/White Book of the Exchequer*, supposedly burned in 1610. I have amended the spelling and sense in line with Verstraten's emendations for ease of the reader's comprehension.

93 - op. cit. I have altered the term "mere Irish" to its modern sense, mere being Latin for *pure*.

94 - See Doyle, 2015, especially pp. 137-138.

95 - Lydon, 1997, p. 24.

# Chapter Four: Comunitatis Galve

1 - Hardiman, 1820, p. 58. For overviews, Hardiman, 1820; Donovan-O'Sullivan, 1942; Nicholls, 1972; NHI, II; Duffy et al, 2001; FitzPatrick et al, 2004.

2 - Donovan-O'Sullivan, 1942, pp. 37-39.

3 - Ó Flaithbheartaigh, 1684, pp. 106-107. For the potato, see O'Riordan, 2001.

4 - chancery.tcd.ie/document/patent/49-edward-iii/84. CIRCLE, CR 49 Edw. III, 84. chancery.tcd.ie/document/patent/9-richard-ii/11

5 - "20 Feb. 1395 Dublin" chancery.tcd.ie/document/patent/18-richard-ii/83 See also Curtis, 1934-35.

6 - Dated 30 January 1387, and "at the request of Thomas s. of Edmund Burgh." (see chancery.tcd.ie/document/patent/12-richard-ii/85).

7 - See "23 Apr. 1387 Tristernagh" - chancery.tcd.ie/document/patent/10-richard-ii/178 and "8 Dec. 1388 Skreen" - chancery.tcd.ie/document/patent/12-richard-ii/85.

8 - NHI, IX, p. 170, Table 38. I am a descendant at least four times from the first William de Burgh in the last seven or eight generations alone, though from quite humble folk! Many in these counties must share my situation.

9 - Donovan-O'Sullivan, 1942, p. 41, quoting page 320 of MS. H.35, Trinity College Dublin.

10 - Donovan-O'Sullivan, 1942, p. 40.

11 - "26 Jan. 1396 Dublin" chancery.tcd.ie/document/patent/19-richard-ii/9

12 - Donovan-O'Sullivan, 1942, p. 41.

13 - Hardiman, 1820, p. 51. "Geoffrey Martyn" is listed in a land inquisition held at Athenry on 31 December 1333 as holding a parcel of land worth six shillings of the Brown Earl in Bak and Glen in what is now County Mayo (see p. 151, *Inquisitions*, 2007, and Hodkinson, 2012). Both he and a Henry Martyn appear to have been natives of Limerick town. Their connection to Thomas Martyn of Galway and Athenry is uncertain. "Geoffrey Martin" is listed a member of a Limerick jury in 1321; see bearers of the name in Hodkinson, 2012. There are dozens mentioned in thirteenth and fourteenth century Anglo-Irish records, and cannot all be related.

14 - Joan Sepishend was not however the last of her name. In 1398, "the tenement inhabited by William Schepishet on the west" in Galway town was mentioned in a deed dated 24th June. See BFR, 1902, pp. 11-12.

15 - See chancery.tcd.ie/document/patent/49-edward-iii/251 and 252.

16 - Verified Martyns with a demonstrable link to the medieval Tribes family have not undergone genetic genealogy, so their origins remain obscure. I have no idea if I am related. My male-line descent begins with my twice-married great-great-great-great grandfather, Laurence Martin, senior (*fl.* 1854) of Kileenadeema, via his eldest son, James (*fl.* 1838-51). At least four distinct Gaelic Martin families are in Connacht alone. Unnecessary fuss concerns spelling i or y. No significance of ethnic, religious, or grammatical identity should be attached to it.

17 - CPR XIII, part I – 1471-1484, pp. 258-59.

18 - Blake, 1915-16, p. 91. See also note 22, this chapter.

19 - chancery.tcd.ie/document/patent/10-richard-ii/74 Does this mean William Martin was not Margaret's son, but a son of Joan (daughter of William) Sepishend? The *marquis* referred to was Robert de Vere, 9th Earl of Oxford.

20 - chancery.tcd.ie/document/patent/10-richard-ii/105. See also chancery.tcd.ie/document/patent/49-edward-iii/84,

21 -Connolly, 1995, p. 160.

22 - Ó Clabaigh's *Regestum*, para 38, p. 210.

23 - op. cit., para 18, pp. 206-07; para 24, p. 208; para 38, p. 210.

24 - op. cit., para , p. 37, p. 210. Brother Colman wonders if *ballach* is not Latin for 'stammerer'? See note 15. The Odhrach bhallach (*Succisa Pratensis*) is known in English as Devil's bit scabious.

25 - op. cit.

26 - BFR, 1902, p. 12, 16.

27 - op. cit. It may be worth mentioning that about any seven out of ten of those who preserved, researched, and passed on Martyn family lore to me in the 1990s, were women. Men like my father, and John Martyn of Mulroog, tended to be a minority. I have found this to be generally the case with all families. All found my youth exceptional.

28 - In 1380, "Clement Laehragh" was "Sheriff of Connaught", BFR no. 6, *Fourteenth Century*, 1902, p. 6. References to his family exists mainly in other Blake deeds.

29 - Hardiman, 1820, pp. 8-9. MacLysaght (1978, p. 20) gives a surprising etymology: "originally Bowdekyn, a diminutive of Baldwin."

30 - *"For every cloth of silk or **baudekin**"* (my emphasis), Hardiman, 1820, p. 58. For etymology, see *Century Dictionary*, London, 1899, p. 35.

31 - Knox, 1904, p. 110.

32 - Blake, 1915-16, p. 81.

33 - GBIG, vol. III, 2003, pp. 78-79 (778.5).

34 - Blake, 1915-16, p. 82.

35 - Blake, 1915-16, p. 81. The best account of the origins of the FitzGeralds appears to be Round, 1902; my thanks to Peter Crooks for a copy. See also "The Children of Nesta", Moody and Martin, eds., 1978, pp. 266-67.

36 - Miles, 1997, p. 15.

37 - Blake, 1915-16, p. 82.

38 - op. cit., p. 82.

39 - Ó Clabaigh's *Regestum*, para 17, p. 206. 40 - BFR. no. 7a, *Fourteenth Century*, 1902, p. 10. Nicholas witnessed BFR no. 6, 1902, pp. 6-7.

41 - Blake, 1915-16, p. 82.

42 - pers. comm. Dr Tyrone Bowes, 24 March 2014.

43 - Walsh, 1992, p. 59. "Ermine, on a saltire, gules, a leopard's face, or.", Hardiman, 1820, p. 10.

44 - chancery.tcd.ie/document/patent/9-henry-v/70: "COMMISSION, by mainprize of James Burgeys of co. Tipperary and Thomas Burton of co. Meath, to Walter, son and heir of Richard Clerk of Galway, also called Richard Bawdekyn of Galway, of custody of the islands called Busheyland and *Goetyland* of the town of Galway; to have for as long as they are in the K.s hand, rendering the extent." For "Thomas Bodykyn and Silma his wife of the

diocese of Tuam", see a Papal document dated 10 February 1429 (*Papal Letters vol. V, 1396-1404*, p. 125).

45 - "Edmund Bodykyn, Provost of Athenry", *BFR no. 40, Fifteenth Century*, 1902, p. 29; "Robert Bodkyn, Provost", *BFR no. 48, Fifteenth Century*, 1902, p. 33.; "Walter Bodykyn, BFR no. 50, Fifteenth Century*, 1902, p. 34.

46 - Blake, 1915-16, p. 82.

47 - Henry, 2002, p. 42; Blake, 1915-16, p. 82-84.

48 - op. cit., both.

49 - *Calendar of Patent Rolls, Richard II*, Vol. V., 1391-1396, London, 1905, p. 394.

50 - op. cit., p. 394. Dr. Freya Verstraten suggested this was "Vienna in the duchy of Austria?" (email, 15 January 2013). The abbey is the Benediktinerabtei unserer Lieben Frau zu den Schotten ('Benedictine Abbey of Our Dear Lady of the Scots'), founded in Vienna in 1155 using Irish monks previously based at St Jakob's, Regensburg. I am indebted to Dr. Diarmuid Ó Rian, who identified him as Heinrich/Henry, Abbot from 1392 to 1399. Ah, Vienna.

51 - chancery.tcd.ie/document/patent/3-henry-v/92

52 - chancery.tcd.ie/document/patent/

53 - BFR no. 32, Fifteenth Century, 1902, p. 25.

54 - Hardiman, 1820, p. 54. John Athy was Soverign of Galway on 10 September 1428 (Blake, 1902, p. 23, 30).

55 - op. cit., p. 14.

56 - op. cit.

57 - chancery.tcd.ie/document/patent/8-henry-v/38:

58 - Hardiman, 1820, p. 14. I take this to mean that Henry Begg Ffrench was of the Frenchs of Wexford, not descended from Walter French of Galway. Nevertheless I cannot find any Henry among the French family in these years.

59 - Colfer, 1987, p. 98.

60 - Colfer, 1987, pp. 65-66.

61 - Dryburgh and Smith, 2005, p. 318, 169, 60

62 - BFR no. 43, Fifteenth Century, 1902, p. 31. "Walter French" is attested in *BFR no. 32, Fifteenth Century*, (dated 13 April 1440), 1902, p. 25). He witnessed *BFR no. 38*, dated 2 April 1444, as one of four named "burgesses of Galway" (op. cit., pp. 27-28), *BFR no. 40*, dated 6 June 1444 (op. cit., pp. 29-30), *BFR. no. 42*, dated 26 July 1444 (op. cit., pp. 30-31), *BFR no. 45* dated 30 September 1445 (op. cit., p. 31), and *BFR no. 45*, dated 1446 (op. cit., p. 32,). "James French, John French", witness *BFR no. 55*, dated 25 October 1453 (op. cit., p. 36).

63 - Hardiman, 1820, p. 12.

64 - Hanks and Hodges, 1988, p. 141.

65 - "died in 1448", op. cit., p. 198. "Julianne Lynch", Blake, 1915-16, p. 92. "William Alleyn", chancery.tcd.ie/document/patent/29-henry-vi/5: "GRANT to Ed' Lynche and William Alleyn, merchants of Galway, of the office of collector of customs of the towns of Galway and Slygoe." 22 April 1451, Dunboyne, Co. Meath.

66 - Fleming, 2013, p. 145. I say "appears" because I cannot locate Edmond in the source cited (Dryburgh and Smith, 2005). Fleming cites BRO P.St S/D/11/1-2, TNA PROB 11/7/85, p. 138 in Dryburgh and Smith.

67 - AFM 1504.14. *The Book of Howth* states "The Earl bestowed 30 tun of wine among the army."

68 - Hardiman, 1820, p. 13.

69 - Hanks and Hodges, 1988, p. 188.

70 - For de Fontes c. 1227-32, see Hogan, 2008, pp. 166-67; for Thomas and Alexander, see *IEP*, p. 592, 221, 245, 260.

71 - For the Limerick Fants, see "Who's Who in Medieval [and] Early Modern Limerick", online. For the two Walter le Enfaunts, see index of *IEP*, p. 681, and Hartland, May 2004, p. 174.

72 - I received this information online in 2014 from descendants of the Fants of Limerick in the USA.

73 - Fleming, 2013, p. 96, 107

74 - NHI II, 1987, p. 498, citing de Azevedo, 1913-14.

75 - GBIG, vol. II, 2003, pp. 418-27 (537.1-540.9). See also Meyer, 1913, p. 176; Mac Giolla Easpaig, 1996, p. 810; Floinn, 2014, p. 199. The surname Kirwan is found elsewhere in Ireland. AFM records an erenagh family attached to the monastery of Lughmhadh (Louth, Co. Louth) *sub anno* 1045 and 1102.

76 - GBIG, vol. II, 2003, pp. 424-25 (539.10).

77 - O'Connell, 1998. I am very grateful to Michael Kirwan of Limerick for providing me with the location of Dunbally. His unpublished article, "The Kirwans of Galway (Part 1)", states that "In the 1842 Ordnance Survey map the site of Doonbally Castle is marked on it (OS M 459 498)." In July 2014 Michael also sent me the *Pedigree of the Kirwan Family* by Denis Agar Kirwan and John Water Kirwan, 1939. Sadly, for the early generations of the family up to Uilliam O Ciordubhain, the authors relied on a pedigree created in 1732 by Charles Lynegar (alias O Luinin), which has almost no historical value and is thus not reproduced.

78 - Byrne, 1973, p. 230.

79 - GBIG, vol. II, 2003, pp. 150-51 (823.1).

80 - op. cit., pp. 420-21 (537.8). For Iarlaithe son of Lugha, see op. cit., pp. 762-63 (734.12). For Moingfhinn daughter of Ciordhubhán, see Herity, 2009, p. 11. Lynch wrongly identified 'Cirdubhani' as Iarlaithe's mother (2006, p. 24).

81 - BFR no. 19, Fifteenth Century, 1902, p. 19.

82 - chancery.tcd.ie/document/patent/10-henry-vi/140: See also Hardiman, 1820, p. 16.

83 - BFR no. 31, Fifteenth Century, 1902, p. 25. There is a slight chance that "William Ogerwayn and Florence Ogerwayn", who held the vicarages and rectories of Kilchreest and Killogilleen in 1491, were Kirwans (see Papal Registers .. 1484-1492, pp. 391-92, 414).

84 - Wardenship, 1944, p. 85, 100.

85 - Hardiman, 1820, p. 199. Uilliam was bailiff again in 1510-11. A Jonock Kyrvan was bailiff 1513-14. Tomas was bailiff 1516-17, 1523-24, and Mayor 1534-35, 1545-46, and 1547-48.

86 - Blake, 1915-16, pp. 92-93. See also O'Connell, 1998.

87 - Blake, 1915-16, p. 93. Hardiman (1820, p. 19) states without citing a source that "This family first settled in Galway, in 1485". "Thomas Mares" was one of four named witnesses to BFR no. 113, Fifteenth Century , dated 28 November 1548 (Blake, 1902, p. 90). Melville (2012, p. 375,), states "A fire also affected the records of the Morris family of Ballinaboy, Clifden. When James Hardiman was writing his History of Galway he approached Captain Anthony Morris, [who] refused to co-operate and claimed that his family's history was already well known. Hardiman reacted by deliberately saying as little as possible about the Morris family in his book."

88 - MacLysaght, 1978, p. 222. See also MacCotter, 2008, which caused me in 2013 to duly amend my own work. Linking the Morris family of Galway with the Meic Muiris is my own suggestion and open to correction.

89 - MacLysaght, 1978, p. 222. For the origins of the forename, see Jenkins, 2013.

90 - See Toorians, 2000.

91 - Martin, 1978, p. 293.

92 - Mullally, 2002, p. 107, lines 2113-2118. See Crouch, 2002, p. 223.

93 - MacCotter, 2008, pp. 297-99.

94 - op. cit., p. 300.

95 - op. cit., p. 303.

96 - op. cit., p. 303.

97 - op. cit., p. 300.

98 - op. cit., p. 300.

99 - op. cit., p. 297.

100 - op. cit., p. 298, 299.

101 - ALCé, 1316.

102 - AC, 1316.

103 - MacCotter, 2008, p. 299.

104 - op. cit., pp. 298-99.

105 - op. cit., p. 301.

106 - Ó Clabaigh's Regestum, para 50, p. 212. A fiant of 20 September 1582 lists "Geoffrey M'Morishe of Derymaclachney", Lackagh. M'Morishe is now Morrissey, another surname found in the Athenry region and attested in PRJI. Though Morris is found in the same area, they are distinct surnames and unrelated families. I suspect that those surnamed Morris in the Athenry area are even unrelated to the Meic Muiris of Crigferter, as PRJI lists in 1618 "Dowell O'Morris Mc Teige oge, Donell O'Morris Mc Mulrony, Teige Mc Thomas O'Morris, and Donnell O'Morris McGilpatrick, all of Clooneloine" ("XV.-35 ... 25 Sep. 15th.") See also page 371.

107 - ALCé, 1271.2; AU 1296; ADdR.

108 - MacCotter, 2008, p. 297.

109 - AC, 1366.12.

110 - See Knox, 1908, pp. 422-23.

111 - See MacDermot, 1996, pp. 458-463.

112 - MacCotter, 2008, p. 303. For the genealogy, see GBIG, vol. III, 2003, pp. 730-31 (1382.2).

113 - MacCotter, 2008, p. 303.

114 - GBIG, vol. I, 2003, pp. 582-83 (255.7-11, and 255. 4).

115 - op. cit., pp. 582-83 (255.4).

116 - Walsh, 2003, p. 202.

117 - Byrne, 1973, p. 236.

118 - Ó Muráile, 2006, pp. 4-5. See also Meyer, 1912, p. 112.

119 - Broderick, 2010, p. 7, 9.

120 - Schrijver, 2005, p. 137.

121 - Corlett, 1999, pp. 43-64.

122 - Hickey, 2011, p. 75.

123 - See *ALCé*, 1242 where Lawless is rendered "Loghbhais", and Knox, 1908, p. 287.

124 - *GBIG*, vol. I, 2003, pp. 612-13 (271.4).

125 - op. cit., pp. 630-31, (278.5). See also op. cit., pp. 582-83 (255.3-11).

126 - See Ordnance Survey Ireland, Discovery Series map 39.

127 - *AFM*, 1273.1.

128 - See Martyn, 2010.

129 - Hardiman, 1820, p. 198. The first Darcy referenced in surviving records is "Cornelius Darcy", mentioned as deceased in a grant dated 18 February 1545 (*Wardenship*, 1944, p. 10). He may be identical with Conchabhar Ó Dorchaidhe (Cornelius=Conchabhar) grandfather of James *Riabhach* Darcy fitz Nicholas. He is the only member the family to bear a Gaelic name, interesting given the lenth of time they had by then lived in Galway. The only other Darcy referenced in these decades is "Christina Dorchi", widow of "John **Butler,** Galway, merchant", and executor of his will, dated 13 November 1556 (*Wardenship*, 1944, p. 10). She may be an ancestor of the brothers Andrew and William Butler who departed Kinsale with the Spanish forces in March 1602. Both were described as 'kearne'; Andrew as "borne in Connought at Galway" (Morgan, ed., 2004, p. 375). "James Butler of Galway, Merchant Ind[igenious]" unloaded cargo at Bristol on 16 July 1595 (Flavin and Evans, 2009, p. 762).

130 - Hoare, 2008, p. 96.

131 - Ó Flaithbheartaigh, 1684, p. 39.

132 - Nicholls, 1972, p. 79. Verstraten (2006, 2011) stresses the importance of gossiprid (god-parenthood) and fosterage in establishing various relationships between Gael and Gall.

133 - Duffy, Edwards, Fitzpatrick, 2001, p. 40, summerising Nicholls, 1972, pp. 2-3.

134 - Edwards, 2001, p. 85. See also Simms, 1987 (pp. 1-2, 49, 75, 83-84, 113, 141-146, 147-150). This may be the actual faultline upon which Gaelic society foundered, not some 'inherent English superiority' nor an 'Irish racial flaw'.

135 - *GBIG*, 14.2, pp. 181, 2003, vol. I, 2003. See also Ó Muraíle, 1996, p. 170, 203. Nobiles ... AC, 1420.9.

136 - Latvio, 2005, p. 70. For social mobility see pp. 82-83, where Latvio comments "In principle [my emphasis], then, the Irish laws allowed the climbing up the ladder of status hierarchy. ... Even those with semi-free or unfree status could reach freedom ... However, the other direction, social mobility downwards, was far more common." (p. 82) Laws and institutions state many principles; enforcement is another matter. See also note 34, Chapter One.

137 - Bhreathnach, 2014, p. 105, 106 (though it should be noted that Bhreathnach's work applies to the era AD 400-1000). For lineage persistence, see Melvin, 2012, in which some of the ruling lineages mentioned in Chapter One had nineteenth-century landlord descendants. On the work of Irish slaves, see Holm, 2005, pp. 430-31. By the 1400s Christian Europeans ceased enslaving each other, enslaving Muslim Europeans and Pagan African instead.

138 - Guinness, 2008, p. 28. During a genealogical conferance at Oranmore in May 2005, Patrick Guinness gave me details on his family DNA results. His biography of his ancestor, Arthur (1725-1803), was published in 2008.

139 - Maginn, 2010, pp. 183-84.

140 - Dunlevy, 1989, pp. 59-64.

141 - *A Discourse* ... 1620, p. 357.

142 - Simms, 2010, pp. 13-17.

143 - Byrne, 1973, p. 175. See Latvio, 2005, p. 82 for the full quote and its context. "Hopefully for the better"; against this is the thesis set out by Emmanuel Goldstein in *The Theory and Practise of Oligarchial Collectivism* (1949), now long out of print but which bluntly dismisses hope and where it is to be found. As one of its editors, O'Brien, correctly stated: "We know that no one ever seizes power with the intention of relinquishing it. Power is not a means, it is an end. **One does not establish a dictatorship in order to safeguard a revolution; one makes a revolution in order to establish a dictatorship.** [my emphasis] The object of persecution is persecution. The object of torture is torture. The object of power is power." (1984, p. 301)

# Chapter Five: Comunitatis Galve

1 - I witnessed this, and was so informed by Tom Kenny, which he confirmed in 2013. For an overview, see *NHI* II and III; Hardiman, 1820; Donovan-O'Sullivan, 1942; Nicholls, 1972; FitzPatrick et al, 2004; Crooks, ed., 2008.

2 - *AC*, 1473.32.

3 - Donovan-O'Sullivan, 1942, p. 48. Tragically little survives.

4 - op. cit., p. 56. The earlier bridge is alluded to in *BFR no. 22, Fifteenth Century*, dated at Galway 16 September 1424,

which mentions "the lands of Richard Athy, near the Great Bridge." See next note.

5 - Westropp, 1912-13, pp. 399-400: "The Church of St. Nicholas was commenced in 1320 and the bridge was built in 1342." He apparently relied on Hardiman's incorrect statement that Eamonn erected the great west bridge in 1342 (Hardiman, 1820, p. 57). Donovan-O'Sullivan (1942, pp. 56-57, note 3) says of this: "Hardiman makes the mistake of placing this Edmond in the 14th instead of the 15th century, and of dating the building of the bridge in 1342 instead of 1442. *Hist. of Galway*, p. 57. Obviously he took his information from John Alexander Lynch, author of Egerton Mss. No. 115, fols. 73-82. The latter, however, has many inaccuracies in dates, and this is one of them. O'Flaherty - *Iar-Connaught* - has the correct date, so has Dutton - *Statistical Survey of Galway*. Edmund Lynch was popularly called Eamon-a-Tuane, i.e., Edmond of the Tuns, from the large quantities of wine he imported. Hardiman's error is a serious one, for ... it antedates the prosperity of Galway, associated with the wine trade, by 100 years."

6 - op. cit., p. 57. Walsh (1996, p. 54) states Edmund's bridge was built over "the upper limit of the ordinary high tides."

7 - Eamonn a Tune appears to be the "Edmund Lynche" who served as sovereign in 1434 (Hardiman, 1820, p. 198), and 1444 (op. cit., p. 198). A Henry Lynch was Provost of Galway on the 6 June 1444, according to BFR no. 40.

8 - *Geffere* was Mayor 1488-89, and apparently 1500-01. Thomas fitz Edmond was Mayor 1492-93. John fitz Edmond was Mayor 1494-95. See Henry, 2002, pp. 58-59. Walter fitz Thomas (Mayor 1505-06, 1513-14), *Jhamys* fitz Geffre (1511-12), *Stevne* fitz Walter (Mayor 1514-15), are thought to be his grandsons. See op. cit., 59-60.

9 - Donovan-O'Sullivan, 1942, p. 51.

10 - CPR XI 1455-64, 3 June 1455, p. 255. See also op. cit., 26 January 1457, pp. 333-334.

11 - op. cit., p. 255.

12 - CPR XII, 1458-71, p. 95, 333.

13 - Donovan-O'Sullivan, 1942, p. 51.

14 - Donovan-O'Sullivan, 1942, pp. 51-52.

15 - BFM no. 67, p. 45

16 - CPR XIII, Part I 1471-1484, p. 258-259.

17 - Donovan-O'Sullivan, 1942, p. 49.

18 - Hardiman, 1820, p. 198, and *Archives*, 1921, p. 284.

19 - Henry, 2002, p. 57. Angela Lynch-Lupton became the eighty-fifth Lynch Mayor of Galway, serving 1989-90 and 1998-99 (op. cit, pp. 198-201). However it is uncertain if she was related to the previous Mayors; her father, William Lynch, was a native of County Cork (conversation with Lynch-Lupton, May 2004). She died in 2007.

20 - *Archives*, 1885, p. 386.

21 - op. cit., p. 391.

22 - op. cit., p. 393.

23 - op cit., p. 394.

24 - op. cit., p. 394. The term *leper* is changed from *lazar* in the original text for clarity.

25 - op. cit., p. 397.

26 - op. cit., p. 398.

27 - op. cit.

28 - op. cit.

29 - op. cit., p. 399.

30 - op. cit., p. 404.

31 - op. cit., p. 406.

32 - op. cit., p. 392 ("Arthur Lynch, mayor, Will[i]am Josse and Antony Lynch, Baylyvis, in anno 1507, being drouned in falling over the west bridge at St. Kateryne day, the sayd yer, the 25 of November."). See also Walsh, 1992, p. 61.

33 - Blake, 1915-16, pp. 102-03. My thanks to Freya Verstraten-Veach for suggesting Switzerland and Luzern.

34 - CSPI 1588-92, p. 250, Theobald Dillon to Sir Richard Bingham: "18 October 1589. At the Cladegh."

35 - O'Dowd (1993, p. 35) quotes Mary Banim (*Here and There Through Ireland*, 1892).

36 - Hardiman, 1820, p. 210, quoting statutes from Corporation Book A.

37 - AFM 1433.9; AC 1426.18.

38 - Cunningham and Gillespie, 2014, pp. 195-196. Thanks to my mother Noreen for this reference.

39 - op. cit., p. 196.

40 - Lydon, 1995

41 - Lydon, 1995; Murphy, 2005, p. 366; Crooks, 2010

42 - Quinn, 1992, p. 284. Quinn believed the two were "corpses", yet nothing in the note indicates they were dead.

43 - O'Neill, 1987, p. 81, 115.

44 - Quinn, 1992, p. 281.

45 - BFR no. 19, Fifteenth Century, 1902, p. 19.

46 - Ó Flaithbheartaigh, 1684, p. 383.

47 - op. cit., pp. 384-86. See also GBIG.

48 - For Stradbally, see CPR, 1401-05, p. 134.

49 - Loeber, 2001, p. 272, citing PRO, SP 46/90, fl. 143. For castles and under-lords, see McNeill, 2001, pp. 355-356.

50 - Ó Flaithbheartaigh, 1684, pp. 71-72. An tIomaire Rua is "the whole western massif from Cruach Phádraic in Mayo to the heads of the bays of south Connemara. (*Connemara: A Little Gaelic Kingdom*, Tim Robinson, 2011, p. 88)

51 - Breen, 2005, p. 115.

52 - Mac Eiteagáin, pp. 203-28. See Breen 2005, Naessens 2007 for Ó Súileabháin, Ó Flaithbertaigh marine lordships.

53 - op. cit.

54 - *BFM no. 59*, p. 38.

55 - AC, 1464.

56 - ALCé, 1410. O'Donovan's *Tribes and Customs of Hy-Maine* states "Le Dail n-Druithne imarchur a fhina o chaladaib an iarthair co h-isdagaib an aird-rig."(p. 90) "The Dal Druithne have the carrying of the wine from the harbours of the west of Connaught [sic] to the seats of the arch-chief." (p. 91) Elsewhere is stated "Ó Gabrán ar Dail n-Druithni" (p. 76). The Dál Druithe ruled part or all of what became Síol nAmchada before the later subborned them and renamed the kingdom; the name (*drúth*, a jester, fool, or comic) hints that they were professional entertainers to greater folk. It comprised what is now Longford barony. Ó Gabráin is now rendered **Smith**, mainly found in and around Loughrea, For "storehouses ... ten battle-standards ...mhínsróll ..." see Russell, 2000, p. 545, 551. Dr. Christy Cuniffe pointed out the Camino symbolism in Kilconnell and Clonfert at the inaugural lecture of the Athenry Historical Network at Athenry Town Hall in September 2015.

57 - AC, 1446. See also Mac Dermot, 1996, p. 98.

58 - AFM, 1444.

59 - Hely Dutton, 1824, pp. 196-197. The streets are identified in O'Dowd, 1985, p. 34.

60 - Dryburgh and Smith, 2005, p. 283, 285.

61 - op. cit., p. 285.

62 - Serradilla Avery, 2007, p. 111.

63 - op. cit., p. 108, 109, 110.

64 - McKenna, 1992, p. 61.

65 - Walsh, 1992, p. 63. See also McCarthy, 2001.

66 - op. cit., p. 64, which goes on to say that "also in the year of his mayoralty, the new tower gate being the south gate of the quay was built." This followed on from the work of Wylliam Martin in 1519-20.

67 - *BFR no. 69, Fifteenth Century*, 1902, pp. 46-49.

68 - op. cit., pp. 46-49.

69 - *BFR no. 68a, Fifteenth Century*, 1902, p. 46.

70 - Henry, 2002, p. 61.

71 - Hardiman, 1820, p. 272. See also Walsh, 1992, p. 61, pp. 78-79.

72 - This is based on the presence of their respective arms in one of the windows. See Higgins and Herkinglee, 1991.

73 - Overlooked in Herkinglee and Higgins, 1991, but both arms are visible in good light.

74 - For Douce, see Lyons, 2002, pp. 73-74; Ó Conchobhair, op. cit., pp. 58-59, 63-64; Ní Mháille, op. cit., pp. 64-65.

75 - op. cit., pp. 59-59, 74. Clyne (1987/1988 and 1990) notes the skeleton of a probable Santiago pilgrim excavated at Tuam in 1986 showed evidence of spinal osteophytosis and osteoarthritis.

76 - Walsh, 1992, p. 60.

77 - O'Neill, 1988, p. 420. Recorded as "Germyn Lynche, of Drogheda, alias "Dermitius Lynsky"" in Symonds, 1921. If Diarmait Ó Loingsigh was his real name then his connection to the Lynch family of Galway is untenable.

78 - FitzPatrick, O'Brien, Walsh, 2004, p. 298.

79 - O'Neill, 1988, p. 420.

80 - op. cit., p. 421.

81 - op. cit., pp. 422-23. For *borrein and knockkylleny*, see Claughton and Rondelez, 2013.

82 - op. cit., p. 423.

83 - op. cit., p. 424.

84 - op. cit., p. 424, 110.

85 - op. cit., pp. 424-35.

86 - op. cit., p. 425.

87 - op. cit., pp. 425-26.

88 - op. cit., p. 426.

89 - op. cit., p. 426.

90 - op. cit., p. 427.

91 - *Archives*, 1921, p. 385. See also Walsh, 1992, p. 60.

92 - Walsh, 1992, p. 60.

93 - Henry, 2002, pp. 58-59.

94 - Hardiman, 1820, p. 72.

95 - op. cit., p. 75. See bibliography for a number of historical articles on the subject, especially by Fr. Mitchell.

96 - See Mitchell, 1966-71.

97 - O'Dowd, 1985, p. 117-119.

98 - Donovan-O'Sullivan, 1942, pp. 42-43.

99 - Walsh, 1992, p. 61, 90. See also Henry, 2002, p. 59.

100- Buckley, 2005, pp.749-68, 806-07.

101 - I am grateful to Roger White, then Rouge Croix Pursuivant, for assuring me of this in a conversation in London, August 1999, as did the former Irish Chief Herald at Oranmore in May 2005.

102 - Hardiman, 1820, p. 7.

103 - op. cit., p. 18.

104 - op. cit., p. 9.

105 - op. cit., p. 12.

106 - This device - the arms of Sheriff Martin Darcy, died 1636 - was mounted on his front door façade in Lower Abbeygate Street. It now stands in the grounds of the Mercy Convent, Francis Street.

107 - Hardiman, 1820, p. 11; "Darcy (D'Arcy), Patrick (1725-79)"; "Darcy, Sir William (c. 1460?-1540)", *DoIB*, vol. 3, p. 51. Sir William's ancestor, John Darcy (d. 1347) of Knaith in northern England. His second wife, Joan de Burgh dowager Countess of Kildare (d. 1359), was mother of William, founder of the Irish branch of the family.

108 – I owe this information to Julie Darcy of Yorkshire.

109 - Hardiman, 1820, p. 19.

110 - O'Hart, Dublin, 1884.

111 - Walsh, 1992, p. 59.

112 - Attested as FitzMartin arms in Burke, 1883, p. 359. See also *The Complete Peerage*, vol. VIII, 1932, pp. 530-39.

113 - Burke, 1883, p. 359. See also Miles, 1998.

114 - Folio 34b of Galway Corporation Book A. "Thomas Marten" appears to be the same man named in a chancery letter dated "9 Sep. 1505" which reads "PARDON to Thomas Martyn of Galway merchant for all manner of treasons ..." (see CIRCLE, http://chancery.tcd.ie/).

115 - Hardiman, 1820, p. 15. Henry Joyce died by 1558, buried in a tomb in the Franciscan (Blake, 1910, p. 231).

116 - op. cit., pp. 17-18.

117 - For Font, see Hardiman, 1820, p. 13; for Morris, op. cit., p. 19; Kirwan, op. cit., p. 17; Skerrett, op. cit., p. 20.

118 - Walsh, 1992, p. 61.

119 - Walsh, 1992, p. 62.

120 - Walsh, 1992, p. 80.

121 – Walsh, 1992, p. 67, 80, 99.

122 - op. cit., p. 62, 92.

123 - See Hynes, 1934-35.

124 - FitzPatrick, O'Brien, Walsh, 2004, p. 81.

125 - *NHI, IX*, p. 320.

126 - op. cit. Seóighe is the form used by NHI.

127 - CPR IX, *1431-1447*, p. 89; CPR XII, *Part II, 1471-84*, p. 769; CPR XII, *1458-71*, p. 405-06; CPR IX, p. 206.

128 - Murphy, 2014, pp. 83-91.

129 - op. cit. pp. 82-83.

130 - CPR XII, *Part II, 1471-84*, p. 508.

131 - op. cit., p. 663.

132 - op. cit., p. 663.

133 - op. cit., p. 663.

134 - *Wardenship*, 1944, p. 8.

134 - Walsh, 1992, p. 62.

136 - op. cit., p. 399.

137 - op. cit., p. 63.

138 - Hardiman, 1820, p. 265.

139 - Walsh, 1992, p. 64.

140 - Hardiman, 1820, p. 82. This plaque survived the demolition of the gate and mill in 1800, and was incorporated into a new building erected at the junction of Shop Street, Church Lane, and High Street. Transcription and translation by Walsh (1992, p. 95, note 103). "Prof. F. Killeen" assisted in translating (Walsh, 1981, p. 52, n. 95).

141 - Walsh, 1992, p. 65: "[1560] ... The within Thomas Martin fitz William built the remotest west gate at the end of the bridge where his arms lieth, for consideration of which work the corporation gave him the plot or ground whereon the small castle and mill lieth, called lately, Turner's mill."

142 - CSPI, 1566-1567, dated 30 May 1566, pp.72-73.

143 - Hardiman, 1820, p. 76-77.

144 - See Hynes, 1934-35.

145 - Henry, 2002, p. 47. An earlier entente was a marriage between Mayor John Blake fitz William (d. 1489) and Anabel de Burgh, daughter of Uilleag Ruadh, the 5th Clanricarde (r. 1430-85). Uilleag Fionn was one of his sons, who in turn was grandfather of Uilleag na gCeann, who married Maire Lynch (see BFM; NHI IX).

146 - Hardiman, 1820, p. 80.

147 - op. cit., p. 81.

148 - AFM 1536.18.

149 - Hardiman, 1820, p. 81.

150 - AFM 1542.21; and Walsh, 1992, p. 64.

151 - Donovan-O'Sullivan, 1942, p. 66, 411.

152 - Hardiman, 1820, p. 82.

153 - op. cit. p. 82. See also Donovan-O'Sullivan, 1944-45. For the warfare, see CSPI, 1509-1573, p. 88.

154 - Flavin, 2013, p. 3. See also Consumption and Culture in Sixteenth-Century Ireland: Saffron, Stockings, and Silk, also by Susan Flavin, Boydell Press, 2013.

155 - Flavin, 20 , p. 24.

156 - Flavin, 20 , p. 14.

157 – see note 38, chapter two.

158 - CSPI, 1509-1573, p.

159 - Admiralty, 1536-1641, p. 3; p. 7; p. 23.

160 - Walsh, 1992, p. 66.

# Chapter Six: The Long War

1 - Donovan-O'Sullivan, 1942, p. 87. I have regularised the spelling.

2 - op. cit. Spelling also regularised.

3 - "Age of Atrocity" is borrowed from Age of Atrocity: Violence and Political Conflict in Early Modern Ireland , eds. Edwards, Lenihan, Tait, 2007 (see bibliography). One statement by them is well worth repeating: "The editors of this volume agree that the best way for historians to prevent history being misused is to provide an accurate record of the past in all its aspects, warts and all – and Ireland's past has sometimes been very warty indeed." (op. cit., p. 18). For overview, Hardiman, 1820; Donovan-O'Sullivan, 1942; chapters I to VI in Atrocity, chapters I to V in NHI, III; Canny, 2001; Connolly, 2007; Lennon, 2005; McGurk, 1997 and 2006; Morgan, 2004, 2004, 2007, 2013. I am especially grateful to Eoin Ó Néill for a critique of a draft of this chapter. His own work (see bibilography) was most useful.

4 - Jarman, 1950-52, 220-222; Gallagher, 2013, pp. 116-117. "ideoque Brittania ...", Jezierski, 2005, p. 167.

5 - Edwards, 2007, p. 34.

6 - NHI, III, p. 199.

7 - Ó Néill, 2013.

8 - Edwards, 2007, p. 76., and Edwards 2009

9 - Recio Morales (1996) notes the first two Jesuits to visit Ulster in 1542 believed Conn Ó Neill and Manus Ó Domnaill "were committed to king Henry VIII of England as head of the church in Ireland and that the entire country was on the point of being lost to the Roman Catholic Church." (p.199). Yet by the 1560s some Irish tied Catholicism into their national identity. See O'Byrne, 2004, p. 182; Walsh, 1989; NHI, vol. III; Connors, 1996.

10 - Ó Corráin, 2011-12, p. 223.

11 - Hart, 2014; Clark, 1989. Campbell (2012, pp. 52-112) goes into some depth discussing Irish and English critiques of each others societies, and comparisions between the Irish and Americans. See also Canny, 2001.

12 - For Irish in English service, see McGurk, 1997, pp. 42-43. For English and Welsh population, and non-English/British in imperial units, see Colley, 2002. For population, see Nicholls, 1987, p. 409.

13 - Lewis, 2014.

14 - This includes both the War of Independence (1919-21, during which my grandparents, great-grandparents, their families and communities, directly experienced state terrorism) and The Troubles (1969-1998). The latter occured because two opposing tyrannies (apartheid Protestant Unionism and militant Catholic Nationalism) needed to sustain their traditions. Thus each sacrificed their own children. So it goes.

15 - Donovan-O'Sullivan, 1942, p. 87.

16 - CSPI, 1566-1567, p. 209-10 ("525 Ralph Rokeby to Sir William Cecil 4 Jan 1570").

17 - Walsh, 1992, p. 65. The term Óg or Óge (as in 'the younger' or 'junior') was used in these generations of the Martyn family to distinguish a grandson from a grandfather of the same name.

18 - Edwards, 2004, pp. 240-41. For the financial aid available to the marshal, see note 56.

19 - CSPI, 1568-71, pp. 243-44. See also ALCé and AFM for these years and events.

20 - op. cit.

21 - op. cit.

22 - op. cit.

23 - op. cit.

24 - op. cit., and pp. 212-213.

25 - CSPI, 1568-71, pp. 243-44.

26 - op. cit.

27 - op. cit., p. 230.

28 - op. cit., pp. 229-30 ("577 Lord Deputy Sidney to the Privy Council 24 Jan 1570").

29 - op. cit., p. 230.

30 - CSPI, 1571-1575, pp. 176-77.

31 - op. cit.

32 - op. cit., pp. 212-213, 243-44.

33 - CSPI, 1571-74, pp. 348-349.

34 - op. cit., p. 391, 392-93.

35 - op. cit., pp. 528-29.

36 - op. cit., p. 529.

37 - op. cit., p. 530. A fiant of Elizabeth I records that a committee was formed "to make enquiry into the statements of a petition by Gregory Botken on behalf of the town of Athynry, co. Galway, that a black rent was levied on the town by the earl of Clanriccard, and that his sons Ullick and John and their followers had seized the goods, and otherwise injured the townsmen". See Fiants – Elizabeth, p. 341. Gregory was one of the Bailiffs of Galway for the term 1569-70 (the other was George Frenche) under Mayor Givane Fante.

38 - op. cit., p. 530.

39 - CSPI 1571-74, p. 302, and CCMI, I, 1515-74, p. 421 (dated Galway, 17 May 1572). Carew ... 1515-1574, p. 421 (dated Galway, 17 May 1572), refers to him as "the Earl's special man". A letter dated 12 July 1580, op. cit., p. 271, calls Lynch "agent here for the Earl of Clanricarde".

40 - CSPI 1571-74, p. 421.

41 - op. cit.

42 - Henry, 2002, p. 43.

43 - op. cit.

44 - CSPI, 1571-74, p. 152.

45 - op. cit., pp. 443-44. How wealthy that may have been remains to be seen. Writing in 1591, Ludolf von Munchausen stated that "Waterford is the noblest of all merchant cities in Ireland, it is here that the richest merchants live. If a merchant or other gentleman owns one thousand pounds, which rarely happens in Ireland, he is considered to be an immensely rich man." (Ó Riain-Raedel, 1998, p. 229)

46 - CSPI 1571-74, pp. 450-51.

47 - op. cit.

48 - Donovan-O'Sullivan, 1942, pp. 99-100. CSPI 1574-85, 16 November 1586 states Jasper Martin was murdered by the Burkes in a town in County Mayo "where certain merchants of Galway dwelt."

49 - op. cit., p. 100.

50 - CSPI 1571-74, p. 550.

51 - CSPI, 1574-85 (dated "30 June, Galway"), p. 108.

52 - CSPI, 1574-85 (dated "9 July, Galway"), p. 97.

53 - Donovan-O'Sullivan, 1942, p. 102.

54 - op. cit., pp. 102-06.

55 - Hardiman, 1820, p. 86.

56 - Robinson, 1986, p. 244. He must have seized the islands by 1574, when Lynches held its its castles of him.

57 - AFM 1580. 26.

58 - CSPI, 1574-85, p. 262, dated 24 October 1580 ("Young William Burke, Clanrycard's son, cannot imbue his hands enough in the English heretics' blood."). See also op. cit., p. 309, 6 July 1581. This sentiment was gruesomely echoed in a statement made at the translation of Tyrone's body at Rome in 1623, when "... both his hands were found perfect. At beholding which the guardian Peter de Roma exclaimed, 'Behold these blessed hands which were often washed in the blood of heretics ..." (Ó Muraíle, 2007, pp. 454-55, ). An obscene sense of sanctity!

59 - CSPI, 1574-85, p. 262.

60 - CSPI, 1574-85, p. 294. A "Walter Wale m'Shane of Court" is mentioned in a fiant of 19 September 1582.

61 - CSPI, 1574-85, p. 301, 308. For Ó Briain, see "Kings and Earls of Thomond, 1168-1657", NHI, vol. IX, p. 153.

62 - Walsh, 1992, p. 67.

63 - ALCé, 1580.18. See also AFM.

64 - See note 55, above.

65 - Fiants-Elizabeth 1558-86, pp. 513-14.

66 - op. cit., pp. 564-65.

67 - op. cit., p. 614.

68 - CSPI, 1574-85, p. 463 ("1583. Aug. 18. Athlone."), and Donovan-O'Sullivan, 1938-39, pp. 29-32, and pp. 36-37. Contrary to her assertion that Martyn "was gaoler in 1580", the manuscript clearly states his post was that of marshal. Googe, in a letter of January 1585 (see op. cit., pp. 37-38) states that the office of town marshal was provided with a jail, "the keepynge off the pledges" (hostages of local lords, surrendered as pledges for the good behaviour) and its allowance – this may explain Donovan-O'Sullivan terming him a jailer.
I believe without William Óge the Martyns would have joined the Athys, Deanes and Fonts in obscurity. He is the certain ancestor of the Dun Guaire/Tullira Castle lineage and possible ancestor to the Ross House/Ballynahinch lineage, two major branches of the Martyns (see family trees). For lands granted to him, see Compossicion, 1936, p. 41, 45, 54, 63, 64. For his term as Mayor, see Henry, 2002, p. 69, almost a word-for-word rendition of notes I gave him on the Martyn Mayors in 2001. My research on the Martyns and the Tribes began in February 1996 with seeing his name for the first time in James Hardiman's History of Galway, and recognising it.

69 - "Seventy men and women" AFM, 1586.1. "Women, boys, peasants, and decrepit persons." AFM, 1586.3. For Cluain Dubhain, see AFM, 1586.2, and ALCé 1586.4. For December 1586, see AFM, 1586.7. Also ALCé 1586.1, 2.

70 - Henry, 2002, p. 69. See also Galway Corporation Book A for Martyn's many signatures during his term of office.

71 - Donovan-O'Sullivan, 1942, pp. 115-16. "In the medieval town such opporutnities for the misappropriation of funds were rife and Galway was manifestly no exception." (Walsh, 1981, p. 37)

72 - AFM, 1582.2.

73 - DoIB, vol. I, p. 40.

74 - AFM, 1582.2.

75 - Walsh, 1992, p. 67.

76 - AFM, 1583.19

77 - Roy, 2001, p. 148. Domhnall mac Dáire Mac Bruaideadha wrote an eulogy for Burke, A mheic, gur mheala t'arma (McManus and Ó Raghallaigh, eds., 2010, p. 15). See also Burke (de Burgh), John, DoIB, vol. I, pp. 39-40.

78 - For John's probable grandchildren, see Jennings, 1947. For his eldest son, Redmond, see DoIB, vol. I, pp. 68-69.

79 - Roy, 2001, p. 154.

80 - Ó Muraíle, 1982, p. 18.

81 - Morgan, 2007, pp. 97-101 (especially 98). Also Douglas, 2009, pp. 33-34.

82 - Morgan, 2007, p. 98. For the bishop's murder, see McGurk, 2006, p. 106.

83 - Donovan-O'Sullivan, 1942, pp. 123-24.

84 - Hardiman, 1820, pp. 93-94.

85 - Walsh, 2003, p. 206.

86 - BFR, 1902, p. 187 ("Blake, formerly of Drum, County Galway").

87 - Walsh, 2003, p. 210.

88 - op. cit., p. 208.

89 - Donovan-O'Sullivan, 1942, pp. 117-18, 122-23, 129-32.

90 - CSPI, 1588-92, p. 144, p. 173.

91 - op. cit., p. 173.

92 - op. cit.

93 - Donovan-O'Sullivan, 1942, p. 116.

94 - *CSPI, 1586-88*, p. 53.
95 - op. cit., p. 68, 69, 105.
96 - *CSPI, 1588-92*, p. 174.
97 - op. cit.
98 - op. cit.
99 - op. cit.
100 - op. cit., pp. 177-79.
101 - op. cit., p. 178.
102 - op. cit., p. 179.
103 - op. cit.
104 – op. cit., p. 181.
105 - op. cit.
106 - "O'Neill, Hugh", *DoIB*, vol. 7, pp. 764-772. "O'Donnell, Red Hugh", op. cit., p. 381. "whipping, branding"
O'Connor, 2004, pp. 60-66. For Ó Neill's relationship with his children and wives, see Lyons, 2007, pp. 41-61.
For the most well-written assesment of Ó Neill's character, motives, and aims, see Connolly, 2007, pp. 227-254.
"England's already debatable survival"; Alford (London, 2012) emphasises how precarious Protestant England's
survival was under Elizabeth I. Like most English (or British) historians even today, Ireland's role is unconsidered
in his account. It is an author's privilege to write as s/he sees fit, yet this continued failure by English/British
writers to integrate the story of Elizabeth's *other kingdom* (!) is baffling – yet from an Irish perspective,
unsuprising. Exceptions include James Shapiro's 1599: *A Year in the Life of William Shakespeare* (London, 2005),
and John Cooper's *The Queen's Agent: Francis Walshingham at the Court of Elizabeth I* (London, 2011).
107 - *CSPI, 1571-75*, p. 377.
108 - *CSPI, 1592-96*, p. 365. See also Walsh, 2003, p. 211.
109 - *AFM*, 1597.1.
110 - op. cit.
111 - op cit.
112 - *CSPI, 1596-98*, p. 221.
113 - *AFM*, 1597.1. Also *CSPI, 1596-98*, pp. 221-22, and Donovan-O'Sullivan, 1942, pp. 132-33.
114 - *AFM*, 1597.1.
115 - *CSPI, 1596-98*, p. 222 ("Oliver Oge French", dated 19 January 1597, Galway).
116 - *AFM*, 1599.15-17.
117 - *CSPI, 1598-99*, p. 56. Perhaps "John Linch of Derrimclaghney, merchant", listed in a "General Pardon" of
12 May 1603 (*PRJI*, p. 18). The writer John Lynch (c. 1599-1677) was also "Joannem Linchaeum, cognomento
Juniorem/John Lynch, known as the younger" (*Com. Rin.*, v, 432; see Campbell, 2008, p. 88).
118 - Morgan, 2013.
119 - Donovan-O'Sullivan, 1942, pp. 139-41. For Ó Neill's exploitation of Catholicism, see O'Connor, 2004.
120 - op. cit., p. 141.
121 - pp. 446-47, *CSPI, 1600*.
122 - op. cit.
123 - *CSPI, 1601-1603*, p. 207.
124 - op. cit.
125 - op. cit., p. 219.
126 - op. cit., p. 220.
127 - op. cit., pp. 399-400.
128 - op. cit.
129 - op. cit.
130 - op. cit.
131 - op. cit., p. 400.
132 - op. cit., pp. 373-74.
133 - pp. 128-29, op. cit (see also p. 89, 130).
134 - op. cit.
135 - op. cit.
136 - op. cit.
137 - op. cit., p. 122.
138 - See Morgan, 2004, and Ekins, 2014, for superb academic and popular accounts.
139 - For English imperialism and the modern creation of the British state and nation, see Canny, 2001; Kearney, 1989

(despite its unfortunate title and regular indiscriminate use of 'Celtic'); Davis, 1999 (ditto 'Celtic', and other reservations); Tombs, 2014. At least as early as the 1640s, 'British' was equated as an ethnic term for English people, deliberatly excluding the Protestant Welsh and Scottish (Canny, 2001, p. 483; also 23-26, 195-197, 205, 236). "Spenser's 'Britain' was therefore England writ large, which would be poised to play a more important role in world affairs once it was in a positon to draw upon the resources 'of all that beare the *British* Islands name.' (op. cit., p. 26). See also *NHI* vols. II, III, IV. While Ireland has always engaged with Britain, it stands apart.

140 - Walsh, 2003, p. 216.

141 - Ekins, 2015.

142 - *NHI, III 1534-1691*, p. 140.

143 - Drawn from Peter Burke's "History as a social memory", in *Memory, history, culture and the mind*, ed. Thomas Butler, Oxford and New York, 1989, p. 106:

144 - See *CSPI* 1602, p. 300, from Mayor Christopher Lynch to Secretary Cecil.

145 - "after 1602"; in August 1602, Blake presented to the Spanish a plan for an invasion of Galway, see Jones, 1950. *"infinitely troublesome"*; Cunningham, 1996, p. 169. "this wretched individual";  see Walsh, 2003, p. 205. BFR, 1902, p. 148, and especially pp. 186-191 (*"Blake, formerly of Drum, County Galway"*) outlines his life, and lists his known descendants down to Valentine Blake fitz Patrick, alive 1782.

146 - Henry, 2002, p. 37. A reference dated 8 May 1614 mentions "James Linch, factor of the said Valentine Blake". Blake had "complained of spoil made of two ships, the one of Lubeck and the other of Callice [Calais], by Capt. Mannering, who pretended a voyage to Binny, whereby he and his partners were endamaged to the value of 3,000l." Mannering "made satisfaction" to Linch (*CSPI 1611-1614*, p. 475). Blake's baronetcy is referenced in *PRJI*, XLV.-12 (p. 546), and LIX.-2, LX.-21 (p. 547).

147 - For Thomas Bodkin fitz Gregory, see BFR no., 15 June 1599. For Gregory Bodkin, S.J., Chapter 7, note 66.

148 - Hardiman, 1820, p. 95.

149 - Henry, 2002, p. 43.

150 - op. cit., p. 49.

151 - Iar Connacht, p. 399.

152 - op. cit., p. 66; Hardiman, 1820, p. xlii. For Lynch's pardon, see *PRJI*, p. 18. "deceased"; Walsh, 1992, p. 103.

153 - See Morgan, 2004, pp. 353-354. He does not appear in "General Pardon" dated 12 May 1603 (*PRJI*, p. 18).

154 - *Compossicion*, p. 41, 45, 54, 63, 64, and Henry, 2002, p. 69. I am grateful to Dr. Joe Mannion for the reference to Martyn's removal and reinstatement as jailer of Galway (TNA SP 63/104/22) and a reminder that he "actually served a second term as sheriff of Co. Galway in 1589" (TNA SP 63/146/35 (ii) & 37). He furthermore passed on a reference (TNA SP 63/104/22, 18 August 1583) in which Barnaby Googe alleged in a letter to Lord Burghley that Martyn "was the ffyrst that ran owte off the ffeylde" at Shrule in 1570. As Googe was not then in Ireland the veracity of this is uncertain. See also Henry, 2002, p. 69 (all of Mr. Henry's published biographies of the Martyn Mayors of Galway were my own almost word-for-word research notes, which I presented to him in 2001). William Óge's will, partly preserved in the Betham Abstracts, reads "Will. Martin of Galway [illegible word] 16 Jan 1592 – 22 May 1593. Brother Francis, wife Elizabeth, father Thomas."

155 - Henry, 2002, p. 69. For his pardon, see *PRJI*, p. 1. Francis's descendants sold the property to their kinsman, Oliver Martyn of Tullira, who sold it to the Gregory family about 1760. They are partly documented in the Betham abstracts. A Francis Martin, buried in Ardrahan graveyard in 1698, may have been of this family.

156 - Hardiman, 1820, p. 211; CSPI 1602, pp. 300-301; For Darcy's denomination, see op. cit., pp. 327-328.

157 - Henry, 2002, pp. 71-72.

158 - *NHI IX*, p. 236. See also Roy, 2001, pp. 158-60, and Ekins, 2014, pp. 272-273.

159 - For the Bingham earls of Lucan, see .

160 - CSPI, 1588-92, p. 476.

161 - The episode, inaccurately known as 'the flight of the Earls', has been exceptionally well recounted in Ó Muraíle, ed., 2007. Cú Chonnacht Mag Uidhir (died Genoa 12 August 1608) was a half-brother of Aodh Mag Uidhir who was killed in action near Cork on 11 March 1600. Rudhraighe Ó Domhnaill (died Rome 28 July 1608) was a younger full brother of Aodh Ruadh, becoming Earl of Tyrconnell on 29 September 1603. Ó Fiach describes him as lacking "Aodh Ruadh's mettle, and was more driven by self-interest." This says more about Ó Fiach's cultural background (similar to my own, which taught us to revere such men) than the motives of the lords, which were nothing if not driven by self-interest (as for Aodh's "mettle", see McGurk, 2006, and Ekins, 2014). See Ó Muraíle, 2007, pp. 434-35 and 423-24. See also Casway, 2003, pp. 56-74, and Ó Dálaigh, 2007, pp. 13-40.

# Chapter Seven: A Golden Age

1 - "It seem to be that the effects of both the local, but destructive, native wars and the more total variety practised by Elizabethan soldiers on the Irish economy and population have been grossly underestimated." (Nicholls, 1987, note 1, p. 410). "We might then suggest that the Irish population in the early sixteenth century was below half a million, perhaps well below that figure, and that as a result of the severe conditions created by war it remained around that level until after 1600." (Nicholls, 1987, p. 409) Against this is Connolly (2007, "Appendix 1: The Population of Medieval and Early Modern Ireland", pp. 404-405) who conclues that the Irish "population in 1500 [was] closer to 750,000 than the half millon often suggested.", with a population of one millon in 1600, 1.5-1.6 millon in 1641. For an overview, see *NHI, III*; Hardiman, 1820; Donovan-O'Sullivan,1942; Clarke, 1966 (2000 paperback edition); Canny, 2001 (2003 paperback); FitzPatrick et al, 2004; Campbell, 2013.

2 *Carew MSS, 1603-1624.*, p. 176.

3 - op. cit., p. 435.

4 - Kearney, 1955, pp. 418-19.

5 - op. cit.

6 - op cit.

7 - op. cit.

8 - *PRJI*, p. 258. See and compare with one on p. 388 to Coman of Athlone and Nolan of Ballinrobe.

9 - *PRJI*, 26 June 1625, p. 582.

10 - *Admiralty, 1536-1641*, p. 3.

11 - Lyons, 2001, pp. 110-12.

12 - Admiralty, 1536-1641, pp. 52-53.

13 - op. cit., p. 57.

14 - op. cit., p. 53-54.

15 - *Admiralty, 1536-1641*, p. 130.

16 - *BFM no. 19, Seventeenth century*, 1902, p. 13.

17 - *BFM no. 50, Seventeenth Century*, 1902, pp. 28-30. A footnote at the bottom of the will testifies his survival: "I John Blake doe revocke the foresaid will in all pointes whattsoever, the tenthy of 9ber 1636; John Blake fitz N."

18 - *Admiralty, 1536-1641*, p. 174.

19 - op. cit., pp. 173-74, 312-13. I am confident that this Andrew Martyn was the first of eleven successive bearers of the name, the last of whom was Andrew Martin (Andrew the 11th) of Eagle Hill House, Abbey-Duniry, Portumna (1852-1932). I am grateful for this piece of family folklore to Andrew the 11th's daughter, Mary Jo Madden nee Martin (born 1922), whom I interviewed at her home in The Nurseries, Taylor's Hill, Galway, in summer 1997. According to her, Andrew the First fled Galway for Dublin due to Cromwell's seizure of Galway. The family purchased Eagle Hill in the 1830s, it remains in the possession of their Burke descendants. The family also had residences in Meelick-Eyrecourt, and Longford Castle.

20 - *Admiralty, 1536-1641*, p. 276.

21 - op. cit., p. 235.

22 - op. cit., p. 236.

23 - op. cit.

24 - op. cit.

25 - op. cit., p. 280.

26 - "foul weather" - *Admiralty, 1642-1660*, p. 2; "extreme storm", *Admiralty, 1534-1641*, p. 280. During the voyage of the Ulster lords in September 1603, Tadhg Ó Cianáin experienced similar conditions to the crew of the *Elizabeth*.

27 - *Admiralty, 1642-1660*, p. 2.

28 - op. cit.

29 - op. cit. *CSPI 1625-32*, p. 281, notes in 1627 a ship was driven into Galway Bay. Its cargo of tobacco and other American goods were seized by the Galwegians, claiming admiralty rights. Tobacco was consumed in Ireland as early as 1600, certainly by 1610. Galway excavations unearthed clay pipes dated to c. 1630.

30 - Dwyer, 2014, p. 9.

31 - *CSP Colonial Series 1574-1660*, p. 115. The other men deposed were "Dan. Fallon" and "Rich. Carpenter". Both surnames were found in seventeenth-century Galway. See *Admiralty, 1536-1641* for Carpenters of Galway.

32 - *Admiralty, 1536-1641*, pp. 261-62.

33 - op. cit., p. 262.

34 - op. cit., pp. 262-63.

35 - op. cit.

36 - *Admiralty, 1536-1641*, p. 321.

37 - op. cit., pp. 252-53.

38 - Ruqia Hassan, born 1985, murdered 2015.

39 - The myth of 'Irish slaves'/'white slavery' in the Americas is a racist fiction, now widespread in the USA and USA based internet sites. It is frightening to note that it has some hold here in Ireland. Its primary source remains Sean O'Callaghan's notorious *To Hell or Barbados* (2000) - though few appear to have read it. Instead many rely on digested versions propagated by online American sites such as GlobalResearch.com and *IrishCentral.com*, written by someone aliased 'John Martin' (since March 2016, the article has being deleted from *IrishCentral.com*, without explanation, apparently as a result of an online petition by over thirty scholars and writers, myself included. O'Callaghan's book seems genuine, yet researching the issue for this chapter sealed a growing suspicion that his book was not factual. This in turn led to heated online arguments between myself and various supporters of the myth, initially during 2012-13. While a number of works do address the actual lives of the West Indies Irish (see below), almost none deal directly with the myth nor rebut it (given the venom they would face, this is understandable). That changed in November 2014 when, for reasons similar to my own, historian and University of Limerick graduate Liam Hogan published online his article "The Myth of 'Irish Slaves' in the Colonies: confusion, conflation, co-option". Hogan has followed this with further articles, all of which rebut this propaganda. An Irish academic who briefly corresponded with me on the subject about 2012 concluded people will believe what they want, despite evidence, and that it is a waste of time arguing with such fools. I understood, but could not agree. Such matters are too serious to remain neutral; they must be fought.
Sources for this section are Akenson, 1997; Beckles, 1990; Block and Shaw, 2011; Canny, 2015; Calder, 1999; Chinea, 2007; Galenson, 1984; Gibson, 2014; Gwynn, 1929, 1932, 1932; Handler, 1973, 2016; Handler and Reilly, 2015; Handler and Shelby, 1973; Hogan, 2014; Hogan, McAtackney, Reilly, 2016; Murphy, 2005; Mullen, 2015; O'Malley, 2012; Reilly, 2014, 2015; Regan, 2016; Rogers, 2007, 2012; Snyder, 2007; Walsh, 2012, possibly the best and most concise essay on the subject.
New studies are *A Tale of Two Plantations: Slave Life and Labor in Jamaica and Virginia* by Richard S. Dunn (2014), *The American Slave Coast: A History of the Slave Breeding Industry* by Constance and Ned Sublette (2015), and *Recovering Scotland's Slavery Past: The Caribbean Connection* by Professor Sir Tom Devine (2015). As I have not read the books I availed of published reviews. The Sublette's contends that slavery - as the major form of property wealth - was a pivotal factor in the economic growth of the thirteen colonies and the subsequent USA. Devine contends Scotland was far more involved in the slave trade that 'memory' allows, and profited greatly (as this book makes plain, I do not believe 'memory' exists, only tradition). Stephen Mullen's "A Glasgow-West India merchant House and the Imperial Dividend, 1779-1867" should also be read.
According to Trinidad historian and Prime Minister Eric Williams, slavery "was not born of racism; rather, racism was the consequence of slavery: ... The reason [for slavery] was economic, not racial; it had nothing to do with the colour of the labourer, but with the cheapness of the labour. ... The features of the [person], his hair, colour and dentifrice, his "subhuman" characteristics ... were only later rationalizations to justify [chattel slavery]." (See *Capitalism and Slavery*, London,1944, pp. 20-21).

40 - See Kennedy, 2016 [2015], pp. 4-5, 81-104, 105-124.

41 - Rogers, 2007, p. 44.

42 - Regan, 2016, p. 37.

43 - Canny, 2015.

44 - Turner, 2014, pp. 10-11. Only in 1868 after the (second?) civil war of 1861-65 did the USA pass the 14th amendment to its constitution, which made anyone born in the USA a citizen. For physical racism, and its applications to Africans, and Irish, see Campbell, 2013, p. 22 (also pp. 1-21), 180, 187, 188, 190-192.

45 - *NHI III*, p. 603.

46 - op. cit.

47 - op. cit. Vagrants and convicts were transported, as were British and Irish rebels in the 1650s (NHI III, pp. 600-01).

48 - Akenson, 1997, pp. 52-53.

49 - Truxes, 1988, p. 20.

50 - de Blacam, 1929, p. 274.

51 - *NHI*, III, p. 604.

52 - Hartnett, 2004, p. 307. Hartnett's "Legitimation and Dissent: Colonialism, Consumption, and the Search for Distinction in Galway, Ireland, ca. 1250-1691" (University of Chicago, December 2010), read in August 2014, anticipated some of my own ideas and themes.

53 - Binasco, 2007, pp. 2-3.

54 - op. cit. This is changing, but much is yet to be done.

55 - Nolan, 1901, pp. 109-23.

56 - *Compossicion*, 1936, p. 54.

57 - *IPRJI*, p. 22, pardon dated 19 April 1603.

58 - For the tribes as landowners, see Ó Bríc, 1974, and Melvin, 1996. Estates listed are in Hardiman, 1820, pp. 7-19.

59 - Connolly, 2007, p. 387.

60 - Connolly, 2007, p. 387.

61 - Leerson, 1986, p. 203.

62 - Leerson, 1986, p. 203. The translation is partly my own.

63 - Gillespie, 1987. "The financial history of early seventeenth-century Ireland ... remains to be explored." (p. 418)

64 - Canny, 2015, p. 133.

65 - Edwards, 2005, pp.95-126.

66 - "political fallout ..." Edwards, 2004, p. 238, and pp. 237-265. See also Ó Siochrú , 2007, pp. 18-21.

67 - Cunningham, 1996, p. 182.

68 - Cunningham, 1996, p. 176.

69 - See Ohlmeyer, 2001. McGrath, 2004, p. 229, comments "The political situation provided the motivation for the length of time the students intended to remain at the inns: merely completing a polite education was no defence against losing property." "This helps to explain the significant role of lawyers in Irish politics." (op. cit., p. 231). *CSPI 1611-1614*, p. 350, records a sour comment by Solicitor-General of Ireland, Sir Robert Jacob, dated 26 May 1613: "The Irish lawyers do more harm than the priests." His wife was a daughter of a Galway Lynch

70 - O'Malley, 1984, pp. 100-102; Ó Siochrú, 1999, p. 239; Campbell, 2013, pp. 40-41. See also chapters 7 to 12 in *NHI III*; and Ó Siochrú, 2001.

71 - Ó Siochrú,, 1999, p. 240.

72 - op. cit.

73 - Ó Siochrú, 1999, p. 241, and 240. "For he that is an Irishman ...", see Gilbert, vol. III , 1885, pp. 301-02.

74 - op. cit., p. 247.

75 - *CSPI 1588-92*, p. 224 ("Summary by Capt. John Merbury of the whole rebellion in Connaught").

76 - Gilbert, 1885, p. 462.

77 - O'Connell, 2001, p. 81, lists his parents and degree.

78 - op. cit., and *DoIB*, vol. 5, p. 643.

79 - Colley, 2002, p.50 (also pp. 43-44, 48-50, 55-56, 75-76).

80 - Colley, 2002, p. 76. Nabil Matar's *British Captives from the Mediterranean to the Atlantic, 1563-1760* (University of Minnesota, June 2014) seems the most comprehensive study available, though its cost prevented purchase.

81 - *DoIB*, vol. 5, p. 643.

82 - Millett, 1965, p. 12, 20, 21, 22, and Fenning, 2000.

83 - *DoIB*, vol. 5, p. 643. *PRJI 1615-25*, p. 496, "one Doctor Lynch, a very learned man, and of great estimation with them [the Dominicans]. He is brother to Sir Harry Lynch." See 1218, 19 May 1624; O'Connell, 2001, p. 82.

84 - O'Connell, 2001, p. 643.

85 - op. cit.

86 - op. cit., p. 644.

87 - op. cit.

88 - Connell, 2001, p. 95.

89 - op. cit., p. 68.

90 - op. cit., p. 81, 95, 82.

91 - op. cit.

92 - See Oranmore and Brown, 1907-08; also Ó Muraile, "Aspects", 1996; and *Antiquary*, 1996.

93 - Ó hAnnracháin, 2003, pp. 143-44. See also Connors, 1996.

94 - Edward, Lenihan, Tait, 2007, p. 9.

95 - op. cit., p. 10.

96 - Connolly, 2007, p. 399.

97 - Doyle, 2015, pp. 128-138. See him also for African Gaeilgeoirí on Monserratt in 1852.

98 - See Cunningham, 2010. If kept strictly to the original title, the work would only have begun in 1541!

99 - Cunningham, 2009, p. 181. Also op. cit. p. 72, 162-3, 182, 334-5.

100 - "Aspects", Ó Muraile, 1996, pp. 176-82.

101 - op. cit. Also Cunningham, 2009, pp. 159-76.

102 - Millett, 1968, p. 56.

103 - Crawford, 2005, p. 502.
104 - op. cit.
105 - op. cit., p. 515.
106 - op. cit.
107 - op. cit., p. 541-42.
108 - CSPI 1625-32, p. 473.
109 - op. cit.
110 - CSPI 1633-47, p. 126. I have updated the spelling of the names as Gaeilge.
111 - Oranmore and Browne, 1907-08, pp. 166-67.
112 - DoIB, vol. 2, p. 903.
113 - Walsh, 1992, p. 68.
114 - op. cit., p. 70.
115 - op. cit.
116 - op. cit, and Gernon, 1620, p. 354.
117 - Gernon, 1620, and Boate, 1652.
118 - Walsh, 1992, p. 71.
119 - op. cit., p. 72.
120 - op. cit.
121 - op. cit.
122 - op. cit.
123 - op. cit.
124 - op. cit.
125 - op. cit.
126 - Donovan-O'Sullivan, 1942, p. 430.
127 – Walsh, 1992, p. 111.
128 - Hardiman, 1820, xxxii-xlii]
129 - CSPI 1625-32, p. 222, 273.
130 - op. cit. p. 222 and 273. Also Admiralty 1534-1641, pp. 167-69, 170, 172, 173; Admiralty, 1642-1660, p. 2.
131 - CSPI, 1633-47, p. 256.
132 - op. cit.
133 - For origins, actions, aftermaths of the 1641 Rebellion: NHI, III, pp. 270-95; NHI, VIII, pp. 231-33;Lydon, 2000, pp. 153-70; Canny, 2001; Edwards et al, 2007, pp. 154-192; Ó Siochrú, 2008, pp. 16-37; Gibney, 2013.
134 - Tanner Letters, 1943, pp. 137-38.
135 - op. cit.
136 - op. cit.

# EPILOUGE

1 – Charles Hudson's review of Bernard Sheehan's Savigism and Civility:Indians and Englishmen in Colonial Virginia, in American Ethnologist, February 1982, p. 217.
2 – Clanricard, 1757, pp. 98-99. See Hardiman, 1820, p. xxx - "Brian Roe Mahon More, Stephen Lynch, Dominick Kirwan and Walter Martin, who had their hands immediately in the effusion of the blood of captain Clark's men", were specifically excluded from the 1651 Terms of Surrender of Galway. The murdered men remain nameless.

# BIBILOGRAPHY:

**Primary Sources:**

"A Galway Hearth Money Roll for 1724", ed. Bernadette Cunningham, *JGAHS*, vol. 56, 2004, pp. 60-74.

*Adomnán of Iona: Life of St Columba, ed. and trans.* Richard Sharpe, London, 1995.

*A Calendar of Irish Chancery Letters, c. 1244-1509*, ed. Peter Crooks, 2012 (see chancery.tcd.ie)

*A Calendar of Material relating to Ireland from the High Court of Admiralty Examinations 1536-1641*, ed. John C. Appleby, Irish Manuscripts Commission, Dublin, 1992.

*A Calendar of Material Relating to Ireland from the High Court of Admiralty 1641-1660*, ed. Elaine Murphy, Irish Manuscripts Commission, Dublin, 2011.

*A Statistical and Agricultural Survey of the County of Galway*, Hely Dutton, Dublin, 1824.

"Account of the Lynch Family And of memorable Events of the Town of Galway. Written in 1815 by John, son of Alexander Lynch" With Introduction by Martin J. Blake, Part II, *JGAHS* vol. VIII, no. 2, 1913-14, pp. 76-93.

"An Account of the Town of Galway", ed. Paul Walsh, *JGAHS* vol. 44, 1992, pp. 47-118.

"An extract from Strafford's inquisition: Galway corporation poperty, 1637", ed. Paul Walsh and Paul Duffy, *JGAHS*, vol. 49, 1997, pp. 49-64.

"An Old Lynch Manuscript", ed. Martin J. Blake, *JGAHS* vol. 8, no. 2 and 4, 1913 and 1914.

*Annals of Clonmacnoise*, ed. Denis Murphy, S.J., Dublin, 1896; facsimile reprint by Llanerch Publishers, 1993.

*Annales Hiberniae* (by James Grace of Kilkenny), ed. Richard Butler, Dublin, 1842.

*Annals of Connacht*, A.D. 1224-1544, ed. A. Martin Freeman, Dublin, 1944.

*Annals of Inisfallen*, ed. Sean Mac Airt, Dublin, 1951.

*Annals of Ireland* by Friar John Clyn, ed. Bernadette Williams, Four Courts Press, Dublin, 2007.

*Annals of Loch Cé*, ed. W.M. Hennessy, two volumes, London, 1871.

*Annals of the Kingdom of Ireland* by the Four Masters, ed. John O'Donovan, six volumes, Dublin, 1851.

*Annals of Tigernach*, ed. Whitley Stokes in Revue Celtique, 1896-97; facsimile reprint by Llanerch Publishers, 1993.

*Annals of Ulster*, ed. S. Mac Airt and G. Mac Niocaill, Dublin, 1984.

"Archives of the Town of Galway", ed. John T. Gilbert, in *Historical Manuscripts Commission, 10th report, appendix V*, London, 1885, pp. 380-520.

*Blake Family Records*, volumes one and two, ed. Martin J. Blake, 1902 and 1905.

*Book of Ui Maine, otherwise called 'The Book of the O'Kellys*, ed. R.A.S. MacAlister, Dublin, 1942.

*Burke's Extinct Peerages*, Sir Bernard Burke, London, 1883.

*Calendar of Documents relating to Ireland 1171-1251*, ed. H.S. Sweetman, London, 1875.

*Calendar of Documents relating to Ireland 1252-1284*, ed. H.S. Sweetman, London, 1877.

*Calendar of Documents relating to Ireland 1285-1292*, ed. H.S. Sweetman, London, 1879.

*Calendar of Documents relating to Ireland 1302-1307*, ed. H. S. Sweetman, London,1881.

*Calendar of Carew Manuscripts, Ireland I, 1515-1574*, eds. J.S. Brewer and William Bullen, 1867.

*Calendar of Carew Manuscripts, Ireland 6, 1603-1624*, eds. Js. Brewer and William Bullen, 1867.

*Calendar of the Justicary Rolls ... of Ireland ... Edward I, 1295-1307*, ed. James Mills, two volumes, Dublin, 1905-14.

*Calendar of the Justiciary Rolls ... of Ireland: I to VII years of Edward II, 1308-14*, ed. Herbert Wood and A.E. Langman; revised by M.C. Griffith, Dublin, 1956.

*Calendar of Patent Rolls, Richard II, Vol. V., 1391-1396*, London, 1905.

*Calendar of Papal Registers vol. XIII, part I 1471-1484*

*Calendar of State Papers Colonial Series 1574-1660*, London, 1860.

*Calendar of the State Papers of Ireland, 1509-1573*, ed. Hans Claude Hamilton, London, 1860.

*Calendar of the State Papers of Ireland, 1574-1585*, ed. Hans Claude Hamilton, London, 1867 (1974 reprint).

*Calendar of State Papers of Ireland 1566-1567*, ed. by Bernadette Cunningham, Dublin, 2009.

*Calendar of State Papers of Ireland 1568-71*, ed. by Bernadette Cunningham, 2010.

*Calendar of State Papers of Ireland 1571-1575*, ed. by Mary O'Dowd, Dublin, 2000.

*Calendar of State Papers of Ireland 1574-1585*, ed. Hans Claude Hamilton, London, 1867.

Calendar of State Papers of Ireland 1586-1588, ed. Hans Claude Hamilton, London, 1877.
Calendar of State Papers of Ireland, 1588-1592, ed. Hans Claude Hamilton, London, 1885.
Calendar of State Papers of Ireland, 1592-1596, ed. Hans Claude Hamilton, London, 1890.
Calendar of State Papers of Ireland, 1596-1598, ed. Hans Claude Hamilton, London, 1893.
Calendar of State Papers of Ireland, 1598-99, ed. Ernest George Athkinson, London, 1895.
Calendar of State Papers of Ireland, 1599-1600, ed. Ernest George Athkinson, London, 1899.
Calendar of State Papers of Ireland, 1600, ed. Hans Claude Hamilton, London, 1903.
Calendar of State Papers of Ireland, 1600-1601, ed. Ernest George Athkinson, London, 1905.
Calendar of State Papers of Ireland, 1601-1603 (addenda, 1565-1654) , ed. Robert Pentland Mahaffy, London, 1872.
Calendar of State Papers of Ireland, 1603-1606, ed. C.W. Russell and John P. Prendergast, London, 1872.
CIRCLE - A Calendar of Irish Chancery Letters c. 1244 – 1509 (see http://chancery.tcd.ie/)
Chartularies of St Mary's Abbey, Dublin, ed. John Gilbert, two volumes, Dublin 1884.
Chronicon Scotorum, ed. and translated by W. M. Hennessy, London 1866 (reprinted Wiesbaden, 1964).
Compossicion Booke of Conought, A. Martin Freeman, ed., Dublin, 1936.
Dictionary of Irish Biography, J. McGuire and J. Quinn, eds., Cambridge, 2009.
Deeds of the Normans in Ireland: La geste de Engleis en Yrlande: a new edition of the chronicle formerly known as The Song of Dermot and the Earl, ed. Evelyn Mullally, Dublin, 2002.
Domesday Book: A Complete Translation, ed. Dr. Ann Williams and Professor G.H. Martin, London, 2002 edition.
Expugnatio Hibernica, ed. A.B. Scott and F.X. Martin, Dublin, 1978.
Fragmentary Annals of Ireland, ed. Joan Radner, Dublin, 1978.
Great Deeds in Ireland: Richard Stanihurst's 'De Rebus in Hibernia Gestis', ed. John Barry and Hiram Morgan, Cork University Press, 2013 (reprinted in paperback, 2014).
Holinshed's Irish Chronicle 1577, Dolmen Press, 1979.
Inquisitions and Extents of Medieval Ireland, P. Dryburgh and B. Smith, 2007.
Irish Exchequer Payments, 1270-1446, Philomena Connolly, Dublin, 1998.
Irish Fiants of the Tudor Sovereigns During the Reigns of Henry VIII, Edward VI, Philip & Mary, and Elizabeth I, ed. Kenneth Nicholls, four volumes, De Búrca, Dublin, 1994.
Irish Patent Rolls of James I, Irish Manuscript Commission, Dublin, 1966.
Leabhar Mór na nGenealach:The Great Book of Irish Genealogies compiled 1645-66 by Dubhaltach Mac Fhirbhisigh, five volumes, ed. and trans. Nollaig Ó Muraíle, De Búrca, Dublin, 2003-04.
Letters and Memoirs, Ulick, Marquis of Clanricard, London, 1757.
Liber Eliensis, ed. E. O. Blake, London, 1962.
Miscellaneous Irish annals, A.D. 1114-1437, ed. Séamus Ó hInnse, Dublin, 1947.
Oxford dictionary of national biography, H. G. C. Matthew and B. Harrison, eds., Oxford, 2004.
Regestum Monasterii Fratrum Praedicatorum de Athenry, Ambrose Colman, O.P., Archivum Hibernicum, vol. I, 1912.
Report on Documents relating to the Wardenship of Galway, ed. Edward MacLysaght, Analecta Hibernica, no. 14, 1944.
"Seanchus Burcach: historia et genealogia familae de Burgo", ed. Tomás Ó Raghallaigh, pp. 50-60, 101-37, 30-51, 142-67, JGAHS vols. 13 and 14, 1922-29, 1928-29.
The Complete Peerage, vol. VIII, London, 1932.
The Tanner Letters, ed. Charles McNeill, Dublin, 1943.
Topographical poems by Seaán Mór Ó Dubhagáin and Giolla-na-Naomh Ó Huidhrín, Dublin, 1943.
Tribes and Customs of Hy-Many, commonly called O'Kelly's Country, ed. and trans. John O'Donovan, Dublin, 1843.

**Secondary sources:**
Adams, G.B., "Prolegomena to a Study of Surnames in Ireland", Nomina vol. 3, 1979.
Akenson, Donald Harman, If the Irish ran the World: Montserrat, 1630-1730, Liverpool, 1997.
Alford, Stephen, The Watchers: A Secret History of the Reign of Elizabeth I, London, 2012.
Athy, Lawrence, Captain George Athy of Galway and Maryland and his Descendants ..., Houston, Texas, 1999 (third edition).

Baldwin, David, *Richard III*, Gloucestershire, 2012 (2013 reprint).

Baillie, Mike, "What are the chances? Hints from the tree-ring record", in *Lost and Found II*: Discovering Ireland's *Past*, ed. Joe Fenwick, 2009, pp. 95-104.

Barlow, Frank, *The Godwins: The Rise and Fall of a Noble Dynasty*, Harlow, 2002.

Becker, Katharina, "Iron Age Ireland – finding an invisible people", in Cooney, Becker, et al, eds., 2009, pp. 353-362.

Beckles, Hillary, "A 'riotous and unruly lot': Irish Indentured Servants and Freemen in the English West Indies, 1614-1733", in *The William and Mary Quarterly*, Third Series, vol. 47, no. 4, October 1990.

Bell, Robert, *The Book of Ulster Surnames*, 1988.

Best, R.I., *The Leabhar Oiris*, *Ériu*, volume 1, 1904, pp. 74–112.

Bhreathnach, Edel, Joseph MacMahon, John McCafferty, eds., *The Irish Franciscans 1534-1990*, Dublin, 2009.

Bhreathnach, Edel, *Ireland in the Medieval World AD 400-1000: Landscape, kingship and religion*, Dublin, 2014.

Blake, Martin J., "An Old Rental of Cong Abbey", *JRSAI, fifth series, vol. 35*, 1905.

Blake, Martin J., "Will of Geoffrey French of Galway, A.D. 1528", *JGAHS vol. 4, no. 4*, 1905-06.

Blake, Martin J., "Sir Peter French", *JGAHS*, vol. 4, no. 4 1905-06, pp. 106-07.

Blake, Martin J., "Obituary Book of the Franciscan Monastry at Galway", *JGAHS*, vol. 6, no. 4, 1910, pp. 222-235.

Blake, Martin J., "French of Duras, Cloghballymore, and Drumharsna", *JGAHS*, vol. 10, 1917-18.

Blake, Martin J.,"Pedigree of Lynch of Lavally, County Galway", *JGAHS*, vol. 10, 1917-18.

Blake, Martin J., "The origins of the families of French of Connaught, with tabular pedigree of John French of Grand-Terre in 1763", *JGAHS* vol. 11, 1920-21.

Block, Kristen, and Jenny Shaw, "Subjects without an Empire: The Irish in the early modern Caribbean", *Past and Present*, no. 2010, February 2011, pp. 33-60.

Boate, Gerard, *Gerard Boate's natural history of Ireland*, [1652] ed. and intro Thomas E. Jordan, New York, 2006.

Boyle, Elizabeth, "Lay Morality, Clerical Immorality, and Pilgrimage in Tenth-Century Ireland: *Cethrur macclérech* and *Epscop do Gáedlaib*", Studia Hibernica 39, 2013, pp. 9-48.

Boyne, Patricia, *John O'Donovan (1806-1861): a biography*, Kilkenny, Boethius press, 1987.

Bradley, John, ed., *Settlement and Society in Medieval Ireland: Studies presented to F.X. Martin, o.s.a.*, Kilkenny, 1988.

Breen, Colin, *The Gaelic Lordship of the O'Sullivan Beare: A Landscape Cultural History*, Dublin, 2005.

Bridgman, Timothy P., "*Keltoi, Galatai, Galli*: Were They All One People?", PHCC, vol. XXV, 2005, pp. 155-162.

Broderick, George, "Kelten und Nicht-Kelten in Britannien und Irland: eine demographische und sprachwissenschaftliche Untersuchung anhand u.a. Ptolemaischer Orts- und Stammesnamen", pp. 17-32, *Akten des 5. Deutschsprachigen Keltologensymposiums*, Zürich, 7.-10. September 2009, eds. Karin Stüber, Thomas Zehnder und Dieter Bachmann, Wien, 2010 (published in English in Nomina 34).

Browne, Bernard, and Kevin Whelan, "The Browne Families of County Wexford", in *Wexford: History and Society*, ed. Kevin Whelan, 1987.

Buckley, Ann, Music in Ireland to c. 1500, Chapter XXI, *A New History of Ireland* volume I, 2005, pp. 744-813.

Byrne, Francis J., *Irish Kings and High Kings*, Dublin, 1973 (2001 reprint).

Byrne, Francis J., "A Note on the Emergence of Irish Surnames", pp. xxxiii-xxxiv, in *IKaHK*, 2001.

Calder, Angus, "Into slavery: the rise of imperialism – A review of Nicholas Canny (ed) *The Origins of Empire: The New Oxford History of the British Empire Volume I*, in *International Socialism Journal* 83, summer 1999.

Campbell, Duncan R. J., "The so-called Galatae, Celts, and Gauls in the Early Hellenistic Balkans and the Attack on Delphi in 280-279 BC", Ph.D thesis, University of Leicester, February 2009.

Campbell, Ian, *Renaissance Humanism and Ethnicity before Race: The Irish and the English in the seventeenth century*, Manchester University Press, 2013 (see also Unpublished Sources).

Candon, Anthony, "Muirchertach Ua Briain, Politics and Naval Activity in the Irish Sea, 1075 to 1119", *Keimelia: Papers in memory of Tom Delaney*, ed. Gearóid Mac Niocaill and P. F. Wallace, Galway, 1988, pp. 397-415.

Canny, Nicholas, *Making Ireland British 1580-1650*, Oxford, 2001.

Canny, Nicholas, review of *A Tale of Two Plantations: Slave Life and Labor in Jamaica and Virginia* by Richard S. Dunn (Harard, 2014), Irish Independent, 6 May 2015.

Canny, Nicholas, review of *Renaissance Humanism* ... by Ian Campbell, *History*, 100, 2015, pp. 132-133.

Carella, Bryan, "Evidence for Hiberno-Latin Thought in the Prologue to the Laws of Alfred", in *Studies in Philology*, vol. 108, Winter 2011, Number 1, pp. 1-26.

Carew, Mairéad, "The Harvard Mission, Eugenics and the Celts", *Archaeology Ireland*, vol. 26, No. 4, Winter 2012, pp. 38-40.

Carew, Mairéad, "Eoin MacNeill and the promotion of Celtic Studies in America", in *Eoin MacNeill: Revolutionary and Scholar*, School of History and Archives, University College Dublin, 2013, www.historyhub.ie

Carey, John, "*Fir Bolg: A Native Etymology Revisited*", CMCS 16, Winter 1988, pp. 77-83.

Carey, John, *The Irish National Origin-Legend: Synthetic Pseudohistory*, Cambridge, 1994.

Carey, John, "Did the Irish Come from Spain?", *History Ireland*, vol. 9, issue 3, Autumn 2001.

Cassidy, Lara M., Rui Martiniano, Eileen M. Murphy, Matthew D. Teasdale, James Mallory, Barrie Hartwell, Daniel G. Bradley, "Neolithic and Bronze Age migration to Ireland and establishment of the insular Atlantic genome", *PNAS Early Edition*, www.pnas.org/cgi/doi/10.1073/pnas.1518445113

Casway, Jerrold, "Heroines or Victims? The Women of the Flight of the Earls", *New Hibernia Review/Iris Éireannach Nua*, vol. 7, number 1, Spring 2003, pp. 56-74.

Caulfield, Séamus, "Celtic Problems in the Irish Iron Age", pp. 205-215, in *Irish Antiquity: Essays and Studies Presented to Professor M.J. O'Kelly*, ed. Donnchadh Ó Corráin, Four Courts Press, Dublin, 1981 (1994 reprint)

Clark, Aidan, *The Old English in Ireland, 1625-42*, Dublin, 2000.

Clark, J. C.D., review of *Nicholas Canny's Kingdom and Colony: Ireland in the Atlantic World, 1560-1800*, in *Irish Historical Studies*, vol. XXVI, no. 104, November 1989, pp. 412-413.

Claughton, Peter, and Paul Rondelez, "Early siver mining in western Europe: an Irish perspective", *Journal of the Mining Heritage Trust of Ireland*, 13, 2013, p. 5.

Clyne, Mirian, "Excavation at St. Mary's Cathedral, Tuam, Co. Galway", *JGAHS*, vol. 41, 1987/1988, pp. 90-103.

Clyne, Mirian, "A Medieval Pilgrim: From Tuam to Santiago de Compostela", *Archaeology Ireland*, vol. 4, no. 3, Autumn 1990, pp. 21-22.

Chapple, Robert M., *A Guide to St. Nicholas's Collegiate Church* Galway, 1996.

Chapple, Robert M., "Celts: art and identity | Some thoughts on an exhibition at the British Museum", 18 November 2015, published online at http://rmchapple.blogspot.ie/2015/11/celts-art-and-identity-some-thoughts-on.html

Charles-Edwards, T.M., *Early Christian Ireland*, Cambridge, 2000.

Chinea, Jorge L., "Irish Indentured Servants, Papists and Colonists in Spanish Colonial Puerto Rico, ca. 1650-1800", pp. 171-181, *Irish Migration Studies in Latin America, Vol. 5, no. 3*, November 2007.

Colfer, Billy, "Anglo-Norman Settlement in County Wexford", in *Wexford: History and Society*, ed. Kevin Whelan, 1987, pp. 65-101.

Colley, Linda, *Captives: Britain, Empire and the World 1600-1850*, London, 2002.

Collis, John, *The Celts: Origins, Myths, Inventions*, Stroud, 2003.

Collis, John, "To be, or not to be, a Celt: Does it really matter?", in Cooney et al (see below), eds., 2009, pp. 233-40.

Collis, John, "Redefining the Celts", in *Kelten am Rhein: Proceedings of the Thirteenth International Congress of Celtic Studies*, 23-27 July 2007, Bonn: Part 2, Philologie: Sprachen un Literaturen, 2010, pp. 33-43. .

Collis, John, "Taking the Celts out of Britain", 2013.

Connors, Thomas, "Religion and the laity in early modern Galway", in Moran and Gillespie, eds, 1996, pp. 131-148.

Comber, Michelle, "Trade and Communications Networks in Early Historic Ireland", *TJIA*, Vol. 10, 2001, pp. 73-92.

Comber, Michelle, *The Economy of the Ringfort and Contemporary Settlement in Early Medieval Ireland*, Oxford, BAR International Series 1773, 2008.

Connoll, Patricia, *The Irish College at Lisbon, 1590-1834*, Dublin, 2001.

Connolly, Philomena, "Irish material in the class of Chancery warrants series I (C81) in the Public Record Office,

London", *Analecta Hibernica* 36, 1995, pp. 135-161.

Connolly, Philomena, *Medieval record sources*, Dublin, 1998.

Connolly, S. J., *Contested Island: Ireland 1460-1630*, Oxford University Press, 2007 (paperback edition, 2009).

Convery, Dorothy, ed. and trans., "Archduke Ferdinand's visit to Kinsale in Ireland, an extract from Le Premier Voyage de Charles-Quint en Espagne, de 1517 a 1518" by Laurent Vital, http://www.ucc.ie/celt, 2012.

Cooney, Gabriel, and Eoin Grogan, Irish Prehistory: *A Social Perspective, 1994* (1999 reprint).

Cooney, Gabriel, Katarina Becker, John Coles, Michael Ryan, Susanne Sievers, eds., *Relics of Old Decency: Archaeological Studies in Later Prehistory*: A Festschrift for Barry Raftery, Dublin, 2009.

Corlett, Christiaan, "Rock Art on Drumcoggy Mountain, Co. Mayo", pp. 43-64, *JGAHS* vol. 51, 1999.

Cosgrove, Art, ed., *A New History of Ireland II: Medieval Ireland, 1169-1534*, Oxford, 1987 (2005 reprint)

Crawford, Jon G., *A Star Chamber Court in Ireland: The Courts of Castle Chamber, 1571-1641*, Dublin, 2005.

Crooks, Peter, "'Divide and Rule': Factionalism as Royal Policy in the Lordship of Ireland, 1171-1265", *Peritia* 19, 2005, pp. 263-307.

Crooks, Peter, ed. *Government, War and Society in medieval Ireland*: Essays by Edmund Curtis, A.J. Otway-Ruthven and James Lydon, Dublin, 2008.

Crooks, Peter, "Representation and Dissent: 'Parliamentarianism', and the Structure of Politics in Colonial Ireland, c. 1370-1420", *English Historical Review* vol. CXXV, no. 512, February 2010.

Crossle, Phillip, "Some records of the Skerrett family, *JGAHS* 25, pt. I, 1931-33, pp. 33-72.

Crouch, David, *William Marshal: Knighthood, War and Chivalry, 1147-1219*, London, 2002.

Cunningham, Bernadette, "Clanricard Letters", pp. 162-208, *JGAHS* vol. 48, 1996.

Cunningham, Bernadette, "A Galway Hearth Money Roll for 1724", *JGAHS* vol. 56, 2004.

Cunningham, Bernadette, "The Louvain achievement I: the Annals of the Four Masters", Bhreathnach, MacMahon, McCafferty, 2009, pp. 177-188.

Cunningham, Bernadette, "The Poor Clare Order in Ireland", Bhreathnach, MacMahon, McCafferty, 2009, pp. 159-176.

Cunningham, Bernadette, *The Annals of the Four Masters: Irish History, kingship and society in the early seventeenth century*, Dublin, 2010.

Cunningham, Bernadette, and Raymond Gillespie, "Manuscript cultures in early modern Mayo", in *Mayo: History and Society*, eds. Moran and Ó Muraíle, Dublin, 2014, pp. 183-205.

Curtis, Edmond, *A History of Medieval Ireland from 1086 to 1513*, 1923 (1978 reprint).

Curtis, Edmond, "The Pardon of Henry Blake of Galway in 1395", *JGAHS* vol. 16, 1934-35, pp. 186-189.

Curtis, Edmond, "Sheriff's Accounts for County Tipperary, 1275-6", *PRIA* 42 (section C), 1934-36, pp. 65-85.

Curtis, Edmond, "Feudal Charters of the De Burgo Lordship of Connacht", in *Féil-Sgríbhinn Eóin Mhic Néill*, ed. John Ryan, Dublin, 1940, pp. 286-95.

Daly, Aoife, "Determining the origin of ancient ships' timbers", in *Colloquium: To sea or not to sea - 2nd international colloquium on maritime and fluvial archaeology in the southern North Sea area, 21-23 September 2006* (eds. Pieters, Gevaert, Mees, Seys). VLIZ Special Publication 32, 2006, pp. 75-81.

de Azevedo, P., "Comercio anglo-portugues no meado do dec. xv", in *Academia das Scienias de Lisboa: Boletim de Segunda Classe*, 1913-14, viii.

de Blacam, Aodh, *Gaelic literature surveyed*, Dublin, 1929.

Defente, Virginie, "The Waldalgesheim Flagon and the Tara Brooch: some considerations of an iconographic tradition", in Cooney, Beker, et al, eds., 2009, pp. 287-290.

Dietler, Michael, "Celticism, Celtitude and Celticity: The consumption of the past in the age of globalization", in *Celtes et Gaulois, l'Archeologie face a l'Historie, I: Celtes et Gaulois dans l'historie, l'historie, l'historiographie et l'ideologie moderne, dir. Sabine Rieckhoff, Bibracte*, 2006, pp. 237-248.

Doherty, Charles, "A road well travelled: the terminology of roads in early Ireland", in *Clerics, Kings and Vikings: Eassays on Medieval Ireland in Honour of Donnchadh Ó Corráin*, Dublin, 2015, pp. 21-30.

Donovan-O'Sullivan, Maureen, *Old Galway: The History of a Norman Colony in Ireland*, Oxford, 1942 (facsimile reprint by Kennys Bookshops and Art Galleries, Galway, 1983).

Donovan-O'Sullivan, Maureen, "The Wives of Ulick, 1st Earl of Clanricarde", JGAHS, vol. 21, 1944-45, pp. 174-83,.

Donovan-O'Sullivan, Maureen, "Some Italian merchant bankers in Ireland in the late thirteenth century", RSAIJ, lxxix, 1949, pp. 10-19.

Donovan-O'Sullivan, Maureen, Italian Merchant bankers in Ireland in the thirteenth century, Dublin, 1962.

Douglas, Ken, The Downfall of the Spanish Armada in Ireland, Dublin, 2009.

Dowd, Marion, and Ruth F. Carden, "First evidence of a Late Upper Palaeolithic human presence in Ireland", in Quaternary Science Reviews 139, 2016, pp. 158-163.

Doyle, Aidan, A History of the Irish Language: From the Norman Invasion to Independence, Oxford, 2015.

Dryburgh, Paul, and Brendan Smith, eds., Handbook and Select Calendar of Sources for Medieval Ireland in the National Archives of the United Kingdom, Dublin, 2005.

Duffy, Patrick J., David Edwards, Elizabeth FitzPatrick, Gaelic Ireland c. 1250-c.1650: Land, Lordship, and Settlement, Dublin, 2001 (paperback edition 2004).

Duffy, Patrick J., David Edwards, Elizabeth FitzPatrick, "Introduction: Recovering Gaelic Ireland, c. 1250-c.1650", in Duffy et al, eds., 2001, pp. 21-76.

Duffy, Seán, Robert the Bruce's Irish Wars: The Invasions of Ireland 1306-1329, Stroud, 2002.

Duffy, Seán, "Gall", in The Encyclopedia of Ireland, Brian Lalor General Editor, Dublin 2003.

Duffy, Seán, Medieval Ireland: An Encyclopedia, New York and Abingdon, 2005.

Dunlevy, Mairead, Dress in Ireland, London, 1989.

Dwyer, Fin, "Food in Early Medieval reland", Irish Independent supplement Brian Boru and the Battle of Clontarf, Saturday 12 April 2014.

Ekins, Des, The Last Armada. Seige of 100 Days: Kinsale 1601, Dublin, 2014.

Ekins, Des, "The real battle of Kinsale: a three-way tussle of titanic egos", The Irish Times, Tuesday 10 February 2015.

Edwards, David, "Collabortion without Anglicisation: The MacGiollapadraig Lordship and Tudor Reform", in Duffy et al, eds., 2001, pp. 77-97.

Edwards, David, ed., Regions and Rulers in Ireland, 1100-1650: Essays for Kenneth Nicholls, Dublin, 2004.

Edwards, David, "Two fools and a martial law commissioner: cultural conflict at the Limerick assize of 1606", in Edwards, ed., 2004, pp. 237-65.

Edwards, David, "A haven of popery: English Catholic migration to Ireland in the age of plantations", in The Origins of Sectarianism in Early Modern Ireland, or Papists and Heretics: debates within and between the Churches of Ireland 1540-1660, eds. Alan Ford and John McCafferty, Cambridge, 2005, pp. 95-126.

Edwards, David, Pádraig Lenihan, Clodagh Tait, eds., Age of Atrocity: Violence and Political Conflict in Early Modern Ireland, Four Courts Press, Dublin, 2007 (2010 paperback edition).

Edwards, David "Some days two heads and some days four", History Ireland, January/February, 2009.

Edwards, David, "The escalation of violence in sixteenth-century Ireland", in Edwards et al, eds, 2007, pp. 34-78.

Fahey, Fergus, "Italian Echoes in the City of the Tribes: Pictorial Map of Galway City", History Ireland, vol. 21, no. 2, March/April 2013, pp. 18-19.

Fenning, Hugh, "Irish Dominicans at Lisbon before 1700: a Biographical Register", Collecteana Hibernica, vol. 42, 2000, pp. 27-65.

Fitzpatrick, Elizabeth, "Native Enclosed Settlement and the Problem of the Irish 'Ring-fort', Medieval Archaeology, 53, 2009, pp. 271-307.

Fitzpatrick, Elizabeth, Madeline O'Brien, Paul Walsh, eds., Archaeological Investigations in Galway City, 1987-1998, Bray, 2004.

Flanders, Steve, De Courcy: Anglo-Normans in Ireland, England and France in the eleventh and twelfth centuries, Dublin, 2008.

Flower, Robin, The Irish Tradition, Lilliput Press, Dublin, 1947 (1994 reprint).

Ford, P. K., "Ul na n-Ulad: Ethnicity and Identity in the Ulster Cycle", Emania 20, 2006, pp. 68-74.

Flanagan, Maire Therese, "The see of Canterbury and the Irish Church", in Irish Society, Anglo-Norman Settlers,

*Angevin Kingship: Interactions in Ireland in the late 12th Century*, Oxford, 1989, pp. 7-55 .

Flanagan, Maire Therese, "Irish kings who submitted to Henry II in 1171-1172", in *Irish Society, Anglo-Norman Settlers, Angevin Kingship: Interactions in Ireland in the late 12th Century*, Oxford, *1989* (1998 special edition), pp. 309-311.

Flannagan, Maire Therese, *Irish royal charters: text and contexts*, Oxford, 2005.

Flavin, Susan, and Evan T. Jones, eds., *Bristol's Trade with Ireland and the Continent 1503-1601: The evidence of the exchequer customs accounts*, 2009.

Flavin, Susan, "Consumption beyond The Pale: Ireland and the Widening World of Goods", 20 , pp.

Fleming, Peter, "Time, Space and Power in Later Medieval Bristol", University of the West of England Bristol, (http://eprints.uwe.ac.uk/22171/), 2013.

Flynn, John S., *Ballymacward: The Story of an East Galway Parish*, [Athlone?], 1991.

Foster, R. F., *Vivid Faces: The Revolutionary Generation in Ireland 1890-1923*, 2014.

Frame, Robin, *Colonial Ireland, 1169-1369*, Dublin, 1981.

Fraser, James E., "From Ancient Scythia to *The Problem of the Picts*", *Pictish Progress: New Studies in Northern Britain in the Middle Ages*, eds. Stephen T. Driscoll, Jane Geddes, Mark A. Hall, 20, pp. 15-45.

Frehan, Pádraic, *Education and Celtic Myth: National Self-Image and Schoolbooks in 20th Century Ireland*, Amsterdam and New York, 2012.

Gallagher, Niav, "The emergence of national identity among the religious of Britain", *The English Isles: Cultral transmission and political conflict in Britain and Ireland 1100-1500*, eds. Duffy and Foran, 2013, pp. 103-117.

Galenson, David W., "The Rise and Fall of Indentured Servitude in the Americas: An economic Analysis", *The Journal of Economic History*, Vol. 44, No. 1, March 1984, pp. 1-26.

Geissel, Hermann, *A Road on the Long Ridge: In Search of the Ancient Highway on the Esker Riada*, Naas, 2006.

Gernon, Luke, *A Discourse of Ireland, anno 1620* (see online sources)

Gibney, John, *The Shadow of a Year: The 1641 Rebellion in Irish History and Memory*, Wisconsin, 2013.

Gibson, Carrie, *Empire's Crossroads: A New History of the Caribbean*, London, 2014.

Gilbert, J. T., *History of the Irish Confederation and the War in Ireland 1641-9*, Dublin, vol. III , 1885.

Gillespie, Raymond, "Peter French's petition for an Irish mint, 1619", *Irish Historical Studies*, xxv, no. 100, November 1987, pp. 413-420.

Gillespie, Raymond, and Gerard Moran, eds., *Galway: History and Society*, Dublin, 1996.

Gillingham, John, "Christian Warriors and the Enslavement of Fellow Christians", in *Chevalerie et Christianisme*, ed. M. Aurell and C. Girbea, Rennes, 2011.

Gillingham, John, "Women, children and the profits of war", *Gender and Historgraphy: Studies in the earlier Middle Ages in Honour of Pauline Stafford*, eds. Janet L. Nelson, Susan Reynolds, Susan M. Johns, London, 2012, pp. 61-74.

Graham-Campbell, J., and M. Ryan, "Anglo-Saxon/Irish relations before the Vikings", J. Graham-Campbell and M. Ryan, *Proceedings of the British Academy*, 157, 2009.

Grimmer, Martin, "Columban Christian influence in Northumbria, before and after Whitby", *Journal of the Australian Early Medieval Society*, vol. 4, 2008, pp. 99-123.

Guinness, Patrick, *Arthur's Round: The Life and Times of Brewing Legend Arthur Guinness*, London, 2008.

Gwynn, Aubrey, "Early Irish Emigration to the West Indies (1612-1643), *Studies* 18, 1929, pp. 377-398.

Gwynn, Aubrey, "Documents relating to the Irish in the West Indies", *Analecta Hibernica* 4, October 1932, pp. 139-286.

Gwynn, Aubrey, "The first Irish Priests in the New World", *Studies* 21, 1932, pp. 213-228.

H., A., "The 'Irish kilt', *The Irish Sword*, Note II, volume 7, pp. 236-237.

Hall, Dianne, "Women and violence in late medieval Ireland", in *Studies on Medieval and Early Modern Women: Pawns or Players?*, eds. Christine Meek and Catherine Lawless, Dublin, 2003, pp. 131-140.

Hammond, P. W., and Anne F. Sutton, *Richard III: The road to Bosworth Field*, London, 1985.

Handler, Jerome S., and Lon Shelby, "A Seventeenth Century Commentary on Labor and Military Problems in Barbados", *Journal of the BMHS*, vol. 34, 1973, pp. 117-121.

Handler, Jerome S., and Matthew C. Reilly, "Father Antoine Biet's Account Revisited: Irish Catholics in Mid-Seventeenth-Century Barbados", in in *Caribbean Irish Connections: Interdisciplinary Perspectives*, Alison Donnell, Maria

McGarrity, Evelyn O'Callaghan, eds., Jamaica, 2015, pp. 33-46.

Handler, Jerome S. "Custom and law: The status of enslaved Africans in seventeenth-century Barbados", in *Slavery & Abolition: A Journal of Slave and Post-Slave Studies*, 2016, pp. 1-23.

Hanks, Patrick, and Flavia Hodges, *A Dictionary of Surnames*, New York, 1988 (1999 reprint).

Hardiman, James, *History of Galway*, Dublin, 1820 (facsimile reprint by Connacht Tribune Ltd., Galway, 1984).

Harris, Amy Louise, and Jon Bayliss, "An Unusual memento from 16th Century Galway", JGAHS vol. 53, 2001, pp. 120-126.

Hart, Emma, review of *Ireland in the Virginian Sea: Colonialism in the British Atlantic* (University of North Carolina Press, 2013),

Hartland, Beth, "The Liberties of Ireland in the Reign of Edward I", in *Liberties and Identities in Later medieval Britain: Regions and Regionalism in History 10*, Boydell and Brewer, 2008, pp. 200-216.

Hartland, Beth, "The Household knights of Edward I in Ireland", *Historical Research*, vol. 77, no. 196, May 2004, pp. 161-177.

Hartland, Beth, "English Lords in Late Thirteenth and Early Fourteenth Century Ireland: Roger Bigod and the de Clare lords of Thomond", *English Historical Review*, Vol. CXXII, no. 496, Oxford, 2007, pp. 318-348.

Hartnett, Alexandra, "The port of Galway: infrastructure, trade and commodities" in FitzPatrick et al, 2004, p. 307.

Henry, William, *Role of Honour: The Mayors of Galway City, 1485-2001*, Galway, 2001.

Henry, William, and Jacqueline O'Brien,, *Galway's Great War memorial Book 1914-1918*, 2007.

Herity, Michael, ed., *Ordnance Survey Letters Galway*, FourMasters Press, Dublin, 2009.

Herriott, Conn, *The Numinous Aquatic: water cult and society in Irish prehistory*, MA dissertation, University of Bristol, September 2005.

Hewer, Stephen, "Free Gaelic people in English Ireland, c. 1250-c.1327, *History Ireland*, November/December 2015, vol. 23, no. 6, pp. 14-17.

Hickey, Kieran, *Wolves in Ireland: A natural and cultural history*, Dublin, 2011.

Higgins, Jim, and Susan Heringlkee, eds., *Monuments of St. Nicholas's Collegiate Church, Galway: A Historical, Genealogical and Archaeological Record*, Galway, 1991.

Hill, J.D., "Re-thinking the Iron Age", *Scottish Archaeology Review*, vol. 1989, pp. 16-24.

Hoare, Kieran, "The Evolution of Urban Oligarchies in Irish Towns, 1350-1534", in *Frontiers and identities: cities in regions and nations, ed. Lud'a Klusakova and Laure Teulieres*, Pisa, 2008, pp. 87-107.

Hoare, Kieran "From Region to Nation: the Development of Irish Nationalist Historiography, 1880-1920", in *Frontiers, regions and identities in Europe*, eds. Steven G. Ellis and Raingard Eber with Jean-Francois Berdah and Milos Reznik, Pisa, 2009, pp. 205-221.

Hoare, Phillip Herbert, *History of the Town and County of Wexford*, volume 3, 1901; vol. 5, 1906.

Hogan, Arlene, *The Priory of Llanthony Prima and Secunda in Ireland: Lands, Patronage and Politics*, Dublin, 2008.

Hogan, Liam, "The Myth of 'Irish Slaves' in the Colonies: confusion, conflation", published online November 2014.

Hogan, Liam, Laura McAtackney, Matthew C. Reilly, "The Irish in the Anglo-caribbean: servants or slaves? Why we need to confront the 'Irish slave' myth and how terminology is not simply semantics", *History Ireland*, volume 24, no. 2, March/April 2016, pp. 18-22.

Holland, Patrick, "The Anglo-Norman landscape in County Galway, Land-Holdings, Castles and Settlements", JGAHS vol. 49, 1997, pp. 159-193.

Holm, Poul, "The Slave Trade of Dublin, Ninth to Twelfth Centuries", *Peritia* 5, 1986, pp. 317-345.

Holm, Poul, "SLAVES", in *Medieval Ireland: An Encyclopedia*, ed. Duffy, 2005, pp. 430-431.

Howe, Stephen, *Empire: A Very Short Introduction*, Oxford, 2002.

Hudson, Benjamin, *Irish Sea Studies 900-1200*, Dublin, 2006.

Hughes, Sam, ""In my sword I trust". A Reeassessment of Irish Iron Age Swords With a Focus on Their Potential Use in Battle", *International Journal of Student Research in Archaeology*, March 2016, vol. 1, no., pp. 159-177.

Hynes, John, "Lynch's Castle, Galway", JGAHS 16, 1934-35, pp. 144-54.

Issac, Graham, "A note on the name of Ireland in Irish and Welsh", *Ériu* 59, 2009, pp. 49-55.

James, Simon, *The Atlantic Celts: Ancient People or Modern Invention?*, 1999.

Jarman, A.O. H., "Wales and the Council of Constance, *BBCS* 14, 1950-52, pp. 220-222.

Jaski, Bart, "The Vikings and the Kingship of Tara", *Peritia* 9, 1995, pp. 310-351.

Jaski, Bart, "Kings over Overkings: Propaganda for Pre-eminence in Early Medieval Ireland", in *The Propagation of power in the medieval west*, eds. M. Gosman, A. Vanderjagt, J. Veenstra, Groningen, 1996, pp. 163-176.

Jaski, Bart, Early Irish Kingship and Succession, Dublin, 2000.

Jaski, Bart, "King and House hold in Early Medieval Ireland", in *Familia and household in the medieval Atlantic Province*, ed. Benjamin T. Hudson, 2011, pp. 89-122.

Jaski, Bart, "Medieval Irish genealogies and genetics", in *Princes, Prelates, and Poets in Medieval Ireland: Essays in Honour of Katharine Simms*, Seán Duffy, ed., Four Courts Press, 2013, pp. 3-17.

Jaski, Bart, "Genealogical tables of medieval Irish royal dynasties" (PDF published online, 31 July 2013)

Jenkins, Phillip, "Maurice, son of Theodoric: Welsh Kings and the Mediterranean World, AD 550-650", *North American Journal of Welsh Studies*, vol. 8, 2013.

Jezierski, Wojtek, "Aethelweardus redivius", in *Early Medieval Europe 2005*, 13 (2), eds. Julia Crick, Catherine Cubitt, Paul Fouracre, Helena Hamerow, Sarah Hamilton, Matthew Innes, Sanuta Shanzer, pp. 159-178.

Johnson, Elva, "Early Irish History: The State of the Art", *IHS*, vol. 33, no. 131, May 2003, pp. 342-348.

Johnson, Penny, *A regional study of Irish early medieval archaeobotanical remains: a case study from Galway*, Royal Irish Academy Archaeological Research Grant, 2013.

Jordan, William Chester, The Great Famine: *Northern Europe in the Early fourteenth Century*, Princeton, 1996.

Kearney, H.F., "The Irish wine trade, 1614-15", *Irish Historical Studies* Vol. IX, No. 36, September 1955.

Kearney, Hugh, *The British Isles: A History of Four Nations*, Cambridge, 1989 (2000 reprint).

Kelly, Eamonn, "The Vikings in Connemara", in *Ireland and the West*, John Sheehan and Donnchadh Ó Corráin, eds, Dublin, 2010, p. 174-187.

Kelly, Maria, *A History of the Black Death in Ireland*, Stroud, 2001 (2004 reprint).

Kelly, Morgan, and Cormac Ó Gráda, "The economic impact of the little ice age", UCD Centre for Economic Research Working Papers Series; WP 10 14 (http://www.ucd.ie/t4cms/wp10_14.pdf) , 16 April 2010.

Kennedy, Liam, *Unhappy the Land: The Most Oppressed People Ever, the Irish?*, Sallins, Co. Kildare, 2016.

Kenny, Gillian, "The power of dower: the importance of dower in the lives of medieval women in Ireland", in Christine Meek and Catherine Lawless, eds., *Studies on Medieval and Early Modern Women: Pawns or Players?*, Dublin, 2003, pp. 59-74.

Kenny, Gillian, *Anglo-Irish and Gaelic Women in Ireland, c. 1170-1540*, Dublin, 2007.

Kinsella, Thomas, *The Táin*, Oxford, 1969.

Knox, Hubert Thomas, *The History of the County of Mayo to the close of the Sixteenth Century*, Dublin, 1908.

Knox, H[ubert]. T[homas]., "Notes on the early history of the dioceses of Tuam, Killala, and Achonry", 1904.

Knox, H[ubert]. T[homas]., "Ardrahan Castle", *JGAHS*, Part II, vol. VII, 1911-12, pp. 73-83.

Koch, John T., "*Ériu, Alba, and Letha*: When was a Language Ancestral to Gaelic First Spoken in Ireland?", *Emania* 9, 1991, pp. 17-27.

Koch, John T., "Celts, Britons, and Gaels – Names, Peoples, and Identities", *Transactions of the Honourable Society of Cymmrodorian*, NS, 2003.

Kowaleski, Mary Anne, "'Alien' Encounters in the Maritime World of Medieval England", *Medieval Encounters*, vol. 13:1, 2007, pp. 96-121.

Larn, Bridget Teresa and Richard, *Shipwreck Index of Ireland*, Surrey, 2002.

Latvio, Riitta, "Status and Exchange in Early Irish Laws", *Studia Celtica Fennica* II, 2005, pp. 67-96.

Leggett, Samantha, "Celticity: Migration or Fashion?", *Vexillum: The Undergraduate Journal of Classical and Medieval Studies*, vol. 2, 2011.

Lennon, Colm, "Richard Stanihurst (1547-1618) and Old English identity", *Irish Historical Studies*, vol. XXI, no. 82, September 1978, pp. 121-144.

Lennon, Colm, *Sixteenth-Century Ireland: The Incomplete Conquest*, 1994 (revised edition, 2005).

Leerson, Joep, Mere Irish and Fior-Ghael: *Studies in the Idea of Irish Nationality, its Development and literary Expression prior to the Nineteenth Century*, Cork, 1986.

Lewis, Stephen, "The Cumbrian Antigones", http://thewildpeak.wordpress.com/ September 2014

Loeber, Rolf, "An Architectural History of Gaelic Castles and Settlements 1370-1600", Duffy et al, eds, 2001, pp. 271-314.

Lucas, Henry S., "The Great European Famine of 1315-17", *Speculum* 5:4, 1930, pp. 343-77.

Lydon, James, *The Lordship of Ireland in the Middle Ages*, Dublin, 1972 (2003 reprint).

Lydon, James, ed., *The English in Medieval Ireland*, Dublin, 1984.

Lydon, James, ed., *Law and Disorder in Thirteenth-Century Ireland: The Dublin Parliament of 1297*, Dublin, 1997.

Lynch, Ronan, *The Kirwans of Castlehacket, Co. Galway: History, folklore and mythology in an Irish horseracing family*, Dublin, 2006.

Lydon, James, "Ireland corporate of itself", *History Ireland*, vol. 3, issue 2, Summer 1995.

Lyons, Mary Ann, "Emergence of an Irish community in Saint-Malo 1550-1710", in O'Connor, ed., 2001, pp. 107-126.

Lyons, Mary Ann, "Lay female piety and church patronage in late medieval Ireland", *Christianity in Ireland: Revisiting the Story*, ed. Brendan Bradshaw and Dáire Keogh, The Columba Press, Dublin, 2002, pp. 57-75.

Lyons, Mary Ann, "The Wives of Hugh O Neill, Second Earl of Tyrone", *Dúiche Néill*, no. 16, 2007, pp. 41-61.

MacCarthy, Anne, "The Image of Ireland in Iberian Galicia in the Early Twentieth Century", *CLCWeb: Comparative Literature and Culture* vol. 13, issue 5, 2011, <http://sx.doi.org/10.7771/1481-4374.1914>

McCarthy, William J.,"Gambling on Empire: The Economic Role of Shipwreck in the Age of Discovery", in *International Journal of Maritime History*, XXII, No. 2, December 2011, pp. 69-84.

MacCotter, Paul, *Medieval Ireland: Territorial, Political and Economic Divisions*, Dublin, 2008.

MacCotter, Paul, "The Prendergast alias MacMaurice lineage of Clanmaurice barony, Co. Mayo", *The Irish Genealogist*, 2008, pp. 292-311.

Mac Eoin, Gearóid, "What Language was Spoken in Ireland before Irish?", in *The Celtic Languages in Contact*, ed. H. L. C. Tristram, Potsdam University Press, 2007, pp. 113-25.

McDonough, Ciaran, "'Death and Renewal': Translating Old Irish Texts in Nineteenth-Century Ireland", *Studi irlandesi*, n4, 2014, pp. 101-111.

Mac Eiteagáin, Darren, "The Renaissance and the Late Medieval Lordship of Tír Chonaill 1461-1555", in *Donegal:History and Society*, 1995, pp. 203-28.

McEvoy, Brian, Martin Richards, Peter Forster, Daniel G. Bradley, "The *longue duree of genetic ancestry*: multiple genetic marker systems and Celtic origins on the atlantic facade of Europe", *American Journal of Human Genetics* 75, 2004, pp. 693-702.

McEvoy, Brian P., and Daniel G. Bradley, "Irish genetics and Celts", *Celtic from the West: alternative perspectives from archaeology, genetics and literature*, Barry Cunliffe and John T. Koch, eds., Oxford, 2010, pp. 107-30.

Mac Giolla Easpaig, Donall, "Early Eccleiastical Settlement Names of County Galway", in *Galway: History and Society*, Moran and Gillespie, eds, 1996, pp. 795-816.

McGinn, Brian, "The Irish in the Caribbean", in *The Encyclopaedia of Ireland*, Dublin, 2003, pp. 157-58.

McGrath, Bríd, "Ireland and the third university: attendance at the inns of court, 1603-1649," Edwards, ed., 2004, pp. 217-36.

McGurk, John, *The Elizabethan conquest of Ireland: The 1590s crisis*, Manchester and New York, 1997.

McGurk, John, *Sir Henry Docwra, 1564-1631: Derry's Second Founder*, Four Courts Press, Dublin, 2006.

McKenna, Patrick, "Irish migration to Argentina", in *The Irish World Wide - History, Heritage, Identity: Volume 1 Patterns of Migration*, London, 1992 (paperback, 1997), pp. 63-83.

McKeon, Jim, "St Nicholas's parish church, Galway: structural and architectural evidence for the high medieval period", *The Journal of Irish Archaeology*, vol. 18, 2009, pp. 95-113.

MacLysaght, Edward, *The Surnames of Ireland*, Dublin, 1978.

McManus, Antonia, *The Irish Hedge School and Its Books, 1695-1831*, Dublin, 2004.

McManus, Damian, *A Guide to Ogam*, Maynooth, 1991 (1996 reprint).

McManus, Damian, and Eoghan Ó Raghallaigh, A Bardic Miscellany: Five Hundred Bardic poems from manuscripts in Irish and British libraries, 2010.

McNeill, Thomas E., "Archaeology of Gaelic Lordship East and West of Foyle", Duffy et al, eds., 2001, pp. 346-356.

MacNeill, Eoin, Early Irish Population-Groups:Their Nomenclature, Classification, and Chronology, Dublin, 1911.

MacNeill, Eoin, Phases of Irish History, Dublin, 1919.

Mac Niocaill, Gearóid, Na Buigéisí IIXVX anois, two volumes, Dublin, 1964.

Mac Niocaill, Gearóid, Ireland Before the Vikings, Gill and Mac Millan, Dublin, 1972.

Mac Niocaill, Gearóid, "The Irish 'charters'", in The Book of Kells: commentary, ed. P. Fox, Luzern, 1990, pp. 153-166.

Melvin, Patrick, Estates and Landed Society in Galway, Dublin, 2012.

Maginn, Christopher, "Gaelic Ireland's English frontiers in the late Middle Ages", PRIA, vol. 110C, 2010, pp. 173-190.

Mallory, J.P., The Origins of the Irish, London, 2013.

Mallory, J.P., In Search of the Irish Dreamtime, London, 2016.

Mannion, Joseph, The Life, Legends and Legacy of Saint Kerrill: A Fifth-Century Galway Evangelist, Athlone, 2004.

Marsden, John, Galloglas: Hebridean and West Highland Mercenary Warrior Kindreds in Medieval Ireland, 2009.

Martin, F.X., "'Obstinate' Skerrett, Missionary in Virgina, the West Indies and England", JGAHS 35, 1976, pp. 12-51.

Martyn, Adrian, "Extracts from the Book of Dead Names", JGSI, vol. 5, no. 4, Winter 2004, pp. 194-106.

Martyn, Adrian, "The Martyn 'Tribe' of Galway", JGSI, vol. 6 no. 1, Spring 2005, pp. 15-19.

Melia, Daniel F., "Global Positioning in Medieval Ireland: Narrative, Onomastics, Genealogy", 2000.

Melvin, Patrick, "The Galway Tribes as Landowners and Gentry", Moran and Gillespie, eds., 1996, pp. 319-374.

Meyer, Kuno, "Die Herkunft der Partraige", Zeitschrift für Celtische Philologie 8, Halle/Saale, Max Niemeyer, 1912.

Meyer, Kuno, "Verschiedenes aus Egerton 1782 (Mitteilungen aus irischen Handschriften)", Zeitschrift für Celtische Philologie 9, Halle/Saale, Max Niemeyer, 1913, pp. 176-77.

Miles, Dillwyn, The Lords of Cemais, Haverfordwest, 1997.

Miles, Dillwyn, A Book on Nevern, Llandysul, 1998

Millett, Benignus, O.F.M., "Catalogue of Volume 294 of the Scritture originali riferite nelle congregazioni generali in Propaganda Archives", Collectanea Hibernica no. 8, 1965, pp. 7-37.

Millett, Benignus, O.F.M., "Catalogue of Irish material in fourteen volumes of the Scritture originali riferite nelle congregazionii generali in Propaganda Archives, Collectanea Hibernica, 1968.

Moody, T.W., F.X. Martin, F.J. Byrne, eds., A New History of Ireland III: Early Modern Ireland 1534-1691, Oxford, 1976 (2005 reprint).

Moody, T.W., F.X. Martin, F.J. Byrne, eds., A New History of Ireland VIII: A Chronology of Irish History to 1976. A Companion to Irish History Part I, Oxford, 1982 (2002 reprint).

Moody, T.W., Martin, F.X., Byrne, F.J., eds., A New History of Ireland IX: Maps, Genealogies, Lists. A Companion to Irish History, Part II, Oxford, 1984 (2002 reprint).

Moran, Gerard, and Raymond Gillespie, Galway:History and Society. Interdisciplinary Essays on the History of an Irish County, Dublin, 1996.

Moran, Pádraic, "Greek Dialects and Irish Identity in the Early Middle Ages", in Early Medieval Ireland and Europe: Chronology, Contacts, Scholarship, Pádraic Moran and Immo Warntjes, eds., Turhout, 2014, pp. 481-512.

Morgan, Hiram, ed., The Battle of Kinsale, Bray, 2004.

Morgan, Hiram, "Disaster at Kinsale", in Morgan, ed., 2004.

Morgan, Hiram, "'Slán Dé fút go hoíche': Hugh O'Neill's murders", in Edwards et al, eds., Dublin, 2007, pp. 95-118.

Morgan, Hiram, "The Establishment of the Irish-Spanish relationship", in Los Irlandeses y la Monarquia Hispanica (1529-1800): vinculos in espacio y tiempo, Eduardo Peduelo Martin and Julia Rodriguez de Diego, eds., Madrid, 2013.

Mullen, Stephen, "The myth of Scottish slaves", March 4, 2016,

Mulligan, Paul, *A Short Guide to Irish Antiquities: Sites shown on Discovery Series Ordnance Survey maps*, 2005.

Mulveen, Jack, "Galway Goldsmiths, Their Marks and Ware", *JGAHS* 46, 1994, pp. 43-65.

Murphy, Margaret, "Parliament" in Duffy, ed., 2005, p. 366.

Murphy, Margaret, "The Archdeacon's Tale", in *Tales of Medieval Dublin*, Sparky Booker and Cherie N. Peters, eds., Dublin, 2014, pp. 83-91.

Murphy, Nathan W., "Origins of Colonial Chesapeake Indentured Servants: American and English Sources", *National Genealogical Society Quarterly*, Vol. 93, No. 1, March 2005, pp. 5-24.

Naessens, Paul, "Gaelic lords of the sea; the coastal tower houses of south Connemara", in *Lordship in Medieval Ireland*, 2007, pp. 217-35.

Naessens, Paul, and Kieran O'Conor, "Pre-Norman fortification in eleventh- and twelfth-century Connacht", *Château Gaillard* 25, p. X-Y, Publications du CRAHM, 2012, pp. 113-22.

Newton, Michael, review of James P. Cantrell's *How Celtic Culture Invented Southern Literature*, e-Keltoi 1, 2006.

Ní Mhaonaigh, Máire, Nósa Ua Maine: Fact or Fiction?", in *The Welsh King and his Court: essays in memory of Glanville R. J. Jones*, ed. T. M. Charles-Edwards, Morfydd E. Owen, and Paul Russell, Cardiff, 2000, pp. 362-381.

Nicholls, Kenneth, *Gaelic and Gaelicised Ireland in the Middle Ages*, Dublin, 1972 (reprinted 2003)

Nicholls, Kenneth, "Gaelic society and economy", Chapter XIV, *NHI II*, 1987, pp. 397-438.

Nicholls, Kenneth, "Woodland Cover in pre-Modern Ireland", in Duffy et al, eds., 2001.

Nolan, John Philip, "Galway castles and owners in 1574", *JGAHS*, vol. I, 1901, pp. 109-23.

Ó Cathasaigh, Tomás, "The First Anders Ahlqvist Lecture – Irish Myths and Legends", in *Studia Celtica Fennica II: Essays in Honour of Anders Ahlqvist*, Helsinki, 2005, pp. 11-26.

Ó Cearbhaill, Diarmuid, ed., *Galway: Town and Gown 1484-1984*, Dublin, 1984.

Ó Corráin, Donnchadh, "Nationality and kingship in pre-Norman Ireland", in *Nationality and the pursuit of national independence: Historical Studies*, XI, ed. T.W. Moody, Belfast, 1978, pp. 1-35.

Ó Corráin, Donnchadh, "What Happened Ireland's Medieval Manuscripts?", *Peritia* 22-23, 2011-12, pp. 191-223.

Ó Cróinín, Dáibhí, *Early Medieval Ireland 400-1200*, London and New York, 1995.

Ó Cróinín, Dáibhí, *The First Century of Anglo-Irish Relations* (AD 600-700), 2004.

Ó Cróinín, Dáibhí, ed., *A New History of Ireland I: Prehistoric and Early Ireland*, Oxford, 2005.

Ó Cuív, Brian, *Aspects of Irish Personal Names*, Dublin, 1986.

Ó Dálaigh, Art, "Flight, departure, or escape of the Earls", *Dúiche Néill*, no. 16, 2007, pp. 13-40.

Ó Donnchadha, Gearóid, *St Brendan of Kerry, the Navigator: His Life and Voyages*, Dublin, 2004.

Ó Donnabháin, Bárra, "An appalling vista? The Celts and the archaeology of late prehistoric Ireland", in *New Agendas in Irish Prehistory: Papers presented in memory of Liz Anderson*, Desmond et al, eds., 2000, pp. 189-196.

Ó Flaithbheartaigh, Ruaidrí [O'Flaherty, Roderick], *Iar Connought*, 1684; James Hardiman, ed., Dublin, 1846.

Ó Floinn, Raghnall, *Franciscan Faith: Sacred Art in Ireland, AD 1600-1750*, National Museum of Ireland Monograph Series 5, Dublin, 2011.

Ó hAnnracháin, Tadhg, "Theory in the absence of fact: Irish women and the Catholic Reformation", in Meek and Lawless, eds., Dublin, 2003, pp. 141-154.

Ó Máille, Tomás, "Ainm na Gaillimhe", *Galvia* I, 1954, pp. 26-31.

Ó Máille, Tomás, "Áitainmneacha na Gaillimhe", in Ó Cearbhaill, ed., 1984, pp. 51-62.

Ó Muraíle, Nollaig, "An Outline History of Co. Mayo", in *Mayo: Aspects of its Heritage*, ed. Bernard O'Hara, Galway, 1982, pp. 10-36.

Ó Muraíle, Nollaig, *The celebrated antiquary, Dubhaltach Mac Fhirbhisigh (c.1600-c.1671): his lineage, life and learning*, Maynooth, 1996.

Ó Muraíle, Nollaig, "Aspects of the Intellectual Life of Seventeenth Century Galway", in Moran and Gillespie, eds., 1996, pp. 176-82.

Ó Muraíle, Nollaig, "Some early Connacht population groups", in *Seanchas: Studies in Early and Medieval Irish Archaeology, History and Literature in Honour of Francis J. Byrne*, ed. Alfred P. Smith, Dublin, 2000, pp. 161-177.

Ó Muraíle, Nollaig, "Settlement and Place-names", in Duffy et al, eds., 2001, pp. 223-245.

Ó Muraíle, Nollaig, "Temair/Tara and Other Places of the Name", in *The Kingship and Landscape of Tara*, edited by

Edel Bhreathnach, Dublin, 2005, pp. 449-77.

Ó Muraíle, Nollaig,"Dubhaltach Mac Fhirbhisigh and County Mayo", *JGAHS* vol. 58, 2006, pp. 1-21.

Ó Muraíle, Nollaig, ed., *Turas na dTaoiseach nUltach as Éirinn: From Ráth Maoláin to Rome. Tadhg Ó Ciánáin's contemporary narrative of the journey into exile of the Ulster chieftains and their followers, 1607-8 (The so-called 'Flight of the Earls')*, Rome, 2007.

Ó Néill, Eoin, "Towards a new interpretation of the Nine Years' War", *The Irish Sword*, Vol. XXVI, number 105, Summer 2009, pp. 241-262.

Ó Néill, Eoin, "The Nine Years' War 1594-1603", in the "Encyclopedia of War", 2012.

Ó Néill, Eoin, "Atrocities in Ireland (16th-17th centuries), in "Encyclopedia of Atrocities", 2013.

Ó Riain-Raedel, Dagmar, ed. and trans., "A German visitor to Monaincha in 1591", *Tipperary Historical Journal*, 1998, pp. 223-233. Reproduced online 2012, http://www.ucc.ie/celt

Ó Riain, Pádraig , Diarmuid Ó Murchadha, Kevin Murray, eag., *Historical Dictionary of Gaelic Placenames:Fascicle 1 (Names in A-/Foclóir Stairiúil Áitainmneachna na Gaeilge: Fascúl 1 (Ainmneacha in A-)*, Irish Texts Society/Cumann na Scríbheann nGaedhilge , Dublin, 2003.

Ó Riain, Pádraig, *A Dictionary of Irish Saints*, Dublin, 2011.

Ó Siochrú, Micheál, *Confederate Ireland, 1642-1649: A Constitutional and Political Analysis*, Dublin, 1999.

Ó Siochrú, Micheál, ed., *Kingdoms in Crisis: Ireland in the 1640s. Essays in honour of Dónal Cregan*, Dublin, 2001.

Ó Siochrú, Micheál, *God's Executioner: Oliver Cromwell and the Conquest of Ireland*, London, 2008.

Ó Tuathaigh, M.A.G[earóid]., ed., *Community, Culture and Conflict: Aspects of the Irish Experience*, Galway, 1986.

O'Brien, David, "The Féni", *Éiru* vol. XI, 1932, pp. 182-83.

O'Brien, William, *Iverni: a prehistory of Cork*, The Collins Press, Cork, 2012.

O'Brien, Niall C.E.J., "Walter Jorz, Archbishop of Armagh", published online 8 July 2014.

O'Byrne, Emmett, *War, Politics and the Irish of Leinster, 1156-1606*, Dublin, 2003.

O'Connell, Jeff, ed., "A manuscript history of the Kirwan family", *Galway Advertiser*, 8 and 15January 1998.

O'Connell, Patricia, *The Irish College at Lisbon, 1590-1834*, Dublin, 2001.

O'Connell, Patricia, *Irish Students at the University of Evora 1618-1719*, Seachas Ard Macha, vo. 20, no. 1, 2004.

O'Connor, Thomas, ed., *The Irish in Europe, 1580-1815*, Dublin, 2001.

O'Connor, Thomas, "Hugh O'Neill: free spirit, religious chameleon or ardent Catholic?", in Morgan, 2004, pp. 59-72.

O'Donovan, John, "The annals of Ireland, from the year 1443 to 1468, translated by Dudley Firbisse ... in the year 1666", *Miscelleny of the Irish Archaeological Society, i*, 1846, p. 249.

O'Donovan, John, *Origin and Meanings of Irish Family Names*, ed. G[eorge]. H. O'Reilly, Genealogical Society of Ireland, Dublin, 2003.

O'Dowd, Peadar, *Old and New Galway*, Galway, 1985.

O'Dowd, Peadar, *Down by the Claddagh*, Galway, 1993.

O'Keeffe, Tadhg, "The Fortifications of Western Ireland, AD 1100-1300, and Their Interpretation", *JGAHS*, vol. 50, 1998, pp. 184-200.

O'Malley, Liam, "Patrick Darcy, Galway Lawyer and Politician, 1598-1668", in Ó Cearbhaill, ed., 1984, pp. 90-109.

O'Malley, Gregory, "Slave Trading Entrepôts and their Hinterlands: Continued Forced Migrations after the Middle Passage to North America", in *Ambiguous Anniversary: The Bicentennial of the International Slave Trade Bans*, David T. Gleeson and Simon Lewis, eds., South Carolina, 2012, pp. 99-124.

O'Neill, Timothy, *Merchants and Mariners in Medieval Ireland*, Bury St. Edmunds, 1987.

O'Neill, Timothy, "A fifteenth-century entrepreneur: Germyn Lynch", John Bradley, ed., 1988, pp. 421-28.

O'Rahilly, T.F., *Early Irish History and Mythology*, Dublin, 1946 (1999 reprint).

O'Sullivan, Aidan, *Crannogs: Lake-dwellings of early Ireland*, The Irish Treasure Series, 2000.

O'Sullivan, Aidan, and Colin Breen, *Maritime Ireland:An Archaeology of Coastal Communities*, Tempus, 2007.

O'Sullivan, Aidan, Finbar McCormick, Lorcan Harney, Jonathan Kinsella, Thomas Kerr, *Early Medieval Dwellings and Settlements in Ireland, AD 400-1100, Vol. I: Text*, INSTAR programme 2010.

O'Sullivan, Aidan, and Tríona Nicholl, "Early medieval settlement enclosures in Ireland: dwellings, daily life and social identity", *PRIA* Vol. 111C, 2010, pp. 59-90.

O'Sullivan, Aidan, Finbar McCormick, Thomas R. Kerr, Lorcan Harney, eds, *Early Medieval Ireland AD 400-1100:The Evidence from Archaeological Excavations*, Royal Irish Academy, Dublin, 2014.

O'Riordan, Thomas, "The Introduction of the Potato into Ireland", *History Ireland*, Spring 2001, issue 1, vol. 9.

Oranmore and Browne, Lord, "Pedigree of the Brownes of Castle MacGarrett", JGAHS vol. 5, 1907-08, part one, pp. 48-59; pp. 165-77, pp. 165-77, JGAHS vol. 5, 1907-08, part two; pp. 227-38, JGAHS vol. 5, 1907-08, part three.

Orpen, G. H., *Ireland under the Normans, 1169-1333*, four volumes, Oxford, 1911-20

Otway-Ruthven, A.J., *A History of Medieval Ireland*, New York, 1968 (reprinted 1980).

Paine, Lincoln, *The Sea and Civilization: A Maritime History of the World*, New York, 2013.

Patterson, Nerys, *Cattle Lords and Clansmen: The Social Structure of Early Ireland*, Notre Dame, Indiana, 1994.

Picard, Jean-Michael, "The French language in medieval Ireland", in The Languages of Ireland", ed. Michael Cronin and Cormac Ó Cuilleanáin, Four Courts Press, Dublin, 2003.

Prestwich, Michael, *Edward I*, London, 1988 (1997 reprint).

Pope, Rachel, "The Celts: Blood, Iron, and Sacrifice"A new BBC series fails to give its subject the depth it deserves", posted at *www.historytoday*, posted 7 October 2015.

Quinn, David B., "Columbus and the North: England, Iceland, and Ireland", *The William and Mary Quarterly*, Third Series, Vol. 49, No. 2, April 1992, pp. 278-297.

Quiggin, E.C., "A Poem by Gilbride MacNamee in Praise of Cathal O'Conor", in *Miscellany Presented to Kuno Meyer*, O.J. Bergin and C. Marstrander, eds, Hall, 1912, pp. 167-77.

Rabbitte, S.J., "The Lynch Memorial in Galway, Commonly Called The Crossbones", JGAHS, vol. 11, no. i, 1918.

Raftery, Barry, "The Celtic Iron Age in Ireland: Problems of Origin", Barry Raftery, *Emania* 9, 1991, pp. 28-32.

Raftery, Barry, *Pagan Celtic Ireland: The Enigma of the Irish Iron Age*, 1994.

Rance, Phillip, "Attacotti, Déisi and Magnus Maximus: the Case for Irish Federates in Late Roman Britain", *Brittania* 32, 2001, pp. 243-270.

Rance, Phillip, "Epiphanius of Salamis and the Scotti: new evidence for late Roman-Irish relations", *Brittania* 43, 2012, pp. 227-242.

Recio Morales, Óscar, "The Irish College of Alcala de Henares (1630-1785) from an European Perspective. A guideline to the Irish Colleges on the Continent: A Counter-Reformation cultural consequence", in *Indagación. Revista de Historia y Arte*, Vol. 2, Universidad de Alcalá, 1996, pp. 197-228.

Recio Morales, Óscar, "What if the earls had landed in Spain? The 1607 flight in the Spanish context", in *The Flight of the Earls*, eds. Finnegan, David, Maire-Claire Harrigan and Eamonn Ó Ciardha, Derry, 2010, pp. 140-146.

Regan, Joe, "'My Father was a Full-Blood Irishman': Recollection of Irish Immigrants in the 'Slave Narratives' from the New Deal's Works Progress Administration (WPA)", *History Ireland*, vol. 24, no. 3, May/June 2016, pp. 35-37.

Reilly, Matthew Connor, "At the Margins of the Plantation: Alternative Modernities and an Archaeology of the "Poor Whites" of Barbados", Ph.D dissertation, Syracuse University, August 2014.

Reilly, Matthew C., "The School of Female Industry: "Poor White" Women and Vocational Education in the Era of Slavery", in *The Journal of the Barbados Museum & Historical Society*, vol. LX, December 2014, pp. 94-118.

Reilly, Matthew C., "The Politics of Work, "Poor Whites", and Plantation Capitalism in Barbados", in *Historical Archaeologies of Capitalism* (second edition), Mark P. Leone and Jocelyn E. Knauf, eds., 2015, pp. 375-397.

Reilly, Matthew C., "The Irish in Barbados: Labour, Landscape and Legacy", in *Caribbean Irish Connections: Interdisciplinary Perspectives*, Alison Donnell, Maria McGarrity, Evelyn O'Callaghan, eds., Jamaica, 2015, pp. 47-63.

Renfrew, Colin, *Archaeology and Language: The Puzzle of Indo-European Origins*, 1987 (1998 edition).

Rice, Gerard, *Norman Kilcloon 1171-1700*, Dublin, 2001.

Richter, Michael, "The Interpretation of medieval Irish history", *IHS*, vol. XXIV, no. 95, May 1985, pp. 289-298.

Robinson, Tim, *Stones of Aran: Pilgrimage*, London, 1986.

Rogers, Nini, "The Irish and the Atlantic slave trade", *History Ireland*, May/June 2007, issue three, volume 15.

Rothwell, W., "'from Oriental Bazar to English Cloister in Anglo-French", *Modern Language Review Supplement: One Hundred Years of 'MLR': General and Comparative Studies*, volume 94, 1999, pp. 647-59.

Round, J. H., "The Origins of the Fitzgeralds", *The Ancestor*, 1902, pp. 119-26 i, pp. 91-98 ii.

Røyrvik, Ellen C., "Western Celts? A genetic impression of Britain in Atlantic Europe", in *Celtic from the West*, Barry Cunliffe and John Koch, eds., Oxford, 2010, pp. 83-106.

Ruiz Zapatero, Gonzalo, "The Celts in Spain: From Archaeology to Modern Identities", Pre-actes du colloque du Collage de France, Juillet, 2006.

Russell, Paul, "*Nósa Ua Maine* 'The Customs of the Ui Mhaine", in *The Welsh King and his Court: essays in memory of Glanville R. J. Jones*, ed. T. M. Charles-Edwards, Morfydd E. Owen, and Paul Russell, Cardiff, 2000, pp. 527-551.

Rynne, Etienne, "Military and civilian swords from the River Corrib", *JGAHS*. 39, 1983-84, pp. 5-26.

Sayles, G.O., "The Siege of Carrickfergus Castle, 1315-16", *Irish Historical Studies*, vol. X, 1956-57, pp. 94-100.

Schrijver, Peter, "Non-Indo-European surviving in Ireland in the first millennium AD", *Ériu*, 2000, pp. 195-99.

Schrijver, Peter, "More on non-Indo-European surviving Ireland in the first millennium AD", *Ériu*, 2005, pp. 137-44.

Schrijver, Peter, *Language contact and the origins of the Germanic languages*, New York-London, 2014.

Schrijver, Peter, "Pruners and Trainers of the Celtic Family Tree: The Rise and Development of Celtic in the light of Language Contact", in XIV International Congress of Celtic Studies, 2015, pp. 191-219.

Sherratt, Susan, "'Ethnicities', 'ethnonyms' and archaeological labels. Whose ideologies and whose identities?", in *Archaeological Perspectives on the Transmission and Transformation of Culture in the Eastern Mediterranean*, Joanne Clarke, ed., 2005, pp. 25-38.

Siggins, Lorna, "Ancient oak track on Galway coast dated to 1700 BC. Evidence suggests Galway Bay is less than 3,700 years old", *The Irish Times*, Tuesday 5 August 2014.

Siggins, Lorna, "Antlers and horse bones dating back 1,500 years found on Galway beach", *The Irish Times*, Monday December 1, 2014.

Sims-Williams, Patrick, "Genetics, linguistics, and prehistory: thinking big and thinking straight", *Antiquity* 72, 1998, pp. 505-527.

Sims-Williams, Patrick, "Celtomania and Celtoscepticism", *CMCS* number 36, Winter 1998, pp. 1-35.

Sims-Williams, Patrick, "Celtic civilization: continuity or coincidence?", *CMCS* 64, 2012, pp. 1-44.

Simms, Katharine, *From Kings to Warlords:The Changing Political Structure of Gaelic Ireland in the Later Middle Ages*, Bury St Edmunds, 1987.

Simms, Katharine, "The Barefoot Kings: Literary Image and Reality in Later medieval Ireland", *PHCC*, 2010, pp. 1-21.

Slavin, Bridgette, "Coming to Terms with Druids in Early Christian Ireland", *ACJ* 9, 2010, pp. 1-27.

Smith, Anthony, *The Ethnic Origin of Nations*, Oxford, 1986

Smyth, Alfred P., ed., *Seanchas: Studies in Early and Medieval Irish Archaeology, History and Literature in Honour of Francis J. Byrne*, Dublin, 2001.

Snyder, Mark R., "The Education of Indentured Servants in Colonial America", *The Journal of Technology Studies*, Vol. 33, Issue 2, Spring 2007, pp. 65-72.

Sproule, David, "Origins of the Éoganachta", *Ériu* 35, 1984, pp. 31-37.

Spufford, Peter, *Power and Profit: The Merchant in Medieval Europe*, London, 2002.

St. George Mark, Gordon, "The Joyces of Merview", Part 1, *The Irish Genealogist*, vol. 8, 1990-95, pp.

Stalley, Roger, "Sailing to Santiago: the medieval *pilgrimage to Santiago de Compostela and its artistic influence in Ireland*", in Bradley, ed., 1988, pp. 397-420.

Stokes, Kaele, "The delineation of a medieval 'nation': *Brittones, Cymry and Wealas before the Norman conquest*", in *Nation and federation in the Celtic World*: Papers from the fourth Australian Conference of Celtic Studies University of Sydney June-July 2001, ed. Pamela O'Neill, pp. 304-316.

Stokes, Whitley, "The Voyage of Mael Duin", Revue Celtique 9, 1888, pp. 447-495; and 10, 1889, pp. 50-95.

Symonds, Henry, "The Irish Silver Coinages of Edward IV", in *The Numismatic Chronicle and Journal of the Royal Numismatic Society, Fifth Series*, vol. 1, no. 1-2, 1921, p. 124.

Tallon, Geraldine, *Court of Claims: Submission and evidence 1663*, Irish Manuscripts Commission, Dublin, 2006.

Tanaka, Miho, "'Nation' Consciousnesses in Medieval Ireland", *Journal of International Economic Studies*, 2010, 3-16.

Thompson, E.A., *Who was Saint Patrick?*, Bury St. Edmunds, 1985.

Tierney, J. J., "The Celtic Ethnography of Posidonius", *PRIA* 60, C, 1960, pp. 189-275.

Tolkien, J. R. R., "English and Welsh", 1955 O'Donnell lecture, in *The Monsters and the Critics and other essays*, ed. Christopher Tolkien, London, Allen and Unwin, 1983 (1997 paperback edition).

Tombs, Robert, *The English and Their History*, UK, 2014.

Thurneysen, Rudolph, *A grammar of Old Irish*, Dublin, 1946 (reprinted 1980).

Toorians, Lauran, "Flemish in Wales", in *Languages in Britain and Ireland*, Glanville Price, ed., 2000, pp. 184-86.

Truxes, Thomas M., *Irish-American Trade, 1660-1783*, Cambridge, 1988.

Turner, Ralph, "Magna Carta in the USA", *Insights on Law and Society* 15.1, Fall 2014, American Bar Association, pp. 6-13.

Tyler, Elizabeth M., *Crossing Conquests: Polyglot Royal Women and Literary Culture in Eleventh-Century England*,

Veach, Colin, "Henry II's grant of Meath to Hugh de Lacy 1172: a reassessment", *Riocht na Mide* 18, 2007, pp. 67-94.

Veach, Colin, "A question of timing: Walter de Lacy's seisin of Meath 1189-94", *PRIA*, Vol. 109C, pp. 164-194, 2009.

Verstraten, Freya, "Both king and vassal: Feidlim Ua Conchobair of Connacht, 1230-65", *JGAHS* 55, 2003, pp. 13-37.

Verstraten, Freya, "Naming practices among the Irish secular nobility in the high middle ages", *Journal of Medieval History* 32, 2006, pp. 43-53 (see also Unpublished Sources).

Villiers-Tuthill, Kathleen, *Beyond the Twelve Bens: A History of Clifden & District 1860-1923*, 1986.

Viney, Michael, "Another Life: Consensus on Irish flora and fauna no longer changing at a glacial pace. DNA evidence indicated array of animals now recognised as distinctly Irish", *The Irish Times*, Saturday February 14, 2015.

Waddell, John, "Celts, Celticisation and the Irish Bronze Age", in *Ireland in the Bronze Age: Proceedings of the Dublin Conference, April 1995*, edited by John Waddell and Elizabeth Shee Twohig, Dublin, 1995, pp. 158-169.

Waddell, John, and Jane Conroy, " Celts and others: maritime contacts and linguistic change", in *Archaeology and Language IV: Language change and cultural transformation*, Blench and Spriggs, eds., London, 1999, pp. 125-137.

Walshe, Helen Coburn, "Enforcing the Elizabethan settlement: the vicissitudes of Hugh Brady, bishop of Meath, 1563-84", in *Irish Historical Studies*, vol. XXVI, no. 104, November 1989.

Walsh, Paul Father, *Irish Leaders and Learning through the Ages*, ed. Nollaig Ó Muraile, Dublin, 2003.

Walsh, Paul, "Foundation of the Augustinian Friary, Galway: A Review of the Sources", *JGAHS* 40, 1985/86, pp. 72-80.

Walsh, Paul, "The Medieval Merchant's Marks and Its Survival in Galway", *JGAHS* 45, 1993, pp. 1-28.

Walsh, Paul, and Paul Duffy, "An extract from Strafford's inquisition: Galway corporation poperty, 1637", *JGAHS* 49, 1997, pp. 49-64.

Ward, Robin, *The World of the Medieval Shipmaster*, Boydell Press, 2009.

Warner, Richard, "The 'prehistoric' Irish annals: fable or history", *Archaeology Ireland* 4 (1), 1990, pp. 30-33.

Warner, R[ichard]. B., "The 'Ernean House", *Emania* 12, 1994, pp. 21-27.

Warner, Richard, "Beehive Querns and Irish 'La Tène' Artefacts: A Statistical Test of their Cultural Relatedness", *The Journal of Irish Archaeology*, vol. 11, 2002, pp. 125-130.

Warner, Richard, "Clogher in late prehistory", in Cooney, Beker, et al, eds., 2009, pp. 507-518.

Warner, R[ichard]. B., "Ptolemy's *Isamnion* promontory: rehabilitation and identification", *Emania* 21, 2013, pp. 21-29.

Welch, Pedro L. V., "Poor Whites in Barbadian History", in *Narratives of the Occluded Irish Diaspora*, eds. Mícheál Ó hAodha and John O'Callaghan, Bern, 2012, pp. 125-148.

Westropp, Thomas Johnson, "Early Italian Maps of Ireland from 1300 to 1600, with Notes on Foreign Settlers and Trade", *PRIA*, Section C, Vol. 30, 1912-13, pp. 361-428.

Williams, Eric, *Capitalism and Slavery*, London, 1944.

Williams, Dr. Ann, and Professor G. H. Martin, eds., *Domesday Book: A Complete Translation*, London, 2002.

Wilson, James F., et al, "Genetic evidence for different male and female roles during cultural transitions in the British Isles", *Proceedings of the National Academy of Sciences of the United States of America*, 2001, pp. 98-99.

# Online sources:

http://www.scribd.com/doc/119379886/a-Genetic-Signal-of-Central-European-Celtic-Ancestry-Preliminary-Research-Concerning-Y-Chromosome-Marker-U152-2

http://www.british-history.ac.uk/report.aspx?compid=43159

Annals of Ulster – http://www.ucc.ie/celt/published/T100001A/index.html, http://www.ucc.ie/celt/published/T100001B/index.html

Annals of Inisfallen - http://www.ucc.ie/celt/published/T100004/index.html

Annals of the Four Masters - http://www.ucc.ie/celt/published/T100005B/index.html

Miscellaneous Irish Annals, Fragment I (Mac Carthaigh's Book) http://www.ucc.ie/celt/published/T100013/index.html

Dominican Annals of Roscommon - http://www.ucc.ie/celt/published/L100015A/index.html

Chronicon Scotorum - http://www.ucc.ie/celt/published/T100016/index.html

Grace's Annals - http://www.ucc.ie/celt/published/T100001/index.html

CIRCLE - A Calendar of Irish Chancery Letters c. 1244 – 1509 - http://chancery.tcd.ie/

"Irish Priests in the West Indies: 1638-1669", http://www.irlandeses.org/imsla2011 7 04 10 Matteo Binasco.

"The Irish in the Caribbean 1641-1837: An Overview", Nini Rogers, pp. 145-56, Irish Latin American Studies, 2007.

"Seville: Between the Atlantic and the Mediterranean, 1248-1492: Pre-Columbus Commercial Routes from and to Seville", Serradilla Avery, Dan Manuel, University of St. Andrews, 2007.

http://hdl.handle.net/10023/340

www.irlandeses.org/imala0711.htm

http://www.limerickcity.ie/media/Who%20was%20who%20in%20medieval%20Limerick.pdf - Brian Hodkinson

"Who Was Who in Early Modern Limerick" - Alan O'Driscoll and Brian Hodkinson

https://www.opendemocracy.net/beyondslavery/liam-hogan%E2%80%98irish-slaves%E2%80%99-convenient-myth

# Unpublished sources:

The Kilfenora Manuscript (NLI Ms. 13, 650), photocopies from Jeff O'Connell of Durras, December 1997.

Campbell, Ian W.S., "Alithinologia: John Lynch and seventeenth-century Irish political thought", thesis, Trinity College Dublin, December 2008 (see Campbell, Ian, for the published version).

Cantwell, Ian, "Climate in Medieval Ireland AD 500-1600", thesis, Trinity College Dublin, 2000.

Kirwan, Andrew, "A Manuscript History of the Kirwan Family", c. 1870 (transcription and edition given to me by Jeff O'Connell of Duras, Kinvara, December 1998; see also O'Connell, Jeff, for printed extracts.)

Ní Bhrolcháin, Muireann, "The Prose Banshenchas", M.A. Thesis, U.C.G. 1980.

Ó Bríc, Brendán M., "Galway townsmen as the owners of land in Connacht 1585-1641", M.A. Thesis, U.C.G. 1974.

Ó Néill, Eoin, "Elizabeth I and the Nine Years' War", read at "Elizabeth I and Ireland" Conference, 12-14 November 2009, University of Connecticut, USA.

Ó Néill, Eoin, "Starvation as a tactic of war", written for Encyclopedia of War, 2012, omitted for editorial reasons.

Verstraten, Freya, "Medieval Views on Acculturation in Ireland", read at Congress of Celtic Studies 1-5 August 2011.

O'Flaherty, Enda, "Archaeological Watermarks: Turlough Floodplains as Communal Spaces and Places of Assembly", National University of Ireland thesis, Galway, 2013.

Walsh, Paul, "Fortifications at Galway 12th-19th Centuries (an archaeological and historical study)", University College Galway, May 1981. "

# INDEX: Unless otherwise stated, all places are of County Galway.

*Tribes of Galway 1124-1642*

*Tribes of Galway 1124-1642*

The Longship, used by 12th-century Irish kings (courtesy Draken Harald Hårfagre Fellowship)

The Cog, used from the 1150s all over Europe and featured on Galway's coat of arms ( courtesy of Wikipedia Commons)

River traffic at the Wood Quay c. 1870, by William Joseph Bond (courtesy of Tom Kenny).
Earlier boats brought people and goods Lough Orbsen and the Gaillimhe

*Young Man Drinking a Glass of Wine by Jan van Bijlert, courtesy of Wikipedia Commons.*

*Restored town house, Kirwan's Lane*

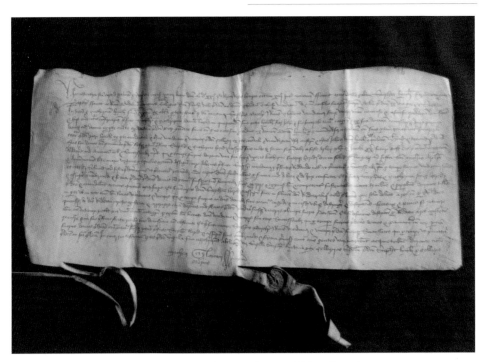

*1485 Mayoralty of Galway grant (courtesy of Galway Diocese)*

*Ó hEidhin's castle of Dún Guaire, Kinvarra, courtesy of Wikipedia Commons*

*Ó Flaithbhertaigh's castle of Aughnanure, Oughterard, courtesy of Jenny Young*

*Lynch's Castle, built in the late 1400's*

*Tigh Neachtain's built in the mid to late 1400's*

All four structures were built thanks to Galway's 15th Century economy

*Galway town officials 1632,  Courtesy of NUI, Galway*

The Civill Irish Woman    The Civill Irish man

*Middle Class Irish woman and man c. 1600 - the woman wears the Gaway blue mantle*

*Three Lynch family Tombs, St. Nicholas' Church*

*1612 Bodkin, Ffrench and Martyn coats of arms, courtesy of the Kings Head pub*

The 1624 Darcy Doorway

Húicéir 'Mac Dara' courtesy of Cumann Húicéirí Na Gaillimhe and Aodan Mac Donnacha

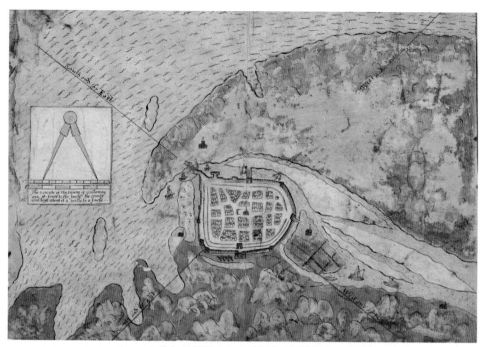

Galway 1589, *courtesy of the British Library*

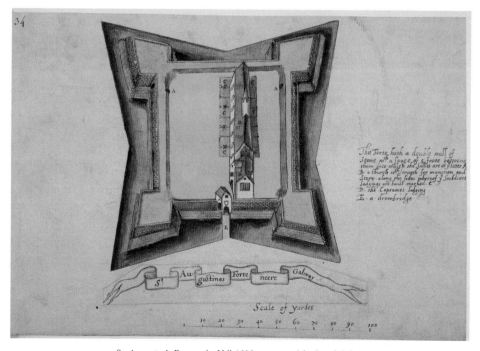

St. Augustine's Fort on the Hill 1603, *courtesy of the British Library*

*Galway 1685, courtesy of the British Library*

A Prospect of Galway

Tribes of Galway 1124-1642